Hawthorne's Habitations

Hawthorne's birthplace, 27 Union St.,
Salem, Mass.

Concord River, with bridge

George's Dock, Liverpool,
nineteenth century

Interior of the Pantheon, Rome, by
Giovanni Paolo Panini or Pannini.

Hawthorne's Habitations

A Literary Life

ROBERT MILDER

OXFORD
UNIVERSITY PRESS

OXFORD
UNIVERSITY PRESS

Oxford University Press is a department of the University of Oxford.
It furthers the University's objective of excellence in research,
scholarship, and education by publishing worldwide.

Oxford   New York

Auckland   Cape Town   Dar es Salaam   Hong Kong   Karachi
Kuala Lumpur   Madrid   Melbourne   Mexico City   Nairobi
New Delhi   Shanghai   Taipei   Toronto

With offices in

Argentina   Austria   Brazil   Chile   Czech Republic   France   Greece
Guatemala   Hungary   Italy   Japan   Poland   Portugal   Singapore
South Korea   Switzerland   Thailand   Turkey   Ukraine   Vietnam

Oxford is a registered trademark of Oxford University
Press in the UK and certain other countries.

Published in the United States of America by Oxford University Press
198 Madison Avenue, New York, NY 10016

Milder, Robert.
Hawthorne's habitations : a literary life / Robert Milder.
p. cm.
Includes bibliographical references and index.
ISBN 978-0-19-991725-9

1. Hawthorne, Nathaniel, 1804–1864—Criticism and interpretation.   2. Hawthorne, Nathaniel,
1804–1864—Homes and haunts.   3. Hawthorne, Nathaniel, 1804–1864—Travel.
4. Hawthorne, Nathaniel, 1804–1864—Themes, motives.   5. Place in literature.
6. Mood (Psychology) in literature.   7. Melancholy in literature.   I. Title.
PS1892.H55M55 2012
813'.3—dc23   2012025139

9 8 7 6 5 4 3 2 1

Printed in the United States of America
on acid-free paper

To the next generations—
Jeff and Nina, Brian and Rebecca,
and Oren

CONTENTS

Preface   ix

Abbreviations for Frequently Cited Sources   xiii

1. Two Hawthornes   3
2. Telling It Slant   28
3. The Wild and the Good   57
4. Undoing It All   90
5. The Problem of New England   115
6. Sisters Act   137
7. In the Belly of the Beast   167
8. Indian Summer   198
9. A Fine Bewilderment   220
10. On the Crust   243

Epilogue: Last Words   268

Notes   273
List of Illustrations   288
Index   291

PREFACE

Regions are not only concrete geographic domains but also conceptual places.

—Joseph A. Conforti, *Imagining New England*

His journals show a sharp-eyed, amused realist, but his imagination, which ripened in the unnatural solitude of his young manhood in Salem, set itself feats of balance on the edge of the unreal that, as the real shadows closed in, he was unable to sustain.

—John Updike on Hawthorne, "Late Works," *Due Considerations*

Prefaces are best kept brief. Some words about my title, *Hawthorne's Habitations*. By "habitation" I mean, first of all, four geographical places that were the scene and literal or figurative subject of Hawthorne's writing: Salem, Massachusetts, his ancestral home and ground of identity; Concord, Massachusetts, where he lived from 1842 to 1845 and came into contact with the Adamic spirit of the American Renaissance, and to which he returned in 1852–53 and again in 1860; England, where he served as consul in Liverpool from 1853 to 1857, absorbing an element of Englishness himself and envisioning a new direction for his work; and Italy, where he lived through most of 1858–59 and was challenged, like Henry James's Americans, by the obliquities of an older, denser civilization morally and culturally distinct from his own. "Habitation" also refers to a mental residence, or region of thought and sensibility rooted in time and place but not dependent on them and having its characteristic attitudes and constellation of themes, which interact with those of other times and places. In this respect, Hawthorne never abandoned any of his habitations; he assimilated them into a self that deepened and expanded as he aged without finding, after the Salem period, a settled physical and metaphysical "home."

As I initially imagined the book, "Salem" and "Concord" were to be the thesis and antithesis of a dialectic that would have its synthesis, or site of collision, in the mature romances. Chapter 3, on Hawthorne at the Old Manse, and chapters 4 and 6, on *The Scarlet Letter* and *The Blithedale Romance*, take their impulse from this idea, though they developed in different, more complex ways than I foresaw. I had a preliminary notion of what I would do with Hawthorne and Rome. The years in England were unknown territory, as were the late unfinished romances. Somehow a reading of these things would take shape.

As it happened, Hawthorne's English experience altered my sense of the contour of his career and my appraisal of the elements within his character. Critical, too, was my immersion in Hawthorne's notebooks, first as a matter of research, then with increasing interest and appreciation, and later as coeditor, with Randall Fuller, of a selection of the American, English, and French and Italian notebooks, *The Business of Reflection* (2009). Except in the scattered hints for stories in *The American Notebooks,* the Hawthorne of the journals is a strikingly different person from the writer of the published fiction. Millicent Bell speaks of the "temperamental nominalism" of Hawthorne the journalizer, "a man for whom the world is exactly what it is and no more."[1] These are not words one would use for the author of *The Scarlet Letter* or "Young Goodman Brown," whose fictive world is what the actual world *isn't* and a good deal more.

All art, journals included, is artifice, but it is one thing to refract an authorial consciousness through a formal literary medium and another to function publicly and privately at radical variance. Emerson's journals are colloquial and rambling, his essays epigrammatic and polished, but the seer in the mature journals is essentially the seer of the published work. This is not the case with Hawthorne, in whom the disjunction between text and notebook is a disjunction between public and private worldviews, indeed public and private selves. Why should a realist, as in his apprehension of experience Hawthorne visibly was, have written the nonrealistic tales and romances he did? When Hawthorne works close to life, he is an extraordinarily keen and lively observer and a graceful stylist; witness not only the notebooks but also "The Old Manse," "The Custom-House," the essays on English life collected in *Our Old Home* (1863), and sections of *The House of the Seven Gables* and most of *The Blithedale Romance*. It was not from necessities of talent, as he sometimes claimed, that Hawthorne wrote romance, nor, after the reclusiveness of the Salem years, was it simply from poverty of experience or by established practice. It was by positive choice and increasingly against the thrust of his life experience and his perception of audience taste.

As my subject developed, Hawthorne's passage through successive habitations came to appear mediated through this fundamental conflict between the naturalist and the idealist or, to use the associated literary terms, the realist and the romancer. By "naturalism" I do not mean the later nineteenth-century literary and philosophical movement but, more simply, a view of experience as secular, material, finite, and shaped by social and psychological forces apart from anything supernatural or immanently teleological. As a form of literary representation, realism for Hawthorne consisted in a fidelity to outward surfaces that did not preclude exploration of their undersides and depths. While ostensibly only a method, however, realism was not philosophically neutral. Openly or by implication, its metaphysics were skeptical, agnostic, morally relativistic, and earthbound—in a word, naturalistic. And in this, however "true" they might be, they were terrifying.

The danger of a book's having two ongoing arguments is that it may end up having no coherent argument at all. The greatest challenge as I wrote and rewrote these chapters was to present the tension between the naturalist and the idealist, the realist and the romancer, as they cut across the four geographical and temporal periods of Hawthorne's career, each with its own opportunities and conflicts, and as they inflected his attitudes on nearly all important matters that define his work—moral, psychological, social, philosophical, religious, aesthetic, sexual. My opening chapter, "Two Hawthornes," establishes the terms of the problem and serves as a prologue. As Hawthorne's life took the form of a physical and mental journey, so the work of describing it resolved itself in the nine succeeding chapters into some combination of outward narrative, psychological biography, and literary interpretation, the chapters varying in content, rhythm, tone, and length according to the nature of their subject.

I would prefer not to anticipate the chapters, which are better left to speak for themselves. Enough to say that while not a formal biography but more than a work of literary criticism, this is a book about a life led in and known primarily through written words—a *literary* life. The notebooks will figure prominently in some sections of the book and implicitly in all; Concord and Europe will receive greater emphasis than in most studies; and Hawthorne's marriage to Sophia Peabody will be an abiding concern, thanks partly to the enabling work of Megan Marshall, Patricia Dunlavy Valenti, and T. Walter Herbert. Among literary figures, Emerson and Margaret Fuller will be foremost, with attention to others whom Hawthorne knew well and had affinities with (Thoreau and Melville) or who provide useful cross-lights on his work (Harriet Beecher Stowe, Washington Irving, Emily Dickinson). Henry James, chiefly in his 1879 *Hawthorne* but also in the transatlantic novels *Roderick Hudson* and *The Ambassadors*, will be a frequent point of reference, and John Updike, one of Hawthorne's most astute readers, a recurrent one. A surprising presence—surprising to myself as well—is Nietzsche, whose theories about culture and morality, offensive as they might have been to the conservative in Hawthorne, came to seem remarkably pertinent to a powerful impulse in his work. Not all of Hawthorne's writing, of course, will receive attention. Many tales and sketches will go unaddressed, as will his biography of Franklin Pierce and his books for children. And except during Hawthorne's residence in England, questions of his politics, insightfully discussed by Larry J. Reynolds in *Devil and Rebels* (2008) and Randall Fuller in *From Battlefields Rising* (2010), will not be a major subject.

Two of the book's chapters, "The Problem of New England" and "In the Belly of the Beast," have previously appeared in or close to their present form, the former in *American Literary History* (2009), the latter in *New England Quarterly* (2011); an early version of "Two Hawthornes" was also published in *New England Quarterly* (2008). I would like to thank editors Linda Smith Rhoads and Gordon Hutner for their encouragement and helpful advice as well as for permission to reprint or adapt the originals. The three anonymous readers for Oxford University Press offered fertile suggestions that helped reshape my final revision of the manuscript, as did Thomas R. Mitchell. My debts to predecessors in Hawthorne studies are numerous, but I would especially like to acknowledge the work of Nina Baym, Millicent Bell, Richard H. Brodhead, Frederick C. Crews, Gloria C. Ehrlich, T. Walter Herbert, Raymona E. Hull, Megan Marshall, James R. Mellow, Richard H. Millington, Thomas R. Mitchell, Philip Rahv, Patricia Dunlavy Valenti, Brenda Wineapple, and Thomas Woodson, as well as the several editors of the Centenary Edition of Hawthorne's writings. I am grateful to the Graduate School of Arts and Sciences at Washington University for a Humanities Research Grant that helped support the project and to Professor Vincent Sherry, Chair of the English Department, and Gary Wihl, Dean of the Faculty of Arts and Sciences, for the adjustment in teaching duties that allowed me to complete the work in a timely fashion. My greatest debt, as always, is to my wife, Gail.

ABBREVIATIONS FOR FREQUENTLY CITED SOURCES

Unless otherwise indicated, all citations of Hawthorne's writings are to the *Centenary Edition of the Works of Nathaniel Hawthorne*, ed. William Charvat et al., 23 vols. (Columbus: Ohio State University Press, 1962–93) and are indicated by volume and page number. The volumes cited are as follows.

1 *The Scarlet Letter*; 2 *The House of the Seven Gables*; 3 *The Blithedale Romance and Fanshawe*; 4 *The Marble Faun*; 5 *Our Old Home*; 8 *The American Notebooks*; 9 *Twice-Told Tales*; 10 *Mosses from an Old Manse*; 11 *The Snow-Image and Uncollected Tales*; 12 *The American Claimant Manuscripts*; 13 *The Elixir of Life Manuscripts*; 14 *The French and Italian Notebooks*; 15 *The Letters 1813–1843*; 16 *The Letters 1843–1853*; 17 *The Letters 1853–1856*; 18 *The Letters 1857–1864*; 21 *The English Notebooks 1853–1856*; 22 *The English Notebooks 1856–1860*

Other Frequently Cited Texts

CWE *The Collected Works of Ralph Waldo Emerson*, ed. Robert Spiller, Alfred Ferguson, et al. *(Cambridge, MA: Harvard University Press, 1971–). Volumes cited are 1 Nature, Addresses, Lectures; 2 Essays, First Series; 3 Essays, Second Series*

ED *The Poems of Emily Dickinson (Reading Edition), ed. R. W. Franklin (Cambridge, MA: Harvard University Press, 1998). Poems are identified by number.*

EMH *Elizabeth Manning Hawthorne: A Life in Letters, ed. Cecile Anne De Rocher (Tuscaloosa: University of Alabama Press, 2006)*

HR *Marion L. Kesselring, Hawthorne's Reading (New York: New York Public Library, 1949). Items are identified by listed number.*

James *Henry James, Hawthorne (1879; Ithaca, NY: Cornell University Press, 1956)*

Mellow James R. Mellow, *Nathaniel Hawthorne in His Times* (Boston: Houghton
     Mifflin, 1980)

NHW Julian Hawthorne, *Nathaniel Hawthorne and His Wife*, 2 vols. (Boston: James
     R. Osgood, 1884)

PRNH Horatio Bridge, *Personal Recollections of Nathaniel Hawthorne* (New York:
     Harper & Brothers, 1893)

WHM *The Writings of Herman Melville*, ed. Harrison Hayford, Hershel Parker, and
     G. Thomas Tanselle, 13 vols. to date (Evanston and Chicago: Northwestern
     University Press and The Newberry Library, 1968–). Volumes cited are 6 *Moby-
     Dick; or The Whale*; 7 *Pierre; or, The Ambiguities*; 9 *The Piazza Tales and Other
     Prose Pieces, 1839–1860*; 12 *Clarel: A Poem and a Pilgrimage in the Holy Land*;
     14 *Correspondence*

WNC Margaret Fuller, *Woman in the Nineteenth Century* (1845; New York: Norton,
     1971)

Hawthorne's Habitations

Two Hawthornes

Throughout his life, Hawthorne led a twofold existence—a real and a
supernatural. As a man, he was the realest of men.... When he entered
upon his work as a writer, he left [the] personality which I have
described entirely behind him.

—George Bailey Loring, *"Nathaniel Hawthorne"* (1880)

The Realist of the Notebooks

He was a keen and accurate observer of men and events, but he seldom
made any direct and extensive use of his observations in his best
writing.... Though he was in many ways an acute self-critic, especially
of the limitations of his stories, Hawthorne did not fully understand
the nature of his gift. He knew his weaknesses well enough but not his
strength.

—Hyatt H. Waggoner, *Hawthorne: A Critical Study*

At a critical moment in *The Blithedale Romance*, just as he prepares to transform
his friends Hollingsworth, Zenobia, and Priscilla into mythic archetypes, narrator Miles Coverdale acknowledges the liberties a romancer takes with the truth
whenever he sets out to "insulate [a friend] from many of his true relations, mag-
nify his peculiarities, inevitably tear him into parts, and, of course, patch him
very clumsily together again. What wonder, then, should we be frightened by the
aspect of a monster, which, after all—though we can point to every feature of his
deformity in the real personage—may be said to have been created mainly by
ourselves" (3:69).

Like Coverdale, Hawthorne the romancer may be said to insulate his characters from the matrix of social reality and fashion them as both more and less
than complete human beings. To one extent or another, Hawthorne's interpreters do the same when they construct a version of him from his published
writings without regard to the context of his voluminous notebooks. As his son
Julian remarked, "the impression produced by his notebooks is oddly different

from that of the romances—a difference comparable in kind and degree to that between the voice in ordinary speech and in singing."[1] The public voice of a writer may vary markedly, of course, from the private. Emerson is sharp and colloquial in his journals, misty and oracular in his essays, and yet his vision of the self and the universe is substantively the same. Hawthorne's is not. To pass from life to art, for Hawthorne, was not simply to assume a different persona; it was to take on a different conception of reality.

To readers coming to the American notebooks of the 1830s from the dark early tales, perhaps the most surprising thing is how un-Hawthornean their writer seems to be. Except in his interspersed notes for stories, Hawthorne looks outward upon experience and is widely inquisitive, ready to take the world as he finds it, sociable (even mildly flirtatious) when away from Salem, and with few indications of the morbidness of the fiction with its quasi-Puritanical contextualization of human frailty. People and places engage him; he shows little interest in contemporary events or ideas, still less in books, and virtually none at all in the historical past, the setting of so much of his early fiction. If in his tales and romances "everything means something else," as W. C. Brownell complained, in his notebooks nothing in life seems to mean anything beyond itself. [2]

Hawthorne's youthful travel notebooks, in particular, show him moving about easily in the world, consorting with all manner of people and observing them with a shrewdness that belies critic E. P. Whipple's ostensibly just remark that Hawthorne's "eye is more certain in detecting remote spiritual laws and their relations, than in the sure grasp of individual character."[3] Visiting his college friend Horatio Bridge in Maine in the summer of 1837, Hawthorne keeps bachelor hall with Bridge and his clever, voluble guest and language tutor, a Frenchman named Schaeffer. He accompanies Bridge to the shanties of the French and Irish laborers in Bridge's employ; he drinks gin and brandy with the locals in a "dingy" country store, "smoking a most vile American cigar" (8:52); he shrewdly gauges the crafty/sincere character of his former classmate Jonathan Cilley, now a congressman and soon to be killed in a duel; he admires "a pretty, black-eyed intelligent servant-girl" (8:59) and flirts with the "frank, free, mirthful daughter of the landlady" in a boardinghouse at seaside Thomaston (8:65); he visits taverns and comments on the range of their clientele: provincial worthies, farmers, drunkards, prostitutes, pimps. As Bliss Perry commented, "there is every evidence that [Hawthorne] was strongly attracted to these broad-backed tavern-haunters and was promptly initiated into their circle."[4]

Hawthorne had developed an affinity for the common in his youth while accompanying his uncle Samuel Manning on horse-buying expeditions—the Mannings, with whom the young Hawthorne lived for most of his Salem years, ran a stagecoach line from Salem to Boston—and his delight in the raffish underside of life remained with him until middle age, when fame, family responsibilities, and Victorian propriety combined to suppress it.[5] "Once a year, or thereabouts," he later told R. H. Stoddard, "I used to make an excursion of a few weeks, in which I enjoyed as much of life as other people do in the whole year's round" (*NHW* 1:97). A master of what James called "the deeper psychology" (James 51), Hawthorne was also gifted with a realist's eye for telling surfaces. As his summer travels of the 1830s led him on picaresque journeys through the towns, villages, and wild, romantic scenery of primitive America, he encountered a colorful array of stage passengers, peddlers, doctors, lawyers, itinerant preachers, and tavern-goers: Chaucerian figures presented with a Chaucerian gusto strikingly at odds with the cool formality of his early tales and described in a prose so easy and graceful as to seem a natural mode of thinking and writing.

In one such encounter, Hawthorne and Bridge are visiting a local tavern when "a soft, simple-looking fellow, with an anxious expression," enters looking for "one Mary Ann Russel—a question which excited general and hardly suppressed mirth; for the said Mary Ann is one of a knot of whores" recently "routed" by the village constable. "Do you want to use her?" the bartender-pimp asks him. It turns out, to the company's hilarity, that the woman is the simpleton's wife and that he is searching for her with the thought of rescuing her and taking her back. "I would have given considerable to witness his meeting with his wife," Hawthorne writes. "On the whole there was a moral picturesqueness in the contrasts of this scene—a man moved as deeply as his nature would admit, in the midst of hardened, gibing spectators, heartless towards him. It is worth thinking over and studying out" (8:58–59). He never did so. The notable thing is that he found the incident worth recording in detail and inscribed it with an artfully Chekhovian mix of objectivity and empathy far removed in style and tone from the recently published *Twice-Told Tales*.

Backwoods America proved endlessly fertile in such "remarkable characters" (8:90, 96), which the notebooks render with humor or pathos (or both) as the case invites. A "traveling 'Surgeon Dentist' "-cum-Baptist preacher heading West, self-educated and full of "self-conceit," entertains Hawthorne with his account of love affairs, providing a brief course in country manners (8:96). A "disagreeable figure," filthy and mutilated, interests him for the signs he shows of former good looks and "a mind once strong and cultivated." " 'My study is man,' said he," as he studies Hawthorne and finds " 'something of the hawk-eye about [him] too'" (8:90, 92). In a Maine tavern Hawthorne encounters a local "blacksmith of fifty or upwards; a corpulent figure, big in the belly, and enormous in the backsides," with "a round jolly face, always mirthful and humorous, and shrewd—and the air of a man well to do, and well-respected, yet not caring much about the opinions of men, because his independence is sufficient to itself" (8:94). "I know no man," Hawthorne concludes, "who seems more like a man—more indescribably human—than this sturdy blacksmith" (8:94–95).

In his romances Hawthorne would celebrate festivals and processions, out-breaks of carnivalesque energy in worlds otherwise contained: New England Election Day in *The Scarlet Letter;* the masquerade late in *The Blithedale Romance;* a street parade in *The House of the Seven Gables;* a frolic in the Villa Borghese, market day in Perugia, and the Roman carnival in *The Marble Faun.* In the notebooks of the later 1830s, sprawling, unkempt America appears itself a carnival for the observer keen enough to relish its moments great or small, orchestrated or impromptu. A Williams College commencement of 1838 is a carnival par excel-lence, wilder and more Bakhtinian in its heterogeneity than anything Hawthorne permitted himself to describe in his fiction. The pageant includes gingerbread sellers; a peddler shrewdly hawking his wares ("this character could not possibly be overdrawn" [8:112]); "people burying their muzzles deep in the juicy flesh of [watermelons]. Cider. Beer" (8:112); half-drunken men wrestling on a green; "a good many blacks," one "a genuine specimen of the slave-negro," another "talking about the rights of his race, yet so as not to provoke his audience" (8:112); "mirth, anger, eccentricity, all showing themselves freely" among the crowd (8:112); "well-dressed ladies…in silks and cambrics"; "country graduates—rough, brown-featured, schoolmaster looking, half-bumpkin, half-scholar"; "the landlord of the tavern, keeping his eye on a man whom he suspected of an intention to bolt" (8:113). This is not the world of Hawthornean romance; it is the world of Chaucer, Cervantes, Rabelais, Brueghel, and George Caleb Bingham.

In contrast to the guilt-obsessed early tales, the notebooks of the period are unperturbed in their voyeuristic attention to the body. Visiting the Maverick House in East Boston in 1835, Hawthorne takes note of "middling-class people" got up in their Sunday best and playing at gentility (8:7), the girls sometimes "showing a good deal of leg in a stocking, and the entire shape of both legs, with the mist of a flimsy gown floating about it."[6] Sexuality near but within the mar-gins of respectability would always fascinate Hawthorne, but in the early note-books (in sharp contrast to later ones) there are few signs of discomfiture. In a scene from "Sketches from Memory" (1835), almost certainly worked up from a lost notebook, Hawthorne listens to and visually imagines a lady undressing for bed behind a curtain on a canal boat. On a stagecoach in the Berkshires he watches the cooings of two newlyweds, the bridegroom taking "little freedoms" with his wife, in which "she seemed to see nothing amiss" (8:86). A dozen years later, attending a Boston performance of "Jack the Giant Killer" staged for "the middling and lower classes," he finds the audience's unabashed behavior "more noteworthy than the play" (8:501). Two women nearby absorb his attention— one "coarse looking, but good-natured," though filthily dressed; the other, finer-featured with "a particularly intelligent and pleasant face," openly nursing a squalling infant with "a perfect naturalness" (8:502). As the women laugh, talk, and freely enjoy themselves, Hawthorne wonders who they are, what class they belong to, and whether they are "reputable as members" of it (8:504). At length he decides that they are.

Little of this vibrant physical world made its way into Hawthorne's fiction. The notebook entries that did produce fiction were the disembodied ideas for stories sometimes inscribed on the same day as colorfully descriptive passages: "To make one's own reflection in a mirror the subject of a story" ("Monsieur du Miroir"); "The race of mankind to be swept away, leaving all their cities and works. Then another pair to be placed in the world, with native intelligence like Adam and Eve, but knowing nothing of their predecessors or of their own nature and destiny" ("The New Adam and Eve"); "A snake, taken into a man's stomach and nourished there from fifteen years to thirty-five, tormenting him most horribly. A type of envy or some other evil" ("Egotism; or, the Bosom Serpent"); "A person to be in the possession of something as perfect as mortal man has a right to demand; he tries to make it better and ruins it entirely" ("The Birthmark"); and so on (8:15, 21, 22, 165). As Dan McCall observes, Hawthorne's notebooks "betray a mind operating at two extremes: either 'An abstraction to be symbolized' or, jotting down a realistically treated incident, 'What can I make of it?' "[7] The problem with the latter was that the result rarely pleased him either as a rendering of the object or as a testament to the meaningfulness he felt literature should have. His long account of a railroad station vendor would eventuate in the sketch "The Old Apple Dealer," which Melville later praised as "conceived in the subtlest spirit of sadness" (*WHM* 9:242) but whose notebook original Hawthorne found wanting: "After all this description, I have not expressed the aspect and character of the old man, in anything like a satisfactory manner" (8:226). Even the Maine blacksmith is called "*indescribably* human," as if for all his care in detailing the man's speech and manner Hawthorne had somehow missed his vital essence.

Did realism require a fineness of perception and expression Hawthorne felt outside his powers? Was reality too variegated or mercurial on its surfaces or too profound in its depths to be seized by *any* verisimilar art? Or was reality unsatisfying in itself, apart from its representation? Hawthorne's achievement with characters like the blacksmith and Jonathan Cilley and with ensemble scenes like the Williamstown commencement show how accomplished a realist he could be. If as tale-writer he turned aside from the actual and immediate, the evidence of the early notebooks indicates that it was not from fastidiousness or aesthetic incapacity; it was by choice.

Why should life have been one thing and its representation in literature quite another? As a youthful admirer of Bunyan, Spenser, and Milton, Hawthorne may have come to identify the literary with the narrative investiture of abstract ideas, but he was also an enthusiastic reader of Shakespeare and Scott, of eighteenth-century novels, and of books like Rousseau's *Confessions* and *La Nouvelle*

Héloise. His preference in painting would be for the verisimilitude of the Dutch and Flemish realists, in literature for the beef-and-ale "novels of Anthony Trollope" (18:229). His observer's eye would sharply record English manners and English poverty; it would register the bewildering mix of splendor and squalor in Italy; it would sketch characters (genially or tartly), describe landscapes and monuments, recount incidents, and comment on the salient qualities of individuals, social classes, and psychological and national types. Yet these materials, too, tended to go unused, to be channeled into nonfiction (*Our Old Home*), or to be employed as local color background for allegorical elements that thematically overrode them (*The Marble Faun*). Even *The Blithedale Romance*, Hawthorne's most realistic work, incorporates notebook materials from Brook Farm largely to subsume them to a constellation of general ideas and archetypes, much as romancer Coverdale subsumes the flesh-and-blood Hollingsworth to "that steam engine of the Devil's contrivance, a philanthropist!" (3:71). The question with Hawthorne's early tales and later with his romances is why the talented realist of the notebooks should prove so little a realist in his fiction.

Ethan Brandism

> But what if the moral order did not really exist? had come to seem a human construction like any other?...The life once *lived* as allegory could disappear into history, becoming fragments to be put together only in a story.
>
> —Alfred Kazin, *An American Procession*

The story in which Hawthorne drew most heavily from his notebooks, "Ethan Brand," is illustrative of the chasm between the realist and the romancer. The idea for the tale derives from two journal entries recorded a few years after the notebook material that provides its subsidiary characters and dramatic setting: "The search of an investigator for the Unpardonable Sin;—he at last finds it in his own heart and practice." And again: "The Unpardonable Sin might consist in a want of love and reverence for the Human Soul; in consequence of which, the investigator pried into its dark depths, not with a hope or purpose of making it better, but from a cold philosophical curiosity;—content that it should be wicked in whatever kind or degree, and only desiring to study it out" (8:251).

The priority of idea to observation calls to mind W. C. Brownell's remark that Hawthorne "did not find sermons in stones. He had the sermons already; his task was to find the stones to fit them."[8] The "stones" were those patterns of moral experience, reflective of traditional Christian values and putatively emanating from the will of God, that *had* to be true if life was to be endurable. With his theme firmly in place, Hawthorne could begin mining his notebook for what

James called "images which shall place themselves in picturesque correspondence with the spiritual facts with which he is concerned" (James 94). The notebook's itinerant Dutchman with a showman's diorama expands into the tale's legendary Wandering Jew, whose coarse gibe at Christ condemned him to endless roaming; a dog chasing its tail becomes a parodic double of Ethan Brand "in pursuit of an object that could not possibly be attained" (11:96). But the allegorical heightening of life materials also entailed their human diminishment. The extended notebook account of a tattered lawyer-turned-soapboiler, who despite his physical and moral degradation shows "a great deal of sense in his talk, and something of elevation in his expression" (8:90), is the origin for the story's lawyer Giles, but the notebook portrait is flattened in the tale and offered chiefly as a foil to Ethan Brand. Similarly, the boy Joe of the notebook—a four-year-old with "the germ of a tavern-haunter, a country roué" and, in later life, an inmate of the state prison and the local poor-house (8:97)—is sentimentalized into a "timorous and imaginative child" (11:97), virtually an artist-to-be, in order to serve as a sensitive register of the terrors of Ethan Brand.

Hawthorne's Berkshire notebook depicts a rude provincial world seen with a naturalist's eye. "Ethan Brand" preserves the lineaments of that world but reconfigures them in the mode of romance, which permits an elevation of speech and action and establishes an appropriate mimetic backdrop for the theme of an Unpardonable Sin. Writing in the heyday of literary realism, W. C. Brownell deprecated what he saw as Hawthorne's flight from the real to the allegorical, in which "the outer world" exists "solely for the sake of the inner" and "meaning" is made "the burden of the story" rather than "the automatic moral complement of its vivid and actual reality."[9] Here, in the relationship between fact and significance, was the crux of the problem. Reality as inscribed in the American notebooks seems to have *no* "automatic moral complement." It hardly seems moral at all beyond the circumstantial case. It simply *is*: a heterogeneous assortment of persons, some admirable, others roguish, still others a mixture of both, thrown together helter-skelter in scenes replete with local interest but devoid of larger consequence.

Allegory is a formal device that ostensibly "beg[s] the question of absolute reality," yet to the extent that it ascribes overarching moral significance to human affairs, it raises the question of whether such significance inheres in life itself or, as Paul de Man argues, is fabricated by the artist over and against life in order to mask or compensate for an intuited vacancy.[10] Beneath its concern with the Unpardonable Sin, "Ethan Brand" intimates just such a vacancy. When its hero peers into the Wandering Jew's diorama, he is startled to see "nothing"; "I find it to be a heavy matter in my show box—this Unpardonable Sin!" the Jew tells him (11:96). "Nothing" may refer to the inner nothingness of one who has cultivated the intellect to the withering of the heart (the tale's explicit moral) or it may imply that the idea of an "Unpardonable Sin" is chimerical. Ethan Brand entertains this doubt himself—"and, strange to say, it was a painful doubt"— when contact with three derelicts from the local tavern so divests experience of grandeur that he wonders whether "the whole question on which he exhausted life, and more than life," is merely "a delusion" (11:93). The moment is one of demystifying skepticism for Ethan Brand, for the notion of an Unpardonable Sin is what guarantees the reality of a transcendent order beyond the petty trespasses of "half-way sinners" like Bartram the lime-burner (11:89). "The dreadful task of extending man's possible guilt beyond the scope of Heaven's else infinite mercy" (11:89) is concomitantly a work of situating man in a religious world and extending his power and majesty, even to the point of abridging divine sovereignty and outdoing God, much as Ethan Brand feels that in boldness of thought and deed he has outdone the Devil (11:89). From spiritual pride and an idealist's contempt for the meanness of ordinary life, Ethan Brand generates an "IDEA" (11:84) that allows him to transmute his cold, inquisitive delving into others into theological Evil and to cast himself as the hero-villain of a cosmic morality play.

Ethan Brand's only (half-)specified crime involves a young woman named Esther, whom he "made the subject of a psychological experiment, and wasted, absorbed, and perhaps annihilated her soul in the process" (11:94). The gravity of even this crime is apocryphal, since Esther has been described as a circus performer about whom "fine stories" filtered back of "her glittering appearance" (11:93). The detail derives from a notebook description of an "underwitted old man" Hawthorne encountered near North Adams whose children and grandchildren worked in a circus and who "recommended" to bachelor Hawthorne "a certain 'maid' of forty years, who had 300 acres of land," upon whom he himself (a widower) evidently had designs (8:89). In "Ethan Brand" (the low comedy shorn away), the granddaughter becomes a daughter who "makes a grand figure in the world" (11:94), so that if a psychic injury was inflicted, it seems not to have been devastating. Along with other particulars in the story (the dog futilely chasing its tail, the "nothing" Ethan Brand sees in the diorama), the allusion to Esther's subsequent life belongs to a pattern of subversion embedded in the story. The injury *ought* to have been devastating for it to carry the moral weight that character and narrator assign to it. Otherwise, as Bartram says, Ethan Brand is a sinner "like the rest of us" (11:90), more culpable chiefly by degree in that his sin is premeditated and coldly intellectual. Beneath his pose of Faustian/ Byronic damnation—"Freely, were it to do again, would I incur the guilt. Unshrinkingly, I accept the retribution!" (11:90)—Ethan Brand may well suspect this himself; his suicide, as Nina Baym suggests, amounts to an act of self-apotheosis designed "to validate the meaning he has imposed on his life" and set "him beyond the reach of a regulating reality."[11]

Ultimately, "Ethan Brand" seems less about a man who commits the Unpardonable Sin than about a man who wants to think that he has and a narrator who goes far toward collaborating with him in his fantasy. In de Man's terms, Ethan Brand is an allegorist who reacts against the prospect of empty naturalism by creating an imagined world fraught with spiritual meaning. What Ethan Brand does *within* the tale, Hawthorne does *through* it, selecting and heightening life materials to body forth a morally charged universe far removed from the ragged but humanly rich one recorded in the tale's notebook sources.

Even as he fashions such a world, however, Hawthorne chips away at it through ironies on the margins of his tale, as if obliged to register a secret suspicion about the verity of the romancer's activity. The impulse to elevate and the impulse to deflate are rooted in the same underlying anxiety about the significance of experience. "Allegory and irony," as de Man said of their relationship generally, are "linked" in "Ethan Brand" by their "common" source in "a truly temporal predicament"[12]—the gap between things and wishful ideas about things. Allegory undertakes to bridge this gap; irony deconstructs the bridge. Understood as a self-conscious expression of ontological desire, allegory of this kind is not a vehicle for deeper truth; it is the representation of an alternative literary universe that author and reader consent to inhabit for the duration of the tale and to which they give what I. A. Richards called "emotional belief"—a belief whose "only justification is its success in meeting our needs"[13]—but which they do not, except nostalgically or sentimentally, confuse with the ways of their lived universe. Without conceptualizing it as such, Hawthorne grasped the "as if" quality of post-Christian allegorical mimesis and was accordingly skittish about the value of his tales even as he insistently shaped them as he did. As a skeptical empiricist, he could not help looking ironically at Ethan Brand; as a would-be religionist lacking the faith of religion, he cultivated romance and Ethan Brandized himself.

The Great Questions of Life

Mr. Brand stopped also, and said with the same soft forwardness, "He doesn't care for the things you care for—the great questions of life."
—Henry James, *The Europeans*

Beyond pointing up the distance between Hawthorne's public and private writings, "Ethan Brand" is instructive because its notion of an "Unpardonable Sin" is the most prominent example of Hawthorne's lifelong belief in the fundamental irreparability of sin, which, next to immortality (with which it was entwined), was the greatest of all "the great questions of life" for him. "Sin" is almost never a concern in his notebook observations of behavior. It defines many of the tales and three of the four published romances (as well as "The Ancestral Footstep") because Hawthorne grasped what Ann Douglas calls "the essential Calvinist truth...that sin itself is the sublime, and that only its enormity puts men on speaking terms with God,"[14] or ushers them into a moral universe in which God and eternal life are possible. While the notebooks display a fascination with the local and idiosyncratic, the fiction, as Yvor Winters remarked, is "far more likely to concern [itself] with the theory of mankind than with the chaos, trivial, brutal, and exhausting, of the actuality."[15] For Winters, Hawthorne's abstractionism was a New England quality, the secular residue of a formerly typological cast of mind. So it was for William Dean Howells, who admired Hawthorne's writing but saw it as impaired by his region's moralizing bias: "New England, in Hawthorne's work, achieved supremacy in romance; but the romance is always an allegory, and the novel is a picture in which truth to life is suffered to do its unsermonized office for conduct; and New England yet lacks her novelist, because it was her instinct and her conscience in fiction to be true to an ideal of life rather than to life itself."[16]

Fidelity to "an ideal of life" is what Mr. Brand of James's *The Europeans* has in mind when he tells the recalcitrant Gertrude that she cares, or ought to care, for "the great questions of life."[17] Mr. Brand is a Unitarian minister in 1840s Massachusetts (Hawthorne's world), a time and place in which liberal theology and social conservatism combined to empty moral experience of what used to be its cosmic dimension but has been reduced to the dry husk of "duty." Hawthorne lived and wrote at the end of a theological tradition, and though he shared little of the religious fervor of his ancestors, he believed, as he said in "The Old Manse," that the musty Puritan tomes were at least "earnestly written" and may have "possessed warmth" in their own time, while "the frigidity" of modern publications like the liberal *Christian Examiner* "was characteristic and inherent" (10:19, 20).

The past for Hawthorne may have possessed a genuine moral weight absent from the present, or (a more vexing doubt) he may have suspected that the actual of any historical period fell short of what the spirit and the imagination required. It is common for a segment of the literary class to view itself as "fragmented" and "hyper-conscious" in relation to a supposedly elemental past. In the mid-to-late nineteenth century, however, transformations of society, along with the decline of traditional idioms of belief, made for an especially widespread feeling of moral dislocation. Spatially larger than the past thanks to increased mobility, the present seemed humanly reduced, as if the expanded physical horizons of life had opened new mental horizons but left the self without a spiritual compass for negotiating them.

Quaint and provincial as it was, the old anthropocentric theology had the virtue of unifying experience sub specie aeternitatis and investing it with grandeur. In Sarah Orne Jewett's *The Country of the Pointed Firs*, published almost half a century after "Ethan Brand," Mrs. Todd and her friend Mrs. Fosdick tell the story of Joanna, a young woman jilted in love, who, after railing inwardly against God, comes to feel that she has "committed the unpardonable sin" and exiles herself to a desolate island in lifelong penance.[18] Joanna lived and suffered long ago, in antebellum times. "Yes," says Mrs. Fosdick, "she was one o' them poor things that talked about the great sin; we don't seem to hear nothing about the unpardonable sin now, but you may say 'twas not uncommon then." Mrs. Fosdick continues: "I expect nowadays, if such a thing happened, she'd have gone out West to her uncle's folks or up to Massachusetts and had a change, an' come home good as new. The world's bigger and freer than it used to be."[19] Going out West to her uncle's is what Howells's Irene Lapham does in similar circumstances, and while she returns not quite "good as new," she is visibly stronger, more sensible, and with prospects of a future. The difference between the realist of "nowadays" (Mrs. Fosdick, Howells) and the romancer with roots in or nostalgia for an older time (Joanna, Hawthorne) is that the former sees life episodically as an ongoing process of growth and development, while the latter sees great events (sins especially) as identity-defining occurrences that happen once and stand as markers for everything that follows.

If the realist's way of regarding experience is pragmatic and future-oriented, it could also seem, for those nurtured in residual ways, to leach meaning from events. To count *as* sin, and therefore to imbue life with significance beyond the matter-of-factly naturalistic, sin had to be definitive in its impress on character and life history. While "the supernatural hardly existed for [Hawthorne] in any realm save that of the fanciful," Philip Rahv observes, he "was none the less unable to free himself from the perception of human destiny in terms of sin and redemption, sacrilege and consecration."[20] Unable and *unwilling*. A feeling of "human destiny"—of life unfolding according to universal laws congruent with traditional religion but not dependent upon it—was what Hawthorne clung to in the absence of orthodox belief. Sin was his conduit to experiential meaning, to cosmic order, to God's Providence, and to the immortality of the soul. Without the reality of sin, there was no transcendent dimension to human affairs, only the anarchic play of desire and circumstance he observed during his youthful travels and recorded in its immediacy with little sense of its bearing on any "great questions of life."

On a Frozen Lake

"It has seemed to me," observed Septimius, "that it is not the prevailing mood, the most common one, that is to be trusted; this is habit, formality, the shallow covering which we draw over what is real, and

seldom suffer it to be blown aside. But it is the snake-like doubt that
thrusts out its head, that gives us a glimpse of reality."

—Hawthorne, *"Septimius Felton"*

Without the supernatural, the natural is a pit of horror.

—John Updike, *interview with Jane Howard (1966)*

In "The Custom-House," apropos of having tried and failed to begin a romance
about the scarlet letter, Hawthorne upbraids himself for the "folly" of attempting
to do so: "The wiser effort would have been to diffuse thought and imagination
through the opaque substance of to-day, and thus to make it a bright transpar-
ency" (1:37). The labor Hawthorne imagines but does not perform is that of the
realist, as the son-in-law he didn't live to know, George Parsons Lathrop, would
describe it nearly twenty-five years later:

> Realism sets itself to work to consider characters and events which are
> apparently the most ordinary and uninteresting, in order to extract
> from these their full value and true meaning. It would apprehend in all
> particulars the connection between the familiar and the extraordinary,
> and the seen and unseen in human nature....Where we had thought
> nothing worthy of notice, it shows everything to be rife with *signifi-
> cance*. It will easily be seen, therefore, that realism calls upon the imagi-
> nation to exercise its highest function, which is the conception of things
> in their true relations.[21]

Dissatisfied with his fictive practice and sensing that his midcentury audience
wanted a more realistic contemporary art, Hawthorne had begun to think of
writing himself out of romance even before "The Custom-House" and *The Scarlet
Letter*. In "Main-street" (1849), his capsule history of Salem presented through
a speaker with a showman's box of representative tableaux, he had voiced his
chronic suspicion that his art of moonlight amounted to little more than fanciful
moonshine. The sketch ends with the showman about to move from "the cold
shadow of antiquity" to "the sunshine of the present" and from "slips of paste-
board" that only distance and a charitable suspension of disbelief can bring to
"spiritual life" to recognizable men and women who walk the streets of present-day Salem (11:81, 63).

The House of the Seven Gables is the deferred fruition of the showman's project.
Despite its famous preface, which has become a reference point for critical dis-
cussions of American romance, the book has "more literal actuality" to it, as
Henry James noted, than either of Hawthorne's other American romances
(James 98).[22] Writing to publisher James T. Fields, Hawthorne acknowledged
this realism when he observed that "many" of the book's passages "ought to be

finished with the minuteness of a Dutch picture, in order to give them their proper effect" (16:371). Reviewers also likened *Seven Gables* to Dutch painting and, in its "sketches of still-life," to the emergent art of daguerreotypy.[23] The book, of course, prominently features a daguerreotypist, and in Holgrave's apologia for his art of "sunshine" (the antithesis of the romancer's chiaroscuro) Hawthorne seems to be defending his own attempt at a mimetic realism reserved until now chiefly for his notebooks. "There is such a wonderful insight in heaven's broad sunshine," Holgrave says: "While we give it credit for depicting the merest surface, it actually brings out the secret character of a truth that no painter would ever venture upon, even could he detect it" (2:91).

Even as he pursues his art of sunshine, however, Hawthorne seems hesitant to stake his success upon it, and in the absence of a continuous novelistic plot he avails himself of the paraphernalia of New England gothic to enliven and diversify his materials and endow them with a significance beyond the dramatic interaction of his characters. "Romance" in *The House of the Seven Gables* is not a sustained midworld between "the Actual and the Imaginary" (1:36), as it had been in *The Scarlet Letter*; it is a treacle of mythiness intermittently poured over the plain cake of realism. Hawthorne's uneasiness with the realist's work is evident from the start in the arch, condescending tone he adopts toward Hepzibah, as if nothing but comic pathos were appropriate for so ungainly a figure. Like a toddler taking his first wobbly steps, Hawthorne seems doubtful not only about "the revelatory value of [his] exterior details" (the realist's method), as Richard H. Brodhead has said,[24] but also about the aesthetic fitness of a subject with "so much of the mean and ludicrous" in it (the realist's content) (2:41). The justification he offers looks ahead to Lathrop's creed, but with a signal difference:

> Life is made up of marble and mud. And, without all the deeper trust in a comprehensive sympathy above us, we might hence be led to suspect the insult of a sneer, as well as an immitigable frown, on the iron countenance of fate. What is called poetic insight is the gift of discerning, in this sphere of strangely mingled elements, the beauty and the majesty which are compelled to assume a garb so sordid. (2:41)

Hawthorne's "poetic insight" is analogous to Lathrop's "imagination" in "its highest function," but where Lathrop's connection between "the seen and unseen in human nature" operates entirely on the level of the secular, Hawthorne needs the assurance of divine "sympathy" if the "mean and ludicrous" in life is to be more than a ghastly affront. Hepzibah sees no token of such sympathy during her moment of greatest trial. Instead, beleaguered by Judge Pyncheon, she has the "wretched conviction, that Providence intermeddled not in these petty wrongs of one individual to his fellow, nor had any balm for these little agonies of a solitary soul, but shed its justice, and its mercy, in a broad, sunlike sweep, over half the universe at once. Its vastness made it nothing" (2:245). Evidence for divine solicitude in *Seven Gables* rests on the intrusive moralizing of the narrator: "But Hepzibah did not see, that, just as there comes a warm sunbeam into every cottage-window, so comes a love-beam of God's care and pity, for every separate need" (2:245). Faithfully represented, experience provides scant ground for faith; faith must be superadded to experience through sentiment and idealizing, or "romance."

In its mixture of marble and mud, novel and romance, rendered experience and asserted meaning, *The House of the Seven Gables* resembles Harriet Beecher Stowe's *The Minister's Wooing* (1859), published at the end of a decade (as *Seven Gables* was toward the beginning) marked by religious anxiety about science's investigations of nature and culminating in Darwin's *The Origin of Species* (1859). In Stowe's book, the high New England themes of piety, sacrifice, and the mysteries of divine government are interspersed with kitchen scenes and the gossipings of the seamstress Miss Prissy, the "two worlds" of "the great and the little, the solemn and the trivial, wreathing in and out, like the grotesque carvings on a Gothic shrine," and joined "only, did we know it rightly" (as implicitly we do not), in a transcendent perspective that "makes all things divine."[25]

Stowe can relax into comic realism because, unlike Hawthorne, she is rooted in Christian faith, which allows her to be more forthright in acknowledging the uncertainty and lurking terror, the visible *un*Christianity, of the sublunary world. The appreciative chapter "Miss Prissy" ends with a memento mori jarringly at odds with its shrewd humor and closer in tenor to Melville's chance-ridden naturalistic universe than to the Calvinist's divinely superintended one:

> You are living your daily life among trifles that one death-stroke may make relics. One false step, one luckless accident, an obstacle on the track of a train, the tangling of the cord in shifting a sail, and the penknife, the pen, the papers, the trivial articles of dress and clothing, which to-day you toss idly and jestingly from hand to hand, may become dread memorials of the awful tragedy whose deep abyss ever underlies our common life. (*MW* 121)

Like Melville, Stowe finds her symbol for the ontological backdrop of life in "the deep, eternal sea,—the treacherous, soft, dreadful, inexplicable sea" (*MW* 42). It is the sea that, by report, kills James Marvyn, heroine Mary Scudder's lover, and to underscore its indifference Stowe has the day that follows Mary's receipt of the news break "calm and fair," with the sea "laughing and dancing with every ripple, as unconsciously as if no other form dear to human hearts had gone down beneath it. Oh! treacherous, deceiving beauty of outward things! beauty, wherein throbs not one answering nerve to human pain!" (*MW* 187).

James, it turns out, is not dead and makes a happy return, but the problem for Mary and for James's distraught, God-arraigning mother—the gulf between human needs and the blithe unconcern of nature—cannot be resolved simply by trust in Providence, as the Marvyns' servant Candace would tautologically have it: "as we's got to live in dis yer world, it's quite clar de Lord must ha' fixed it so we *can*" (*MW* 202). Why "*must*" he, if "he" there is? A faith grounded in nothing more substantial than human need, Stowe understands, is tenuous. In order for the universe to be more than a random play of forces, God must be felt across nature as an active presence in human life. "The point" we need "to be sure of," James Marvyn says in relation to the biblical Jacob, is not merely that God exists but that he "care[s] anything about men, and would do anything to help them" (*MW* 298). There must be a reciprocal interchange between God and ourselves. The ascending part of this interchange is human prayer; the *de*scending part is God's response, displayed visibly through material favors or invisibly through bestowed spiritual strength. "The genuineness of religion," as William James wrote, "is indissolubly bound up with the question whether the prayerful consciousness be or be not deceitful."[26] The communication between ourselves and God must be mutual and it must be credibly ratified.

For Stowe, answered prayers are proof of a realm beyond nature and of the centrality of human beings to its design. As a literary realist, Stowe cannot import a responsive God into her fictional world; God enters her work by way of "romance," through counterrealistic authorial intrusions and manipulations of plot. As narrator, Stowe confronts the fact that prayers *do* go unanswered by positing "established laws for prayer," one or another of which may have been "neglected" by the disappointed pray-er (*MW* 312); as plot-maker, she substitutes an offstage deus ex machina for narrative plausibility to show God's benign superintendence of human affairs. During his long absence at sea, James Marvyn comes to make a Jacob-like compact with God—if He will interest himself in Marvyn and "be [his] Friend and Protector," Marvyn will do his best to serve Him—and Marvyn is gratified to discover that apparently "*Somebody* did attend even to [his] prayers" and arranged matters fortunately on his behalf (*MW* 298). "*Somebody*" took pains not only to save him amid shipwreck but also to return him to New England "quite rich" and in the nick of time to win Mary (*MW* 324). For those who can strike such a bargain with God, religion's proof is in the payment.[27]

The flaw in Stowe's science of prayer is that those nearest to despair and in most need of divine aid are least likely to be in the pious frame of mind required to secure it. Seeking assurance as his mother lies dying in July 1849, Hawthorne finds "so much gloom and ambiguity" attending death in old age "that it opens no vista for us into Heaven" (8:425); even his daughter Una's talk of her grandmother "going to God" only prompts a wishful, "Would to God it were to be so! Faith and trust would be far easier than they are now" (8:430).[28] Una's own near-death from malaria in 1859 would be even more trying for Hawthorne and unrelieved in the days of crisis by anything like his wife's resignation to the will of God. In *Seven Gables*, oppressed by Judge Pyncheon and anxious about Clifford, Hepzibah finds "her faith… too weak; the prayer too heavy to be thus uplifted. It fell back like a lump of lead, upon her heart" (2:245). In place of answered prayer, Hawthorne relies upon plot to help characters who cannot help themselves and who look in vain to Providence for assistance or even for moral strength. Hepzibah is delivered in timely fashion by the death of Judge Pyncheon, and she is made rich by the equally timely death in Europe of the judge's only son and heir.

"Religion," John Updike remarks, "is our persistence," in the face of material evidence "that we are insignificant accidents within a vast uncaused churning, in feeling that our life is a story, with a pattern and a moral and an inevitability."[29] Understood not as a fictional subgenre but as an *activity*—a mode of treating experience that gives it pattern, moral, and at least an aura of inevitability— "romance," or romanc*ing*, may also be such a "persistence." The *Somebody* who manages affairs in *The Minister's Wooing* and *The House of the Seven Gables* is the godlike author, whose intervening hand administers a comforting narrative and moral resolution even as the realized worlds of the books attest to naturalistic indifference. At once realist *and* romancer, Hawthorne, like Stowe, would have it both ways. Faithful to experience in his presentation of character and homely circumstance, he is *un*faithful to it in structuring events so as to reassure himself and his audience of life's inherent order and meaning. As realist, he demystifies the idea of Providential design by having Holgrave ascribe the bloody deaths of Colonel Pyncheon and Judge Pyncheon to a "physical indisposition in the Pyncheon race," which old Matthew Maule shrewdly drew upon for his curse (2:304); as romancer, he has Holgrave speak of the judge's death as consumma- tional, an "event pre-ordained, happening inevitably, and so fitting with past occurrences, that it could almost have been prophesied" (2:303).

The notion that history has an immanent moral logic will be so sketchily developed in *Seven Gables* that Hawthorne sees fit to undercut his "moral purpose"—to illustrate how "the wrong-doing of one generation lives into the successive ones" (2:2)—virtually as soon as he announces it. The real cause of transgenerational Pyncheon tragedy, as F. O. Matthiessen observed, is "not the original curse on the house, but the curse that the Pyncheons have continued to bring upon themselves" through greed, arrogance, class oppression, envy, and lust.[30] "When romances do really teach anything," Hawthorne writes, as if con- ceding the point, "it is usually through a far more subtle process than the osten- sible one" of a moral (2:2).

What, then, *does Seven Gables* teach? For Stowe, as for many readers then and later, the book's vitality lay in its "succession of Rembrandt pictures, done in words instead of oils"[31]—pictures of Hepzibah, Phoebe, Judge Pyncheon, and, most subtly, Clifford, whom Melville found "full of an awful truth throughout.... He is no caricature. He is Clifford" (*WHM* 14:186). In one of the most delicate sections of psychological analysis in the book, Hawthorne tries to calibrate the peculiar mix of elements in Clifford's sentiment toward Phoebe. His feeling is not exactly paternal; it is not disinterestedly aesthetic; nor, despite his pleasure in her budding womanhood, can it quite be called sexual. It is something elusively compounded of all of these things and of other feelings still more ineffable. "But we strive in vain to put the idea into words" (2:142), Hawthorne writes in exasperation, as he had of the old apple dealer and the Maine blacksmith. As art, he finds the realist's work of psychological precision extraordinarily taxing; as morality, he finds it insufficient. If he *had* succeeded in delineating Clifford's feelings to his satisfaction, what, by his own measure of truth, would he have accomplished? A delineation of Clifford's feelings. As Melville said, Clifford is Clifford.

For reviewer Henry T. Tuckerman, such delineations were enough. The genius of *Seven Gables* resided in its characters, who "symbolize[d] the poles of human existence" but also represented distinct regional types; Clifford, for example, was "the man of fine organization and true sentiments environed by the material realities of New England life" (Tuckerman 348). A Boston-born New York critic writing in *The Southern Literary Messenger,* Tuckerman saw *Seven Gables* as a work about the nature of "New England character in its elemental state," with "all its frigidity, its gloom, its intellectual enthusiasm and its religious aspiration" (Tuckerman 348). At the same time, the book radiated outward for him to transregional themes like "mesmerism and socialism," "family tyranny," and moral inheritance, and to "beautiful revelations" about human nature (Tuckerman 348). Pointedly ignoring its gothic excesses and nearly everything that comprises its "romance"—ancestral curses, magic mirrors, secret compartments, hints of supernatural agency—Tuckerman ascribes the success of *Seven Gables* to the realist's "fidelity to local characteristics" and to an "earnestness of feeling" that eschewed "melo-dramatic development" (Tuckerman 348, 349). His view of mimesis—the grounding of literary meaning in the actual and immediate—resembles Goethe's, which is the antithesis of Hawthorne's in his top-down allegorical moods. "There is a great difference," Goethe wrote,

> between a poet's seeking the particular from the general and his seeing the general in the particular. The former gives rise to allegory, where the particular serves only as an instance or example of the general; the latter, however, is the true nature of poetry: the expression of the particular

without any thought of, or reference to, the general. Whoever grasps the particular in all its vitality also grasps the general, without being aware of it, or only becoming aware of it at a late stage.[32]

Why didn't Hawthorne confine himself to the Goethean "particular" Tuckerman admires in *Seven Gables*? At its highest, the achievement of realism is the revelation of what Lathrop calls the "full value and true meaning" of the natural objects before it. In Edwin H. Cady's words, realism shifts its "vision… from an upward to a level plane where it focuse[s] upon man and his life in the world."[33] It does not try to perform the office of religion or to fill the void of significance felt in religion's absence. For the postbellum generation reacting against the mentality and literary practice of the fathers, this was realism's great strength; for Hawthorne, it was its limitation, which troubled him all the more because realism seemed to have the weight of truth on its side. By the time of *Seven Gables*, he wished to engage himself more concretely with the world around him, but he feared the naturalistic implications of realism, disliked what he considered its aesthetic meanness and poverty of spirit, and employed it restrictedly as a pictorial technique, unwilling to trust it as a site and vehicle for meaning and an implied reading of experience. In Hepzibah's frustrated appeal to Providence, the vision of the realist "thrusts out its head" with "snake-like doubt" (13:11), as it periodically will throughout Hawthorne's work, and gives voice to what William James would call the "sadness [that] lies at the heart of every merely positivistic, agnostic, or naturalistic scheme of philosophy":

> For naturalism,… mankind is in a position similar to that of a set of people living on a frozen lake, surrounded by cliffs over which there is no escape, yet knowing that little by little the ice is melting, and the inevitable day drawing near when the last film of it will disappear, and to be drowned ignominiously will be the human creature's portion.[34]

This is where literary and philosophical realism pointed for Hawthorne: to the frozen lake. From *Fanshawe* (1828), whose lovers Edward Wolcott and Ellen Langton fade into oblivion, to *Grimshawe* (1861), whose misanthropic hero raves of coming from and returning to "nothingness" (12:356), Hawthorne's fictions rest on a barely concealed intuition of the void.

Despite his reputation in his own time and for most of the century after his death, Hawthorne was not a Christian in the sense of having a deep and abiding belief in established doctrine or an interest in or respect for the institutional Church. Even, or especially, liberal religion left him indifferent. The minister at Salem's Unitarian North Church beginning in 1847 was Octavius Brooks Frothingham, a convert to the broad theism of Theodore Parker and as *literary* a clerical presence (he would be chairman of the Salem Lyceum) as could be found in provincial New England. Even before he came to Salem, Frothingham was known to Hawthorne, having "closed" a sermon in Boston to dramatic effect, Sophia Hawthorne reports, "with three pages quoted from my husband's Fancy's Show Box" (16:172). There is no record of Hawthorne attending Frothingham's church or cultivating his acquaintance, though Frothingham reports seeing him frequently on the street.[35] Clerics discomfited Hawthorne even more than literary men; worse, they bored him.

Hawthorne's religion had three essential planks: he believed in the existence of God; he believed in an afterlife and eternal judgment; and he believed in the long-term Providential superintendence of history and the immanence of moral law. He believed in these things not on the basis of evidence but in its absence, and not on the ground of faith but of tenuous hope. What William James called "the will to believe" was, in Hawthorne, as in James himself, fundamentally a *need* to believe. He felt the frozen lake cracking beneath his feet.

The Return of Romance

> Man lives in an environment that we call nature, and he also lives in a society or home, a human world that he is trying to build out of nature. There is the world he sees and the world he constructs, the world he lives in and the world he wants to live in.
>
> —Northrop Frye, *Fables of Identity*

Whatever their roots in temperament, talent, or New England tradition, the moral and metaphysical idealizations of romance served Hawthorne instrumentally as a refuge against the threefold horrors of naturalism: the horror of universal meaninglessness; the horror of death and oblivion; and the horror of enthrallment to bodily drives, particularly the sexual.

For Hawthorne, as for his age, the site of the ideal in the actual world was the chaste spiritual woman, whose countertype, the earthy erotic woman, was a powerfully attractive but cautionary example of the energies of wild, unsublimated nature. Dan McCall finds "an intimate connection between [Hawthorne's] aesthetic ideal of how art should 'spiritualize' life and his responses to women."[36] Both were transmutations of reality. Hawthorne's notion of the "ethereal essence" (1:165–66) of woman was his ultimate romance, or rather his foundational one, since morality, the soul, eternal life, and God himself all depended upon it.

In practice, such idealizing meant not only relocating the spiritual from the pulpit to the middle-class home—Hawthorne's symbol of the "human world that [man] is trying to build out of nature"[37]—but also endowing its everyday activities with the glow of the sacramental. Early in *The Minister's Wooing*, Harriet

Beecher Stowe celebrates what New Englanders called "faculty" (*MW* 3), a feminine genius for bringing order and beauty to domestic affairs with the lightest perceptible touch. Mary Scudder has faculty *and* she is radiantly religious, but Stowe, Christian to the marrow, feels no call to conflate the two.[38] Phoebe Pyncheon of *Seven Gables* also has faculty, "a kind of natural magic" that draws out "the hidden capabilities" of her surroundings and gives them "a look of comfort and habitableness" (2:71). Phoebe's sunny domesticity, however, *is* her religion, or the core of what Hawthorne most values in it, though he dutifully has her attend church and say her morning prayers. The phrase "angel in the house" (Hawthorne would greatly admire Coventry Patmore's 1854 poem of that title, which he bought for Sophia) is more than a cultural cliché with Phoebe. "By her sweet breath and happy thoughts," Phoebe purifies the House of the Seven Gables "of all former evil and sorrow" (2:72) in a single night (negating in the process Hawthorne's theme of an enduring curse upon it). "There was a spiritual quality in Phoebe's activity," Hawthorne writes, that made the mundane and the "squalid" seem "pleasant, and even lovely" (2:82). While firmly planted in the "real" (2:141)—solid, convention-bound actuality—Phoebe also embodies the ideal and is the avatar of a middle-class democratic future in which "woman's office" would be "to move in the midst of practical affairs, and to gild them all—the very homeliest, were it even the scouring of pots and pans—with the atmosphere of loveliness and joy" (2:80). Hawthorne can venture such language because he knows his religion of domesticity is shared by his audience; the difference is that for him it truly comprises a religion, or the nearest thing he has to one.

The return of romance: except in his notebooks (and occasionally even there), Hawthorne's response to the problem of hard actuality was to silver it. *Seven Gables* is more a novel than a romance, but in the pivotal chapter "Phoebe's Good Bye" romance asserts itself, not as a form of storytelling (as in Holgrave's tale of Alice Pyncheon) or an alleged historical curse, but as an elevated mode of feeling and perceiving. Dramatically, the chapter is a garden love scene between Holgrave and Phoebe; morally, a meditation on the growth of a soul (Phoebe's); and politically, a rejection of root-and-branch reformism (Holgrave's). Above all, however, its celebration of moonlight articulates a way of apprehending the world in which, as Hawthorne said in "The Custom-House," the "details" of ordinary reality, "so completely seen, are so spiritualized by the unusual light" that they seem disembodied and come to "acquire dignity thereby" (1:35). In "Phoebe's Good Bye," as the exterior features of the time-worn house are "transfigured" by moonlight with "a charm of romance" (2:213), the characters' interior lives are also transfigured. Without transcending the actual (like religious art) or disclosing its essence (like realistic art), moonlight (romance) divests experience of the sordid and wearisome and allows the responsive sensibility to enter a hallowed world that seems its proper and joyful abode (2:213). "Could I keep the feeling that now possesses me," Holgrave exclaims, "the garden would every day be virgin soil" (2:214).

This is the underlying function of "romance" in *Seven Gables*: to crystallize Holgrave's feeling of wonder through the creation of an aesthetically distilled textual world, which, without being religious in invoking the supernatural, is capable of kindling the emotions of religion in characters and readers alike, whether the emotions be those of romantic love (as here) or of awe at the benign operations of moral and historical law. Against the earthly pull of realism and its implied metaphysics, romance confirms belief in life's intrinsic meaning, in cosmic justice, and in the immortality of the soul. It is an elixir that, performing the work once reserved for grace, awakens the idealizing impulse in the self and prompts at least a transient facsimile of redeemed vision. Although Hawthorne "could never feel that America was a new world,"[39] in "Phoebe's Good Bye" he has love generate a new world for the lovers, or rather he has language evoke the *aura* of such a world as it transmutes the prosaic into the quasi-spiritual. Romance is Hawthorne's vehicle for (in Richard Poirier's words about "great" American texts) "stabiliz[ing] certain feelings and attitudes that have, as it were, no place at all except where the writer's style can give them one."[40]

Such idealizations were essential for Hawthorne, for in inscribing them he made them affectively real and lived in their glow. But not steadily or permanently. Most of a decade removed from his own idyll at the Old Manse, Hawthorne in *Seven Gables* can no more sustain the beatifying vision than Holgrave ("Could I keep...") foresees that he can. The book "darkens damnably toward the close," he wrote James T. Fields in November 1850, "but I shall try hard to pour some setting sunshine over it" (16:376). Pour he did, though more by force of will than through the autointoxication of "Phoebe's Good Bye." Sophia was not the only reader to enthuse over the "unspeakable grace and beauty" of the book's conclusion with its "ethereal light, and...dear home-love-liness and satisfaction" (*NHW* 1:383). Hasty and implausible as it is, the ending of *Seven Gables* completes the triumph of romance over realism—in Northrop Frye's terms, of the world of desire the artist constructs over the world of nature he inhabits.

Has Hawthorne transcended the real or simply evaded it? "The creative and the neurotic reactions to experience are both dissatisfied with what they see," Frye remarks: "they both believe that something else should be 'there'; they both attempt to remake the world of experience into something more responsive to their desire."[41] Is "romance" an expression of creative insight or of neurotic fear? This is a question Hawthorne could never resolve and would never cease to ask.

Beautiful Illusions

> Something might be true even though it is harmful and dangerous in
> the greatest degree; it might in fact belong to the basic make-up of
> things that one should perish from its full recognition. Then the
> strength of a given thinker would be measured by the amount of "the
> truth" that he could stand. Or, to say it more plainly, to what degree he
> would *need* to have it adulterated, shrouded, sweetened, diluted, and
> falsified.
>
> —Nietzsche, *Beyond Good and Evil*

The "Hawthorne" I have been describing is not the Christian moralist of older
readings, the depth psychologist of Frederick C. Crews's *The Sins of the Fathers*,
the New England historian of Michael J. Colacurcio's *The Province of Piety*, the
romantic liberationist of Nina Baym's body of work, or the social, cultural, or
political commentator of historicist readings like Larry J. Reynolds's *Devils and
Rebels*. He is a self-divided man known on one side through his fiction, on
another through his notebooks and letters, who senses from experience that naturalism may be the order of things but can neither live comfortably within its
confines nor transcend them through religious belief.

That Hawthorne shrouded, sweetened, and even falsified what struck him as
the truth is evident from the discrepancies between his published writings and
the notebook entries that are sometimes their direct source. Even in his early
sketches, Rita K. Gollin notes, he often hedged his claims on subjects like immortality with linguistic *dis*claimers that introduced doubt into what was overtly
intended as "conventional affirmation."[42] The ready account is that the expressions of belief are for his audience, the hints of unbelief from himself, but this
simplifies Hawthorne's engagement with the felt truth. In the closing scene of
Heart of Darkness Conrad's Marlow is asked by Kurtz's Intended to repeat his
dying words ("The horror! The horror!").[43] Marlow loathes a lie, but as he stands
in the darkening room with "only [the Intended's] forehead...illumined by the
indistinguishable light of belief and love" (*HD* 158), he feels that a lie is
demanded not simply to spare her but also to preserve the civilization she represents, groundless as it may be. Women, he had said earlier, "are out of it—should
be out of it. We must help them to stay in that beautiful world of their own, lest
our own gets worse" (*HD* 115). Marlow lies to maintain beautiful illusions (not
least his own about women) against the nihilism of the dangerous-true.
Hawthorne was a Marlow, protectively lying to the world, but he was also the
Intended, who required to be lied to, sometimes even by himself.

I have focused chiefly on the private and idiosyncratic in Hawthorne, but the
problem Hawthornean romance ontologically addressed—that of establishing a
post-theological ground for moral and spiritual belief or finding an emotive

replacement for it—was endemic to an age characterized, as Richard H. Brodhead observes, by the "movement from a vision of the world as governed from above by a divine order to a vision of it as governed from within by its own inherent laws."[44] In some fashion, nearly all of Hawthorne's major literary contemporaries found themselves poised between a naturalism that simultaneously attracted and repelled them and a supernaturalism they could neither assent to in traditional terms nor affectively renounce. On fundamental matters of God's existence and the nature of the soul, they were ambivalent, perplexed, vacillating, and self-contradictory, with the consequence that their literary attitudes are often provisional, inconstant, or indeterminate. Does Emerson's "light" in the mind (the oversoul) come "from within [naturalism] or from behind [supernaturalism]" (*CWE* 2:161)? Does Thoreau firmly believe that there is "no higher heaven than the pure senses can furnish, a *purely* sensuous life"?[45] Emily Dickinson, that "The 'Bird within the Hand'" (Heaven on earth) is "Superior" to the one uncertainly in "The 'Bush'" (*ED* #1021)? And Melville, that "the Problem of the Universe" is like the Freemason's "mighty secret," which turns out "to consist in a triangle, a mallet, and an apron,—nothing more!" (*WHM* 14:186)? For each of these writers, naturalism at its best was an open, adventurous posture of the self in a dynamic universe but one that could not be steadily maintained against the thought of annihilation and the lingering appeal of the absolute. Even Whitman, who "was able to spell out the first invigorating syllables of a naturalistic credo," Newton Arvin observes, "recoiled from its full and final exactions, and fell back... upon an intuitionalist theism" that was his substitute for Judeo-Christianity.[46]

Nietzsche put the issue squarely when he asked whether our "desires and passions" mightn't be taken as "'givens'... *sufficient* for understanding the so-called mechanistic (or material) world."[47] As an analyst of character (with Dimmesdale, for example, or in *The Blithedale Romance*), Hawthorne explored the "sufficiency" of naturalistic accounts of behavior. Is "thinking," as Nietzsche claims, "nothing but the interrelation and interaction of our drives" within the framework of what education and environment have made us (*BGE* 42)? Is sin an objective reality or only a subjective fact of consciousness? If the latter, do moral values exist outside the mind, which is doomed to dust? And if dust is indeed our destination, why not acknowledge the fact and make naturalism the ground for a rich, creative, sin-emancipated life in time?

Nietzsche's words are from *Beyond Good and Evil*, whose title suggests "the self-surpassing of morality" that Nietzsche regards as the "long secret labor which is in store for the subtlest, most candid, also most malicious consciences of today" (*BGE* 38). Hawthorne had the first of these qualities, often the second, and at least vicariously the third (how else could he create the spirited iconoclasts he did?); but he also had another, ontological dread, that caused him to doubt whether anything could matter at all if one "transcended" Good and Evil.

The dark heroines of his romances (Hester, Zenobia, and Miriam) share nothing of this dread and welcome the dismantling of the moral and social order as an occasion for building a more satisfying one. Through them, Hawthorne gives play to the Nietzschean prospect of a life-affirming naturalism, and in each instance, after opening a vista of freedom and possibility, he defensively pulls back and closes it, only to reopen it in his next romance.

As Hawthorne aged, the stakes involved with naturalism increased for him, complicated by his European experience, his encumbered personal and professional life, his nostalgia for a more footloose time, and his awareness that, having drawn his lot, no second chance would be forthcoming for him or, if it did come, that he was too old, too tired, and too cautious to avail himself of it. With its appeal to the senses, physical and aesthetic, Italy was his consummate dark heroine, and resistance to its siren song came at a high price. Hilda in *The Marble Faun* is a tepid substitute for someone who has known the plenitude of Rome and felt the charisma of Miriam; but Rome and Miriam were too dangerous to countenance for long, even in wishful fantasy. To the older Hawthorne, the naturalist's life-in-the-moment seemed an empty cup, both on the side of pain and death, which had become more real to him, and on the side of joy, which had become less. "God himself cannot compensate us for being born, in any period short of eternity," he wrote in January 1855: "All the misery we endure here constitutes a claim for another life;—and, still more, all the happiness, because all true happiness involves something more than a mortal capacity for the enjoyment of it" (21:153). A claim, however, was simply a feeling of entitlement; it guaranteed nothing and might go as unheeded as Hepzibah's prayer.

Against the pull of experience, Hawthorne in his final years continued to labor (unsuccessfully) at romance, though aware that the public taste had changed and that his sensibility and writerly bent had undergone a marked shift toward realism during his English residence. He persisted with romance partly by force of habit or engrained literary identity,[48] but also because romance, with its beautiful illusions, was his instrument for shoring up his tottering faith that the universe was what it should be, a divinely appointed order, rather than the chaos it visibly seemed.

Delia Bacon was an American woman who conceived the idea that Shakespeare's plays were written by a group of prominent Elizabethans, Sir Francis Bacon chief among them, to insinuate a subversive political philosophy that could not be propounded openly or under their own names. Her speculations led her to England and, through the mediation of Hawthorne's sister-in-law Elizabeth Peabody, to Hawthorne himself, who was impressed by her character and eventually underwrote the publication of her "most remarkable" book (22:91).[49] In time, Hawthorne came to regard Bacon as "unquestionably... a monomaniac" whose ideas were "erroneous" (5:106, 104), possibly even insane. And yet, he allowed in *Our Old Home,* Bacon was "in a certain sense" right. "Shakespeare has surface beneath surface," and Bacon's achievement was to recognize "a depth" in the plays that "scholars, critics, and learned societies, devoted to the elucidation of his unrivalled scenes, had never imagined to exist there" (5:106, 116).

What especially fascinated Hawthorne about Bacon was the imagined process by which a philosophy antipathetic to her native beliefs gradually established itself in her mind "without [her] volition—contrary to [her] volition—and substitut[ed] itself," on some level of consciousness and expression, "in place of everything that originally grew there" (22:92). Hawthorne calls such a development unexampled, yet it has strong affinities with his own relationship to naturalism—with a difference. If Delia Bacon grew hostage to a reading of Shakespeare's plays that usurped the "religious doctrines in which she had been educated" (22:92), Hawthorne, reacting self-protectively, grew hostage to his need to *contain* such a usurping vision. Even so, the vision developed as it would, abetted in the 1850s by the reimmersion in gritty reality that came with his consular duties and by his exposure to the physical and moral phenomena of Europe. Reading his account of Delia Bacon and the philosophy that took possession of her, one wonders how far Hawthorne was thinking of the naturalism that more than ever, late in life, bid to take possession of him.

Telling It Slant

Be true! Be true! Be true! Show freely to the world, if not your worst,
yet some trait whereby the worst might be inferred!

—Hawthorne, *The Scarlet Letter*

Tell all the truth but tell it slant

—Emily Dickinson, #1263

"Salem"

It was my fortune or misfortune...to have some slender means of supporting myself; and so, on leaving college, in 1825, instead of immediately studying a profession, I sat myself down to consider what pursuit
in life I was best fit for....And year after year I kept considering what
I was fit for, and time and my destiny decided that I was to be the writer
that I am. I had always a natural tendency...toward seclusion; and this
I now indulged to the utmost, so that, for months altogether, I scarcely
held human intercourse outside of my own family; seldom going out
except at twilight, or only to take the nearest way to the most convenient solitude, which was oftenest the seashore....I doubt whether so
much as twenty people in the town were aware of my existence.

—Hawthorne to R. H. Stoddard (1853)

Returning from college to another Massachusetts town, Thoreau would ask,
"What may a man do and not be ashamed of it? He may not do nothing, surely,
for straightaway he is dubbed Dolittle!—aye! christen[s] himself first."[1]
"Nothing" was precisely what Hawthorne would have liked to do—"Oh that
I was rich enough to live without a profession," he wrote his mother from
college (15:79)—and what to outward eyes he did do for most of a dozen years.
Though his Manning relatives seem to have been indulgent—Hawthorne had
little contact with his father's family—Gloria C. Erlich is right to feel that
Hawthorne internalized their mercantile values and, like Owen Warland in
"The Artist of the Beautiful," judged himself unmanly and wanting by their

measure.[2] It was not entirely in jest that he referred to himself as "an idler" in "The Custom-House" and, through the ventriloquized voice of his Puritan ancestors, heaped scorn on his vocation as " 'A writer of story-books!' " (1:10). In truth, it was not the dead Puritans who oppressed him but their living descendants, the practical Yankees. The opprobrium was chiefly in his own mind; so far as his actual neighbors went, he seems, unlike the gadfly Thoreau, to have enjoyed a benign invisibility.

Surveying this period, his son Julian professed amazement at the "extraordinary undemonstrativeness" Hawthorne showed at a time when youth, talent, and the fluidity of the American world seemed to make anything possible (*NHW* 1:184). Here he was, Julian marvels, "content" to spend his days in "a meditative solitude...musing over the theories and symbols of life" and "writing cool and subtle little parables" about them (*NHW* 1:82–83). The solitude having ended with the publication of *Twice-Told Tales* in 1837, Hawthorne explained it to Longfellow, a former Bowdoin classmate and recently the author of an instrumental review, as a happenstance: "By some witchcraft or other—for I really cannot assign any reasonable why or wherefore—I have been carried apart from the main current of life, and find it impossible to get back again" (15:252). Much of the witchcraft had to do with Hawthorne's shyness, which developed, according to his sister Ebe, "only after his return to Salem [from college], and when he felt that he could not get away from there, and yet was conscious of being utterly unlike everyone else in the place, that he began to withdraw into himself" (*EMH* 145). Like Emily Dickinson's reclusiveness, Hawthorne's was also a quiet but firm rebellion against contemporary role expectations—in his case, from a "repugnance to commercial life" that led him to reject the idea of entering "his Uncle Manning's counting-house" (*PRNH* 67)—and a means for securing an insulated domestic space in which to write.

Given Hawthorne's social *ir*relation to the town—the actual Salem was a livelier and more diverse place than Hawthorne later allowed[3]—Salem as a "habitation" should be understood less as an objective physical and cultural locale than as a psychological one. Salem for Hawthorne was the Mannings; it was the regimen of school and duty as opposed to the freedom of Raymond, Maine, where he lived for a time in his youth; above all, it was the "haunted chamber" in the Herbert Street house to which he returned in 1825 and where he wrote nearly all of his early tales and sketches. "If ever I should have a biographer," he told Sophia Peabody during their courtship, "he ought to make great mention of this chamber in my memoirs, because so much of my lonely youth was wasted here; and here my mind and character were formed" (15:494).

His words are apt. Although Hawthorne would leave Salem to reside in Boston in the later 1830s, in Concord in 1842, and in the Berkshires (and countless places thereafter) in 1850, Salem never left him. Freed from it outwardly, he did all he could to efface it inwardly, repeatedly adjuring college friend Horatio Bridge to burn his letters, and himself destroying "quantities of [his] private journals in which all the ups and downs of his early and earlier life were written down."[4] He succeeded so well that the ten years after his graduation from Bowdoin are "almost void of biographical documents" (15:37), including a mere twelve letters prior to his assuming an editorship in Boston in 1836. Most of what is known about his early character and private circumstances comes from belated recollections by Bridge, Ebe, and Elizabeth Peabody.

The paradox of Hawthorne's relationship to Salem is that the self he sought to leave behind was, as he knew, the core of his literary being. As he told Cornelius Mathews and Evert Duyckinck in 1841, "I do not believe that I shall ever write any more—at least, not like my past productions; for they grew out of the quietude and seclusion of my former life; and there is little probability that I shall ever be so quiet and secluded again" (15:600). Ebe felt that he wrote better in Salem than in Concord (*EMH* 24); even Hawthorne, temporarily reestablished "in the old chamber where I wasted so many years of my life," was obliged to admit to Bridge in 1845, "I find it rather favorable to my literary duties" (15:122). After struggling to write "The Old Manse" *at* the Old Manse, "forth came this sketch, of its own accord" (16:152), when Hawthorne was settled in Salem. *The Scarlet Letter*, of course, was written in Salem, and *The House of the Seven Gables*, written in Lenox, was *about* Salem. Toward the end of his life, having begun, then abandoned, an English romance, "The Ancestral Footstep," Hawthorne returned to it in later drafts, "Etherege" and "Grimshawe," both of which open with a long section in Salem. As a setting, the town is incidental to the manuscripts' plot and themes; what Hawthorne seems to have sought, as inspiration, was the "Salem-note," the "Salem-idea."

If Hawthorne could not live with Salem, he suffered creatively when he tried to live without it. During his newlywed idyll at the Old Manse, "Salem" took its toll in the tepidness of much of his work or else found its outlet in sketches about human frustration or misery. Financial worries aside, Hawthorne was happy at the Manse; he was delighted with marriage; he felt reborn. Yet he could not help suspecting that, given the nature and conditions of his talent, he had sold his literary birthright for domestic content. If he was mistaken in this, it was because he underestimated the tenacity of Salem, which had not died but simply, for a season, estivated. Salem would be with him, *in* him, and in his writing until the last, even during his European years. As his first habitation, extending well into his thirties, it was his formative one. As Edwin H. Miller observes, he "never left his dwelling place except physically."[5]

A Muffled Shriek

Without any effort of his will, or power to restrain himself, he shrieked aloud.

—Hawthorne on Dimmesdale, *The Scarlet Letter*

Hawthorne's "problem"...concerns the possibility or desirability of self-exposure.

—Joel Porte, *In Respect to Egotism*

For readers who value complexity over simplicity, symbolism over allegory, Hawthorne's aesthetic development during the Salem years confounds all expectations. After a halting start in *Fanshawe* and tales like "The Hollow of the Three Hills," Hawthorne soon found his vein—so much so that by the end of 1829, when he sent Samuel Goodrich "The Gentle Boy," "Roger Malvin's Burial," "My Kinsman, Major Molineux," and an early version of "Alice Doane's Appeal" ("Young Goodman Brown" may also belong to this period), he was, as a tale-writer, at the height of his powers. The best work often comes first, and it can hardly be coincidental that, as James R. Mellow notes, "the darker side of Hawthorne's mind seemed reserved for [these] early tales," whose "presiding themes...—the secret springs of shame, the hidden nature of guilt, the communion of sinners—speak of the tormented mind" (Mellow 57).

Why was this vein so prematurely exhausted, abandoned, suppressed, or renounced? "Torment" may have been the very reason. Hawthorne's anxiety about writing such tales extended to displaying them under his own name. First published anonymously, "Young Goodman Brown," "Roger Malvin's Burial," and "My Kinsman, Major Molineux" were all withheld from the original and expanded editions of *Twice-Told Tales*; the first two would be published in *Mosses from an Old Manse* (1846), the last in *The Snow-Image* (1851), when Hawthorne had reached the bottom of the well. He could hardly have been ignorant of their worth. Habitually secretive, he may have feared that the tales revealed too much, and yet, like many with a secret, he was driven to flirt with self-disclosure.

Midway through *The Scarlet Letter* Dimmesdale thinks to relieve the pressure of secret sin by mounting the scaffold late at night and symbolically proclaiming his guilt to the town, confident that no one will see him; he even shrieks aloud, in a muffled way, no doubt, as the urge toward self-exposure is checked by the fear of humiliation. Hawthorne's closing moral—"Be true! Be true! Show freely to the world...some trait whereby the worst might be inferred!" (1:260)—is misleading. Dimmesdale has been doing this all along, berating himself as "altogether vile, a viler companion of the vilest, the worst of sinners, an abomination, a thing of unimaginable iniquity"—for which, as he knew ("subtle, but remorseful hypocrite that he was!"), his congregation would revere him all the more (1:143–44). His sermons betray nothing specific about himself, but as they penetrate to their listeners' hearts they are remarkable for their sympathetic insight into human frailty. Altogether, Dimmesdale's relationship to the public is analogous to Hawthorne's in his literary prefaces as he takes the reader into his confidence, or plays at doing so, while "still keep[ing] the inmost Me behind its veil" (1:4), and in many of his tales and sketches, whose fictive "touches," as Melville said, "furnish clews, whereby we enter a little way into the intricate, profound heart where they originated" (*WHM* 9:242).

Years before *The Scarlet Letter* Hawthorne had prefigured Dimmesdale in the Reverend Hooper of "The Minister's Black Veil," who by donning a piece of black crepe did show something "whereby the worst might be inferred." A veil conceals, but it also draws attention to a mystery of concealment and invites speculation. Hooper's veil, the story suggests, is connected to a young woman recently dead, but whether it is indicative of sin or sorrow, and of sin or sorrow as it pertains to Hooper personally or to the human race, is left ambiguous. So is the meaning of the tale's subtitle, "A Parable," which may be taken to refer to universal sinfulness and dissimulation (Hooper's "I look round me, and lo! on every visage a Black Veil!" [9:52]) or to private obsession. Hooper may be right about human nature *or* he may find the world dark because he views it through the interposing medium of the black veil, which "give[s] a darkened aspect to all living and inanimate things" (9:38). The truly constitutive veil, in either case, is not the material one that covers Hooper's face but the psychological one that shades his mind and temper. The question the story raises is the one implicit in Hawthorne's darker writings as a group: does their preoccupation with sin and guilt represent an authorial insight into human nature or a filtration of experience through their creator's own black veil?

Hawthorne's fondness for assuming veils and pointedly announcing their presence is a mannerism so frequent and insistent as to demand attention. In "The Old Manse," having guided readers on a tour of his outward premises and, it seems, of his inward ones, Hawthorne turns on them gratuitously in a betrayal of established intimacy:

> How little have I told!—and, of that little, how almost nothing is even
> tinctured with any quality that makes it exclusively my own! Has the
> reader gone wandering hand in hand with me, through the inner pas-
> sages of my being, and have we groped together into all its chambers,
> and examined their treasures or their rubbish? Not so. We have been
> standing on the green sward, but just within the cavern's mouth, where
> the common sunshine is free to penetrate, and where every footstep is
> therefore free to come. I have appealed to no sentiment or sensibilities,

save such as are diffused among us all. So far as I am a man of really individual attributes, I veil my face. (10:32–33)

Why break the spell of a companionable preface to gloat over reticences that would otherwise go unnoticed? Like Dimmesdale on the scaffold, Hawthorne seems compelled, if not to lift, then momentarily to flaunt, the veil he conceals himself behind. To explore Hawthorne is almost inevitably to be drawn into the game of hide-and-seek he plays with the world. So it was for contemporaries who knew him. "There were not more than two or three persons in the world to whom he could disclose himself freely," his son Julian remarked (*NHW* 1:90). Jonathan Cilley, one of his circle of friends at Bowdoin, was not among them: "I love Hawthorne, I admire him; but I do not know him. He lives in a mysterious world of thought and imagination which he never permits me to enter."[6] Even Julian confessed his surprise when as an adult he first read Hawthorne's writings and found himself "constantly unable to comprehend how such a man as I knew my father to be could have written such books. He did not talk in that way; his moods had not seemed to be of that color."[7] With literary men Hawthorne was especially guarded, his friendship with Melville a rare and partial exception. When the young William Dean Howells asked Oliver Wendell Holmes about Hawthorne, whom Howells was about to visit, Holmes replied, "Ah, well! I don't know that you will ever feel you have really met him. He is like a dim room with a little taper of personality burning on the corner of the mantel."[8] When they did meet, Howells found Hawthorne full of "a dark repose" and "shadowy kindness" but "shy to the point of discomfort" and all but impenetrable.[9]

Hawthorne's elusiveness has not kept readers from trying to know him and sometimes believing they do. The cult of personality began early, with the first reviews of *Twice-Told Tales*. For Andrew Preston Peabody in *The Christian Examiner* (1838), the author of the writings was omnipresent, "and we feel, after the perusal of this little volume, as if we had always been familiarly acquainted with him."[10] Edgar A. Dryden opens *The Poetics of Enchantment* with the question, "Who is Nathaniel Hawthorne?"[11] Biographer Edwin H. Miller describes himself as "seek[ing] to lift the veils with which Hawthorne guarded self and art but only partially succeed[ing]."[12] Brenda Wineappple presents Hawthorne as "a man of disclosure and disguise" who is "aching to confess but too proud, too obstinate, too ashamed to do so."[13] Confess what? Wineapple doesn't say.

Julian Hawthorne blandly asserted that Hawthorne's "closet" was empty of "skeletons" (*NHW* 1:v), but from the first some believed otherwise. Reviewer Charles Fenno Hoffman thought he detected "some rending and ever-remembered sorrow" haunting Hawthorne's thoughts in *Twice-Told Tales* and "color[ing] them with the shadow of their presence."[14] So did Hawthorne's friend and legal advisor George S. Hillard, who after reading *The Scarlet Letter* wrote to inquire how, "with so thoroughly healthy an organization" as he presented to the world, he should "have such a taste for the morbid anatomy of the human heart, and such knowledge of it, too. I should fancy from your books that you were burdened with secret sorrow; that you had some blue chamber in your soul, into which you hardly dared to enter yourself" (15:79). Melville, too, harbored suspicions. In *Clarel* he wondered whether the "coyness" of the Hawthorne-based Vine "bordered not on fear— / Fear or an apprehensive sense? / Not wholly seemed it diffidence / Recluse" (*WHM* 12: I, 29:46–49); and late in life he told Julian "he was convinced that there was some secret in [Hawthorne's] life which had never been revealed, and which accounted for the gloomy passages in his books"—an insinuation Julian deflected by turning it back on Melville, who (he said) had "many secrets untold in his own career."[15]

Sorrow or sin—should we even inquire? Hooper regards intrusion behind the veil as a violation of what rightly belongs to eternity. Sophia Hawthorne agreed. "The veil he drew around him no one should lift," she told Annie Fields, shortly after Hawthorne's death (8:682). Fields later expanded on the hint: "Hawthorne's inner life was largely his own: neither wife nor child nor friend shared freely in his experiences.... [H]is whole heart seems to have unveiled to no living soul."[16] Hawthorne's "vocation is to observe & not to be observed," Sophia told her sister Mary Mann (*NHW* 1:271), preempting all inquiries and echoing Hawthorne's own expressed wish to be "a watchman, all-heeding and unheeded" (9:192).

Nonetheless, when the watchman signals his presence and "beckons us forward into the cavern of his deepest soul,"[17] as Frederick C. Crews says, he forfeits his claim to immunity; he becomes an element in the work itself, integral to its meaning and effect. Describing himself in the preface to *The Snow-Image* as "a person who has been burrowing...into the depths of our common nature, for the purposes of psychological romance," Hawthorne mocks the idea that "a little preliminary talk" about externals amounts to anything confessional: "These things hide the man, instead of displaying him." Yet having said this and withdrawn behind the veil, he comes forth again and concedes that writing is indeed self-revelatory, if one knows how to read it: "You must make quite another kind of inquest, and look through the whole range of [an author's] fictitious characters, good and evil, in order to detect any of his essential traits" (11:4). "I am there," Hawthorne all but announces: "find me!" The arch invitations extend to his private writings. "Like the epistolary novels of the eighteenth century that enchanted his youth," editor Thomas Woodson notes, "Hawthorne's correspondence is often a self-conscious game of purposeful disclosures and reticences"; "Reluctance...conspire[s] with Revelation alternatively to show a vision and to draw a veil" (15:7, 10).

It would be surprising if Hawthorne's psychological themes were *not*, in displaced form, confessional. Writing to Longfellow in 1837, he complained of a "lack of materials" for fiction, having "seen so little of the world" and therefore having "nothing but thin air to concoct my stories of" (15:252). Although he would always purport to be "telling what is common to human nature, not what is peculiar to myself" (15:613), his position in the formative Salem years resembles that of his reclusive speaker in "Sights from a Steeple," who "can but guess" about "the mystery of human bosoms" (9:192); his knowledge of others is rooted in knowledge of himself. As Oliver Wendell Holmes put it, "Count it no marvel that he broods alone / Over the heart he studies,—'tis his own"[18] Even the prosy Mary Mann recognized as much: "He always puts himself into his books. He cannot help it."[19]

Workshopping

Hawthorn [*sic*] invites his readers too much into his study, opens the process before them. As if the confectioner should say to his customers Now let us make the cake.

—Emerson, *Journals and Miscellaneous Notebooks* (1846)

In none of his early writings is Hawthorne more present, if subtly disguised than in "The Haunted Mind." The sketch amounts to a tour of his creative workshop before the fabulist has set about clothing his themes in narrative particulars. On a frigid midnight its speaker awakens to find himself a spectator of his own dreamworld. The conscious mind has been given a privileged glimpse into the unconscious and permitted to act as the self's psychoanalyst, probing the symbolic dream-work in its role as clinical observer while obscuring its discoveries in allegorical abstractions, since the analyst is also the analysand unwilling to have its secrets exposed. The core of the fictive experience was Hawthorne's own. "Do you never start so suddenly from a dream that you are afraid to look round the room, lest your dream-personages...should have thrust themselves out of dream-land into the midst of reality? I do, sometimes" (15:318), he wrote Sophia from his Salem chamber in 1839. In "The Haunted Mind" (published earlier) "you" takes the form of second-person narration as Hawthorne distances himself from his material and weaves a claim of common reference into the rhetoric of the work itself. "In the depths of every heart," he writes,

there is a tomb and a dungeon, though the lights, the music, and revelry above may cause us to forget their existence, and the buried ones, or prisoners whom they hide. But sometimes, and oftenest at midnight, those dark receptacles are flung open. In an hour like this, when the mind has a passive sensibility, but no active strength; when the imagi-

nation is a mirror, imparting vividness to all ideas, without the power of
selecting or controlling them; then pray that your griefs may slumber,
and the brotherhood of remorse not break their chain. (9:306)

Tombs, dungeons, caverns, catacombs, labyrinths: these are Hawthorne's
characteristic metaphors for the unconscious, a proto-Freudian repressed or willfully *suppressed* whose contents surface in reverie or dreams when the restraints
of waking consciousness are relaxed. Even dreams, of course, have their vigilant
dream-censor; in "The Haunted Mind" censorship is doubled (the dreamer's, the
controlling artist's) as disinterred memories and wishes are channeled into an
allegorical procession generic enough to pass for Everyman's and, in keeping with
Hawthorne's "characteristic turn to the abstract when the revelation threatens to
become too personal,"[20] to preclude identification with himself.

"Everyman" means precisely that. Although Young Goodman Brown's wife,
Faith, admits that "a lone woman is troubled with such dreams and such thoughts,
that she's afeared of herself, sometimes" (10:74), "The Haunted Mind" implicitly distinguishes male and female. Indeed, the transgressions of its dreamer are
primarily *against* women and, while not literally sexual, are clothed in a language
of sexual victimization all the more striking for its tenuous relation to the allegorized subject. "There is your earliest Sorrow, a pale young mourner, wearing a
sister's likeness to first love, sadly beautiful, with a hallowed sweetness in her
melancholy features, and grace in the flow of her sable robe" (9:306–7). The
conceit seems labored ("Sorrow" a *"sister"* to "first love"?) until one recalls
Frederick C. Crews's remark that in Hawthorne's tales "*suppression* always has
the psychological consequences of *repression*: the denied element reappears in
imagery and innuendo" (Crews 20). The figure of Hope turned to Disappointment
similarly appears as "a shade of ruined loveliness, with dust among her golden
hair, and her bright garments all faded and defaced," while "the fiend" described
as possibly coming to the dreamer's bedside is clothed "in woman's garments,
with a pale beauty amid sin and desolation, and [lying] down by [his] side," or,
alternatively, appears "in the likeness of a corpse, with a bloody stain upon the
shroud" (9:307). The language of despoiled virginity is so remote from the
abstractions it purports to illustrate that it effectively displaces them and becomes
itself the locus of meaning. The third figure in the procession is Fatality, "a demon
to whom you subjected yourself by some error at the outset of life, and were
bound his slave forever, by once obeying him"; the fourth is Shame (9:307). Is
Hawthorne, with a muffled shriek, emblematizing a guilt-ridden habit of sexual
fantasy that debases the dreamer and the dream object alike?

Philip Young has argued that the shadowy guilts in Hawthorne's early writings are rooted in the fact of incest with his sister Ebe.[21] Physical incest seems
unlikely, if only because a man of Hawthorne's character would never have gotten

over it. Incestuous fantasy is possible. Living in the Manning household and meeting few eligible women, Hawthorne may have turned in imagination toward the dark-haired Ebe and she, also a recluse, toward him. Hawthorne admired Ebe, "whom [he] often said had more genius than himself" (*PRNH* 38), while she on her side was deeply devoted to him. According to Julian, Ebe was "the Machiavelli" who "resolved to do what she could to prevent" Hawthorne's marriage to Sophia Peabody (*NHW* 1:197, 198), ostensibly because she felt the semi-invalid Sophia not "strong enough to fulfil the duties of married life" (*NHW* 1:198) but also from a contempt for Sophia's sunny temperament, Ebe herself being a confessed admirer of Milton's Satan, with "other predilections of a similar kind" (*EMH* 94). Ebe's congratulatory letter to Sophia on her engagement is frigid to the point of insult, which is how Sophia took it, to judge from Ebe's pro forma apology the next month (*EMH* 64, 65). Even in her old age, Ebe spoke hostilely of Sophia: "she is the only human being whom I really dislike: though she is dead, that makes no difference; I could have lived with her in apparent peace, but I could not have lived long; the constraint would have killed me" (*EMH* 182). Gloria C. Erlich finds "a powerful sexual motive" in Ebe's "possessiveness" (Erlich 88), but whether this was more than resentment at the loss of a cherished brother—whether a pattern of quasi-incestuous feelings and fictive themes can be taken to imply actual incest, as Young believes—Erlich is hesitant to say (Erlich xv–xvi).

Hawthorne addresses fantasized transgression in another workshop sketch, the oddly contrived "Fancy's Show Box," subtitled "A Morality." "What is guilt?" the sketch begins: "A stain upon the soul. And it is a point of vast interest, whether the soul may contract such stains, in all their depth and flagrancy, from deeds which may have been plotted and resolved upon, but which, physically, have never had existence" (9:220). The chief literary source for the sketch is Jeremy Taylor's *Ductor Dubitantium; or, The Rule of Conscience*, which Hawthorne borrowed from the Salem Athenaeum in June 1834 (*HR* #432). The critical passage is this: "The act of the will alone, although no external action or event do follow, is imputed to good or evil by God and men."[22]

Although Hawthorne adopts the stance of disinterested inquirer, the sketch unfolds with the rigor of a defense attorney's plea on behalf of a hapless client. In one vignette, the sketch's hypothetical Mr. Smith stands haughtily over an innocent girl he has seduced. The scene is "a record merely of sinful thought, which never was embodied in an act," yet the recollection causes the older Mr. Smith an "extreme" pang of conscience (9:223). In another vignette, an act *is* performed— Fancy, Memory, and Conscience accuse Mr. Smith of murder for having thrown a bottle at a companion's head during a drunken quarrel—but the bottle missed, the incident came to nothing, and the two men later laughed over it. For Taylor, the want of physical injury would be morally irrelevant: a "sin begins within, and the guilt is contracted by what is done at home, by that which is in our power.... For as the external act, God for ends of His own providence does often hinder it; and yet he that fain would, but cannot bring his evil purposes to pass, is not at all excused, or the less a criminal before God."[23] "Fancy's Show Box" takes the opposite position: morally as well as legally, the act with its consequences is *all* that matters, though subjectively the "pain" Mr. Smith feels is "quite excruciating" (9:224).

Like the allegorical procession in "The Haunted Mind," the fabricated crimes of Mr. Smith are a red herring. Their real function is to help the narrator establish a principle of culpability that may tacitly be applied elsewhere. Editing Hawthorne's notebooks after his death, his wife excised the word "squalid" from a remark about his Salem room—"In this dismal and squalid chamber, FAME was won."—"squalid" retaining traces of its historical connotation of "impure, morally polluted, morally shameful."[24] The word is especially resonant within the cultural context of the 1830s ("Fancy's Show Box" appeared in 1836), a decade marked, as Stephen Nissenbaum says, by an "unprecedented public apprehensiveness about human sexuality" and particularly about masturbation.[25] Solitary, idle, and imaginative, men of letters were thought to be unusually susceptible to this practice. In S. A. Tissot's *A Treatise on the Diseases Produced by Onanism* (1760; trans. New York, 1832), the "ill effects" of masturbation are likened to those suffered by "the literary man who fixes his attention wholly on the subject." The relationship is also causal: "by engrossing the thoughts, [the imagination] can excite them, and desire leads to the act," which is "more pernicious" because it lacks the excuse of physiological need.[26] In 1828, soon after creating the reclusive scholar Fanshawe, Hawthorne checked out Chandler Robbins's *Remarks on the Disorders of Literary Men; or, An Inquiry into the Means of preventing the Evils usually incident to Sedentary and Studious Habits* (HR #372). He may also have known the Reverend John Todd's *The Student's Manual* (1835)—reviewed in *The New-England Magazine* at a time when Hawthorne was a regular contributor—which gravely warns young men against the polluting "habit of revery" and the influence of "bad books" (including Hawthorne's beloved Waverley novels) that "will leave a stain upon the soul which can never be removed."[27]

Coincidentally or not, "Fancy's Show Box" opens with an echo of Todd— guilt is "a stain upon the soul"—and with a prospectus of its subject evocative of Todd's bête noire, masturbation:

> Must the fleshly hand, and visible frame of man, set its seal to the evil designs of the soul, in order to give them their entire validity against the sinner? Or, while none but crimes perpetrated are cognizable before an earthly tribunal, will guilty thoughts—of which guilty deeds are no more than shadows—will these draw down the full weight of a con-

demning sentence, in the supreme court of eternity? In the solitude of a
midnight chamber, or in a desert, afar from men, or in a church, while
the body is kneeling, the soul may pollute itself even with those crimes,
which we are accustomed to deem altogether carnal. If this be true, it is
a fearful truth. (9:220)

The degree of Hawthorne's investment in his subject is indicated by the care
he takes in framing it. Since few would contend that evil thoughts deserve the
same punishment as evil acts, the answer to the sketch's yes/no propositions—is
action necessary to give guilty thoughts "their *entire validity* against the sinner"?
may the soul "contract such stains, *in all their depth and flagrancy*," without
action? will "guilty thoughts…draw down the *full weight* of a condemning
sentence"?—must almost certainly be no. Hawthorne presents the case so as to
ensure acquittal. If its veiled subject is indeed masturbation, he leaves it further
unclear whether his opening words pertain to sexual fantasies potentially leading
to masturbation (guilt residing in the carnal act, not the wayward thought) or to
sexual thoughts in and of themselves (self-pollution even while kneeling in a
church). While most antimasturbation writers of the 1830s focused on the
physical practice, extremists like Sylvester Graham attacked desire itself as
blameworthy and debilitating.[28]

The notion that we are guilty, or may *feel* guilty, for our thoughts as well as our
deeds is a point of congruence between Christianity, Freudianism, and a persis-
tent strain in Hawthorne's moral thought. It is the position he took years later in
Our Old Home when he recounted the story of an American doctor of divinity—
"a fine-looking middle-aged gentleman, a perfect model of clerical propriety"
(5:25)—who called upon him at the consulate in Liverpool only to stumble in a
week later piteously degraded after a long binge. "It was the deepest tragedy
I ever witnessed," Hawthorne writes, adding: "I leave it to members of his own
profession to decide whether it was better for him thus to sin outright, and so to
be let into the miserable secret what manner of man he was, or to have gone
through life outwardly unspotted, making the first discovery at the judgment-
seat" (5:29–30). Even before his physical debauch, Hawthorne implies, the minister was morally that "manner of man."

Whether or not Hawthorne felt himself "that manner of man," "Fancy's Show
Box" is shaped by the need to air and allay anxieties about errant thoughts. In
arguing for the moral blamelessness even of fixed intentions, Hawthorne likens
a proposed "scheme of guilt" to "a train of incidents in a projected tale…. Thus a
novel-writer, or a dramatist, in creating a villain of romance and fitting him with
evil deeds, and the villain of actual life, in projecting crimes that will be perpetrated, may almost meet each other, half-way between reality and fancy. It is not
until the crime is accomplished, that guilt clenches its gripe upon the guilty

heart and claims it for its own" (9:225–26). "Apparently exonerating the fanta-
sizer of evil by comparing him to the romancer," Nina Baym remarks, "Hawthorne
in fact implicates the romancer in guilt" (Baym 67)—implicates, then quickly
acquits, since the physical deed alone is the determinant of guilt.

In this late, seemingly casual analogy, Hawthorne lays bare the exculpatory
impulse behind his sketch. Aside from sexual anxieties, or rather in relation to
them, his concern is with the guilt attached to fiction-writing. To a residually
Puritan distrust of the imagination Hawthorne joined a Freudian sense of literature as a symbolic enactment of desire rooted in "ambitious wishes" or "erotic
ones" and aimed at covertly gratifying them.[29] Dreams, daydreams, fantasies,
random thoughts, fugitive images, and the fetal origins of fictive plots—such
irruptions into consciousness were bizarre and often disconcerting, but they
assumed moral weight for Hawthorne only when the will took responsibility for
them by electing to dwell upon them. And yet, as writer, dwell he did. In "giving
a sort of material existence" to upwelling thoughts, as he wrote in "The Devil in
Manuscript," the artist entered into a perilous game not unlike the sorcerer's in
raising evil spirits (11:171). His writer Oberon (his own chosen nickname in his
correspondence with Horatio Bridge) expresses a "horror at what was created in
[his] own brain": "That scribbled page describes shadows which I summoned
to my bedside at midnight; they would not depart when I bade them; the gray
dawn came, and found me wide awake and feverish, the victim of my own
enchantments!" (11:174). Artist, dreamer, and sinner converge here in the
figure of a self-damning conjuror who summons up internal powers of darkness
he cannot control. What the dreamer of "The Haunted Mind" involuntarily
does in sleep—throw open the "dark receptacles" of the unconscious (9:306)—
the writer willfully does in his fiction, procuring the pleasures of peering at or
vicariously indulging in the forbidden even as he sternly condemns it. In this
border region between physical event and purely mental event, degrees of innocence and guilt are uncertain. The writer has *done* nothing yet feels *as if* he has
and as if the world (in the person of the acute reader) might detect it. He is
terrified of being caught and guiltily wants to be caught. He denies the overt
self-implication of his work and suggests its more subtle self-implication. He
veils himself and points to the veil.

After the mid-1830s Hawthorne grew increasingly chary about visiting this
equivocal region. "Lights and shadows are continually flitting across my inward
sky," he told Sophia in May 1840, "and I know neither whence they come nor
whither they go; nor do I inquire too closely into them. It is dangerous to look
too minutely at such phenomena. It is apt to create a substance, where at first
there was a mere shadow" (15:462). "Fancy's Show Box" is his effort to persuade
himself that fictionalizing dark thoughts counts only as a "shadow." So far as we
are all fictionalizers (or fantasists), moreover, the shadow is universal. The upshot

of this belief is the generous tolerance associated with Hawthorne despite the fact that in literature and life he could be stiffly severe. "Man," his sketch concludes, "must not disclaim his brotherhood, even with the guiltiest, since, though his hand be clean, his heart has surely been polluted by the flitting phantoms of iniquity" (9:226). Psychologically, he has moved to absolve the fantasist (or tale-writer) of lingering guilt: because fantasy is universal and, *as* fantasy, blameless, no one need feel condemned or self-condemned by motions of the mind.

Displacement

> Displacement takes two forms: first, a latent element may be *replaced*... by something more remote, something of the nature of an allusion; and secondly, the *accent* may be transferred from an important element to another which is unimportant.
>
> —Freud, *Introductory Lectures on Psycho-Analysis*

> By displacement I mean the techniques a writer uses to make his story credible, logical motivated or morally acceptable—lifelike, in short.
>
> —Northrop Frye, *Fables of Identity*

Though not among Hawthorne's earliest sketches, "The Haunted Mind" and "Fancy's Show Box" are outcroppings of the bare schema of his work. Halfway between these sketches and the artful tales themselves is Hawthorne's ur-tale, the patched-together and uncollected "Alice Doane's Appeal."

The original "Alice Doane" was among the tales Hawthorne sent Samuel Goodrich late in 1829; it may even have been written at Bowdoin, since Ebe claimed to have seen it in the summer of 1825 (*NHW* 1:124). Adapting his plot of wizardry and false accusation from Spenser—with notable "variants" of his own, as John W. Shroeder notes: "The erotic fantasy becomes incest and the homicide becomes parricide"[30]—Hawthorne makes the traducer and would-be seducer of Alice, Walter Brome, the unknown twin brother and psychic double of Leonard Doane. Similar yet complementary in character, the two are "like joint possessors of an individual nature, which could not become wholly the property of one, unless by the extinction of the other" (11:272). Leonard's jealousy and hatred of Walter, whom he feels Alice "must inevitably love" because of Walter's resemblance to *him*, is aggravated to the point of madness by Leonard's recognition that "the germ of all the fierce and deep passions" in Walter lives in himself (11:271). By killing Walter, Leonard is not only destroying Alice's slanderer and his own sexual rival; he is also slaying the offending part of himself embodied in his double and, at the same time, *introjecting* that part as he takes on the incest wish latent in his devotion to Alice. Gazing at the face of his victim, Leonard sees the features of his father, slain by Indians, glaring at him as if in reproach. Literally, Leonard has recognized the common biological parent in the lineaments of the murdered son; figuratively, like so many of Hawthorne's sinners, he has committed a kind of moral parricide. He has thrown off the prohibitions of paternal authority (here the incest taboo), reveled for a moment in orgiastic freedom ("my spirit bounded, as if a chain had fallen from it and left me free" [11:273]), then recoiled in horror at the recognition of evil in himself. Aside from his remorse for Walter's death, Leonard is burdened by "a deeper sense of some unutterable crime, perpetrated, as he imagined, in madness or a dream"—a psychic censor keeps him from recognizing the incest wish—and he is tempted through a crazed logic of vengeance, outrage, ritual sacrifice, and self-purification "to meditate violence against the life of Alice" (11:273–4), the source of his forbidden desire and now the scapegoat for his guilt.

The most problematic character in "Alice Doane's Appeal," because dramatically the most superfluous, is the old wizard, a figure "with fiendish ingenuity in devising evil, and superhuman power to execute it" (11:270), to whom Leonard tells the story and who is presented as being somehow responsible for it. A representation of the unconscious—"that portion of the mind which drives men to do things they find abhorrent" (Crews 54)—the wizard is also, as the scripter of events, an embodiment of the authorial imagination, which in generating the incest plot is as "senseless as an idiot and feebler than a child" (11:270) before the impulses that command it, like the passive dreamer of "The Haunted Mind." What the artist actively can and does do is shape the compulsions of incest fantasy into a self-serving fable. Called to judgment in the climactic crowd scene, the wizard must let it be known that Alice (Ebe?) is guiltless of incest and therefore that Leonard and Walter (Hawthorne?) are also guiltless of incest, whatever they may have wished or intended to do. As in "Fancy's Show Box," Hawthorne parades the hidden imaginings of the psyche in order to demonstrate that they are *only* imaginings, lacking the weight of punishable deed.

The incest plot probably comprised the whole of the original Alice Doane story. In recasting the tale nearly ten years later, Hawthorne added the quasi-autobiographical frame that stands as a bridge between its minimally displaced gothic psychodrama and the world of his historical tales. Like Hawthorne himself during his postcollege years, the narrator of "Alice Doane's Appeal" is an outsider in present-day Salem, alienated from its commonplace prosperity and cultivating a counteridentity associated with its guilty past. The two girls he brings to Gallows Hill are surrogates for his townspeople, oblivious to "legend or tradition" (11:267), and for his largely feminine gift-book audience. The girls are spellbound as he reads the tale until he tries to connect its gothic paraphernalia to contemporary reality, at which point they break out in incredulous laughter. Unmanned and reduced to a trivial entertainer, the storyteller tries again, this time with a tableau of the "blood-thirsty" Cotton Mather presiding over the execution of the witches (11:279). His new effort succeeds; he reaches "the seldom trodden places of [the girls'] hearts" (11:280) and provokes the requisite tears. The writer has found his usable genre (historical romance), his setting (the dim but veritable past), and his dramatic theme (Puritan New England's obsession with sin and punishment). In powerfully affecting his representative audience, he has joined past to present and exchanged his position of cultural marginality for the role of "keeper of the collective conscience and prophet of a better society."[31] By turning the girls' mockery into dependence—trembling, they "seized an arm on each side"; their tears were a "sweeter victory" still (11:279, 280)—he has also established a necromantic sexual power over them (like wizard Maules's power over Alice and Phoebe Pyncheon in *The House of the Seven Gables*, but benign) and remasculinized an effeminate vocation.

Nina Baym sees "Alice Doane's Appeal" as "chronicl[ing] the narrator's discovery of how to write American gothic" (Baym 38). Since Hawthorne had been successfully working in the gothic years before he revised "Alice Doane," it would be more proper to call the tale an apologue of his discovery of how to channel private obsessions into historically garbed (and psychically guarded) universals.[32] We can never know what caused Hawthorne, first, to write of incest, then to divert attention away from it by a shift to the Salem witch trials; what we *can* note is that the materials of this crude, fractured tale represent, as Hyatt H. Waggoner says, "blocks of feeling which Hawthorne afterwards learned to build together into unified structures."[33] It has been observed that "Alice Doane's Appeal" has close affinities with "Young Goodman Brown" and "My Kinsman, Major Molineux." "All three" stories, Lea Newman observes, "have a common intent (dramatization of perilous unconscious states, among them sexual guilt and patricide), a common structure (question, quest, revelation), and common devices and stage properties (journeys, illusions, visions, devils, crowds of fiends, public illumination)."[34] The signal moment in each occurs when the props of conventional morality are removed and the protagonist feels licensed to indulge sexual or aggressive impulses that have tempted him all along. A central ambiguity in the tales is whether the discovery of evil they recount has reference to human sinfulness generally or to a disordered individual's self-revelation and outward projection of sin. The scenes testifying to universal sinfulness—the assembly of the wicked dead in "Alice Doane's Appeal," the black mass in "Young Goodman Brown," the climactic crowd scene in "My Kinsman, Major Molineux"—are apocryphal. They may be spectral appearances evoked by demonic powers, they may be illusions wrought by the characters' psyches, or they may simply be dreams; all that the protagonists can know for certain is the capacity for evil revealed within themselves.

This, too, is all that writer Hawthorne can know. Wanting broad experience and generalizing about humanity largely from introspection, he cannot be sure whether the fallenness he sees around him is truly there or, as with Reverend Hooper, is partly or wholly a function of his own black veil. His artistic task, as suggested by the reworked "Alice Doane," is to suppress this latter possibility as it threatens to reflect upon himself. He must externalize the internal, publicize the private, and do so in a way that fulfills both Freud's and Northrop Frye's ideas of displacement. Psychologically, he must substitute one thing (in this case, incest) with another (history); aesthetically, he must clothe a core fantasy in social particulars to "make his story credible, logical motivated [and] morally acceptable—lifelike, in short."[35]

The Salem Masterplot

> The plotting of the individual or social or institutional life story takes on new urgency when one no longer can look to a sacred masterplot that organizes and explains the world.
>
> —Peter Brooks, *Reading for the Plot*

In a notebook entry of 1842 Hawthorne outlined a sketch he would never write but whose pattern informed several of his previous tales and would provide the structural framework for at least the first and last of his published romances.

> The human Heart to be allegorized as a cavern; at the entrance there is sunshine, and flowers growing about it. You step within, but a short distance, and begin to find yourself surrounded with a terrible gloom, and monsters of divers kinds; it seems like Hell itself. You are bewildered, and wander long without hope. At last a light strikes upon you. You press towards it yon, and find yourself in a region that seems, in some sort, to reproduce the flowers and sunny beauty of the entrance, but all perfect. These are the depths of the heart, or of human nature, bright and peaceful; the gloom and terror may lie deep; but deeper still is this eternal beauty. (8:237)

In lieu of what Peter Brooks calls a "sacred masterplot" for interpreting experience, Hawthorne evolved his own masterplot, a variation on the Christian theme of Paradise, Paradise Lost, and Paradise Regained but one whose secularized subject was the moral and psychological journey of the self.[36] The lines of the traditional pattern remained, as a new edifice may be built upon structural pillars of an old, but the plot was detheologized and remained loosely Christian chiefly in its sense of sin. A second entry from the same day also bears upon the masterplot: "To write a dream, which shall resemble the real course of a dream, with all its inconsistencies, its strange transformations, which are all taken as a matter of course, its eccentricities and aimlessness—with nevertheless a leading idea running through the whole" (8:240).[37]

"Young Goodman Brown" and "My Kinsman, Major Molineux" are Hawthorne's archetypal excursions into the cavern of the heart. Their subject is that of "The Haunted Mind," the confrontation with buried desire that occurs through the portal of dreams. The tales have the lurid surrealism of dreams; they make open reference to dreams; their protagonists wonder whether part or all of their night's experience might be a dream; and as fictive performances they may even be regarded as dreams, or representations of essentially mental actions transposed to a historical world. Their author has not held a mirror to reality, even remote historical reality; he has "dream[ed] strange dreams, and [made] them look like truth" (1:36). As Robin's "evening of ambiguity" unfolds (11:222), he feels that its pageant has been staged specially for him, just as Young Goodman Brown finds himself and his "Faith" the focal initiates at a black mass. The stories are symbolic monodramas whose subordinate characters are purely adjunctive, like the shadowy figures in a dream charged with embodying psychic cathexes or advancing the illogical logic of the dreamplot.

Outwardly, Young Goodman Brown travels into the forest to attend a witches' sabbath; Robin crosses a river from country to city and joins in the humiliation of Major Molineux; Leonard Doane kills his offending alter ego, Walter Brome; Reuben Bourne abandons his father-figure Roger Malvin to die in the forest, marries his "father's" daughter, and enters the world of concealment and guilt; and Reverend Hooper (his initiating experience having occurred before the story begins) assumes a black veil. Whatever the tales' physical action, their moral one is the discovery of and response to unconscious wishes within the self. Q. D. Leavis calls Young Goodman Brown's journey the one that all of us "must take alone, in dread, at night, . . . away from home and the community, from conscious, everyday social life, to the wilderness where the hidden self satisfies, or is forced to realize, its subconscious fears and promptings in sleep."[38] The same might be said for the journeys of other protagonists in the tales, as later for those of Hester and Dimmesdale in *The Scarlet Letter*, Donatello and (vicariously) Hilda in *The Marble Faun*, and (also vicariously) Phoebe in *The House of the Seven Gables*. The development of the soul through sin and/or suffering is Hawthorne's signal theme, it is his *Salem* theme, and it is his masterplot. It will persist in moral outline through thirty years despite the inflections it receives with new characters and new fictional situations, and despite life experiences in Concord, England, and Italy that might have been expected to challenge or supplant it.

What of the lighter strain in Hawthorne's writing invoked by Jane Tompkins in arguing that critics misrepresent his canon when they construct it from allegedly "great short stories" like "Young Goodman Brown" to the neglect of sentimental ones like "Little Annie's Ramble," widely admired in its own time?[39] Contemporary reviewers commented on both types of works, sometimes juxtaposing them. In an 1845 essay, Evert A. Duyckinck passes from one story to the other, finding that Hawthorne "makes amends for [the] gloomy night-picture [of 'Young Goodman Brown'] by the sunshine of his 'Little Annie'"—a sketch "so cheerful" and "so full of pleasant imagery" as to merit quotation in its entirety.[40]

The two faces of Hawthorne have typically been seen as opposites, save by Melville, who intuited their deep interconnection (*WHM* 9:242). Ostensibly, "Little Annie's Ramble" is the obverse of "My Kinsman, Major Molineux," a five-year-old child's daytime journey into "the mystery of the great world," escorted by an avuncular, quasi-autobiographical speaker who "delight[s] to let [his] mind go hand in hand with the mind of a sinless child," his own mind presumably being of a different cast (9:121, 122). Protected by her innocence, Annie *sees* innocently; the worldly narrator does not. For him, a doll in a toy store gazing out her window "upon many ladies" prompts the severe reflection that such ladies "are also toys,...though they wear grave visages" (9:125). Even young Annie, however, is instinctively made "unquiet" by monkeys in a menagerie with their "wild and dark resemblance to humanity" (9:127), as if nature were staging a grotesque parody of human pretensions.[41] At the end of their ramble, "after wandering a little way into the world," Annie (unlike Robin) is able to "return [to childhood] at the first summons, with an untainted and unwearied heart." The narrator himself cannot; life has told upon him, innocence is behind, and he has "gone too far astray for the town crier to call [him] back!" (9:129).

In intention, "Little Annie's Ramble" may be precisely what it seems: a celebration of the restorative effect of "spend[ing] an hour or two with children" (9:129). Yet even in such an innocuous daylight frolic, the outlines of Hawthorne's night-journey replicate themselves, as if they were a structuring principle of his moral imagination regardless of subject and genre. Bunyan was a favorite of Hawthorne's youth, and in place of a Bunyanesque journey toward the celestial city, Hawthorne came to fashion a pilgrim's progress of his own, with characters ranging themselves morally according to how they negotiated the soul-passage into which sin or sorrow inducted them. The "ramble" little Annie takes anticipates the journey she will take again, without childish immunity, "when life settles darkly down upon" her (9:129), as it has upon the narrator. Situated, it appears, midway through the cavern, the narrator plays at returning to its mouth, but he cannot even vicariously go back. He can only "struggle onward" (9:129), with no hint within the sketch of "bright and peaceful" depths lying ahead (8:237).

And Hawthorne himself? During the Salem years what position did he occupy within the passage he describes? Henry James felt that a "magnificent little romance" like "Young Goodman Brown" could mean "nothing as regards Hawthorne's own state of mind ... for the simple reason that, if it meant anything, it would mean too much" (James 81). This is what troubled Hawthorne, both privately and in relation to his audience: that his tales might mean, or be taken to mean, "too much." In "Young Goodman Brown" the inducement the devil holds out to potential converts is the voyeuristic power to pierce others' veils and "know their secret deeds" (10:87). Young Goodman Brown seems to resist the devil's bribe, yet on returning home he sees sin everywhere, prima facie evidence that the devil has planted his corrosiveness in him. Psychologically, this is what "devil-worship" means: an obsession with darkness so overwhelming as to skew one's apprehension of life. In *The Scarlet Letter* Hester is tempted to feel that her sin gives "her a sympathetic knowledge of the hidden sin in other hearts," and it is greatly to her credit, Hawthorne says, that she struggles to resist "such loss of faith" (1:86–87). If this is so, what is one to make of a writer who founded a career on a Paul Pry exploration of hidden sin?[42]

The paradox that beset Hawthorne as he worked to establish a moral template for his writing was that the supposition of universal fallenness through which he sought to normalize and exculpate irruptions from his haunted mind might redound upon himself in a peculiarly damning self-indictment. What could be said about Reverend Hooper—that he saw a black veil on every face because he looked at every face through a black veil—might be said about him. As Hooper becomes a more profound, sympathetic, and eloquent psychologist due to his wanderings in the midregion of the cavern, so did Hawthorne in his dark early tales. But this does not mean that he wished to dwell there or, as the publication history of the tales indicates, to be known as *having* dwelled there. What he wished was to seem and to be normal.

The Marriage Group

> I am sick to death of depicting humanity without having any part or lot in it. ... Is an artist male, anyhow?
>
> —Thomas Mann, "Tonio Kröger"

> For the ironical romantic fixes the eyes of poetry upon the world, and the eyes of the world upon poetry; and by virtue of this romantic squint, it is now poetry and now the world that comes to nothing.
>
> —Erich Heller, "The Realistic Fallacy"

Hawthorne's cavern entry is dated June 1, 1842, slightly more than a month before his marriage to Sophia Peabody. If Hawthorne could write of "flowers and sunny beauty" at the cavern's heart (8:237), it was because he felt them imminently within his grasp. "Salem" would soon be behind him—forever, he hoped.

"The Haunted Mind" had ended with just such a prospect as the wakened dreamer imagines "how pleasant in these night solitudes, would be the rise and fall of a softer breathing than your own, the slight pressure of a tenderer bosom, the quiet throb of a purer heart, imparting its peacefulness to your troubled one" (9:308). The influence of the envisioned woman brings with it the icons of sunny domesticity. The speaker's icy winter night becomes "the sunny rain of a summer" day; he pictures a hearth, children, rainbows, and birds in spring; the nightmare realm of half-consciousness becomes "a flowery spot, on the borders of sleep and wakefulness," and he is filled with "a pervading gladsomeness and beauty" (9:308). The foul cavern of the dreamer's heart has been purified and redeemed through its association with the sweet conventionalisms of domestic life.

Years before he met Sophia Peabody, Hawthorne created a Sophia-figure as the instrument for his deliverance from "Salem." Fantasy aside, he seems to have doubted he would ever marry. What James R. Mellow calls "the unwritten prohibition against love and marriage that thwarts so many of his heroes" (Mellow 43) stemmed from his feeling that marriage was not merely the sign and source of normalcy, but also its moral reward. One earned the right to marry by solidity of character and a healthy extroversion that claimed a place in the world—or, wanting these things, by a leap of faith that marriage would produce them. Hawthorne had neither the extroversion nor the faith. Like his artist-hero Oberon, he felt himself by destiny "a solitary man." In November 1813, at age nine, he incurred a foot injury that left him severely lame for more than a year, soon after which, his sister Ebe recalled, he suffered "another long illness": "It was during these two long confinements that he acquired the habit of constant reading" and grew distant from the world. "Undoubtedly," Ebe reflected, "he would have wanted many of the qualities which distinguished him in after life, if his genius had not been shielded in childhood" (*EMH* 99, 100). In Ebe's telling, Hawthorne's history resembles that of Sophocles' Philoctetes (bitten on the foot by a venomous snake), which Edmund Wilson reads as a parable of the socially marginalized artist: "The victim of a malodorous disease which renders him abhorrent to society and periodically degrades him and makes him helpless is also the master of a superhuman art which everybody has to respect and which the normal man finds he needs."[43]

Fanshawe (1828) is Hawthorne's Philoctetes, save that its afflicted hero, rather than rescuing others through his gift, is himself rescued through the memorializing gift of his chronicler. Still more, it is his "Tonio Kröger," Thomas Mann's fable of the self-doubting artist in a world of contented philistines. "When does one begin to feel the curse" of literature, Tonio Kröger asks: "Early, horribly early.... It begins by your feeling yourself set apart, in a curious sort of opposition to the nice, regular people; there is a gulf of ironic sensibility, of knowledge, of skepticism, disagreement between you and the others; it grows deeper and deeper, you realize that you are alone; and from then on *rapprochement* is simply hopeless.[44]

The "nice, regular people" in *Fanshawe* are represented by Edward Wolcott, a handsome and well-bred but otherwise unremarkable student at Harley College (Bowdoin), and Ellen Langton, the college president's beautiful ward. Its Tonio Kröger is Fanshawe, a version of the collegiate Hawthorne: proud, withdrawn, introspective, with "a nobleness on his high forehead, which time would have deepened into majesty"—"would have" signaling that Fanshawe's "thin, pale cheek" and "bright eye" are marks of the consumption or (according to theories of the day) the hyperstudiousness that will prematurely kill him (3:346).[45] Like Hawthorne at Bowdoin and later in Salem, Fanshawe "scorned to mingle with the living world, or to be actuated by any of its motives," secretly nourishing a "dream of undying fame" (3:350).

The plot of *Fanshawe* is empty contrivance. Its live concern is whether Fanshawe should remain faithful to his character and ambitions at the cost of loneliness and an early death or seek an "earthly happiness" with Ellen Langton that would restore him to society and possibly to health (3:353). Wolcott is evidently made for Ellen, who, though finer than others in her world, is also "formed to walk in the calm and quiet paths of life, and to pluck the flowers of happiness from the way-side" (3:353). (Hawthorne will retell the story of this triad in "The Artist of the Beautiful" and, late in life, in the unfinished "Septimius Felton".) Through an unlikely course of events, Fanshawe rescues Ellen from the story's villain; in gratitude and with admiration for his character, Ellen offers herself to him; but he, rightly gauging her nature and his own, declines, though to "refuse [her hand] was like turning from an angel, who would have guided him to Heaven" (3:458). The question is whether such happiness *is* heaven. Wolcott and Ellen go on to marry; domesticity weans Wolcott away from whatever "worldly distinction" he might have had; and after "a long life of calm and quiet bliss," the two pass away and leave "no name behind them" except as subordinate figures in Fanshawe's tragedy (3:460). Fanshawe himself soon leaves "a world for which he was unfit" (3:460), his dream of fame realized only in his epitaph: "THE ASHES OF A HARD STUDENT AND A GOOD SCHOLAR" (3:460).

If the name "Fanshawe" suggests "fantasy of Hawthorne," what fantasy does the story enact? Ebe noted that "all through his boyhood, everything seemed to conspire to unfit [Hawthorne] for a life of business" (*EMH* 140). Through the history of Fanshawe, Hawthorne converts his feeling of alienation into a passive-aggressive drama of career rejection; he proclaims what Erik H. Erikson calls a "negative identity," marked by "a scornful and snobbish hostility toward the roles offered as proper and desirable in one's family or immediate

community."[46] Michael Davitt Bell sees the young Hawthorne turning the negative to a positive by cultivating the deviant status of romancer as "an objective
correlative for the outcast's rage against society."[47] In pre-Romantic 1820s New
England, however, deviance was rare and without a bohemian subculture to sustain it. Nor, lacking "brass," as Horatio Bridge told him, did Hawthorne harbor
an "outcast's rage"; instead, he suffered an outcast's want of "confidence" (PRNH
74), which disposed him to identify with those whom he felt condemned him.
Like Tonio Kröger, he would forever remain "a *bourgeois* who strayed off into art,
a bohemian who feels nostalgic yearnings for respectability; an artist with a bad
conscience": "a bourgeois *manqué*."[48]

It is not surprising that one who felt so ill-adapted to the world should have
dwelt on death, especially since he also believed that the artist's posture, "graceful now" in youth, "would be ridiculous in middle life" (11:316). According to
Ebe, Hawthorne "said, after he had begun to write, that he had not expected to
live to be twenty-five" (EMH 140). *Fanshawe* was published the year he turned
twenty-four. Erikson notes that "in extreme instances of delayed and prolonged
adolescence" (and Hawthorne's postgraduation years in Salem were nothing if
not that) "the young person may feel simultaneously very young and in fact baby-
like, and old beyond rejuvenation."[49] This is the world-weariness felt by the
unworldly Fanshawe, by Oberon in "The Devil in Manuscript" and "Fragments
from the Journal of a Solitary Man," and by Hawthorne himself, who in Bridge's
words "never look[ed] at the bright side with any hope or confidence" (PRNH
73). What oppresses Fanshawe is not his present obscurity so much as the unremitting labor needed to overcome it—"the eternity of improvement" he sees
lying "before him," "a weary way, without a resting place, and without a termina-
tion" (3:350). Given such a prospect, it might seem preferable to throw off the
burden and die, as Bridge feared Hawthorne might "some day" choose to do
(PRNH 72).[50] Suicidal impulses, however, may also be therapeutic. "The assump-
tion that life could actually be made to end with the end of adolescence or at
tentatively planned later 'dates of expiration' is by no means entirely unwelcome,"
Erikson remarks, "and, in fact, can become the only condition on which a new
beginning can be based."[51] In this respect, killing off Fanshawe—and doing so
again when he destroyed whatever copies of the book he could, having become
"before 1832…thoroughly ashamed of it" (EMH 150; v. PRNH 68)—was
Hawthorne's way of killing off an unwanted identity in lieu of killing himself.

Because marriage, the socially integrative counterpoint to suicide, was not a
serious option for Hawthorne until the later 1830s, the question of whether or
not to marry was essentially one of competing value systems and ways of life.
The feelings of loneliness and insubstantiality voiced by Oberon were
Hawthorne's own, echoed in letters and later in reminiscences of the time.
"Merely skimming the surface of life," Oberon says,

I know nothing, by my own experience, of its deep and warm realities.... The truly wise, after all their speculations, will be led into the
common path, and, in homage to the human nature that pervades them,
will gather gold, and till the earth, and set out trees, and build a house.
But I have scorned such wisdom. I have rejected, also, the settled, sober,
careful gladness of a man by his own fireside, with those around him
whose welfare is committed to his trust and their guidance to his fond
authority. Without influence among serious affairs, my footsteps were
not imprinted on the earth, but lost in air. (11:314)

Alison Easton sees the Salem Hawthorne reacting against his "illusory and
dreamlike" solitude by idealizing a domestic "reality" ungrounded in any "experiential sense of a solid, substantial world."[52] In fact, he considered the subject
from various sides, by no means all ideal. Late in "Fragments" Oberon admits to
having "had day-dreams even of wedded happiness" (11:327), but at twenty-
four (close to Hawthorne's own self-appointed terminus) he feels death
approaching. In a notebook entry of 1835, having long outlived this grim
prophecy, Hawthorne proposed a story "to represent the process by which sober
truth gradually strips off all the beautiful draperies with which imagination has
enveloped a beloved object, till from an angel she turns out to be a merely ordinary woman" (8:11). In "The Canterbury Pilgrims" a wife describes the mutual
falling out of love that follows "a year or two" of marital happiness: "by-and-by,
he'll grow gloomy, rough, and hard to please, and you'll be peevish, and full of
little angry fits, and apt to be complaining by the fireside" (11:130). The wife's
speech doesn't prevent the young lovers in the tale from going on "to mingle in
an untried life" (11:131), but it does ironically bracket their hopefulness within
worldly disillusion. On the other hand, the aging bachelor Ellenwood in "The
Wedding Knell"—"a shy but not quite a secluded man; selfish, like all men who
brood over their own hearts...; a scholar, throughout life, though always an
indolent one": in short, Hawthorne as he might become—is belatedly redeemed
from "an aimless and abortive life" by an autumnal marriage (9:27–28).

Hawthorne's subtlest and most ambiguous treatment of the marriage question
is "The Village Uncle," a small masterpiece of the period, rarely discussed.
Originally titled "The Mermaid," the tale has its source in Hawthorne's 1833
summer flirtation with a Swampscott shopgirl named Susan, whom, "in his
fanciful way" (Ebe recollected), he called "a 'Mermaid'" (*EMH* 80). The tale is
cast as the deathbed monologue of its narrator, in youth a writer much like
Oberon but one who renounced his solitary vocation to marry a fisherman's
daughter and become a fisherman himself. Its subtitle, "An Imaginary Retrospect,"
seems superfluous, since its narrator is obviously fictitious, unlike the semiautobiographical "I" of sketches like "Sunday at Home" and "Sights from a Steeple."

The tale seems Hawthorne's own imaginary retrospect as he faces a divide, projects himself forward along the conventional path, and looks back, assessing his choice. Hawthorne is serio-fancifully testing out a life possibility and reporting on it to himself: what if he *had* married the Swampscott mermaid or *did* marry someone like her?

Set on Thanksgiving night, the sketch is the uncle's thanksgiving for choosing his present life over his former one:

> Oh! I should be loath to lose my treasure of past happiness, and become once more what I then was; a hermit in the depths of my own mind; sometimes yawning over drowsy volumes, and anon a scribbler of wearier trash than what I read; a man who had wandered out of the real world and got into its shadow, where his troubles, joys, and vicissitudes were of such slight stuff, that he hardly knew whether he lived, or only dreamed of living. (9:311)

In old age the former writer has "become the patriarch, the Uncle of the village," joined to others across generations by common sympathies (9:318–19), but at what cost? His first vision of Susan had clothed her in fancy, "a daughter of the viewless wind" and "akin to the race of mermaids" (9:312). This was the poet at work, until fact proved her to be "nothing but a pretty young girl" struggling to hold her petticoats in place (9:312). The narrator's hope, partially realized early in their marriage, is of a happy commingling of his dreamy inwardness and her solid actuality: "She gave me warmth of feeling, while the influence of my mind made her contemplative. I taught her to love the moonlight hour," while she led him to feel a "deeper poetry" by "the quiet hearth" in what was "the dearest hour of all" (9:316–17). The relationship between Holgrave and Phoebe in *The House of the Seven Gables* is prefigured here, but where *Seven Gables* will end with an engagement, leaving readers to imagine (or not) the couple's afterlife, "The Village Uncle" explores the consequences of domesticity for the apostate artist. The narrator's village is not merely simple; it is downright coarse, its handful of cottages seemingly "cast up by the sea, with the rock and marine plants it vomits after a storm" (9:219). The uncle himself has shrunk to fit this world; once a man of books and reveries, his literature now consists of "the almanac," and like his neighbors he has come to regard the local "pedagogue" as the repository of "all human erudition" (9:223).

Hawthorne's rendering of this complacent "spinner of long yarns" (9:222) is comic-pathetic, but the mood alters when the uncle bids his family look into a pool of water to see how Heaven is reflected everywhere. As he himself looks, the faces of Susan and the children all "seemed to fade away and vanish around me, leaving a pale visage like my own of former days, within the frame of a large looking glass" (9:318). The pieties he sought to illustrate suddenly disappear; his family suddenly disappears; his essential self is revealed to be the artist he disavowed. On his deathbed, too, the solid figures around him through which he had sought to rescue himself from insubstantial dreams grow insubstantial themselves, and displacing them in his mind's eye is "the book that [he] flung down, and the sheet that [he] had left half written, some fifty year ago" (9:322).

From its opening image of the hearth-fire heaped with logs to sustain the appearance of "household mirth" against "the outer darkness" (9:310), "The Village Uncle" raises questions about the enduring, the valuable, and the true as set against a backdrop of nothingness. His family dim and indistinct to his dying eyes, the uncle is returned to "myself alone" (9:227). All else seems a delusive dream, his rich communal life no more palpable now than his youthful imaginings. In as stark a moment as any in Hawthorne's fiction, the uncle feels the "gloom and terror" a "magician" might "after dismissing the shadows that had personated dead or distant people, and stripping his cavern of the unreal splendor which had changed it to a palace" (9:322–23). *This* is the irreducibly real. There will be moments like this scattered throughout Hawthorne's writings, public and private. Hawthorne refuses to end "The Village Uncle" with such a void, but he does not know how to fill it. His first of two morals, privileging the fanciful over the real, breaks up against the hard facts of life: "The slight tissue of a dream can no more preserve us from the stern reality of misfortune, than a robe of cobweb could repel the wintry blast" (9:323). But his second moral, privileging the real over the fanciful—"In chaste and warm affections, humble wishes, and honest toil for some useful end, there is health for the mind, and quiet for the heart, the prospect of a happy life, and the fairest hope of Heaven" (9:323)—has already been discounted by evidences of that life's boorishness and evanescence.

Mann's Tonio Kröger, though living as an artist, gives his "deepest and secretest love...to the blond and blue eyed, the fair and living, the happy, lovely, and commonplace."[53] In certain moods Hawthorne did the same, yet ultimately he had no more faith in the sufficiency of his Edward Wolcotts, Ellen Langtons, and Swampscott mermaids than he did in that of Oberon. Marriage forced the question of how to live to a head, but until he met Sophia Peabody, Hawthorne had no answer to it and no cause to press for one.

Roads Taken, and Not

When the book was done, he sent it to Goodrich to publish, but Goodrich declined to undertake it—it was two volumes—but said...the editor of *The New England Magazine* would take some of the stories. So they tore up the book, and Hawthorne said he cared little for the stories afterwards, which had in their original place in the

"Storyteller" a greater degree of significance; and he got little or nothing
as pay. Then, as nobody reviews stories in magazines, it did not serve
the purpose of introducing him into the world of letters.

—Elizabeth Peabody in Moncure Conway, *Life of Hawthorne*

As soon as I could, I ran upstairs to her and said, "Sophia, you must get
up and dress and come down! The Hawthornes are here, and you
never saw anything so splendid as he is,—he is handsomer than Lord
Byron!"

—Elizabeth Peabody, in Julian Hawthorne,
Nathaniel Hawthorne and His Wife

In the late summer of 1832 Hawthorne made a journey through northern New
Hampshire and Vermont and across central New York State to Niagara Falls with
the idea of writing a book, he told Franklin Pierce, that would win him "an
(undoubtedly) immense literary reputation" (15:224). Hawthorne had high
hopes for the collection he would call "The Story Teller," which he composed
between late 1832 and June 1834 and sent off to printer Samuel Goodrich. As
described in the ruefully titled "Passages from a Relinquished Work," the plan
was for something genuinely new: a volume of framed tales that would "contain
a picture" of the itinerant storyteller's "vagrant life, intermixed with specimens"
of the tales themselves, sketches of "the circumstances in which each story
was told," and descriptions of the American scenery Hawthorne had recently
traveled through and almost certainly described in notebooks not extant
(10:408).[54]

Through the kind of editorial malfeasance and ill luck that plagued
Hawthorne's early publishing career, the project fell through, and though several
of the pieces were published separately in *The New-England Magazine* in late
1834 and 1835, Hawthorne lost the opportunity to come before the public as
the author of a multigeneric and multitonal work that would present a balanced
sample of his gifts. Beyond affecting his spirits and extending his reign as "the
obscurest man of letters in America" (9:3), the collapse of "The Story Teller" had
important consequences for his stance as a writer. Instead of bringing his talents
for romance and realism into harmonious relation, it further divided them.
In 1837, traveling to Maine for an extended visit with Horatio Bridge, Hawthorne
kept the journal that is the first great surviving testament to his powers as a
recorder of actual life. In 1837 he also published *Twice-Told Tales*, a carefully
culled volume that omitted both his realistic travel writings and two of the darker
pieces that appeared in *The New-England Magazine* and were presumably part of
"The Story Teller," "The Devil in Manuscript" and "Young Goodman Brown."

Given his selections and exclusions, Hawthorne had reason to allow that
Twice-Told Tales had "the pale tints of flowers that blossomed in too retired a
shade" (9:5). Bridge noted that "there was much more of fun and frolic in

[Hawthorne's] disposition than his published writings indicate" (*PRNH* 6). With the authorial self-presentation of *Twice-Told Tales*, the man who delighted in the variegated human spectacle went underground, visible at most on the edges of his work. Hawthorne's published writings would now be one thing, his observations of actual life another. Whether it was a cause of this bifurcation or only an apt symbol, the breakup of "The Story Teller" signifies a watershed moment: the dissociation of Hawthorne's literary personality.

Though not a popular and only a modest critical success, *Twice-Told Tales* "had the effect," as Hawthorne told R. H. Stoddard in 1853, "of making [him] known" in and around Salem and obliging him "to come out of [his] owl's nest" and perform a part in the world. He became, so he said, "pretty much like other people" (*NHW* 1:98), or at least made an effort to appear so. While he might continue to inhabit or visit Salem, its status as a defining identity was dethroned, and with it the character and circumstances that generated his early work. With the distance of fifteen years or so, Hawthorne could view his "long seclusion" as "the kind of discipline which my idiosyncrasy demanded" (*NHW* 1:98). By then he had published his third romance and was soon to leave for Liverpool as American consul. He could afford to look graciously on an identity he believed (erroneously) he had outgrown.

Soon after its publication, *Twice-Told Tales* came to the notice of Salemite Elizabeth Peabody, who eventually managed to "establish visiting relations with so eccentric a household" (*NHW* 1:178). Hawthorne and his two sisters called on the Peabodys in November of that year, and while Hawthorne did not meet Sophia on that occasion, "he did call again," Elizabeth reported, "and this time she came down" to greet him (*NHW* 1:178). Hawthorne "looked at her intently.—he did not realize how intently," Elizabeth wrote, while Sophia felt "so strong a magnetic attraction upon her, that instinctively, and in self-defence as it were, she drew back and repelled him" (*NHW* 1:180). By early 1839 Hawthorne and Sophia had come to an understanding, which would last about three and a half years and become known to Hawthorne's family only shortly before the marriage in July 1842. Although each of the lovers had reasons for delay and concealment—Sophia's recurrent headaches; Hawthorne's financial situation; his professed reluctance to upset his family; perhaps a complicating prior relationship with Sophia's sister Elizabeth[55]—the greater hesitation seems to have been on Hawthorne's part, as if he were reluctant to trade the idealizations of courtship for the realities of marriage.

The long engagement gave Hawthorne ample time to fabricate myths of himself and his Salem life. The public myth, offered later to Stoddard for general consumption, was that, "strange as it may seem," he "had lived a very tolerable life" during these reclusive years, had "always seemed cheerful, and enjoyed the very best bodily health" (*NHW* 1:97). The private myth, developed gradually in the courtship letters he wrote Sophia during this period, is a lover's fairy tale. This is its gist:

> So now I begin to understand why I was imprisoned so many years in this lonely chamber, and why I could never break through the viewless bolts and bars; for if I had sooner made my escape into the world, I should have grown hard and rough, and been covered with earthly dust, and my heart would have become callous by rude encounters with the multitude; so that I should have been all unfit to shelter a heavenly Dove in my arms. But living in solitude till the fullness of time was come, I still kept the dew of my youth and the freshness of my heart, and had these to offer to my Dove. (15:495)

The writer of these words is not "pretty much like other people." His voice is the poignant, lyrical voice of Oberon in "Fragments from the Journal of a Solitary Man," but now of Oberon-in-love. Chaste courtship would not be Hawthorne's conduit to a sturdier relationship to the world; rather, it would invite him to exchange the romance of dark imaginings for the romance of sentimental ones. In this respect, "The Haunted Mind," which begins with the dreamer's wintry descent into the cavern of his psyche and ends with his summery deliverance through the pure woman, is a parable of the entire Salem period, not least of Hawthorne's efforts to escape it.

3

The Wild and the Good

> I found in myself, and still find, an instinct toward a higher, or, as it is
> named, spiritual life, as do most men, and another toward a primitive
> rank and savage one, and I reverence them both. I love the wild not less
> than the good.
>
> —Thoreau, *Walden*

Circling Back

> [Marriage] would renew your youth—you would be a boy again, with
> the deeper feeling and purposes of a man.
>
> —Hawthorne to Horatio Bridge (May 3, 1843)

It is late summer 1842 and Hawthorne has been living at Concord's Old Manse for nearly two months. "Oh, that I could run wild!" he exclaims in his notebook: "that is, that I could put myself into a true relation with nature, and be on friendly terms with all congenial elements" (8:358). Newly married and happier than he had been since his childhood, Hawthorne felt himself delivered from a place (Salem), an identity (the solitary writer of postcollege years), and a literary manner (historical and psychological romance) that had grown oppressive and creatively fallow. Time and place seemed to invite him to create himself anew. Tending his beans and summer squash, he compared his days to Adam's in Paradise and expressed a kinship with the "many ancient sages and heroes" who had likewise cultivated beans (8:329). Periodically, Emerson came by to visit, sometimes with a companion—Margaret Fuller, perhaps. He bought Thoreau's boat, the *Musketaquid* of *A Week on the Concord and Merrimack Rivers*, which he promptly rechristened the *Pond Lily* and came to manage with passable skill. He took walks with Emerson, fished with Ellery Channing, bathed in Walden Pond; he perused *The Dial*, if only "after dinner...as a soporific" (8:371); he studied German. For the most part, he simply enjoyed. "My life, at this time," he wrote, "is more like that of a boy, externally, than it has been since I was really a boy" (8:331).

The phrases "run wild" and "like that of a boy" recall Hawthorne's life at his mother's house in Raymond, Maine, in the summer of 1816 and again for several months in 1818–19 before he grudgingly returned to his Manning relatives in Salem to attend school. In Raymond "I ran quite wild, and would, I doubt not, willingly have run wild till this time," he remarked in 1853 (*NHW* 1:95). In truth, Hawthorne "spent, all told, no more than nine months at Raymond" by Arlin Turner's count,[1] but the process of mythmaking began almost immediately and the period would be etched in his mind as an idyll of liberty and delight. "How often do I long for my gun, and wish that I could again savagize with you," he wrote his sister Louisa from Salem in 1820: "But I shall never again run wild in Raymond, and I shall never be so happy as when I did" (15:119).

Raymond and Salem, "the geographical poles of young Hawthorne's life," were also the imaginative poles,[2] as Quincy and Boston would later be the young Henry Adams's. Country and town, summer and winter, were felt symbols of freedom and confinement, sensuous delight and sober discipline, *e*xpression and *re*pression, "balanced," in Adams's words, "like lobes of the brain."[3] The duality, Adams felt, was endemic to New England with its "harshness of contrasts and extremes of sensibility,—a cold that froze the blood, and a heat that boiled it" (Adams 727)—and to the New England race, puritanical by heritage yet deeply responsive to the possibilities of life in a new world. "Winter was always the effort to live; summer was tropical license": "two hostile lives," the carefree and the dutiful, that bred in the New Englander a chronically self-divided nature (Adams 728).

Hawthorne typically lived for the pleasures of summer and complained bitterly of "our…New England winters, which leave so large a blank—so melancholy a death-spot—in lives so brief that they ought to be all summer-time" (11:81). "Early in his career," James R. Mellow notes, Hawthorne "discovered that the summer was an unfavorable time for writing.… He once confessed that it was only when the autumn leaves began to color that he could bear to settle down to his desk. In the summers, he traveled" (Mellow 48) or, save when necessity obliged him to work, he lazed. Summers also had a way of commencing as early as April and extending well into autumn. During his first year at the Manse there are no surviving journal entries between November 24, 1842, and March 31, 1843 (Hawthorne was writing fiction) and no fiction undertaken between May and early November. "As the casement ascends," he wrote in "Buds and Bird-Voices," his 1843 celebration of spring,

> forth into infinite space fly the innumerable forms of thought or fancy, that have kept me company in the retirement of this little chamber, during the sluggish lapse of wintry weather.… In the spring and summer time, all somber thoughts should follow the winter northward.… The old, paradisiacal economy of life is again in force: we live, not to think, not to labor, but for the simple end of being happy; nothing, for the pre-

sent hour, is worthy of man's infinite capacity, save to imbibe the warm
smile of heaven, and sympathize with the reviving earth. (10:148–49)

The tale Hawthorne published just prior to "Buds and Bird-Voices" was "Little
Daffydowndilly," a children's fable about a would-be idler who "loved to do only
what was beautiful and agreeable" (11:200) and is made to learn the necessity of
toil. Writing was often toil for Hawthorne after his first rush of creativity in the
late 1820s and early 1830s; it could also involve a revisitation of parts of his mind
he preferred to let alone. In "Buds and Bird-Voices" he is not simply closing his
writing desk for the season; he is happily bidding farewell to a class of imaginings
that the sun dissipates as surely as it does the winter snow.

Consciously or not, as Adams might have said, New Englanders like
Hawthorne were shaped by the extremities of their climate and came to project
upon it or emblematize through it their constitutional ambivalence toward
nature, human nature, and the prospect of a "natural life," churchless, undeformed by notions of sin, and dedicated to the soul's fulfillment within time
rather than beyond it. Emerson drew upon a symbology ingrained in his auditors'
imaginations when he began the Divinity School Address with an appeal to "this
refulgent summer [in which] it has been a luxury to draw the breath of life" and
against which he set the wintry image of a pulpit "formalist" (the aptly named
Barzillai Frost, unidentified in the text) preaching with a snowstorm outside
(*CWE* 1:76, 85). Emerson used the seasons to represent the rival parties of
Memory and Hope: "We are reformers in spring and summer; in autumn and
winter we stand by the old; reformers in the morning, conservers at night" (*CWE*
1:184, 186). In "Buds and Bird-Voices" Hawthorne does the same: winter is a
faithless conservative "cling[ing] tremulously to the remembrance of what has been";
spring, "with its outgushing life," "the true type of the Movement!" (10:158).

The root difference between figurative "winter" and "spring," as Emerson and
Hawthorne both understood, was a belief or disbelief in Original Sin or its psychic
equivalent, the conservative allowing that the reformer "would talk sufficiently to the
purpose, if we were still in the garden of Eden" (*CWE* 1:196). As early as Anne
Bradstreet's "Contemplations," the New England writer is recalled from a pagan or
deistic worship of bountiful nature ("More Heaven than Earth was here, no winter &
no night") by reminders of Adam's and Cain's sins with their legacy of moral winter
and their accompanying threat of eternal night.[4] In Hawthorne's imagination, winter
was associated historically with the Puritan past, morally with sin and guilt, culturally
with repression, and affectively with the gloom of his Salem chamber.

Within the dialectic of Hawthorne's American career, the Manse period, with
its emphasis on contemporary rather than historical subjects and its exploration
of themes of reform, represents an antithesis to the Salem years. Initially linked
to Raymond, spring and its fruition, summer, were revived for Hawthorne in

Concord, where, as he wrote Margaret Fuller in February 1843, "the circle of my life seems to have come round, and brought back many of my school-day enjoyments; and I find a deeper pleasure in them now than when I first went over them. I pause upon them, and taste them with a sort of epicurism, and am man and boy together" (15:671).

It was largely chance (the death of the incumbent minister) and the encouragement of Emerson and Elizabeth Hoar that brought Hawthorne to the Old Manse, but there was scarcely a town in America that could have provided a more powerful counterweight to Salem. Although Emersonianism was never a serious temptation for Hawthorne, he was right to acknowledge that "it was impossible to dwell in [Emerson's] vicinity, without inhaling" at least some of the heady atmosphere of his thought (10:31). His affinity with Transcendentalism was not a matter of ideas but of participation in a common cultural moment bounded on one side by "The American Scholar," the founding of *The Democratic Review* (Hawthorne's chief literary outlet during the Manse years), and the Panic of 1837, and on the other by the failure of Brook Farm, the Wilmot Proviso, and the beginning of the Mexican War.[5] For a brief decade or so, to Massachusetts intellectuals, nearly anything seemed possible amid the social and spiritual forces vying for ascendancy. It was "an unquiet period," Hawthorne wrote in "The Hall of Fantasy," "when mankind [was] seeking to cast off the whole tissue of ancient custom, like a tattered garment" (10:180).

Though scarcely a reformer by temperament or conviction, Hawthorne could empathize with the reform spirit because he too was engaged in shedding an old garment (Salem), which in some sense was New England's collective garment. Private season and season of history converged for a time to put Hawthorne in unusual consonance with the age and to imbue his notebooks and at least some of his published writing with the morning atmosphere that is the distinguishing mark of American Renaissance texts. Having lived for years among shadows and felt himself a shadow, Hawthorne was now happily grounded in the "real." He was "much more willing to die than two months ago," he told Margaret Fuller in August 1842, "for he had had some real possession in life, but still he never wished to leave this earth; it was beautiful enough."[6]

A Natural Life

> Men nowhere, east or west, live yet a *natural* life.... [Man] needs not only to be spiritualized, but *naturalized*, on the soil of earth. Who shall conceive what kind of roof the heavens might extend over him, what seasons might minister to him, and what employment dignify his life!... Here or nowhere is our heaven.
>
> —Thoreau, *A Week on the Concord and Merrimack Rivers*

Nature is hard to be overcome, but she must be overcome.
                                                        —Thoreau, *Walden*

In his renewed love for "this earth," the Concord resident Hawthorne most resembles is Thoreau, "a young man with much of wild original nature still remaining in him" but also "a keen and delicate observer of nature," which rewards him with "secrets which few others are allowed to witness" (8:353–54). In time Hawthorne would tire of Thoreau's prickliness—"he is the most unmalleable fellow alive," he told Evert Duyckinck in July 1845—but he never lost admiration for Thoreau's intimacy with nature and his "great qualities of intellect and character" (16:106).

Passages of the Manse notebook of August 5, 1842–October 6, 1843 read uncannily like a Hawthornean *Walden*. Like Thoreau in leaving Concord on Independence Day, 1845, Hawthorne, in settling there three years earlier, was also declaring independence from a former life and attempting to meet the world afresh. "Why should not we also enjoy an original relation to the universe?" Emerson had asked in *Nature* (*CWE* 1:7), a work composed, according to Hawthorne, in the same "delightful little nook of a study" he himself was now occupying (10:5), and in which, a month into his tenancy, he wrote, "It is as if the original relation between Man and Nature were restored in my case" (8:332).

The parallels between Hawthorne's "original relation" and Thoreau's are especially striking in view of the differences in sensibility between the two men. The Concord River seems to Hawthorne "like an open eye in earth's countenance" (8:320); Walden Pond is "earth's eye" for Thoreau.[7] The river is "like a strip of sky set into the earth, which is so etherealized and idealized that it seemed akin to the upper regions" (8:312); Walden is "sky water" that mediates between heaven and earth and "betrays the spirit that is in the air" (*W* 188). Hawthorne cultivates his bean field like the classical agriculturalists (8:329); so does Thoreau. Hawthorne notes the rise and fall of the river, as Thoreau records the fluctuations of the pond. Hawthorne praises Walden's water as "the very purest liquid in the world" (8:337); he observes the halting progress of spring; he sees the April flooding of the river as "the formation of a new world" (8:385), as Thoreau sees the melting sandbank. Hawthorne's previous accounts of nature had been largely pictorial; he now shows a Thoreauvian delight in the microchanges of the year ("Oh, how blest should I be, were there nothing to do! Then I would watch every inch and hair's breadth of the progress of the season; and not a leaf should put itself forth... without my noting it" [8:380]), along with a Thoreauvian disposition to find analogies between nature and spirit.

For both writers, the basis of a "natural life" is simple, receptive *being*. In "Sounds" Thoreau sits in his doorway in what his "fellow-townsmen" would regard as "sheer idleness" and gives himself to the impressions of the day (*W* 112). Hawthorne is similarly conscious of spending his time "in what the world would call idleness," yet he, too, "cannot feel" the time "to have been spent amiss"; if only for the term of a summer, "it is good to live as if this world were Heaven" (8:334). In a later entry he seats himself alone in Concord's Sleepy Hollow to "await such little events as may happen" (8:245). He enjoys the play of sunshine and shadow, but chiefly, like Thoreau, he luxuriates in the sounds of the day. He hears the chirpings of the birds and "the tinkling of a cow-bell," which, like the Sunday church bells audible at Walden, is mellowed by distance and becomes "musical" (8:248). His morning idyll, like Thoreau's, is interrupted by "the long shriek, harsh, above all other harshness," of a locomotive, which recalls to him the world of "men of business" and "all unquietness" (8:248, 249). Leo Marx makes the incident a symbol of the intrusion of the "machine" into antebellum America's pastoral "garden"[8] (the railroad came to Concord that very year, 1844), but the lesson Hawthorne evolves from his day is quite different. As the train passes and he turns his eyes to fungi on the ground, then to a colony of anthills, it strikes him "how narrow, scanty, and meagre, is this record of observation, compared with the immensity that was to be observed.... How shallow and scanty a stream of thought, too—of distinct and expressed thought—compared with the broad tide of dim emotions, ideas, associations... sometimes excited by what was around me" (8:250). The natural world seems inexhaustibly to repay those who attend to it; in Thoreau's words, it provides "a drama of many scenes and without an end" (W 112).

For the naturalist at ease with himself and with life in time, this drama may be sufficient. "We need pray for no higher heaven than the pure senses can furnish, a *purely* sensuous life," Thoreau wrote in *A Week on the Concord and Merrimack Rivers*.[9] By "purely" Thoreau means "thoroughly" or "exclusively," with nothing of the super-sensuous added to it; as David Robinson says, Thoreau's "quest to see, hear, and touch God" is his way of figuring "a reawakened life in the world" of time.[10] But "purely" for Thoreau also means "cleanly" or "chastely" (sens*uous* but not sens*ual*), for cleansed being is his precondition for secular beatitude. "Impurity"—distrust of the body and its appetites—is the snake in this naturalist's Eden. Echoing Hawthorne's "Egotism; or, The Bosom Serpent," Thoreau plays upon this trope when he describes himself in his journal as having swallowed a snake as he "drank at stagnant waters once": "I caught him by the throat & drew him out & had a well day after all."[11] A well day, however, did not guarantee a well life. Thoreau's disgust for our "reptile and sensual" nature, as he calls it in "Higher Laws" (W 219)—his obsession with purity and impurity, cleanliness and filth, continence and dissipation—stems from his view of moral life as a continual warfare between exalting and degrading impulses. The pivotal chapters in *Walden*, "The Ponds," "Baker Farm," and "Higher Laws," are his effort to abet the process of ascent by purging himself not of the materialism and conventions of society, but of the uncleanness attached to bodily life wherever it is lived.[12] Although "Higher Laws" begins by eulogizing the wild "not less than the good" (*W* 210), increasingly it comes to identify the wild with our "slimy, beastly" life of "eating and drinking" (*W* 218), Thoreau's stand-in for the appetite that disturbs him most and emerges as the chapter's more pressing subject—sexuality.

When Thoreau writes startlingly, "Nature is hard to overcome, but she must be overcome" (*W* 221), he is referring to nature as it is reproduced within ourselves in animal appetites and drives. No longer a complement to the good, the wild so conceived is its antagonist. The moral paradox on which *Walden* rests, or perhaps totters, is its appeal to *external* nature as a vehicle for cleansing and sublimating *internal* nature. Yet what if external nature is itself tainted by impurity, as Thoreau came to feel in 1852–53 as he returned to the *Walden* manuscript after a lapse of three years? Guilty about his own felt impurities—even involuntary erections and nocturnal emissions shamed him—Thoreau came to find impurity in natural phenomena instinctively repulsive to many (noxious odors, slime, mushrooms, reptiles) but without moral significance. Most disquieting to him was nature's flagrant sexuality, "blazon[ed]" in the visible parts of flowers, in the "Phallus impudicus... & other phallus-like fungi" that recalled obscene scribblings on privy walls (*TJ* 4:308), and in certain "orange-colored toadstools... cumber[ing] the ground" that led him to wonder whether "the earth [were] in her monthly courses" (*TJ* 4:288). "To correspond to man completely," he speculated, "nature is even perhaps unchaste herself. Or perhaps man's impurity begets a monster somewhere, to proclaim his sin" (*TJ* 4:309). Divided inwardly between lower and higher impulses, the "wild" and the "good," Thoreau saw his division mirrored in the natural world. On one hand, nature seemed undefiled and undefilable, "a perennial spring" (*W* 175); on the other, it contained elements of noisome filth that reminded him of his own filth.

To read portions of the Manse notebook as a *Walden*-esque exploration of a "natural life" is to become cognizant of Thoreauvian anxieties as well as of Thoreauvian delights. A lifelong seeker of correspondences, and burdened with a residue of sexual unease even in his present conjugal happiness, Hawthorne found in or projected upon nature a Janus-faced purity/impurity that troubled him both as a revelation about nature and, by analogy, as a reinforcement of doubts about human nature. His physical and moral bête noire was the sluggish Concord River, which resembled nothing so much as "one of the half torpid earthworms" he used for bait (8:320). "A domain of sexual filth," T. Walter Herbert calls Hawthorne's "vision of the river," linking it to the "prurient lassitude" decried in contemporary antimasturbation tracts as they bore on the solitary, introverted life still fresh in his memory.[13] Bathing in Walden Pond after "a good deal of mud and river-slime had accumulated on [his] soul," Hawthorne felt that "not only [his] corporeal person, but [his] moral self, had received a cleansing" (8:337). It was the river, however, not the pond, that his life at the Manse physically and metaphysically abutted and whose placid beauty and repellent muck became the reference point for his reflections on nature. Two river flowers, the white pond lily and the yellow lily, fascinated him as emblems of human character. Though both were rooted in river mud, one drew "loveliness and perfume" from it, the other filth and stench. "I possess...a human and heavenly [pond] lily, and wear it in my bosom," he wrote of Sophia, as if of a talisman: "Heaven grant that I myself may not be symbolized by its yellow companion" (8:319).

Thoreau, too, was drawn to moralizing correspondences, but Thoreau could also regard nature nonanthropocentrically both in its delicate minutiae and as a grandly functioning ecosystem. Wanting Thoreau's gifts as a naturalist, Hawthorne had *only* the lens of moral analogy, which turned out to be disconcertingly heterodox when applied to natural facts. Tending his garden, he feels "bitterly angry" at the squash bugs that devastate his crop and is puzzled that "Nature has provided such a host of enemies for every useful esculent." Why should weeds be allowed to thrive "with such tenacity of life" that there seems "a sort of sacredness about them"? "Perhaps," he suggests, "if we could penetrate Nature's secrets, we should find that what we call weeds are more essential to the well-being of the world than the most precious fruit or rains." Systemic good, he realizes, may not be congruent with narrowly human good—a nascent ecologism. Ever the moralist, however, he goes on: "This may be doubted, however; for there is an unmistakable analogy between these wicked weeds and bad habits and sinful propensities which have overrun the moral world; and we may as well imagine that there is good in one as in the other" (8:388).

Hawthorne writes half in jest, but only half. Where Thoreau, viewing nature, could wish to see our human "limits transgressed" (*W* 318), Hawthorne wishes to see them confirmed by a universe comprehensible through and illustrative of moral pieties. He cannot speculate freely about nature, for to do so is either to end in conundrum (as with the squash bugs) or to be drawn into a naturalism so vast and impersonal as to confound notions of an intelligible cosmic order. The problem of the squash-patch, microcosmically, is either that of theodicy (why has God permitted evil?) or of the *irrelevance* of theodicy within a material universe neither designed for human beings nor answerable to their needs.

Attractive as it was, the idea of "a *purely* sensuous life" was oxymoronic to Hawthorne, first, because the (male) senses could never be pure and, second, because the more closely he observed and marveled at nature, the less reliable it seemed as a divine sermon or a touchstone for ethical living. Sexual fecundity, not sexual purity, was nature's way, nor was nature readable in ways consonant with traditional belief. In the end, a "natural life" seemed precisely that: a life of natural*ism*, or at most of a natural religion so vacated of Providence, morality, and heaven as to be tantamount to atheism. One could not draw moral and spiritual meaning *from* nature; at best, one brought it *to* nature and culled from nature's workings only so much as was salutary and safe.

Ideality

> I have never elsewhere had such an opportunity to observe how much
> more beautiful reflection is than what we call reality.... I am half con-
> vinced that the reflection is indeed the reality—the real thing which
> Nature imperfectly images to our grosser senses. At all events, the dis-
> embodied shadow is nearest to the soul.
>
> —Hawthorne, on reflections in the Concord River,
> *The American Notebooks*

The counterweight to the "natural" throughout the Manse period is the "ideal,"
associated with Sophia, or Hawthorne's construction of Sophia. Recounting a
solitary evening walk less than a month after their marriage, Hawthorne wishes
that Sophia had been with him, for then he "should have looked through the
medium of her spirit" and had "a far deeper sense of beauty" (8:322). Imaginatively,
Sophia *had* been with him, as she would be again when he ascended a hill and
looked down on the oft-maligned Concord River, observing both the physical
scene and its reflections in the water. The latter appeared to him the "more charming" because, being "unsubstantial, they assumed the Ideality which the soul
always craves, in the contemplation of earthly beauty" (8:321). A few weeks later
Hawthorne returned to the subject, praising the reflections "arrayed in ideal
beauty, which satisfied the spirit incomparably more than the actual scene," and
which, he speculated, may be more real than the reality itself (8:360).

Between these passages in the collaborative notebook Hawthorne kept with
Sophia (each read the other's contributions) is a related entry of hers: "The river
was perfectly still & soft, taking all the trees and the heavens captive in its depths,
where we decided that they were more real than those we could touch & see
above; as least *as* real—why not?"[14] There is hardly a better example of what
Patricia Dunlavy Valenti calls "the antiphonal quality" of the Manse notebook:
"one spouse calls, the other answers."[15] "*We decided*," Sophia writes. Approaching
each other from opposite ends of the philosophical and temperamental spectrum, husband and wife meet at moments like this on Sophia's ground and speak
in Sophia's idiom. "Ideality" had not been a serious concern in Hawthorne's early
writings, public or private. Neither a Platonist nor a Transcendentalist, it is
doubtful he could have specified what the word meant for him. Yet if one side of
the Concord Hawthorne is the celebrant of sense experience who "for the present.... like[s] this earth better than Paradise itself" (15:679), another is the aco-
lyte of the soul who deprecates material life and gives allegiance to the "ideal."

"Ideality" belongs to the second phase of Sophia's influence on Hawthorne;
the first phrase centered upon deliverance. "Oh, my Dove," Hawthorne told
Sophia in July 1839: "I have really thought sometimes, that God gave you to me
to be the salvation of my soul" (15:330). The 109 extant love letters Hawthorne

wrote during their courtship develop the implications of this thought as he at once submits to Sophia in her spiritual superiority ("Thou art ten times as powerful as I, because thou art so much more ethereal" [15:606]) and asserts his practical dominion over her. Writing to her in May 1839, he professes an "awe" of her that he "never felt for anybody else" and that "converts my love into religion"; yet "this awe (or whatever it is)," he quickly adds, "does not prevent me from feeling that it is I who have charge of you, and that my Dove is to follow my guidance and do my bidding" (15:317). In simultaneously exalting female nature and subordinating it to male authority, Hawthorne was typical of his age, class, and region. His motive, however, seems not so much power as anxiety, or power rooted in anxiety. "Since writing the above," his letter continues,

> I have been asleep, and I dreamed that I had been sleeping a whole year in the open air; and that while I slept, the grass grew around me. It seemed, in my dream, that the very bed-clothes which actually covered me were spread beneath me, and when I awoke (in my dream) I snatched them up, and the earth under them looked black, as if it had been burnt—one square place, exactly the size of the bed clothes. Yet there was grass and herbage scattered over this burnt space, looking as fresh, and bright, and dewy, as if the summer rain and the summer sun had been cherishing them all the time. (15:317–18)

A connoisseur of dreams, Hawthorne feigns puzzlement over this one and asks Sophia its meaning; but lest she pick up its hint of voluntary or involuntary sexual pollution—a prospect more disturbing for what it might imply about her innocence than disclose about his guilt—Hawthorne peremptorily waives the subject: "But it is a silly dream, and you cannot expound any sense out of it" (15:318). The confession has done its therapeutic work, and Sophia needn't have fathomed it; it is enough for them to feel that his unworthiness has blackened the earth and that her sympathy and trust have cleansed it. "My surest hope of being a good man, and my only hope of being a happy man," he told her a few months into their engagement, "depends on the permanence of our union" (15:305).

Hawthorne was aware of how well Sophia fit his preconceptions of the redemptive woman; "I have found a reality, though it looks very much like some of my own dreams," he wrote Evert Duyckinck in November 1843 (16:9). He was less aware of how far this likeness was due to his re-creation of her and to her complicity in the process. Culturally, this, too, was representative. If the "politics of purity recruited women to the task of allaying male sexual anxiety,"[16] as T. Walter Herbert says, its idiom of spirituality spoke to women as well by inviting them to idealize themselves as domestic redeemers, or what Harriet Beecher Stowe called "soul-artists."[17] "A good man's faith in you, fair lady, if you ever have it, will make you better and nobler even before you know it" (*MW* 8), Stowe wrote in *The Minister's Wooing* with a characteristic blend of sentiment and canniness. Stowe's hero, James Marvyn, voices the canniness—"there's nothing surer to hook a woman than trying to save a fellow's soul" (*MW* 25). James *is* elevated by his love for Mary Scudder, who "represent[s] to [him] a sphere higher and holier than any in which [he has] ever moved, and stir[s] up a sort of sighing and longing in [his] heart to come towards it" (*MW* 43). On Mary's side, a natural religiosity is deepened and focused by her proud awareness of "the immortality of a beloved soul hanging upon her" (*MW* 43), a soul with latent magnanimities uniquely developable by her, and one that also happens (as in Hawthorne's case) to be incarnated in a wondrously handsome body. Each character comes to realize a higher self by striving to be worthy of the other's faith as they enact their accepted parts of sinner and redeemer. What begins as half-illusion develops into a beneficently symbiotic reality.

In his courtship letters to Sophia, Hawthorne assumes James's role and assigns Sophia Mary's. "My dear Sophie," he writes in March 1839, "your letters are no small portion of my spiritual food, and help keep my soul alive, when otherwise it might languish unto death, or else become hardened and earth-encrusted" (15:291). No one could read her letters, he continues, "without feeling the influence of [her] character throughout his own—purifying his aims and desires, enabling him to realize that there is a truer world than this feverish world around us, and teaching him how to gain daily entrance into that better world. Such, so far as I have been able to profit by it, has been your ministration to me. Did you dream what an angelic guardianship was entrusted to you?" (15:291). Hawthorne writes with a lover's ardor, he flatters Sophia as a woman of her class and tradition is most susceptible of being flattered, and he ennobles himself in her eyes through the loftiness of his sentiments. He earns the coronation she will give him as "Apollo" even as he consecrates her as his celestial "Dove."

Precisely how Sophia responded to this myth is largely a matter of inference, since Hawthorne burned her courtship letters before the family left for Europe in 1853 and very few of her other letters of the period survive. Disabled by periodic headaches since the age of twelve, Sophia suffered an equivalent of Hawthorne's long years of seclusion, save that in her case the deprivations were not social (the Peabody women were active, intellectual, and widely connected) so much as vocational: an exemption from most domestic obligations and from the teaching career followed by her mother and two older sisters. Gifted and intelligent, Sophia early on seems to have gauged the possibilities before her and, like another gifted New England woman, Mary Moody Emerson, said to herself, "I am glad I have nothing, as I can't have much."[18] Megan Marshall notes that Sophia's "headaches first became incapacitating when Elizabeth and Mary went out to work and Sophia glimpsed the conditions of 'independant' life for her self-supporting sisters."[19] Conducting a school was exhausting, unremunerative, precarious, and socially humbling, and in her own form of gender rebellion (analogous to Hawthorne's against a business career) Sophia "may have preferred remaining an invalid in her mother's care to becoming a schoolteacher—or even an artist."[20]

The latter vocation was a genuine possibility. Sophia's talent as a copyist was recognized in the emerging art world of Boston, whose middle-class patrons were eager for competent reproductions of paintings they would never otherwise see, let alone hang on their walls. Sophia's work was saleable. Mostly self-taught and insecure about her productions, however, she approached her art (original work especially) with anxiety, which could trigger her migraines. "I always go through the valley of the Shadow of death in painting every picture," she wrote in 1843, near the end of her artistic career, "& the more worth the picture has, the more dismal is my journey," though it might end at "the delectable mountains."[21]

Insulated in her private space and ministered to by family, Sophia had little incentive to test the uncertain waters of professionalism or, given the example of the feckless Peabody males, the dubious waters of marriage (*NHW* 1:179, 186). Hawthorne rescued her from an invalid's narcissism, as she rescued him from an aesthete's solitude. Elizabeth Peabody reports that "a great change took place in Sophia" during her walks with Hawthorne, which "worked like animal magnetism upon her, suspending" for a time "the chronic pain in her head."[22] The relief wasn't constant—she was treated periodically by mesmerists almost to the day of her wedding—but "immediately upon arriving at the Manse, she declared herself to be completely free from headaches."[23] Like Hawthorne, she believed herself re-created through marriage. "I feel new as the Earth which is just born again," she wrote in the spring of 1843: "I rejoice that I am, because I am his, wholly, unreservedly his" (*SPHAN* 134).

In envisioning their wedded life, Hawthorne had held out the prospect of artistic collaboration: "we will paint pictures together—that is, our minds and hearts shall unite to form the conception, to which your hand shall give material existence" (15:397–98). Just prior to the marriage Sophia told a friend, "He has a study & I a studio, one over the other, & while he is in the hands of his Muse in the morning, I shall be subject to mine.... Then after noon we shall meet to interchange the thoughts that have visited us from the Unknown deep."[24] The reality proved otherwise. "By the end of 1843," Sophia "ruefully notes that [Hawthorne] retired habitually to his study after breakfast,"[25] while she, pregnant with Una, found herself "rather nervous," not in the mood to paint, and often unable to accomplish much when she tried to.[26] After Una's birth in March 1844, she ceased to paint pictures at all.

Julian claims that Sophia "never had any jealousy of [Hawthorne's] study and books" (*NHW* 1:248). If her letters can be trusted, she even came to glory in his ascribed genius, as years earlier she had characterized herself as "a planet that shines by borrowed light."[27] Luanne Jenkins Hurst titles her account of Sophia's wifely ministrations "The Chief Employ of Her Life,"[28] a phrase that resonates sharply against Margaret Fuller's contemporary notion of "self-impulse," which held that woman's chief employ was her own inner growth, not to be sacrificed in self-effacing relation to husband and family. It may have been a consciousness of dereliction that caused Sophia to react as hostilely as she did to Fuller's *Woman in the Nineteenth Century*: "It seems to me that if she were married truly, she would no longer be puzzled about the rights of woman. This is the revelation of woman's true destiny and place, which never can be *imagined* by those who do not experience the relation" (*NHW* 1:257). Hawthorne himself would hardly express the view more forcibly.

Sophia professed to believe that "*truly*" married persons like herself and Hawthorne "pass into perfect spheres & sail off into the infinite on their own account, complete in themselves" (*SPHAN* 139). The effect of the Manse years was to convert such "perfect spheres" into complementary *hemi*spheres. Beneath its celebration of his parents' marriage, Julian's *Nathaniel Hawthorne and His Wife* reveals how each spouse sought to compensate for, even to valorize, the deficiencies of the other. Sociable by nature, Sophia had to accommodate herself to Hawthorne's *a*sociability, even to the point of defending him from the criticism of her mother and sisters. For his part, as Elizabeth Peabody noted, Hawthorne had to be "ever on the watch to ward off from her the hurts to which she was liable from those moral shocks given by the selfishness and cruelty she could never learn to expect from human beings" (*NHW* 1:248). *She* protected *him* from the "abomination of visiting" (Sophia's words to her mother), accepting his reserve as a condition of his genius (*NHW* 1:270); *he* helped keep *her*, Elizabeth believed, a moral child and even considered her unworldliness "her supreme charm" (*NHW* 1:248).

Intellectually, Sophia was not merely immune to contagion from Hawthorne's gloom; she denied its very existence in him, maintaining that the themes in his writings had nothing to do with his personal character. Influence within the marriage tended to flow in the opposite direction, from wife to husband. Early in their courtship Hawthorne had imagined a kind of spiritual telepathy by which Sophia might transmit to him "some purer feeling, some more delicate sentiment, some lovelier fantasy, than could possibly have had its birth in my own nature, and therefore be aware that my Dove was thinking through my mind and feeling through my heart!" (15:294). More than simply a ministering angel operating on him from outside, Sophia is seen as an internalized presence that elevates his percipient being. In moments like this, she is not, as Leland S. Person, Jr. claims, "a long-buried, alternative self, a friendly alter ego that he was just rediscovering";[29] she is a benign but entirely foreign presence who temporarily takes possession of him and becomes what he occasionally calls her in the letters, "mine own self."

Thomas Woodson ascribes "the idealistic passion of Hawthorne's love letters" partly to his fascination with "the 'tyrannising Unity'" Sophia found "in every thing," as she told her sister Elizabeth in 1838.[30] "I suppose," she wrote, "that when every subject becomes a perfect circle to the mind, there shall be no more discord or error in it."[31] A few months later she enlarged on the subject as she reflected on her "habit of viewing things through the 'couleur de rose' medium": "suddenly, like a night-blooming cereus, my mind opened, and I read in letters of paly golden-green words to this effect: The beautiful and good and true are the only real and abiding things—the only proper *use* of the soul and nature. Evil and ugliness and falsehood are *abuses*, monstrous and transient. I do not see what is *not*, but what *is*, through the passing clouds. Therefore, why is not my view more correct than the other?" (*NHW* 1:183–84). Her optimism appears all the more inviolable for having been recorded after a day of intense pain. This was characteristic. Sophia coped with bodily evil as she coped with natural evil, by taking "the whole problem of life" as a "unit" and subsuming harsh particulars to faith in an overarching benevolism (*NHW* 1:183). "Evil is the shadow & exception to the heavenly order of things," she told Hawthorne's sister Louisa: "Well-being is the law, & like the sunshine usually pervades" (16:56–57).

Alien as they were to him, James R. Mellow feels, Hawthorne "seems to have been infected by Sophia's high-minded attitudes toward life" (Mellow 237). If so, it was an influence he gratefully embraced. "Peace overflows from your heart into mine," he wrote Sophia in April 1839: "Then I feel there is a Now—and that Now must always be calm and happy—and that sorrow and evil are but phantoms that seem to flit across it" (15:299). For one who had lived long and drearily behind a black veil, the "'couleur de rose' medium" was a happy relief. Floating on the Concord River, Sophia finds it hard to "imagine that there [is] mud & fire & rock under our little boat" (*SPHAN* 130). Hawthorne typically finds such things hard to *forget*, yet at times, under her influence, he does forget and can sound remarkably like her. Exhilarated by a "soft and sunny" April day, Sophia takes it as proof of divine beneficence. As the birds "sang without end—I felt inclined to respond 'Yes, yes, yes—I know it I know it! There never was such a sun, such an air, such a sky, such a GOD! I know it, my dear little fellow worshippers'" (*SPHAN* 134). On a "glorious" September day Hawthorne could write as if he knew it, too:

> On such days, it is impossible not to love Nature; for she evidently loves us. At other seasons, she does not give me this impression; or only at very rare intervals; but in these happy autumnal days, when she has perfected her harvests, and accomplished every necessary thing that she had to do, she overflows with a blessed superfluity of love. It is good

to be alive now. Thank God for breath—yes, for mere breath!—when it is made up of such a heavenly breeze as this.... There is a pervading blessing diffused all over the world. I look out of the window, and think—"Oh perfect day! Oh beautiful world! Oh good God!" And such a day is the promise of a blissful Eternity; our Creator would never have made such weather, and have given us the deep hearts to enjoy it above and beyond all thought, if He had not meant us to be immortal. It opens the gates of Heaven, and gives us glimpses far inward. (8:393)

Hawthorne's "Thank God for breath—yes, for mere breath!" recalls the opening of Emerson's Divinity School Address, "In this refulgent summer it has been a luxury to draw the breath of life" (*CWE* 1:76). But where Emerson passes from sensory delight to natural religion through the evocation of a universe of interlocking laws, Hawthorne moves emotively from euphoria to professed belief. "What plays the mischief with the truth," Melville would write him of such ecstasies, "is that men will insist upon the universal application of a temporary feeling or opinion" (*WHM* 14:194): a mood was not the basis for a metaphysics. Hawthorne allows as much when he observes that "such days" and the emotions they kindle are the exception, not the rule. His common sense obliges him to put a brake on his enthusiasm. His conduit to faith takes the form rather of the quasi-rational construction (to recur in his writing) "God would not have done such-and-such unless..."

Scornful as he was of Emerson's cloudy mysticism, it is surprising that Hawthorne should have been so responsive to Sophia's and so indulgent of his own. In passages like the above, his sturdy realism drops away and he becomes purveyor of an "ideality" vacant of intellectual content and at odds with his impatience with humbug in other matters. Does Hawthorne truly believe, as he writes in the sketch "A Select Party," that "the dominions which the spirit conquers for itself among unrealities, become a thousand times more real than the earth whereon they stamp their feet, saying, 'This is solid and substantial!—this may be called a fact!'" (10:58)? What can such an idea mean beyond the truism that the beliefs we live by have a constitutive mental reality for the believer? The sentimentality in Hawthorne's early work had been conventional and primarily audience-directed. The sentimentality of the Manse period—a quasi-Platonism grafted onto a mind otherwise sharply observant, down-to-earth, critical, and ironic— seems domestically induced.

The tension during Hawthorne's years in Concord, to be enacted in its fiction, is between a sensuous attachment to the real and a vague yearning for the ideal. Hawthorne wants a "natural life" (the wild) but doesn't fully trust it, and he wants a "spiritual life" (the good) but has no distinct idea of what it consists in or how and where to find it.

Naturalizing Convention

> We are to revise the whole of our social structure, the state, the school,
> religion, marriage, trade, science, and explore their foundations in our
> own nature.... What is a man born for but to be a Reformer, a Re-maker
> of what man has made...?
>
> —Emerson, "Man the Reformer"

The immediate problem for Hawthorne at the Old Manse was how to make a living as a writer, since discarding an old way of life meant discarding an associated literary practice. The New England past was so interwoven with his Salem life that to mine it for material was to recall a self only precariously behind him. Of the twenty-two newly written pieces published in *Mosses from an Old Manse*, none deal with Puritan New England, and only "Egotism," "The Birth-mark," and "Rappaccini's Daughter" verge on the darkness of the early tales. Determined to write about the present just as he was to live in it, and publishing chiefly in the Jacksonian *Democratic Review*, Hawthorne found a subject in the tendencies of the age and an authorial role as commentator on America's ongoing experiment in reform. His characteristic productions of the period are neither tales nor sketches but miniature anatomies, cast in the form of fantasies or dream-visions, that survey classes of people and modes of life, ring changes on the theme of innovation, and explore the inheritance from the past and the prospects for the future.

In three lectures on "The Times" delivered in December 1841, Emerson had located the social moment within the struggle between "the two omnipresent parties of History, the party of the Past and the party of the Future" (*CWE* 1:172), represented for him in contemporary America by the reformer (one type of which was the Transcendentalist) and the conservative. "The castle, which conservatism sets out to defend, is the actual state of things, good and bad. The project of innovation is the best possible state of things" (*CWE* 1:185). Whether or not Hawthorne was acquainted with Emerson's lectures, his meditations on reform take place within a similar frame. One of the first pieces he wrote at the Old Manse, "The Hall of Fantasy," turns on the opposition between ideas in the mind (what ought to be) and resistant material facts (what is) and adopts a position toward reformers much like Emerson's: although their ideals may be laudable, their practice is narrow, self-conceited, and fanatical to the borders of insanity (10:180; *CWE* 1:176). Fanaticism is also a theme in "Earth's Holocaust," which echoes the Emersonian tension between reformer and conservative in its depiction of "the Titan of Innovation—angel or fiend, double in his nature, and capable of deeds befitting both characters" (10:400). In "The Times" Emerson had used the device of "a portrait gallery" (*CWE* 1:170) to give voice to the division within himself between an old faith and a new skepticism. In "Earth's Holocaust," with its sanguine but slightly obtuse narrator, its overenthusiastic reformers, its "grave man" of discriminating sense, and its cynical "dark-visaged stranger" (10:382, 403), Hawthorne does the same, save that the sketch's reformism represents what is new in him and its skepticism what is old.

In a notebook entry of 1836, Hawthorne had proposed a story in which "the race of mankind [was] to be swept away" and a new "human pair to be placed in the world, with native intelligence like Adam and Eve, but knowing nothing of their predecessors or of their own nature and destiny. They, perhaps, to be described as working out this knowledge by their sympathy with what they saw, and by their own feelings" (8:21). "The New Adam and Eve," a touchstone for Hawthorne's 1840s stance toward reform, develops this idea, but in keeping with the Emersonian project of revaluating traditions and institutions in light of essential human nature, it opens by putting the imagination to work to deconstruct "those iron fetters, which we call truth and reality," and help distinguish what is "natural" in "our present state and circumstances" from what "is merely the interpolation of the perverted mind and heart of man" (10:247). "Perverted" is an ambiguous, ideologically freighted word; it can mean "morally corrupt" (evil in the heart; the conservative's argument for social restraints) or it can mean "turned aside from the true and the good" (evil as a function of flawed social arrangements; the progressive's argument for reform). "The New Adam and Eve" seems to take the latter position, setting the norm of nature against what it calls "artificial error" (10:255).

As standards of undeformed humanity antecedent to and apart from culture (as if such a thing were possible), Adam and Eve are vehicles for arraigning a social system gone astray, due largely to money; as embodiments of "the instincts and intuitions" that give rise to social practices, they are also winnowing devices for separating whatever "wisdom and simplicity" inheres in those practices from the "elaborate perversities" that have come to encrust them (10:248). Banks, courts of law, and prisons come in for predictable criticism, but otherwise Hawthorne works with a light hand. On matters of gender especially, the "natural" turns out to be remarkably like the conventional. Adam is drawn more strongly than Eve "toward the material world" and has the livelier "appetite and animal instincts" (10:249, 259). He is the character of intellect, she of "tenderness and moral sense" (10:253). Politically, he rules, she moderates his rule (10:253). He is fascinated by a library, she gravitates toward ornamental dress, toward flowers and "fashionable poetry," toward a sewing basket, a pianoforte, a nursery, and a broom (10:251, 264, 257–58).

Not least, in view of the Manse period's attitudes toward body and spirit, the actual and the ideal, both figures (but Adam especially) look upward toward heaven and are sensible of "the soul's incongruity with its circumstances" (10:266). While Eve seems content with Adam, Adam, like other Hawthorne males, longs for transcendence. "Why is the world so unfit for our dwelling place?" he asks Eve (10:257). Adam feels they have "strayed away" from a celestial "home," and while he acknowledges "the necessity of keeping the beaten track of earth" for a time (10:250), he aspires beyond time to eternity and beyond the body to the soul. Eve takes the matter of an afterlife with quiet assurance; linked to nature more intimately than Adam, she is drawn instead toward populating the earth with children (10:257). Written during Sophia's first pregnancy (which would end in miscarriage), "The New Adam and Eve" is already evincing the gender divide rooted in maternity that will make Hawthornean woman, for all her heavenliness, a creature of nature and Hawthornean man, for all his physicality, an aspirant toward the ideal.

Having promised what seems a root-and-branch inquiry into social arrangements, Hawthorne ends by naturalizing domestic pieties, conveniently severed from their economic base. He solves the world's problems of sin and error much as experience seemed to have solved his own, through the "cure" of "Love!" (10:254). After a sweeping indictment of capitalist selfishness in "Man the Reformer" (1841), Emerson had also appealed to love—"Let our affections flow out to our fellows; it would operate the greatest of all revolutions" (*CWE* 1:158)—but for Emerson "love" carried the Edwardsian connotation of a gracious reorganization of being that radiated outward toward all creation and was socially transformative in its consequences. For Hawthorne love has its source, center, and limit in conventional marriage, which regenerates private life in a way that all but obviates matters of outward reform.

Written as an afterthought to frame and nominally to unify the pieces in the collection, "The Old Manse" is Hawthorne's celebration of domesticity and capsule resolution of the tensions between tradition and reform. Rummaging through books in the Manse's attic on a rainy day, Hawthorne finds, as Emerson had in "The American Scholar," that "thought grows moldy. What was good and nourishing food for the spirits of one generation, affords little sustenance for the next" (10:19; v. *CWE* 1:57). But Hawthorne wants little to do with modern books either, whether of the rational Unitarian or the visionary transcendental sort. He and Sophia are like his fictive Adam and Eve, "who, having no reminiscences, save dim and fleeting visions of a pre-existence, are content to live and be happy in the present" (10:266). In "The Old Manse" Hawthorne's first act as householder is to brighten the walls of his residence with "a cheerful coat of paint, and golden-tinted paper-hangings," and replace "the grim prints of Puritan ministers" with pictures of a Raphael Madonna and Lake Como (10:5). A Calvinist parsonage is made over into a contemporary middle-class home and its tenant, formerly a man of shadows, into a middle-class husband. Hawthorne is shedding the personal as well as the cultural past and fashioning a backdrop of comfort and genteel aestheticism for the next scene of his life.

The lure of wildness is represented in "The Old Manse" by those "strange and happy times" on the river with Ellery Channing "when we cast aside all irksome forms and strait-laced habitudes, and delivered ourselves up to the free air, to live like the Indians or any less conventional race, during one bright semi-circle of the sun" (10:21). Describing one such excursion, Hawthorne rehearses the archetypal American Renaissance action of severing oneself from society and venturing forth to nature to take the measure of life and reassess the prospects of the self. "The chief profit of those wild days," Hawthorne writes, resided less in any particular discoveries than "in the freedom which we thereby won from all custom and conventionalism, and fettering influence of man on man. We were so free to-day, that it was impossible to be slaves again tomorrow" (10:25). The act of emancipation, however, is quickly succeeded by one of willed reincorporation. Returning to the Manse, Hawthorne finds his "speculative extravagances" rebuked by its venerable solidity. The house "had grown sacred, in connection with the artificial life against which we inveighed"; it was "a home"—*his* home—and as such, like the social institutions that seem to have arisen from human needs, it could be renovated from within through love without serious structural alteration, "all the artifice and conventionalism of life" being "but an impalpable thinness upon its surface," with "the depth below…none the worse for it" (10:25).

While responsive to the Emersonian call to slough off the past, Hawthorne is wary of the indeterminacies of a structureless future and ends by upholding a rejuvenated version of established forms. Writing of spring in "Buds and Bird-Voices," he openly paraphrases Emerson in *Nature*—Emerson: "why should we grope among the dry bones of the past?" (*CWE* 1:7); Hawthorne: "Why may not we be permitted to live and enjoy, as if this were the first life, and our own the primal enjoyment, instead of treading always on these dry bones and mouldering relics…?"—only to meet Emerson's radical question within a conservative answer: "from the aged accumulation of which springs all that now appears so young and new" (10:152). "There is no decay," he writes: "Each human soul is the first-created inhabitant of its own Eden. We dwell in an old moss-covered mansion, and tread in the worn footprints of the past, and have a clergyman's ghost for our daily and nightly inmate; yet all these outward circumstances are made less than visionary, by the renewing power of the spirit" (10:153).

From the Manse period onward, reform for Hawthorne would essentially be a matter of regeneration through love within the framework of social institutions. In *The House of the Seven Gables*, the radical Holgrave, a would-be house-burner as radical Democrats were called barnburners, is wooed back to an admiration for architectural and societal "permanence" (2:315) through the agency of Phoebe, whose sunny domesticity has already purified the old Pyncheon house and dissolved two hundred years of Puritan gloom. Anchored to his own Phoebe, Hawthorne at the Manse felt at home with himself and the world and actuated by little of the reformer's indignation at the inequities of things. Resacralized convention, he came to believe, was the most genuine form of the "natural," not in Thoreau's sense of living close to nature and in harmony with its rhythms but as representing what Providence and human instincts seemed to intend for the race.

Aside from Sophia's miscarriage in February 1843 and an ongoing shortage of cash (the magazines paid late, if at all), the honeymoon phase of the Manse period, extending through the birth of Una in March 1844, was the happiest time of Hawthorne's adult life. On the occasion of their first anniversary each spouse inscribed a celebratory love message in their joint notebook. Hawthorne: "We never were so happy as now—never such wide capacity for happiness.... Methinks this birth-day of our married life is like a cape, which we have now doubled, and find a more infinite ocean of love stretching out before us" (8:390). And Sophia: "Our state is now one of deeper felicity than last 9th of July. Then we had visions and dreamed of Paradise—Now Paradise is here & our fairest visions stand realized before us. We are happier than we knew, or perhaps than we know now, for who can tell what is to come?" (*SPHAN* 142). For Sophia especially (Hawthorne was more reticent on such matters), marriage promised to combine the lives of the spirit and the flesh. "What a wondrous instrument [the body] is for the purposes of the heart," she exclaimed in her notebook (*SPHAN* 133). For a time, at least, the wild and the good must have seemed to be one.

The Life within a Life

> In some of his moods, strange to say, he prided and gloried himself on being marked out from the ordinary experience of mankind, by the possession of a double nature, and a life within a life.
>
> —Hawthorne, "Egotism; or, the Bosom Serpent"

In "The Christmas Banquet" Roderick Elliston tells the story of an annual assembly of ten of the world's most miserable, a banquet established by an eccentric benefactor to give voice to "the stern or fierce expression of human discontent" that might otherwise go unheard (10:285). As a man who has himself "wandered like one astray in a dark cavern" (10:284), Elliston, restored to domestic happiness with his wife Rosina, is a fit teller for such a tale. The story "Egotism; or, The Bosom Serpent," written nine months earlier, details Elliston's wanderings and deliverance and ends with the reunited couple looking brightly ahead. "The past," Rosina says, "dismal as it seems, shall fling no gloom upon the future" (10:283). And yet it does: Elliston writes "The Christmas Banquet." *Hawthorne* writes "The Christmas Banquet."

"The Christmas Banquet" is by no means anomalous among the Manse sketches. "Though Hawthorne's married life at the Old Manse appears on the surface to have been ideal," Larry J. Reynolds observes, "an undercurrent of dis-ease pervades the *American Notebooks*."[32] It also pervades a number of the tales and sketches. The more closely one examines the Manse writings, the more one is struck by the oddity that a writer so visibly happy should dwell so persistently on *un*happiness. "The Procession of Life," composed immediately after "Egotism," begins with life figured as "a festal or funereal procession" (10:207). The sketch that follows is almost entirely funereal—a litany of woes that reaches beyond the particulars of individual lives to an arraignment of life itself. Rejecting the classification of humanity by wealth, occupation, and degree of intellect, the sketch marshals people into columns according to disease, sorrow, affliction, and guilt, especially secret guilt. "The Good" are mentioned only to cite their diffidence in coming forth, "most conscious" are they "of error and imperfection"; the ranks of Love are also shy and marked less by brotherhood than by mutual antagonism, with "each sect surround[ing] its own righteousness with a hedge of thorns" (10:217). The largest group of sufferers are those who have made "some great mistake in life" or who by some inner failure find themselves "continually at cross-purposes with the world" (10:219). The grand Pilgrim's Progress of collective humanity turns out to be "a toilsome and doubtful march toward death," beyond which—"we know not" (10:222).

A similarly dark vision informs the "The Intelligence Office," a fable about a bureaucratic subdivision of Providence in which "all human wishes seemed to be made known, and, so far as destiny would allow, negotiated to the fulfillment" (10:328). In practice, destiny allows very little; the bureau is chiefly a depository for unanswered prayers and disregarded complaints, like the Dead Letter Office in Melville's "Bartleby, the Scrivener." A main grievance is the want of "fit" between desires and circumstances, whether in the matter of "yearnings for I know not what," of vocation ("I want my place!—...my true place in the world!—my proper sphere!—my thing to do" [10:323]), or—strangely, for a newlywed—of marriage, which "in ninety-nine cases out of a hundred" is entered into without any profound sympathy (10:324).

Where the somber writings of the Salem years center upon sin or guilt, those of the Manse period tend to focus on life's dissatisfactions and abortive mischances. Some of the unhappiness is rooted in temperament, some in outward conditions. In "The Christmas Banquet" Hawthorne describes various psychological types impaired by their constitutions: the depressive man, without "energy [of character] to struggle against the heavy despondency to which his temperament rendered him liable" (10:287); the hypersensitive one, whose slightest contacts with the world rub painfully against a "diseased heart" (10:287); the moral hypochondriac, who sees sin everywhere, like Young Goodman Brown or Reverend Hooper in "The Minister's Black Veil"; the disillusioned idealist turned misanthrope who rails at humanity like Timon; and the sole perennial guest, Gervayse Hastings, a man of cold heart and torpid sensibilities excluded from life's joys and sufferings alike. Still another class of the wretched are made so by their life-situations, including three—a philanthropist, a consumptive seamstress, and a "woman on unemployed energy" (10:303)—who prefigure Hollingsworth, Priscilla, and Zenobia of *The Blithedale Romance*.

What does all this suffering mean? "Tell me what is beneath it, and what your real agency in life, and what your influence upon mankind?" a truth-seeker demands of the Intelligencer. Why, nothing at all is beneath it, he is told in reply: "The desire of man's heart does for him whatever I seem to do" (10:336). The "intelligence office" proves to be a *non*-intelligence office. There is no design to things; people do as they do; they act according to how they are made or how life hems them in; and they suffer for things they choose, for things that befall them, or for no definite reason at all beyond vague longings, "feverish" passions, object-less sorrows (10:324), or nocturnal dreads. Why should a man who seems to have had most of his own wishes astonishingly filled be writing about the Vanity of Human Wishes?

Elliston's reference to having "wandered like one astray in a dark cavern" (10:268) recalls Hawthorne's uses of that image, first in "The Haunted Mind" and again in the notebook entry encapsulating his "Salem masterplot" ("The human Heart to be allegorized as a cavern" [8:237]). The latter envisions a happy outcome to the journey from innocence through gloom and terror to a higher innocence. In practice, few of Hawthorne's characters complete the journey, and only one of those may be called a sinner—Elliston, whose sin is obscure and directed chiefly against himself.

"Egotism" is sometimes read as a loose allegory of Hawthorne's own "newly found marital happiness" and/or his deliverance from "what in Hawthorne's day...was considered the curse of solitary manhood," masturbation, both as a debilitating sexual habit and as a cause or symptom of psychological introversion, or egotism.[33] The book Elliston is shown reading in the story, Jeremy Taylor's *Ductor Dubitantium*, had been a main source for "Fancy's Show Box," whose exploration of guilt-ridden fantasy had covert reference to masturbation; Elliston is even given the "unwholesome look" and sickly greenish white pallor that contemporary tracts associated with masturbators (10:268–69). The curious thing about the story is that, through no apparent necessity of plot or theme, Hawthorne makes Elliston a married man. For unspecified reasons, Elliston has "willfully shattered" his domestic happiness and lived apart from his wife for nearly four years (10:271).

"Egotism" was written in February 1843, during Sophia's first pregnancy, a time when conjugal relations were out of the question (given contemporary mores), so that the sexual insinuations of the story may have been occasioned by a guilty relapse into premarital habits. Yet another kind of "relapse" may also have been involved. Although the Manse notebook gives the impression of uninterrupted marital bliss, in fact, after the first several months husband and wife "spent a good deal of time apart," with Hawthorne visiting his family in Salem and Sophia hers in Boston, not always concurrently.[34] Life at the Manse without Sophia was trying for Hawthorne; returning to Salem was even more so. During one visit, shortly after her miscarriage and Hawthorne's completion of "Egotism," Sophia went to stay with her family in Boston, Hawthorne with his in Salem— "where," he said, "I resumed all my bachelor habits for nearly a fortnight, leading the same life in which ten years of my youth flitted away like a dream" (8:368). If the visit showed Hawthorne "how much changed" he was from earlier days (8:368), it also reminded him, as earlier and later visits did, that beneath these changes, waiting to surface whenever the regulative influence of domesticity was removed, was the self he hoped he had outgrown. Despite his efforts to incorporate her into his being, Sophia did not make her way into Hawthorne's heart as an abiding principle of grace. Her influence was chiefly *upon* him, not *within* him, and it waned in her absence.

Although Elliston loathes the reptile in himself, he is strangely attached to it. Whatever the nature and origin of his obsession, he comes to regard it as the mark of his "individuality" (10:273), indeed of his distinction. Initially he tries to conceal his snake by "estrang[ing] himself from all companionship"; later he actively flaunts it to "establish a species of brotherhood between himself and the world" on the ground of common guilt (10:271, 274). His fixation renders him preternaturally sensitive to the real or fancied sins of others, and he assumes the role of moral gadfly, "grappl[ing] with the ugliest truth that he could lay his hand on, and compel[ling] his adversary to do the same" (10:277–78). In this, he seems a malign version of Reverend Hooper in "The Minister's Black Veil"; still more, he seems a version of Hawthorne, who in his Salem phase projected obscure guilts into fictional plots and universalized them for his audience into a common liability to sin.

Through Elliston, Hawthorne is asking whether the themes of his younger self represent a penetrating insight into human nature or evidence of a neurosis to be cured. Elizabeth Peabody believed that Sophia's optimism caused Hawthorne "almost...to doubt whether his own power to gaze steadily at the evils of human character, and analyze them, were really wisdom, or a defect of moral sensibility" (*NHW* 1:248–49). He had long wondered this himself. Now, alongside Sophia's bright gaze, his own dark one seemed especially morose. Whether read as a fable of Hawthorne's redemption through marriage or of his *re*-redemption after a period of physical or sexual separation, "Egotism" is Hawthorne's effort to expel (yet again) the guilt-burdened introversion that had marked his former life and on some level was still operative in him. Elliston feels he might be saved if "for one instant" he could "forget" himself and escape the "diseased self-contemplation" responsible for his condition (10:283). He does.

Restored to Rosina (whose name evokes Sophia's "couleur de rose" sensibility), Elliston is "restored to his right mind" (10:283), as, cathartically, Hawthorne is restored through the symbolic action of his tale.

But not entirely. Although Elliston's "former sad experience" has given him privileged "insight into the gloomy mysteries of the human heart" (10:284), it does not explain why in his present happiness he (and Hawthorne) should choose to write about them. In arranging the selections in *Mosses from an Old Manse*, Hawthorne positioned "The Christmas Banquet" (narrated by Elliston) immediately after "Egotism," and "The New Adam and Eve" immediately before it. Whether by design or by chance, the pieces constitute a rough allegory of Hawthorne's interior life at the Manse. In the first, newlywed Hawthorne sloughs off the past and inhabits the world like a prelapsarian Adam; in the second, remnants of the old self resurface and are purged through the vehicle of plot; and in the third, the purgation having been only partially effective, the darker self withdraws to a more sequestered level of being and expresses itself in tableaux of thwarted selves inwardly disjoined or at variance with their circumstances.

"Most men seek to impose some cunning falsehood upon themselves for truth," Hawthorne has his Intelligencer say (10:335). Hawthorne's "cunning falsehood" was the air of contented domesticity he assumed for himself and before the world. "My youth comes back to me here," he wrote Evert Duyckinck from Salem in October 1845, "and I find myself, sad to say, pretty much the same sort of fellow as of old" (16:126). Despite the transformation he felt marriage had wrought, Hawthorne came to regard this Salem "fellow" as at bottom who he was, all else—wife, children, position in the world, modest reputation, happiness itself—being, if not exactly a veneer, then at least a kind of ongoing performance. He did all he could to avoid meeting his former self, down to refusing to visit his sister in Salem after returning from Europe. At any stage of his life, to return to Salem, even in thought, was not merely to evoke an unwanted ghost from the past; it was to feel starkly unveiled in the present, as if all that separated him from his Salem self were the life-structures he had made with Sophia.

And Sophia herself? Rosina in "The Christmas Banquet" is an unperturbed auditor of Elliston's manuscript; Sophia herself called the sketch "very extraordinary—perfectly original & very profound."[35] For both women, the morbid content of the tale was distinct from the personal character of their husband. Sophia was pleased to believe that literature was literature and marriage, marriage, and that even in the intimacy of marriage spouses as extraordinary as her husband were entitled to unplumbed depths. Part of the tacit contract between herself and Hawthorne was that she should never pry into the recesses of his soul and he never let his darker moods and opinions intrude upon family life. They kept to their roles, Sophia so faithfully as to assume hers even in letters to her family. With Hawthorne, the outward serenity of married life (economics excepted) seems to have led him to compartmentalize himself. On some level, he had long "live[d] two ... different lives" (16:395), as he wrote Sophia in 1840, claiming that his outward life was perfunctory and only his relationship with her deeply real. Now there was yet another "life," hidden even from Sophia, a "life within a life" (10:274) reserved for his work and only fitfully to be acknowledged even there.

Julian maintained that Sophia's "lofty and assured ideals kept [Hawthorne] to a belief in the reality and veracity of his own" (*NHW* 1:40). Kept him, it might be truer to say, to a willed persuasion they *were* his own. It was against such self-apostasy that Hawthorne tacitly protests when he has his testator endow the Christmas banquet "to perpetuate his own remonstrance against the earthly course of Providence, and his sad and sour dissent from those systems of religion or philosophy which find either sunshine in the world, or draw it down from heaven" (10:285). "Sunshine" seems a mild gibe at Sophia, but Hawthorne's true object of scorn is his own complicity with her sentimental fictions. In his eagerness to put "Salem" behind him, he has, he understands, wandered away from the man he most deeply is and from the springs of his art.

"Theodore"

> But Theodore, whose natural tendency was toward skepticism, felt himself almost injured and insulted by the Veiled Lady's proposal that he should pledge himself, for life and eternity, to so questionable a creature as herself.
>
> —Hawthorne, *The Blithedale Romance*

> People never do get just the good they seek. If it come at all, it is something else, which they never dreamed of, and did not particularly want.
>
> —Hawthorne, *The Blithedale Romance*

In three of his letters to Sophia from Brook Farm, Hawthorne playfully signed himself "Theodore De L'Aubépine" (15:584, 586, 592). He had been nicknamed M. de. l'Aubépine (French for hawthorn) by Horatio Bridge's French tutor when he visited Bridge in Maine in 1837, and he would adopt the name as a literary pseudonym in his preface to "Rappaccini's Daughter."[36] "Theodore" was Sophia's suggestion for the son born to them in 1846. Hawthorne claimed not to like the name (15:585), yet he liked (or perhaps disliked) it enough to use it for the Coverdalesque hero of "Zenobia's Legend" in *The Blithedale Romance*. Zenobia's Theodore is a skeptic whose reservations about the Veiled Lady keep him from making the act of faith needed to win her, just as Coverdale, who claims to have loved Priscilla but wonders if she is really the ethereal maiden of his imaginings, woos her with halfhearted advances destined to fail. His denials notwithstanding, Coverdale is also in love, or in lust, with Zenobia for the opposite quality, her voluptuous sexuality, which both allures and unsettles him. To Coverdale, Zenobia at Blithedale (not in town) represents physical human nature (the wild), Priscilla spiritual human nature (the good). With more courage to grasp the real, Coverdale would have loved Zenobia and taken the wild *as* the good; with greater trust in the ideal, he would have won Priscilla and put the wild out of his mind. As it is, fearing the natural, which he yearns for, and only half believing in the spiritual, which he professes to revere, he cannot fully commit himself to either and so loses both.

Hawthorne in the early 1840s is Theodore de l'Aubépine. "Theodore" is the doubting idealist within him, "l'Aubépine" (creator of the dangerously erotic Beatrice Rappaccini) the ambivalent naturalist. The name is a metonym for Hawthorne's self-division at the Manse and for the conflicts he would fictionalize in the three most important tales he wrote there: "The Birth-mark," "The Artist of the Beautiful," and "Rappaccini's Daughter."

Zenobia and Priscilla, half sisters, are extremes of womanhood, or rather projections *upon* womanhood of a bifurcated male sensibility unable to reconcile the sexual and the spiritual. Early in their engagement Hawthorne took to addressing Sophia as his "Wife," partly to legitimize his sexual feelings for her. Sophia the "Dove" was his angelic redeemer, but by August 1839 his fantasy and/or her behavior had spawned a psychic double, "naughty Sophie Hawthorne," with whom Hawthorne and his Dove conducted a kind of epistolary ménage à trois. "Yes, mine own Dove," he wrote in October 1839, "whether you like it or no, that naughty little person must share our pillow" (15:357). Initially, "naughty" implied willful or disobedient, but as Sophia's resistance assumed piquancy it became increasingly erotic. Hawthorne wished to unify his two Sophias—"methinks a woman...who should combine the characteristics of Sophie Hawthorne and my Dove would be the very perfection of her race," he told her (15:358)—and in so doing unify the sexual and spiritual impulses within himself, but the two women continued to displace one another in his imagination, leaving him "in a state of dynamic tension" between notions of wifely "purity" and wifely "naughtiness."[37]

Instead of resolving this tension, marriage, Patricia Dunlavy Valenti suggests, exacerbated it by incarnating Hawthorne's "immaterial longings" in an actual "female body."[38] With the birth of Una in March 1844, Hawthorne found himself with yet another aspect of Sophia, the figure whom he would later designate "Mama" and who established her identity *as* a mother almost immediately. Sophia's notebook entries after Una's birth deal almost exclusively with child-rearing, as do her letters to her mother and sister Mary (herself a recent mother), down to details about breast-feeding and infant bowel movements. For Hawthorne, Una's birth was less a celebratory beginning than a bittersweet end. Fatherhood "ought not to come too early in a man's life—not till he has fully enjoyed his youth—for methinks the spirit can never be thoroughly gay and carefree again," he wrote George Hillard shortly after Una's birth (16:22–23). After twenty months at the Manse, the reality principle, represented by fatherhood, responsibility, and cohabitation with a practical-minded caregiver, asserted its claims; the Edenic interlude was over.

It may have ended fully a year before that, during the months of Sophia's first pregnancy. To Aylmer in "The Birth-mark," written in January 1843, the crimson hand on his wife Georgiana's cheek symbolizes her "earthly imperfection"—aesthetically, the flaw in her beauty; ontologically, her "liability to sin, sorrow, decay, and death"; and spiritually, the defect that mocks his idealization of her, "degrading [her] into kindred with the lowest and even with the very brutes" (10:37, 39). It has also been read sexually as signifying menstruation (crimson) or masturbation (a hand) as well as eroticism generally. Aylmer's loathing of the birthmark is so intense, so tangled in its elements, and so entwined with attitudes expressed elsewhere by Hawthorne that it is difficult to assign a single meaning to it other than under the general rubric "biology."[39] The story's object of revulsion seems the entire physiological basis of life as it converts heavenly angels into creatures of material nature.

Nina Baym upbraids the Hawthorne hero for the "deeply warped" activity of trying "to purify [his] woman by separating her in some way from her body."[40] This is the view Hawthorne seems to take at the close of "The Birth-mark": had "Aylmer reached a profounder wisdom, he need not have flung away the happiness which would have woven his mortal life of the selfsame texture with the celestial" (10:56). But there are ambiguities, so many in fact that the tale all but deconstructs itself. Georgiana, Aylmer's victim, "exult[s]" in the "honorable love" that destroys her, "so pure and lofty that it would accept nothing less than perfection nor miserably make itself contented with an earthlier nature than he had dreamed of" (10:52). Even as she lies dying and tasks Aylmer with rejecting earth's "best," she assures him he has "aimed loftily," "done nobly," and should "not repent" (10:55). Her words resemble a notebook remark of Sophia's about Hawthorne: "he is so seldom satisfied with any thing—weather, things, or people....His demand is for perfection, & nothing short can content him."[41] Noting "woman's recognition" in the Manse writings "that she does not measure up to her would-be lover's ideal," Larry J. Reynolds wonders whether "Sophia ever [felt] such rejection and hurt."[42] If she did, she would likely have depersonalized the feelings, as Georgiana does in believing that it is not her body or fallible self that Aylmer recoils at so much as the flawed conditions of material life. Driven by "his strong and eager aspiration toward the infinite" (10:49), Aylmer must inevitably fail in this and other experiments, not merely because Georgiana is human clay but also because *he* is human clay. His tragedy—a representative one—is that of "the composite man, the spirit burdened with clay and working in matter," and subject to "the despair that assails the higher nature in finding itself so miserably thwarted by the earthly part" (10:49).

As both a cautionary tale about transcendent idealism *and* a rueful eulogy of it, "The Birth-mark" bears doubly on Hawthorne's life at the Manse. The happiness Aylmer might have had is Hawthorne's happiness, but so is the idealism that looks beyond it in the belief (as Hawthorne later wrote) that "all true happiness involves something more than the earth owns" (21:153). Valenti sees the Manse stories as "repeatedly declaim[ing] the man's disappointment in the woman he imagined to fulfill [his] aspirations,"[43] a theme she takes (contra Baym) as reflecting Hawthorne's partial identification with his idealizing males. In what respect might Sophia have fallen short? Probably not sexually, for she seems to have been more comfortable with her body than Hawthorne was with his. Whatever disenchantment he felt more likely involved his "Dove," whose aura of heavenliness necessarily dimmed in day-to-day living, punctuated by the round of pregnancy, miscarriage, pregnancy again, and motherhood with all their physical exigencies. It is as though Theodore kissed the Veiled Lady and found her, not hideous, as he feared, but simply the same in kind as everyone else.

The irony of marriage for Hawthorne was that women, imagined conduits to the infinite, had the practical effect of making life *finite*. "Why do you bring in the names of these women?" (3:135) Hollingsworth asks Coverdale in *The Blithedale Romance*, impatient that his friend should introduce romantic relations while he is unfolding the grand scheme of his life's work. "The Hawthorne woman is very much a being of flesh," Nina Baym writes in praise of the type: "She is...always 'natural' in the sense of being artless, unself-conscious, and generally rooted in life and content with it,"[44] while the Hawthorne man is not. The point in question with the Manse writings (and later with the romances) is not the terms of the opposition—men as abstractionist, women as "natural"—but the attitude(s) adopted toward it. Does Hawthorne take issue with his aspirant men, as Baym has it, or does he compulsively reenact their ambivalence toward the body—or both?

Aspiration versus finitude is the theme of "The Artist of the Beautiful," begun in March 1844, within two weeks of Una's birth. The early sections of the story dwell on what by then was a residual subject for Hawthorne, the artist's struggle with utilitarian society, whose contempt he internalizes as chronic self-distrust. The more pertinent issues are whether Owen Warland can have art and domesticity both and whether Annie Hovenden, as representative woman (?), is refined enough to mediate between the artist's delicate spiritual organization and the coarse masculine world. "There were no such attributes in Annie Hovenden as [Owen's] imagination had endowed her with," Hawthorne states flatly. And yet, he adds, had Owen won Annie and seen her "fade from angel into ordinary woman," he might have been thrown back upon his art with renewed energy; alternatively, if Annie *had* fulfilled his idea of her (a possibility just discounted) he might have "wrought the Beautiful" out of "mere redundancy" of joy (10:464).

Owen is a Theodore who doubts his Veiled Lady and hesitates to kiss her before someone else does. Hawthorne himself made the act of faith, wed his Veiled Lady, and for a time seemed to have the satisfactions of butterfly and baby at once. Or did he? Aside from claiming Sophia's attention and pulling *her* into the finite, Una proved a temperamental child whom Hawthorne watched solicitously as if she were a seedling that might or might not develop into a beautiful flower. His writing was also problematic. Owen Warland creates the beautiful in solitude and is both transfigured in the process and vindicated by the product, which, as Robert Danforth says, "beat[s] all nature" (10:474). Neither triumph was fully Hawthorne's at the Manse. Apart from the struggle to wrest a living from his work, he had difficulty finding subjects; the conceits behind the sketches were often thin or labored; and if in quantity the writings amounted to a respectable body of work (Hawthorne felt they didn't), in quality most readers have shared Melville's opinion that as a group they are inferior to those in *Twice-Told Tales* (WHM 14:181). Hawthorne agreed. "I thank God, I have grace enough to be utterly dissatisfied with them," he wrote Horatio Bridge in February 1846: "I am ashamed—and there's an end" (16:140).

In writing of Owen's victory, Hawthorne vicariously participates in it; he also makes it his own, for "The Artist of the Beautiful" is one of his finest stories. Such success is rare in the Manse period, however, and it may have been a lonely success. The ebony box Owen carves to encase his artwork shows a boy chasing a butterfly that turns into a winged spirit and ascends heavenward, with the boy following in pursuit, alone. The image plays off another from early in the period— a "butterfly soaring upward" in "The New Adam and Eve," as if in response to Adam's intuition that "our allotted task is no other than to climb into the sky" (10:267, 260). In "The Artist of the Beautiful," Adam's "our" becomes Owen's "my," and his ascent is accomplished in monastic solitude. When Hawthorne wrote the tale, the time was long past when he and Sophia dreamed of collaborating as artists or meeting at the end of the day to share their work-in-progress. His realm was the study, hers now the nursery. As Sophia grew more narrowly domestic, Hawthorne's writing replaced his Dove as the site of the ideal, yet even within and toward his art he showed himself a "Theodore": "The Artist of the Beautiful" is his only tale to exalt the creative process in Romantic fashion and one of the very few of the period whose art testifies to its glow.[45] Writing was Hawthorne's craft; it was his business; it was not his surrogate religion. With his Dove now earthbound in motherhood, he had no religion.

Thwarting Nature

> Blessed are all simple emotions, be they dark or bright! It is the lurid
> intermixture of the two that produces the illuminating blaze of the
> infernal regions.
>
> —Hawthorne, "Rappaccini's Daughter"

After the joys of the early months at the Manse subsided, Hawthorne negotiated
the conflict between the wild and the good by settling for a diluted version of
both that left him, for the most part, quietly content. His greatest work would
come when he grew *dis*content—when desire, chafing against confinements of
his own making or choosing, conjured up the possibility of a passionate naturalism, sensuous, earthy, and free. When the woodcarver of "Drowne's Wooden
Image" manages his lone feat of genius, his muse is an exotic woman rich in complexion, with "dark eyes," a "voluptuous mouth," and "a look made up of pride,
coquetry, and a gleam of mirthfulness" (10:314). Hawthorne, too, attained to
genius by falling in love with proud, voluptuous, dark-eyed women, but in his
case the love-objects were of his own creation.

"Rappaccini's Daughter," the penultimate story written at the Manse, marks
the initial appearance of the "mythic being, the incarnation of hidden longings
and desires," that Philip Rahv calls "The Dark Lady of Salem."[46] Provokingly
sexual yet also chaste, if language as heated as Hawthorne's is consonant with
chastity—"She looked redundant with life, health, and energy; all of which
attributes were bound down and compressed, as it were, and girdled tensely, in
their luxuriance, by her virgin zone" (10:97)—Beatrice Rappaccini promises to
combine the heavenliness of the Dove with the eroticism of "naughty Sophie
Hawthorne." Yet rather than work to reconcile body and spirit, Hawthorne's tale
confounds them in ways that epitomize the tension of the Manse period and
betray his own irresolution.

"It is the inward thought alone that renders the body either material or angel-
ical," Sophia wrote in her Manse notebook (*SPHAN* 133). This is the theme of
"Rappaccini's Daughter," save that Hawthorne seems less sure of Sophia's "alone."
Is the sexual body poisonous or is "poison" a function of the fastidious or prurient mind? The latter possibility centers on the hero Giovanni's construction of
Beatrice, as his "wonder-working fancy" and commingled "love and horror"
build upon his observation of the baneful effects of her touch (10:98, 105). "Oh,
was there not, from the first, more poison in thy nature than in mine?" (10:127),
Beatrice bitterly asks Giovanni, a judgment anticipated by the narrator's progres-
sively harsh depiction of Giovanni's "venomous" heart (10:122, 124). If Beatrice's
alleged poison is her healthy eroticism as it fascinates and repels a squeamish
male, then "Rappaccini's Daughter" may indeed be about a perverse denial of

instinct—in Nina Baym's phrase, "thwarted nature."[47] Yet Beatrice's poisonousness is not simply the product of Giovanni's lurid imaginings. Even as Hawthorne chides his lover for a lack of faith, he presents the beloved, in body at least, as warranting such lack of faith.[48] Beatrice acknowledges the poison herself; plants wilt and animals die under its influence; Hawthorne makes it a textual fact.

If manuscript evidence survived, it would be instructive to follow the development of "Rappaccini's Daughter" as its emphases emerged during the writing. Julian reports that when Hawthorne "read the as yet unfinished manuscript" to Sophia and was asked about its ending—"is Beatrice to be a demon or an angel?"—he replied, "with some emotion," "I have no idea!" (*NHW* 1:360). His uncertainty was more than a literary matter; he could not decide whether he most loved or feared his alluring heroine and whether he wanted to eulogize, contain, sublimate, or destroy her. Like Hester, Zenobia, and Miriam after her, Beatrice is a middle-aged man's evocation of the magnificently erotic woman he never had, and the turns his story takes—its evolving portrayals of Beatrice and Giovanni and the increasing prominence given its narrator as a moralizing presence—seem virtually an exercise in fantasy management.

Despite her air of "simplicity and sweetness" (10:102), Beatrice as initially presented is by no means ingenuous. Her "intimate embrace" of the purple-flowered plant she knows is deadly (10:102)—of the "sister" whom she "nurse[s]" and "serves"[s], whose "perfumed breath" is her "breath of life," and with whom she identifies even in her choice of dress and color (10:97, 102)—is a celebration of her own dangerously luxuriant sexuality. Hawthorne celebrates it, too, even as he hints at the "strange peril" that links "flower and maiden" (10:98), a peril that seems as much his as Giovanni's. If his first response to Beatrice and her fictive descendants is to linger appreciatively on their bodies, his second is to slap his hero, his readers, and himself on the wrist for doing so. His third response is to rid himself of temptation and its related guilt by ostracizing, killing off, or otherwise neutralizing its provoking object. Years later in Italy he would react similarly to Titian's Magdalene, all but fondling her through his graphic prose before dismissing her as a strumpet and her creator as "a very good-for-nothing old man" (14:334).

"Rappaccini's Daughter" sets the pattern. Through Giovanni, Hawthorne plays out his erotic fascination with Beatrice, then dissociates himself from its accompanying anxieties by making a vilified Giovanni the scapegoat for his own inability to reconcile body and spirit. By giving weight to Beatrice's words— "though my body be nourished with poison, my spirit is God's creature, and craves to be loved" (10:125)—Hawthorne proclaims her moral innocence and with it his own. He aligns the values of the story with her lofty idealism and diverts his conflicted obsession with her body into a chaste reverence for her soul. But the concession this strategy exacts—allowing that her body, the human or female body, is indeed "nourished with poison"—is enormous. Instead of embracing sexuality as natural and healthy, Hawthorne inscribes his own version of mind/body dualism. He is able to angelicize Beatrice only by dematerializing her, or doing what Baym says his flawed heroes do, separating woman from her body. He even has Beatrice verbally perform the act herself.

Beyond sexuality, narrowly conceived, poison in "Rappaccini's Daughter" functions like Georgiana's crimson hand in "The Birth-mark"; it symbolizes the hero's (and author's) uneasiness with the facts of corporeal life as they relate to the putative life of the soul. When Beatrice tells Giovanni to disregard stories about her and believe only what he sees with his "own eyes," Giovanni thinks immediately of the things he *has* seen with his eyes, whereupon Beatrice "with queen-like haughtiness" amends her plea: "if true to the outward senses," an observation or suspicion "still…may be false in its essence" (10:111, 112). Ignore the testimony of experience, she tells him; facts are not a pathway to belief but an impediment to it; let faith prevail. Late in the story the narrator intrudes to record just this idea: "There is something truer and more real, than what we can see with the eyes, and touch with the finger" (10:120). Giovanni's fault— the sign of an inferior nature "groveling among earthly doubts" (10:120)—is that he cannot make or sustain a counterexperiential act of faith. When, however, he does approach such an act, refusing to admit that Beatrice's grasp has produced the "burning and tingling agony in his hand" (10:114–15), Hawthorne turns on him contemptuously and charges him with denial: "Oh, how stubbornly does love" or pretended love "hold its faith, until the moment come, when it is doomed to vanish into thin mist!" (10:115). Is faith a matter of true visionary transcendence, as the idealist in Hawthorne proclaims, or of self-delusion in the face of irrefutable evidence, as the realist objects?

There is no obvious way of reconciling these passages, which proceed from Hawthorne's own temperamental division, nor is it easy to square Giovanni's curative purpose in offering Beatrice what he takes to be an antidote—he would relieve her body of poison, restore her to "the limits of ordinary nature," and enable their "earthly union and earthly happiness," which presumably includes sexual happiness—with the scorn Hawthorne heaps upon it, nominally because of Giovanni's "blighting words" at discovering that Beatrice has infected him (10:126). Unlike Aylmer, who wants to perfect Georgiana by desexualizing her, Giovanni wants to normalize Beatrice in order to *re*sexualize her, his modest physical advances having been rebuffed with a look "so sad" and "so stern" as to preclude further ones (10:116). Beatrice concedes the basis for Giovanni's late anger and revulsion—"I, it is true, am the horrible thing thou namest me" (10:124)—and is stung only by his charge that she infected him knowingly, yet how is he to guess that rather than wish to marry him she had meant (disingenuously) only to "be with [him] a little time" and then "let [him] pass away" (10:125)? After encouraging Giovanni's love, Beatrice upbraids him for thinking she sought to entrap him. "You ought to have loved ME, not my body," she says, in effect. The narrator agrees. Where Giovanni would unite spirit and matter in a detoxified Beatrice, the story berates him for failing to choose spirit *over* matter. In presenting the "ugly mystery" of her poisoned body as "but an earthly illusion" beyond whose "mist of evil…the real Beatrice was a heavenly angel" (10:122), "Rappaccini's Daughter" allows that the material body is indeed corrupt, that the "real" self exists apart from it, and that spiritual love is to be realized fully only beyond time.

There may be another way of considering the story, more radical as cultural critique. Commonly taken as a metaphor for female sexuality, Beatrice's poisonousness may instead be a quality superadded to her sexuality. The plants in Dr. Rappaccini's garden are not natural but hybrid—a "monstrous offspring of man's depraved fancy" as it meddles with nature and creates "only an evil mockery of beauty" (10:110). Beatrice may also be such a hybrid. Innocent itself, her sexuality has been *made* poisonous by the interventions of culture as embodied in the patriarchal Dr. Rappaccini, on whom blame is leveled at the end. In this reading, Giovanni's misgivings would not be those merely of his own shallow heart; they would be representative misgivings inbred in males by a reigning mind-set that privileges knowledge and control of nature and regards female sexuality as profoundly disruptive. "Poisoning" woman's body—that is, treating her body *as if it were* poisonous and perpetuating structures of belief that confine it narrowly to an unnatural garden—may be man's way of containing female power in the service of what he understands to be "civilization."

If this is indeed Hawthorne's theme, the question remains whether he is critiquing an ideological discourse or revealing his own embeddedness in it. Does he mean to deconstruct culture and return to nature? to advance *beyond* culture toward a higher version of nature? The difficulties with positing a "natural" Hawthorne are, first, that it demands a selective reading of ambiguous, self-contradictory texts and, second, that it ignores the interpretive pressures of notebooks and letters, which portray a vastly different sort of man. To argue for a liberationist Hawthorne is to attend exclusively to a single side of the approach/avoidance conflict that characterizes his mature work. In "Rappaccini's Daughter" Hawthorne comes to terms with the equivocal Beatrice by sending her off to paradise, letting canonization perform the practical work of exorcism. He has not exposed his hero's nervous Manichaeanism so much as, in his handling of materials, he has exposed his own. He has set the physical body *against* the celestial soul, the wild *against* the good, and cast his lot with the latter. The battle, however, has barely begun.

Bowdoin College, ca. 1823

Sophia Amelia Peabody, age 23, etching by S. A. Schoff

Nathaniel Hawthorne, age 36, by Charles Osgood, 1840

Emerson's House, Concord, Mass.

Margaret Fuller, engraving ca. 1840–1880

The Old Manse, Concord, Mass.

Salem Custom House, ca. 1850

Una and Julian Hawthorne, ca. 1850, daguerreotype by unknown photographer

Hawthorne 1852/53, by
George P.A. Healy

The Wayside, Concord (house Hawthorne bought in 1852)

4

Undoing It All

Very few people are capable of being independent; it is a privilege of the strong.... For he who walks into a labyrinth; he increases a thousandfold the dangers which are inherent in life anyway. And not the smallest of his dangers is that no one can witness how and where he loses his way, falls into solitude, or is torn to pieces by some troglodytic minotaur of conscience.

—Nietzsche, *Beyond Good and Evil*

With this symbol, I undo it all, and make it as it had never been!

—Hester Prynne in *The Scarlet Letter*

Salem, Concord, and the Death of Mrs. Hawthorne

For a long time, I knelt there, holding her hand; and surely it is the darkest hour I ever lived. Afterwards, I stood by the open window, and looked through the crevice of the curtain. The shouts, laughter, and cries of the two children had come up into the chamber, from the open air, making a strange contrast with the death-bed scene. And now, through the crevice of the curtain, I saw my little Una of the golden locks, looking very beautiful; and so full of spirit and life, that she was life itself. And then I looked at my poor dying mother; and seemed to see the whole of human existence at once, standing in the dusty midst of it. Oh what a mockery, if what I saw were all,—let the interval between extreme youth and dying age be filled up with what happiness it might!

But God would not have made the close so dark and wretched, if there were nothing beyond; for then it would have been a fiend that created us, and measured out our existence, and not God. It would be something beyond wrong—it would be insult—to be thrust out of life into annihilation in this miserable way. So, out of the very bitterness of death, I gather the sweet assurance of a better state of being.

—Hawthorne, *The American Notebooks* (July 29, 1849)

Art arises, it may be, from the death-denying portion of the psyche deeper than reason's reach.

—John Updike, "Late Works," *Due Considerations*

In chapter 11 of *The Scarlet Letter,* Hawthorne sets aside his arch, external perspective on Dimmesdale and penetrates into what he calls "the interior of a heart" (1:13). He describes the moral and physical debilitation of Dimmesdale under the burden of sin and hypocrisy. He shows the paralyzing introspection that afflicts the guilt-ridden Protestant consciousness, the unavailing and monkishly *un*-Protestant penances with which Dimmesdale punishes himself in lieu of the needful act of public confession, the self-loathing and self-estrangement that arise from the discordance between his inward and outward selves, and, paradoxically, the newly achieved ministerial efficacy consequent on these very agonies, which awaken in him an empathy with the broad community of sinners.

Situating *The Scarlet Letter* within Hawthorne's trials of mid-1849—the prolonged turmoil surrounding his removal from the customhouse and, in the midst of the crisis, the death of his mother on July 31, 1849—James R. Mellow finds the romance the work of a "changed man and writer" whom late events have "afforded... an understanding of the secret psychological springs of guilt" (Mellow 307). In fact, aside from the circumstance of Dimmesdale's total concealment, the substance of "The Interior of a Heart" is contained in Hawthorne's portrait of Reverend Hooper in "The Minister's Black Veil." Dimmesdale is a Hooper whose "veil" is immaterial and inward, Hooper a Dimmesdale who displays the outward token of guilt but never openly confesses. The psychology behind Dimmesdale does not represent a new departure for Hawthorne so much as a reprise of familiar themes. Even Dimmesdale's hypocrisy and corrosive guilt are prefigured by Reuben Bourne's in "Roger Malvin's Burial."

Why should Hawthorne have returned to a subject that in the Manse period he had deliberately put behind him? It is difficult to imagine Hawthorne creating Dimmesdale in Concord, or indeed anywhere other than in Salem. To reinhabit Salem was, beneath the quiet domesticity of his custom house years, to rouse the dormant self of the early tales. Even so, it may have required trauma—*economic* trauma (his official "guillotining") and *psychic* trauma (a panicked sense of mortality and ontological dread)—to overcome his repugnance toward that self, deliver him from his literary doldrums, and evoke the long-suppressed anatomist of painful emotions.

If Dimmesdale fictively belongs to Salem, Hester does not, save in recalling the unnamed adulteress of "Endicott and the Red Cross" with a resplendently stitched scarlet *A* on her breast but with no dramatic function in the tale. Nina Baym argues that "a work following so immediately on the death of a mother" and "featuring a heroine who is a mother" seems likely to have been "inspired by that death" and constitute "a complex memorial" to the deceased.[1] "A memorial" seems far-fetched, given the differences in character between Elizabeth Manning Hawthorne and Hester Prynne; but "inspiration," yes, insofar as the allegorical design of the narrative may be an oblique response to anxieties raised by Elizabeth's death. Sophia Hawthorne reported that her "husband came near a brain fever" after sitting by mother's bedside (*NHW* 1:352). Beyond grief and a regret for whatever failings may have belonged to the relationship—in Hawthorne's case, for the "sort of coldness of intercourse" that had subsisted between his mother and himself "ever since [his] boyhood" (8:429)—the death of a lone remaining parent, even in a child's middle age, may precipitate a crisis that extends beyond personal loss. By removing a barrier between himself and death, loss sharpens the child's sense of vulnerability, occasions a stock-taking of his life, and may even prompt an interrogation of life itself. "The death of old age is the consummation of life," Hawthorne wrote as Elizabeth lay dying, "and yet there is so much gloom and ambiguity about it, that it opens no vista for us into Heaven" (8:425). Settled comfortably in England six years later, he remembered the "very nervous state" in which he wrote *The Scarlet Letter*, "having gone through a great diversity and severity of emotion, for many months past" (21:340).

Even in the serenest of times, faith and trust did not come easily to Hawthorne, and as he sat by his mother's bedside in what he called "the darkest hour I ever lived" (8:429), they seemed to come haltingly, if at all. Roberta Weldon sees "culture" for Hawthorne as "born out of the tension between the knowledge of our mortality and the desire to forget, remake, or recover from this knowledge."[2] If not an instrument for outright denial, culture in this respect involves the substitution of what Weldon calls "the most necessary of necessary fictions" for the ineluctability of horrific fact.[3] The fictions may be direct, about the afterlife, or indirect, about a beneficently ordered universe that answers to the needs of the soul. Because immortality, the issue most urgently at stake, is also the least determinable, one looks for evidence of design elsewhere, in history and patterns of moral experience. Hawthorne could not attain to God through a positive act of belief, nor was he supported by the fellowship or creed of a church. What he could do, as writer, was shape a fiction permeated with moral law that testified to the workings of Providence and the reality of the soul. As always for Hawthorne, such an order rested upon the fact of sin, a theme he had long avoided except in "Ethan Brand," composed in Salem late in 1848. Within weeks of his mother's death, he returned to the subject, writing so "*immensely*" that Sophia was "almost frightened" (*NHW* 1:353–54).

Form is a vehicle for vision, and by illustrating how reality operates it may create at least a simulacrum of cosmic order capable of warding off intuitions of chaos. Brenda Wineapple observes that the "smoldering emotions" of *The Scarlet Letter* "are so volatile that Hawthorne regulates them in the book's shapely design," its twenty-four chapters "symmetrically organized" around the three scaffold scenes that enact its exemplary drama of sin and repentance.[4] But there are resistances and demurrals. The fears that led Hawthorne to instantiate the moral law in the logic of his plot are countered by a hunger for life that strains against the confinements of that law. "Is this not better... than what we dreamed of in the forest?" Dimmesdale asks Hester as he prepares to mount the scaffold. Although Hester claims to "know not" (1:254), she clearly wants no part of otherworldly renunciation, nor have a substantial number of the book's readers, both in its own time and later. What smolders most within *The Scarlet Letter* is a profound ambivalence about what, in the face of problematic eternity or oblivion, *is* "better." On one side, a dread of nothingness led Hawthorne to pattern his book upon the supposed inexorabilities of law (Dimmesdale on the scaffold); on the other, a feeling of suffocation made him yearn for freedom, spontaneity, and passion despite the fact that they ended in death (Hester in the forest). What Philip Rahv calls Hawthorne's "submerged intensity and passion—[his] tangled imagery of unrest and longing for experience and regret at its loss"[5]—derive from this clash between natural and supernatural impulses in him, that is to say, between "Concord" and "Salem." The latter gives *The Scarlet Letter* its allegorical design and ostensibly Christian meaning, the former its air of frustrated desire and, in places, its muted rebellion.

The Prison Door

Each settlement of the Pilgrims was a little piece of the old world, inserted into the new.

—Hawthorne, "Sir William Phips"

As if striking a heavy minor chord, *The Scarlet Letter* opens with the rusty, weather-stained prison door. The time is 1642, and although the town of Boston is scarcely more than a dozen years old, the impression conveyed is of an Old World mentality imprinted on the openness of a pristine continent. Against this "black flower of civilized society," Hawthorne sets the red flower of nature, "the wild rose-bush" (1:48). Black and red; civilization and nature; constraint and freedom; superego and libido: these are the terms within which the narrative will unfold.

Through these threshold symbols Hawthorne adumbrates what Nina Baym identifies as the conflict within each of his four completed romances, that "between passionate, self-assertive, and self-expressive inner drives" associated with nature "and the repressing counterforces that exist in society and are also internalized within the self."[6] Extending across time, place, and cultural idiom, the conflict centers upon the nature of the human personality and the degree of external coercion and internal self-control required for social order. Emerson designated the rival parties that "divide the state" and the mind those of

"Innovation" and "Conservatism" (*CWE* 1:184); T. E. Hulme called them "romantic" and "classic," the former holding that "man is intrinsically good, spoilt by circumstance," the latter that "he is intrinsically limited, but disciplined by order and tradition to something fairly decent."[7] Christianity, according to Hulme, takes a "classical" view of humanity, ideologies of liberation from Rousseau onward a "romantic" one.

Ostensibly "classical" in their skepticism, the opening paragraphs of "The Prison-Door" wind back upon themselves in ways that signal ambiguities to come. "The founders of a new colony, whatever Utopia of human virtue and happiness they might originally project," Hawthorne begins, "have invariably recognized it among their earliest practical necessities to allot a portion of the virgin soil as a cemetery, and another portion as the site of a prison" (1:47). Why should this be so? Does human sinfulness make for criminality or, by proscribing culturally undesirable behaviors, do societal *laws* establish criminality? If the latter, must prisons always be necessary? The phrase "have invariably recognized" (as distinct from "invariably recognize") is descriptive only and suggests a uniformity of historical experience that may or may not extend into the future. While the prison door, emblematic of "the whole dismal severity of the Puritanic code of law" (1:52), has crumbled to dust over time, the rosebush, symbol of nature with its "deep heart" (1:48), has improbably survived. Is Hawthorne implying that actions defined as criminal are historically contingent and may lose their stigma as society evolves toward a norm of empathetic nature? *Is* nature empathetic or is "the stern old wilderness" (1:48), as Hawthorne also calls it, kind only in its indifference to societal judgments?

After striking a somber initial note, the "The Prison-Door" becomes increasingly relativistic, romantic, and antinomian. Legend has it that the rosebush "sprung up under the footsteps of the sainted Ann Hutchinson" (1:48), a disputatious figure in Hawthorne's 1830 sketch "Mrs. Hutchinson" but here an apostle of nature's freedom. The chapter's concluding words, "a darkening tale of human frailty and sorrow" (1:48), enclose any Hutchinsonian promise within a frame of impending gloom, but it remains uncertain what stance the book will take toward its tragic materials. Will it be historicist and progressive ("romantic"), essentialist and conservative ("classic"), or, like "Rappaccini's Daughter," so at odds with itself to be almost indeterminable?

A-religio Medici

[In *The Scarlet Letter*] it is not Hester or Dimmesdale that really interests us, but the spectacle of the human mind open to the retribution of violated law, and quivering in the agonies of shame and remorse. It is

the law and not the person that is vitally conceived....As an illustration
of the Divine order on which our conventional order rests, it is the
most moral book of the age.

> —E. P. Whipple, unsigned review of *The Blithedale Romance*,
> *Graham's Magazine* (1852)

"May it not be possible," asked Septimius, "to have too profound a
sense of the marvelous contrivance and adaptation of this material
world, to require or believe in anything spiritual?"

> —Hawthorne, "Septimius Felton"

From the moment her sin separates her from the community, Hester Prynne is
described as "wander[ing], without rule or guidance, in a moral wilderness; as
vast, as intricate and shadowy, as the untamed forest" (1:199). Hester is not the
only wanderer in *The Scarlet Letter*. By virtue of a resistance to Puritan Boston
that implies a distrust of all institutionalizations of morality, Hawthorne, too,
casts himself adrift from established norms even as he holds Hester to a traditional measure of sin. Darrel Abel finds three "systems" of reality at work in
Hawthorne's writing—God's, nature's, and society's.[8] The difficulty in *The
Scarlet Letter* is that the first system is inaccessible, the second amoral, and the
third historically relative. In arraigning the Puritan identification of "religion
and law" (1:50), Hawthorne dismantles the authority of scripture as a basis for
civic morality; on biblical grounds, the severest of the Puritan women have precedent for wanting to execute Hester, as Hawthorne knew from the instance of
an adulterous couple hanged in 1640s Massachusetts Bay despite biblical coun-
terexamples cited by some of the magistrates in their arguments for leniency.
The moral law is not unequivocably clear from scripture; it is not educible from
nature; and it is not correlative with the laws and customs of any historical
society. "The law we broke, indeed," D. H. Lawrence snorted of *The Scarlet
Letter*: "You bet! Whose law!"[9]

In the opening marketplace scene, a standard is implied through the figure of
a young wife who understands that sin is an internal matter to be addressed not
by law and civil punishment but by individual sinners in the privacy of their
hearts. The wife is an authorial plant, but though she never reappears in the book
Hawthorne makes a point of informing us that she has died. A quality of wisdom
and compassion has departed from New England life, the seedbed for Hawthorne
of American life. The second and third generations of Puritans, we're told, were
narrower and gloomier than the first, and their legacy has continued to cast its
shadow over the New World down to the present.

In the absence of creditable religious, legal, institutional, or cultural embodiment, moral law in *The Scarlet Letter* comes to reside in the consciousness of the
narrator. It is he who intervenes with a one-sentence paragraph to counter
Hester's freethinking ("The scarlet letter had not done its office" [1:166]); he

who moralizes on Hester's taking up the discarded *A* by the brook-side; he who obliges Hester, against the grain of her character, to reassume the letter at the last (1:263); and he who insists on "a space between" Hester's and Dimmesdale's graves, as if the breach made by sin precluded even a symbolic reunion after death (1:264).

For reviewer E. P. Whipple, the sternness of *The Scarlet Letter* was its distinguishing moral and aesthetic strength: Hawthorne "has made his guilty parties end, not as his own fancy or his own benevolent sympathies might dictate, but as the spiritual laws, lying back of all persons, dictated to him."[10] Later in the century, with such "laws" in mind, genteel critics sometimes invoked Hawthorne by name or implication as a foil to what they regarded as the materialism and tacit unbelief of emergent realism. "The older art of the world," Hamilton Wright Mabie wrote in an 1885 review of William Dean Howells's *The Rise of Silas Lapham*,

> is based on the conception that life is at bottom a revelation; that human growth under all conditions has a spiritual law back of it; that human relations of all kinds have spiritual types behind them; and that the discovery of these universal facts, and the clear, noble embodiment of them in various forms, is the office of genius and the end of art.[11]

The title of Mabie's review, "A Typical Novel," rests on a pun, for his quarrel with Howells's "typical" (representative) book is that it is not "typical" at all in the sense that books like Hawthorne's were. Mabie's "spiritual types" recall Puritan typology and Jonathan Edwards's eighteenth-century "Images or Shadows of Divine Things," but without the underpinnings of Reformation cosmology they lack status and ontological "site." Mabie does not claim that the "spiritual law" behind human development is Providentially ordained and regulated, but neither can he countenance the alternative of naturalistic psychology. Still less can he imagine a pragmatic rehabilitation of core Western values detached from ideas of the transcendent. The realists' denial that outward facts "conform to the unbroken order of the Universe" amounts for Mabie to "practical atheism applied to art."[12] Yet what can Mabie's "spiritual law" signify when notions of correspondence and divine immanence are no longer even discussable except in the terms of vaporous idealism?

The threat of naturalism that gives urgency to Mabie's essay also informs *The Scarlet Letter* thirty-five years earlier as Hawthorne works to affirm the universality of spiritual laws over and against his realist's apprehension of experience. Inhabiting a God-imbued seventeenth-century world, Roger Chillingworth has no doubt about the status of types when he appeals to immutable law in rejecting Hester's plea that he spare Dimmesdale: "By Thy first step awry, thou didst plant the germ of evil; but, since that moment, it has all been a dark necessity. Ye that have wronged me are not sinful, save in a kind of typical illusion; neither am I fiend-like, who have snatched a fiend's office from his hands. It is our fate. Let the black flower blossom as it may!" (1:174). Chillingworth has his own motives for pleading necessity—he has made a life of tormenting Dimmesdale and is unwilling to renounce it or accept the attendant guilt—but his notion of the characters' fates as "typical" is deeply engraved in the romance itself, if never confidently so. As Millicent Bell observes, Hawthorne deals with types "as though they were figures of speech in a spoken or written text" rather than "privileged signs deriving from a transcendent presence."[13] He *would* have the latter, "transcendent presence," yet lacking both a Puritan faith in divine inscriptions of reality and a Transcendental faith in its spiritual luminousness, he must rely on writerly artifice to establish what his metaphysics cannot and what his burgeoningly novelistic sense of character led him to regard, even in literature, as quaint and anachronistic.

The psychologist and the allegorist within Hawthorne strain against one another and contend for primacy both in representational technique and in implicit worldview, the psychologist viewing experience as an interplay of character and circumstance, the allegorist as an enactment of laws of the soul. In "The Child at the Brook-side," for example, Pearl returns from playing in the forest to find Hester in strange intimacy with Dimmesdale, her hair unbound and the scarlet letter missing from her breast. She reacts as any child of her age and situation might; she throws a tantrum. Hester understands this perfectly: "Children will not abide any, the slightest, change in the accustomed aspect of things" (1:210). The scene is naturalistic and unfolds convincingly as such. But as Pearl makes Hester reaffix the scarlet letter, the narrator interjects, "So it ever is, whether thus typified or no, that an evil deed invests itself with the character of doom" (1:211). "Thus typified" overlays the incident with a level of meaning extrinsic to its dramatized content; "or no" qualifies the claim and retreats to the defensible ground of fancy. The invocation of typology is metaphorical, not metaphysical, but it assumes an air of metaphysics when it introduces a note of fatality ("So it ever is") beyond the particulars of Hester's case. Without giving credence to typology, Hawthorne has availed himself of its prerogatives to pontificate on moral absolutes, secure in the allegorist's exemption from the demands of verisimilitude and dramatic "proof."

The objections of Henry James and others that Hawthorne was not a realist are only partially true of *The Scarlet Letter*. Hawthorne is an admirable realist in passages of analysis in "Hester at Her Needle," "Another View of Hester," "The Interior of a Heart," and "The Minister in a Maze." He was never primarily or comfortably a realist, however, because psychology—or psycholog*ism*: realism as applied to the portrayal of character—was insufficient to establish, even worked *against* establishing, the ordered universe in which he wanted to believe. In his study of the emergence of psychology in the earlier nineteenth century, Edward S. Reed notes the contemporary concern that a "science of the soul" might "contain the seeds of ideas that would undermine religion." Sensitive to the charge of materialism, Reed argues, psychologists sought to align their discipline with "important religious beliefs." Alongside dominant theories, however, was "an 'underground psychology,'" associated with thinkers like Erasmus Darwin, that took a more openly materialist view.[14] Because of their interest in the actualities of character, novelists were especially likely to become "underground" psychologists, whatever their formal beliefs. The protagonists of "Young Goodman Brown" and "My Kinsman, Major Molineux" are only slightly individuated characters and therefore eligible to the uses of allegory, but with more subtly conceived figures like Tobias Pearson in "The Gentle Boy" and Reuben Bourne in "Roger Malvin's Burial" Hawthorne enters the domain of the psychological novelist and his characters become arresting case studies rather than moral exempla. Within the larger, denser, more closely imagined form of the romance, it was particularly difficult to restrict characters to an allegorical role. Hawthorne tries to contain Chillingworth—"In a word, old Roger Chillingworth was a striking evidence of man's faculty of transforming himself into a devil, if he will only, for a reasonable space of time, undertake a devil's office" (1:170)—but even Chillingworth sometimes steps outside his assigned function and assumes a psychic life of his own.

Throughout *The Scarlet Letter* Hawthorne must pull himself back from the precipice of psychologism in order to maintain the allegorical significance of his romance. In chapter 12, "The Minister's Vigil," he presents the guilt-ridden Dimmesdale "extend[ing] his egotism over the whole expanse of nature" as he takes a rosy apparition in the meteor-lit sky as "a revelation, addressed to himself alone" (1:155). The scene is a masterpiece of psychological projection, complete in itself, but Hawthorne will not let it stand as such; he proceeds to objectify the celestial A by having the sexton mention it to Dimmesdale the next morning. Perhaps he is trying to suggest that what Melville calls "nature's cunning alphabet" (*WHM* 7:342) is not self-interpretive but must be construed by individuals in their closeted psyches. Yet by giving the letter an outward existence, he seems also to be reaching beyond subjectivism and, without implying that God judges sinners on the canvas of nature, intimating the presence of a moral order inherent in Creation. As projection, the celestial A belongs to *The Scarlet Letter* as a psychological novel embedded in the historical consciousness of its characters; as supernatural emblem, it belongs to what W. C. Brownell called "a drama of the soul . . . measurably independent" of individuals, society, and history.[15]

It might be argued that Hawthorne's generic achievement in *The Scarlet Letter* is to preserve the balance between psychological novel and allegorical romance.[16] The genres, however, are markedly *im*balanced: as psychologist, Hawthorne works meticulously and with extraordinary insight; as allegorist, intermittently and by heavy-handed intrusion. Nonetheless, the allegory seems so central to his design that the book could scarcely have been executed without it. Hawthorne supplements or overrides psychological realism not because he questions its explanatory power but because, like Hamilton Wright Mabie on Howells, he is uncomfortable with its ethical neutrality and lurking "atheism." Situating Hawthorne "at the threshold" of modern ideas of cognition even while "formally committed to older views," Millicent Bell finds him voicing a Derridean skepticism about the relationship between signifier and signified.[17] His deepest doubt, however, is about not the stability of the sign, but about the reality of the transcendent order it purports to signify. Perhaps there are *only* signs.

It is against this suspected nominalism, or naturalism, that the allegory of *The Scarlet Letter* sets itself. In his confession on the scaffold, Dimmesdale ratifies the book's motif of types when he casts his life-drama as an illustrative history of redemption staged by a merciful God who inflicts pain in the service of repentance and ultimately of salvation. Beyond celebrating his own spiritual victory, Dimmesdale's myth addresses the largest anagogical dimension of the narrative, in which Chillingworth-as-Devil is given free rein to do whatever mischief he will. Evil, the book's theodicy implies, is provisional within a beneficent teleology that is triumphant within as well as beyond human time. A reluctant accessory to Dimmesdale's grand egocentric pageant, Hester is herself made to accede to the force of law when she returns to Boston and takes up the scarlet letter. Whatever political meaning her gesture may have,[18] morally it is designed to symbolize Hester's recognition of and submission to a moral order that does not so much overrule private will as inwardly take possession of it.

Even as he willfully enforces his meaning, however, Hawthorne is ambiguous, as though obliged by honesty to ironize the triumph of law. Beyond his coyness about the reality and origin of Dimmesdale's scarlet *A*, he leaves it unclear whether the minister's dying speech has reference to anything more than his own and Puritan culture's reigning eschatology. Indeed, his entire portrait of Dimmesdale may be read as an exercise in historical psychology. "A true priest, a true religionist" (1:123), Dimmesdale is a thoroughly socialized being whose thoughts and feelings take shape, as reviewer George Bailey Loring put it, "from the society in which he moved, and from which he received his engrafted moral nature."[19] In this light, questions of "sin" and "evil" seem secondary, if not irrelevant; the writhings we observe are those of a mind within its own conceptual prison. When Dimmesdale apostasizes from Puritan morality by agreeing to flee with Hester, he does not escape his inbred worldview but simply inverts his position within it; the man of piety becomes demonic, tempted "to do some strange, wild, wicked thing or other," at once in violation of his nature and emanating from some "profounder" part of it (1:217).

In Freudian terms, the "total change of dynasty" that occurs in Dimmesdale's "interior kingdom" (1:217) amounts to a usurpation of the ruling superego by the id, newly empowered by his "deliberate" yielding to "what he knew was deadly sin" (1:222). The critical words are "what he knew." Within his own mental universe, Dimmesdale has indeed sold himself to the devil (1:222). The question is whether anything exists *outside* his mental universe, or outside anyone's. Do we inhabit an objective moral world or only a multitude of *subjective* ones? Is Hawthorne's proto-Freudian mapping of the psyche—an unconscious of sexual, aggressive, and otherwise tabooed impulses precariously held in check by a socialized conscience—to be taken as paradigmatic of human nature or merely as illustrative of the psychodynamics of persons like Dimmesdale shaped by a severely repressive society? And if the latter, might other, non-Puritanical individuals like Hester function by a different, healthier, and perhaps culturally prophetic psychic economy?

"Hawthorne was well aware," Harry Levin writes, "that the sense of sin is more intimately related to inhibition than to indulgence; that the most exquisite consciences are the ones that suffer most; that guilt is a by-product of the very compunction which aims at goodness and acknowledges higher laws."[20] Yet if sin is operative only in proportion to the intensity with which it is felt, can it be called "sin" at all and *are* there "higher laws"? Hester mistakes her partner in love when she assumes he is also a partner in freethinking and social rebellion: "what hast thou to do with all these iron men, and their opinions?" (1:196). Hester would have Dimmesdale an "iron man" of another sort, such as Hawthorne imagines when he writes of the guilt that drives Dimmesdale to the scaffold in the dead of night, "Crime is for the iron-nerved, who have their choice either to endure it, or, if it press too hard, to exert their fierce and savage strength for a good purpose, and fling it off at once!" (1:148). So far as these words ascribe Dimmesdale's torment to his unfitness to carry off the role of transgressor, they are anomalous within the text and for that reason particularly telling. Dimmesdale knows that if he were "an atheist,—a man devoid of conscience,—a wretch with coarse and brutal instincts," he "might have found peace, long ere now" (1:191); but so, Hawthorne implies, might he have found it had he been a man of strength and iconoclastic vision. "For a *good* purpose," Hawthorne insists: in a single phrase he deconstructs the controlling moral scheme of his book, as if he were outing with a secret and normally unspeakable thought.

"We need a critique of all moral values; the intrinsic worth of these values must, first of all, be called into question,"[21] Nietzsche announced in *The Genealogy of Morals*. Hester would have agreed. So, in certain moods, would Hawthorne. Like Dimmesdale temporarily breathing the "freer atmosphere" of Chilling-worth's conversation, Hawthorne sometimes took a "tremulous enjoyment" in speculations that appalled his ontologically fearful self (1:123). Melville recognized this truant quality in him and in *Clarel* made the Hawthornesque Vine a Paul Pry of dangerous ideas. Hawthorne's remark on the "iron-nerved" is typical of a store of opinions he kept to himself except when weariness, exasperation, despair, or a vein of "freakish mockery, elfin light" (*WHM* 12:1, 30:109), called them forth. If in frequency such remarks constitute a subordinate strain in Hawthorne, in sinew they seem particularly close to the veiled man whom even his wife confessed not to know. "I like a look of Agony, / Because I know it's true," Emily Dickinson begins one of her poems (#339). One likes a look of heterodoxy in Hawthorne for much the same reason.

"In their researches into the human frame," Hawthorne writes of physicians like Chillingworth, "it may be that the higher and more subtile faculties of such men were materialized, and that they lost the spiritual view of life amid the intricacies of that wondrous mechanism, which seemed to involve art enough to comprise all of life within itself" (1:119). A similar process may occur with researchers into the mind. Writing *The Scarlet Letter* led Hawthorne more deeply than ever into the recesses of human nature, and as he explored his characters' feelings, motives, impulses, and layers of rationalization and self-delusion, together with the historical forces acting upon and within them, he came to find the interpretive power of "underground psychology" more compelling than the shadowy universals he set out to illustrate. Psychologism seemed "art enough," except for the purposes he most wanted art to serve.

Skepticism has no resting place. In loosing himself from conventional religion early in life, Hawthorne found himself a reluctant wanderer trying to uphold Providence, moral law, and the immortality of the soul against the overwhelming testimony of experience. The more acute his naturalist's sense of cosmic anarchy, the more urgent his need to contain it and the more likely his doubts to erupt on the margins of his text or even, as in the forest scenes, near the epicenter. Reticent about such matters in life, in his writings he gravitated toward them as if by compulsion, employing his dark heroines, in particular, to destabilize orthodoxies and champion a freer life to be enjoyed in their absence. As much as he needed assurances of order, he felt hemmed in and devitalized by its requirements. In a retrospect of his career, the usually sympathetic Whipple found his work somber to the point of "misanthropy": Hawthorne "had spiritual insight, but it did not penetrate to the sources of spiritual joy."[22] In Hester, Hawthorne created a potential source of joy. If she were a wanderer "in a moral wilderness" (1:199), so, if truth be told, was he. Might the absence of certitude—*a*-religion—be made the foundation for a new religion?

Hester in the Forest

What makes itself felt in a human community as a desire for freedom may be [a] revolt against some existing injustice, and so may prove favorable to a further development of civilization.... But it may also spring from the remains of their original personality, which is still untamed by civilization and may thus become the basis in them of hostility to civilization. The urge for freedom, therefore, is directed against particular forms and demands of civilization or against civilization itself.

—Freud, *Civilization and Its Discontents*

In "The Old Manse" Hawthorne pays tribute to Emerson as "a poet of deep beauty and austere tenderness" from whose philosophy he "sought nothing" (10:31); as a Concord neighbor, he sought scarcely more. Emerson mystified, bemused, and ultimately bored Hawthorne, yet without the spur of Emersonian iconoclasm *The Scarlet Letter* might have been a folio version of "The Minister's Black Veil." Whether or not Emerson was consciously in Hawthorne's mind as he wrote his book, his presentation of Hester engages itself with Emersonian notions of self-reliance, Emersonian prospects for "an original relation to the universe" (*CWE* 1:7), Emersonian assumptions about the mind, and Emersonian hopes for a renovated America.

When Hester says, "With this symbol, I undo it all" (1:202), she is doing more than divesting herself of an imposed stigma of sin; she is figuratively throwing off the entire structure of social values amid which she has lived. After seven years of what Emerson would call "conforming to usages that have become dead" to her (*CWE* 2:31), Hester in the forest scene discards the scarlet letter, unbinds the dark, luxuriant hair that symbolizes her suppressed nature, and undertakes, as Emerson said, to "build" her "own world" (*CWE* 1:45). She repudiates the past—Puritan America's as well as her own—and seeks to be "happy and strong" (Emerson's words) in the only way that Emerson believed a person could, by living "with nature in the present, above time" (*CWE* 2:39).

"Nothing is at last sacred but the integrity of your own mind" (*CWE* 2:30), Emerson proclaims in "Self-Reliance," a sentiment Hester might have amended to read, "nothing but the motions of your own heart." In its exhortation to "cast off the common motives of humanity" and trust oneself "for a taskmaster" (*CWE* 2:43), Emersonian self-reliance looks back to the antinomianism of Anne Hutchinson, as Emerson well understood; the Transcendentalist, he writes, "easily incurs the charge of antinomianism by his avowal that he who has the Lawgiver, may with safety not only neglect, but even contravene every written commandment" (*CWE* 1:204). "Little accustomed, in her long seclusion, to measure her ideas of right and wrong by any standard external to herself"

(1:159), Hester, who is linked to Anne Hutchinson, comes forth an antinomian when she tells Dimmesdale, "What we did had a consecration of its own" (1:195). "Consecration" implies sacredness, and in conferring sanctity on an act of passion, Hester makes it the body and blood of a new eros-centered religion. If, as Emerson says, "power is, in nature, the essential measure of right" (*CWE* 2:40)—power as fullness of being arising from a harmonious alignment with the laws of the universe, including the law of one's self—it is difficult to judge Hester in the forest as anything *but* "right." She is wondrously attuned to herself and to nature, her "sex, her youth, and the whole richness of her beauty" returning to her after long dormancy, and nature signaling its approval with a "flood of sunshine" (1:202). In Emerson's moral universe, governed by the law of compensation, behavior generates its own immediate consequences. By our acts we are "instantly" enlarged or contracted; we go "out of acquaintance" with our essential being or we grow further into it (*CWE* 1:78). Hester, it seems evident, grows into it.

Hester's "consecration" does not refer solely to an act in the past; it applies to the life she intends to lead with Dimmesdale in the future. A. N. Kaul voices the reaction of many readers when he writes, "the important thing...is to realize how fully the novel aligns our sympathies with Hester, and how completely it endorses, as a means of both heavenly and earthly redemption, her plan of withdrawing from the stern Puritan colony."[23] By "earthly redemption" I take Kaul to mean temporal happiness, by "heavenly redemption" something like moral right. The stakes involved are enormous, for if as readers we empathize with Hester we become complicit antinomians ourselves, bestowing approval on an adulterous relationship whatever its moral and social implications.

In her study of Hutchinson and New England dissent, Amy Schrager Lang notes that in 1636 and again during the Great Awakening the theological heterodoxies of antinomianism spilled over into social heterodoxies that seemed to bode "the end of traditional social relations."[24] So it appeared to Hawthorne as he viewed the mid-seventeenth century through the agitations of the mid-nineteenth. The social relations at risk for him were those of gender, both externally (the position of women in society; their political, civil, vocational, and domestic relations to men) and internally (the relationship between "masculine" and "feminine" elements within the human personality). In "Earth's Holocaust" his narrator is "startled" to find that "highly respectable" women have proposed to exchange their garments for men's and assume "the manners, duties, offices, and responsibilities of the opposite sex" (10:389). As in Hutchinson's time, deviation from traditional gender roles is associated with free love, as zealots at the sketch's bonfire burn their marriage certificates and claim themselves "candidates for a higher, holier, and more comprehensive union" than time-honored marriage (10:394).

As the outgrowth of a "freedom of speculation" more subversive of Puritan hegemony than her adultery itself (1:164), Hester's plan for a new life is an expression of ideology as well as of desire. Literally, what Hester proposes is escape; symbolically, it amounts to revolution. Her plan builds upon and proto-typically enacts the social critique set forth earlier in the book when Hawthorne had her reflect on women's past and present condition and the difficulties of ameliorative change:

> As a first step the whole system of society is to be torn down, and built up anew. Then, the very nature of the opposite sex, or its long hereditary habit, which has become like nature, is to be essentially modified, before woman can be allowed to assume what seems a fair and suitable position. Finally, all other difficulties being obviated, woman cannot take advantage of these preliminary reforms, until she herself shall have undergone a still mightier change; in which, perhaps, the ethereal essence, wherein she has her truest life, will be found to have evaporated. (1:165–66).

The gender revolution Hawthorne describes resembles the one outlined by Margaret Fuller in *Woman in the Nineteenth Century* (1845), a book Fuller was in the process of developing from her *Dial* essay "The Great Lawsuit" when she stayed with the Hawthornes at the Old Manse in July 1844. For both writers, the successive phases of this revolution involve, first, the dismantling of legal and institutional impediments to women's equal participation in society (Fuller: "We would have every arbitrary barrier thrown down. We would have every path laid open to Woman as freely as to Man"); second, a revision of role conceptions governing what women are capable of doing and may appropriately do (Fuller: "you ask me what offices they may fill...; let them be sea-captains, if you will"); and third, an alteration in women's psychological being that will enable them to transcend their domestic sphere and compete with men in the public world (Fuller: in "the present crisis" preference goes to the active, "masculine" side of female character, symbolized by the goddess Minerva) (*WNC* 248, 276, 264).

Hawthorne's account of Hester as feminist begins with apparent sympathy, but as the passage unfolds, its identification with woman as victim gives way to an uneasiness about the internal changes necessary for or consequent upon woman's entrance into the public sphere. Hester's speculations are dismissed as a sign of gender deviance, her "marble coldness" a function of her life having turned unnaturally "from passion and feeling to thought" (1:164). Hester does, Hawthorne allows, feel deeply; her nature is "a well-spring of human tenderness" toward the afflicted (1:161). But such love is of a nunlike variety (agape), and it cannot prevent the "sad transformation" that leaves nothing for love of a differ-ent kind (eros) "to dwell upon" or for "Passion" to "dream of clasping in its embrace" (1:163). From his own conflicting impulses, Hawthorne has boxed Hester in. He chides her for her unwomanly intellection but forbids her the eroticism that would "keep her a woman" (1:163) even as he laments the loss of that eroticism. Having traced the logic of feminist reform to its projected endpoint (the de-etherealization of female character), he finds himself torn between the irreconcilable values of social justice, female sexuality, and female spirituality. His way of resolving the matter is to dispatch it with an emphatic one-sentence paragraph—"The scarlet letter had not done its office" (1:165)—that clamps the lid on the Pandora's box he has incautiously opened.

He would raise the lid twice again, with Zenobia in *The Blithedale Romance* and Miriam in *The Marble Faun*. The pattern in all three books is similar. True to a type that looks back to the dark, thwarted heroines of Sir Walter Scott, Hawthorne's heroines are passionate, intellectual, creative, eager for life, and of vast possibility. His distinctive variation on the theme is to bind his women by a tie from their past that prevents them from fulfilling themselves through the culturally sanctioned channel of conjugal love. Their various sublimations (Hester's needlework, Zenobia's writing, Miriam's art) provide only limited satisfaction. Chafing against the limits of their condition, they become freethinkers, feminists, and would-be reformers. What they truly want, however, is erotic love, in pursuit of which they become lawbreakers and are banished from the community through ostracism, death, or moral rejection by the normative characters of their world.

Why did Hawthorne tell variants of this story three times? Feminism was emergent in 1840s America, and through Margaret Fuller especially it spoke to him with an imperativeness that no other reform movement did.[25] It was not the person of Fuller or even the issue of female rights that gave "the woman problem" its urgency for him; it was woman herself as an earthy, sexual being who called forth the earthy and sexual in man, and whose demand for the free development of her nature signified, in the largest terms, a plea for the unfettering of the human personality. Beyond their roles as feminist challenges to patriarchy and embodiments of eros, Hawthorne's dark heroines have a more sweeping and radical function; they call into question the institutionalized assumptions that have dominated Western culture for nearly two millennia. Of Hester, Hawthorne writes: "the world's law was no law for her mind" (1:164); of Zenobia: "She made no scruple of oversetting all human institutions" (3:44). As an ideologist and actional perpetrator of revolt, Miriam is the boldest of all. The true threat, or promise, of the dark heroine is not that she is a transgressor but that she comes to regard transgression as a "passport" (1:199) to moral and social emancipation.

Nearly eighty years before Freud's *Civilization and Its Discontents*, Hawthorne is asking whether the rebellious woman proclaiming her nature and suing for her rights is the avatar of a new human personality and ultimately of a new social order or a splendid atavism whose unsublimated eroticism is a threat to the community. Naturalizing the biases of contemporary patriarchy, Freud identified women with "the interests of the family and of sexual life" and viewed them as fundamentally antagonistic to civilization, whose "higher psychical activities" required instinctual sublimations "of which women are little capable."[26] Shunted "into the background by the claims of civilization," women develop "a hostile attitude toward it,"[27] as Hawthorne has Hester do ("thus much of woman was there in" her) when she watches Dimmesdale "moving proudly past" in the Election Day procession, "so remote from her own sphere, and utterly beyond her reach" (1:239). In the forest she had been Dimmesdale's intimate and equal, indeed by force of character his superior; now she is invisible to him and peripheral to the public world in which he has his being.

Where Freud saw women's opposition to civilization as retrograde, Hawthorne is of two minds about it. "Thou hadst great elements" (1:173), Chillingworth says to Hester of her wasted potential. In the forest scene these elements are realized. Joining eros (her love for Dimmesdale) to intellect (her outsider's critique of society), Hester has not regressed to the precivilized; she has glimpsed a life— her own, the New World's, all humanity's—beyond the life of repressive Christendom and is acting to bring it about.

The Foreverness of Sin

If [Hawthorne] meant to teach the sinfulness of Hester's sin—the great and divine obligation and sanctity of a legal marriage contract, and the monstrous depravity of a union sanctioned only by affection, his book is the most sublime failure of the age. Hester Prynne...is the most glorious creation of fiction that has ever crossed our path.

—Jane Swisshelm, review of *The Scarlet Letter*, *Saturday Visitor* (1850)

Although we are expected to love and pity Hester, we are not invited to condone her fault or to construe it as a virtue. More a victim of circumstances than a wilful wrongdoer, she is nevertheless to be held morally responsible....This is harsh doctrine, but there is no escape from it short of unflinching repudiation of the moral ideas which give man his tragic and lonely dignity in a world in which all things except himself seem insensate and all actions except his own seem mechanical.

—Darrel Abel, *The Moral Picturesque*

In an 1850 review of *The Scarlet Letter*, George Bailey Loring—Harvard-educated surgeon, soon-to-be postmaster of Salem, and later state representative, congressman, United States commissioner of agriculture, and ambassador to Portugal: a sober establishment figure and "not a Transcendentalist"[28]—reads

Hawthorne's romance in a way that Hawthorne seems on the brink of developing it but doesn't. Loring begins with a scathing critique of Puritanism that focuses on its denial of the "sensuous element of human nature": "Zest of life was no part of the Puritan's belief. He scorned his own flesh and blood. His appetites were crimes" (Loring 136). Far from seeing this sensuousness as merely physical, Loring regards it as "the foundation" of the love of beauty and of "the highest apprehension of religious fervor" (Loring 136). Like Hawthorne, he rebukes the Puritans for their severity toward Hester, but while nominally uneasy with "what is called the guilt of this woman," he questions whether it *is* guilt and seems disposed to agree that by the law of "holy love," which "man's heart recognizes, whether society will or not," Hester's relationship with Dimmesdale did have a consecration of its own (Loring 140). For Loring, the lovers' sufferings are a consequence not of moral law but of social law, which in Dimmesdale's case has been internalized "by education alone" (Loring 137) and in Hester's hardly even by that. Where Hawthorne has Hester submit to an acknowledged need for penitence, Loring sees little for her to be penitent about:

> We dare not call that a wicked perversity, which brought its possessor into that state of strong and fiery resolution and elevation, which enabled her to raise her lover from his craven sense of guilt, into a solemn devotion to his better nature. She guided him rightly, by her clear vision of what was in accordance with the holiest promptings of her true heart. Aided by this, she learned what all his theology had never taught him— the power of love to sustain and guide and to teach the soul. This bore her though her trial; and this, at that glowing hour when both rose above the weight which bowed them down, tore the scarlet letter from her breast, and made her young and pure again. (Loring 142)

Beyond suggesting the diversity of contemporary opinion, the value of Loring's essay is to divest the judgments of *The Scarlet Letter* of the air of impersonal necessity that struck readers like Whipple and to illustrate how, even within the confines of its tragic plot, the book might have taken, and for some readers did take, a celebratory stance toward Hester as lover and prophetess. To document her "holy exaltation," Loring reproduces the long paragraph in which Hester discards the scarlet letter and the sun bursts forth "as with a sudden smile of heaven" (1:203). His quotation breaks off just before the opening of the next paragraph: "Such was the sympathy of Nature—that wild, heathen Nature of the forest, never subjugated by human law, nor illumined by higher truth—with the bliss of the two spirits!" (1:203; Loring 142).

With these words, Hawthorne draws back from Loring's *Scarlet Letter* and encloses his narrative within a moralism distinct from Puritan society's but hardly less exigent and prohibitive. The sentence is one of his many efforts to contain what he has unleashed with Hester. Coming, however, at a moment when the narrative enlists readers powerfully on her behalf, it has the effect of an abrupt intrusion of the reality principle, a dashing of raised hopes, even—so far as the "gladdening sunshine" invites us to identify with the lovers (1:203)—a sober reprimand. If "we endorse the 'sympathy of nature' nonetheless,"[29] as Sacvan Bercovitch says we do, it is against the narrator's explicit caution. What the scene causes us to desire is checked by what the narrator reminds us we shouldn't desire. Hawthorne is responsible for both effects; both are strongly felt; but it is the moralist who rhetorically overrules the dramatist and bids to have the determining say.

In a classic essay, "Scarlet A Minus," Frederic I. Carpenter takes Hawthorne to task for failing to distinguish between "romantic immorality" (Hester as law-breaker) and "transcendental idealism" (Hester as Emersonian heroine shriven in the confessional of her own law).[30] Carpenter does not consider whether Hawthorne might have weighed the distinction and found it empty, viewing the Transcendentalist as a deluded Romantic who mistakes the promptings of the ego (or libido) for those of God. This is the charge that Anne Hutchinson's accusers brought against her and that Emerson entertained and airily dismissed about himself: "On my saying, What have I to do with the sacredness of traditions, if I live wholly from within? my friend suggested—'But these impulses may be from below, not from above.' I replied, 'They do not seem to me to be such; but if I am the Devil's child, I will live then from the Devil'" (CWE 2:30).

Naturally austere and descended from eight generations of New England clerics, Emerson could be confident that deviltry was highly unlikely. He was equally confident about the revelations of the soul: "We know truth when we see it, from opinion, as we know when we are awake that we are awake" (CWE 2:166). We know it not by active agency but because it imposes itself upon us in moments of insight and commands both our cognitive understanding and our affections and volitions (CWE 2:167). The truly self-reliant individual—the one drawing upon the transpersonal soul, not willfully asserting the private ego—is thus ipso facto God's child and not the Devil's. Emerson can describe the highest virtue as "impulsive and spontaneous" (CWE 2:78) because his moral psychology is grounded in a theory of knowledge that identifies the genuine motions of the self with the influx of the soul. "Either God is there" in our intuitions "or he is not there" (CWE 2:78). Emerson believes we can tell.

In The Scarlet Letter, Hester cannot tell, Hawthorne insists, though she comes to believe she can. While only a year younger than Emerson, Hawthorne passed his formative years relatively untouched by the strains of Romantic thought newly arrived from Europe. In 1827, when Emerson was hailing Sampson Reed's Swedenborgian Observations of the Growth of the Mind as a latter-day revelation,

Hawthorne was enlarging his acquaintance with the Scottish Common Sense philosophers he had read at Bowdoin.[31] Emersonian self-reliance—or *soul-reliance*—seemed groundless to him because his conception of the mind included no faculty that enabled it to transcend sense experience and received morality and grasp truth by direct intuition. The sloughing of convention that Emerson saw as the primal act in a lifelong pilgrimage toward truth was, for Hawthorne, a baptism into chronic uncertainty, dangerous for anyone but particularly so for those baptized through sin. "Shame, Despair, Solitude!" Hawthorne writes: "These had been [Hester's] teachers—stern and wild ones,—and they had made her strong, but taught her much amiss" (1:199–200). The objects of Hester's scorn include some that deserve to be scorned (the pillory, the gallows), at least one that is iconic and does not (the fireside), and others whose status is equivocal (the clerical band, the judicial robe, the church), depending on how the office is filled. Hester, it is implied, rejects them all, without discrimination. The physical and social isolation that has intellectually "set her free" (1:199) leaves her estranged from whatever elements of wisdom and salutary restraint may inhere even in deeply flawed institutions and with no alternative means for distinguishing truth and right from their beguiling counterfeits: self-delusion, rationalization, wishful thinking, and desire.

In Loring's *Scarlet Letter* the power of love is moral compass enough; in Hawthorne's, so far as love is transgressively sexual, it is the problem. The voice that counsels Hester to flee with Dimmesdale is not, for Hawthorne, "from above" but "from below," a libidinal "I want" that Hester sets in place of the communal "thou shalt not." Before the destabilizing power of sexuality, even Emerson hedged his radical claim that "the only right is what is after my constitution, the only wrong what is against it" (*CWE* 2:30). "Especially the crimes that spring from love, seem right and fair from the actor's point of view," he wrote in "Experience," "but, when acted, are found destructive of society" (*CWE* 3:45). Antinomianism for Emerson stopped at the bedroom door—or short of the bedroom door: although Margaret Fuller was assumed to be virginal during her New England years, she was suspect to Emerson for a temperamental "energy" that seemed "too much a force of blood."[32]

Sexual puritanism was a regional heritage, but with insight into what Loring calls the "beautiful and holy" that may belong even to an "apparent violation of virtue and chastity" (Loring 140) it might, for some, be overcome. The forest scene is the pivot on which *The Scarlet Letter* turns. Having come with Hester to the verge of cultural prophecy—a new social order freed from traditional absolutes and shaped according to human needs—Hawthorne may cast his lot with her, as Loring enthusiastically does, or he may retreat. In his handling of feminist reform in "Another View of Hester" he had retreated; in "A Flood of Sunshine" and "The Child at the Brook-side" he retreats again. Affectively he stands with

Hester—readers like Loring are responding to genuine signals in the text—but morally he cannot countenance the thought that her adultery had, and her proposed life with Dimmesdale *will* have, "a consecration of its own" (1:195).

As a legacy of his prolonged bachelorhood with its shadowy guilts, Hawthorne would forever be hypersensitive to sexual irregularity, which included everything outside monogamous heterosexuality. Though in name the Unpardonable Sin for him was a cold intellectual prying into the human heart, in practice it was female impurity. A casual remark on English bankrupts, occasioned by the troubles of his London friend Francis Bennoch in 1857, is revealing: "They will be like a woman who has once lost her chastity; no after life of virtue will take out the stain" (22:430).

Entwined with Hawthorne's squeamishness and sexual anxiety was something like a lifelong metaphysical fetishism. In a sketch of the Compsons, Faulkner describes family "honor" as resting "precariously" for Quentin on his sister Caddy's "maidenhead as a miniature replica of all the whole vast globy earth may be poised on the nose of a trained seal."[33] So, for Hawthorne, morality, Providence, and the immortality of the soul rested on the individual and collective chastity of spiritual woman. The conflict Philip Rahv identifies in Hawthorne "between a newborn secular imagination, as yet untried and therefore permeated with the feeling of shock and guilt, and the moribund religious tradition of old New England"[34] involved more than the tenacity of the Calvinist past; it derived from a fear of nothingness raised periodically to crisis proportions by events like his mother's death yet ever-present for him as an abyss just below the solid surface of life. The reality of a cosmic order depended for Hawthorne on the reality of a moral order, which in turn depended on female virtue. In organizing *The Scarlet Letter* upon a quasi-typological pattern of sexual sin and repentance Hawthorne sought to confirm this order for himself as if mimesis could work backward, the textual reality providing assurances of the extratextual one.

A paradox of *The Scarlet Letter* is that its most radical chapters ("Another View of Hester," "The Pastor and His Parishioner," "A Flood of Sunshine") are also among its most conservative as the force of Hester's iconoclasm provokes a commensurate check. When Hester urges Dimmesdale to "Begin all anew!" (1:198), she is challenging the narrator's claims that her adultery was like "a new birth" whose "chain" of "iron links...never could be broken" and that "the breach" made by "guilt...into the human soul" leaves a "ruined wall" that can "never, in this mortal state, [be] repaired" (1:80, 200–201). Hester would deny these *nevers*, as would many readers, past and present. People do come to terms with guilt; they put past deeds behind them; they survive, heal, and develop; they move on to other, sometimes better lives. But not in Hawthorne's world. Neither in *The Scarlet Letter* nor elsewhere in his fiction does Hawthorne allow his transgressors to repair the ruined wall or live in forgetfulness of it. Hester's darkest moment occurs when she trivializes the scarlet *A* to Pearl ("'I wear it for the sake of its gold thread!'"), at which point, the narrator interjects, "a stern and severe, but yet a guardian spirit, ... now forsook her; as recognizing that, in spite of his strict watch over her heart, some new evil had crept into it, or some old one had never been expelled" (1:181). In the final scaffold scene, hoping for at least a celestial reunion, Hester tells Dimmesdale they "have ransomed one another" by public humiliation and private "woe" (1:256). Dimmesdale will have nothing of it, nor will Hawthorne, who refuses to allow the lovers' dust "to mingle" (1:264). For sin to be veritable, and therefore a warranty of universal order, the ruined wall had to be irreparable in the sense that one never ceased to live in relation to it, even in penitence and partial rehabilitation. It was not enough that Dimmesdale praise the workings of law on the scaffold; Hester must also be made to acknowledge them, and so Hawthorne returns her to Boston and penitence "of her own free will" (1:263), factitious as such penitence seemed both to contemporary champions of Hester like Jane Swisshelm and contemporary critics like Orestes Brownson.[35]

As It Had Never Been

> Does the interrelation between freedom and repression ... really constitute the principle of civilization? ... Or does this interrelation result only from a specific historical organization of human existence?
>
> —Herbert Marcuse, *Eros and Civilization*

"With this symbol, I undo it all, and make it as it had never been!" Hester exclaims in the forest (1:202). In one sentence Hawthorne conjoins romantic optimism and counterromantic unillusion. Hester means "*as if* it had never been," expunging history with an Emersonian confidence that "in nature every moment is new; the past is always swallowed and forgotten; the coming only is sacred" (*CWE:* 1:189). By omitting "if" and leaving the reference of "it" ambiguous, Hawthorne gives the sentence a second meaning. Hester says, in effect, "I make the present as the past—my past, any past, the human past—never was. Here in the forest I make an ideal life such as has never been led." With these words, we return to the ambiguities of "The Prison-Door." *Could* such a life be led? And on what foundation?

Critical as Hawthorne is of the theocratic conflation of religion and law, he inscribes no alternative source of authority in the historical world of *The Scarlet Letter* and implies none in the outside world of its readers. The conflict in *The Scarlet Letter* between repression and antinomian freedom is not, as Hawthorne presents it, between bad and good but between bad and probable worse. The tragedy of human beings' social situation is that they live, or always have lived, within the neither/nor of confinement and anarchy. If *The Scarlet Letter* inclines toward control of instinct, an internalized form of confinement, it is not because Hawthorne is a conservative by positive conviction but because he felt that virtually any structure was preferable to none at all. He was a skeptic, the uneasy bedfellow of the conservative, but a skeptic graced or plagued with the yearnings of a romantic.

Hester's closing prophecy of "some brighter day" when "a new truth" about gender relations "would be revealed" (1:263) can be taken in a variety of ways: as her effort to wring consolation from her sufferings and from woman's generally; as Hawthorne's own historical meliorism; as his "liberal" co-optation of the threat of dissent;[36] as his conservative evasion of immediate reform; or simply as his attempt to palliate the book's final gloom. Hawthorne adapted Hester's prophecy from the same source as her feminist protest, Fuller's *Woman in the Nineteenth Century*. Addressing herself to Mary Wollstonecraft and George Sand, Fuller proclaims what Hawthorne through his dark heroines would thrice dramatize: "Such beings as these, rich in genius, of most tender sympathies, capable of high virtue and a chastened harmony, ought not to find themselves, by birth, in a place so narrow, that, in breaking bonds, they become outlaws" (*WNC* 75). Social arrangements are deeply at fault, but so, Fuller adds, are women like Wollstonecraft and Sand, who "must be severe lawgivers to themselves," their "lives...unstained by passionate error" (*WNC* 77). Hester's recognition that "the angel and apostle of the coming revelation must be a woman, indeed," but "lofty" and pure (1:263), is a substantive paraphrase of Fuller, whose judgment of Wollstonecraft and Sand ("society has a right to outlaw [such women] until she has revised her law" [*WNC* 77]) is even more severe than Hawthorne's of Hester.

With Fuller's argument in mind, Hawthorne was able to contain his sense of the justice and inevitability of feminist reform within a stern insistence on sexual orthodoxy. That society was wrong, he and Fuller agreed, did not mean that its lawbreakers were right, merely that they were driven to extremity by the constrictions of their situation. Nonetheless, on essential matters of woman's nature and role Fuller is the radical, Hawthorne the conservative. By assigning his prophetess the task of illustrating "how sacred love should make us happy, by the truest test of a life successful to such an end!" (1:263), Hawthorne returns woman to the sphere of the affections and implicitly of sanctified marriage. In Hawthorne's gender utopia there will be no feminine "independence of Man" (*WNC* 175), no female sea captains, and no Minerva-like androgyny; women will remain properly "ethereal." Where Fuller, moreover, writes in the belief that "a new manifestation is at hand" (*WNC* 20), Hawthorne postpones reform until "Heaven's own time" and reassigns its agency from proselytizers like Fuller to the slow, internal development of culture that will make "the world...ripe for it" (1:263). "As it has never been" did not necessitate "as it may never be," but it implied that the process would be evolutionary, not revolutionary, and that it would take place within the framework of universal law, without which life was emptiness and horror.

Afterward

[Hawthorne] was haunted not only by the guilt of his desires but also by the guilt of his denial of them.

—Philip Rahv, "The Dark Lady of Salem"

When Hawthorne finished *The Scarlet Letter*, he could not have anticipated returning to a heroine like Hester. Like Dimmesdale after his Election Day sermon, he was exhausted by what the occasion demanded of him. Though projected two centuries backward into the past, the book came nearer the core of his internal conflict (moral and metaphysical order versus freedom in nature) than anything he had previously written.

Elizabeth Peabody told Sophia of an acquaintance's remark that in *The Scarlet Letter* Hawthorne had "purified himself by casting out a legion of devils into imaginary beings."[37] Dimmesdale was one such devil insofar as he embodied the sexual guilts of the Salem years, compounded by who knows what subsequent imaginings. Chillingworth was another devil, representing, along with the near-contemporaneous Ethan Brand, the artist's sin of clinically delving into the heart. A third devil was Pearl, whose wildness drew upon a mercurialness in Una that disconcerted Hawthorne and led him to project a normalization for his fictive elf-child in lieu of a remedy for his actual one.[38] But the chief devil to be cast out—like Beatrice Rappaccini, devil or angel?—was Hester, whom Hawthorne loved and feared both for what she was and what she called forth in him.

To rid oneself of devils, of course, one must first be possessed by them. What Peabody's correspondent shrewdly guessed of Hawthorne is what Perry Miller claims of the antebellum romance as a genre: through the figure of its dark heroine it "becomes a method for exorcising the demonic...by giving the demon full play, and then letting the eternal verities subdue it by the obstinacy of inertia."[39] This would be the pattern of Hawthorne's four published romances, each of which holds out a promise of the transformative only in the end to "demonize" it and reinstate a moral and social conservatism. "The obstinacy of inertia" may seem a dull place to reside, but when "the eternal verities" have only a tenuous "as if" quality, as they did for Hawthorne, it was preferable to the whirl of chaos.

In *The House of the Seven Gables*, Hawthorne's dark heroine would be replaced by a dark hero, Holgrave, who, if more sweepingly radical than Hester in wanting "everything to begin anew" (2:179), is psychologically safer in that, being male, he raises no feminist issues and arouses no desire. The dream of a "natural" life has been put in abeyance. Hawthorne's intention now is to inscribe a thoroughly conventional life and to try to live it himself. Through Phoebe (one of his nicknames for Sophia), he rejects both the morbid past and the utopian future and settles for a sunny middle-class domesticity that he hopes will provide a via media between the denials of the prison door and the license of the forest.

Stability, however, would not content Hawthorne for long. If, as Brenda Wineapple says, he "was a fastidious man who depended on regulation...as if to contain or curb his own sense of the underside of things,"[40] he was also a chronically restless man who wearied of people and places, chafed against the regulation he sought, and periodically liked to peer into the underside precisely *because* it terrified him. Having structured *Seven Gables* to celebrate conjugality, he reacted against its bourgeois values in *The Blithedale Romance*, which develops the constellation of themes adumbrated with Hester. With their new interests and horizons, the years in England and Italy might have been expected to put the subject to rest, but in *The Marble Faun* Hawthorne returned to his dark heroine yet again, with a still more fascinated sense of her allurements and of her danger. With each successive telling, his grasp of the issues she evoked grew more comprehensive and penetrating until, with Miriam, she became a vehicle for interrogating Christendom and, indeed, life itself, as Hawthorne had been incipiently forced to do a decade earlier as he stood by his mother's deathbed.

5

The Problem of New England

It is impossible to write a story of New England life and manners for a
thoughtless, shallow-minded person. If we represent things as they are,
their intensity, their depth, their unworldly gravity and earnestness,
must inevitably repel lighter spirits, as the reverse pole of the magnet
drives off sticks and stones.

—Harriet Beecher Stowe, *The Minister's Wooing*

Here where the wind is always north-north-east
And children learn to walk on frozen toes,
Wonder begets an envy of all those
Who boil elsewhere with such a lyric yeast
Of love that you will hear them at a feast
Where demons would appeal for some repose,
Still clamoring where the chalice overflows

And crying wildest who have drunk the least.
Passion is here a soilure of the wits,
We're told, and Love a cross for them to bear;
Joy shivers in the corner where she knits
And Conscience always has the rocking-chair,
Cheerful as when she tortured into fits
The first cat that was ever killed by Care.

—Edwin Arlington Robinson, "New England"

Salem, Yet Again

But there is a fatality, a feeling so irresistible and inevitable that it has
the force of doom, which almost invariably compels human beings to
linger around and haunt, ghost-like, the spot where some great and
marked event has given the color to their lifetime; and still the more
irresistibly, the darker the tinge that saddens it.

—Hawthorne, *The Scarlet Letter*

Toward the end of "The Custom-House" Hawthorne dismissed Salem with
wishful finality: "Henceforth, it ceases to be a reality of my life. I am a citizen of
somewhere else" (1:4). He had thought he put Salem behind him when he mar-

115

ried, settled at the Old Manse, and reinvented himself as a writer and man. In the fall of 1845, however, life returned him to Salem like a "bad half-penny" (1:12), and it was in Salem, after his mother's death, that he wrote *The Scarlet Letter* during a period of "shock and strain" from which his son Julian felt "his physical energies perhaps never fully recovered" (*NHW* 1:358). The ending of "The Custom-House" was intended as a farewell to Salem both as a residence and as a mental habitation associated with an identity and a literary practice. But physical separation was not enough. Even in self-exile in the distant Berkshires, Salem remained for Hawthorne both a weight and a gravitational pull. "Mr. Hawthorne thinks it is *Salem* which he is dragging at his ankles still," his wife reported of his gloomy spirits on August 1, 1850, more than two months after the move to Lenox.[1] By early September Hawthorne had begun *The House of the Seven Gables*, his Salem book, which also ends with a decisive break from the town. His first removal in "The Custom-House" had been incomplete; the separation had to be performed again.

I use "Salem" synecdochically for "New England" because in Hawthorne's imagination the two were entwined despite his broad acquaintance with the region from his youthful travels. "Salem history haunted him," Margaret B. Moore remarks,[2] but beyond his fascination with seventeenth-century Salem witchcraft, what was the nature of his personal engagement with the New England past? "The historical sense," T. S. Eliot remarked, "involves a perception, not only of the pastness of the past"—its difference from ourselves; its over-and-doneness—"but of its presence."[3] Almost alone among classic American writers (Faulkner and Stowe are the chief exceptions), Hawthorne shared this twofold historical sense. With something like Eliot's "pastness of the past" in mind, Michael J. Colacurcio describes the "intention...in the best of [Hawthorne's] early tales" as "the wish to recover the affective quality of human lives lived under conditions or assumptions different from those which prevailed in his own later and more liberal age. Or, alternatively," he adds, echoing Eliot's notion of "presence," it is "the desire to re-enact the subtle process by which a solid but often unlovely past had thrown its long and often darkening shadow an equally solid and apparently sunnier present."[4] These are quite different impulses. Both may express themselves in a Hawthorne fiction, as they do in *The Scarlet Letter*, but they make for different emphases and belong to complementary thematic enterprises. One is concerned with the past *as* past (Hawthorne as regional historian, with New England as the fountainhead of America), the other with the intellectual and psychological legacy of the past for its descendants (Hawthorne as cultural anthropologist).

Those who see Hawthorne as preoccupied with local history other than as material for fiction will be surprised by its near-entire absence from the American notebooks. The history that mattered privately for him—"the major ligature between culture and literary text," as Leonard N. Neufeldt observed with Thoreau—was "the problem of vocation."[5] The young man who, as Henry James said, "must have proposed to himself to enjoy" became an anthropologist perforce from the frustrations of living and writing in a society that made small "provision" for enjoying (James 24). Describing his 1860 meeting with Hawthorne during his literary pilgrimage to New England, William Dean Howells recalled that Hawthorne "spoke of the New England temperament, and suggested that the apparent coldness in it was also real, and that the suppression of emotion for generations would extinguish it at last."[6] Hawthorne was not referring to New England's past so much as to its present and future, and his prolonged silences and "shadowy kindness," which made Howells's "spirits sink,"[7] testify to the inhibitions of feeling and expression that afflicted Hawthorne himself, notwithstanding the exhortations to sympathy that run through his work.

The enduring "problem of New England" for Hawthorne had little to do with the witch trials except symptomatically or with other remembered (or forgotten) episodes in regional history; as he said in "Alice Doane's Appeal," "we are a people of the present and have no heartfelt interest in the olden time" (11:267).[8] Practically, as lived experience, the New England past asserted itself for Hawthorne in what history, climate, and religion combined to make of the mind and temperament of its people, himself included. New England was the starvation of the senses, the imagination, the feelings, and the erotic nature consequent on living in a post-Puritan world. It was the mental place that Hawthorne inhabited and the "place" that inhabited him wherever else his physical and cultural wanderings might take him.

Hawthorne was aware of this and, on the levels of consciousness subject to will, struggled within and against it. *The House of the Seven Gables* is the culmination of his open engagement with Salem, both personally ("Salem" as a symbol for his years of seclusion) and culturally ("Salem" as a miniature of New England civilization). To the extent that the individual life is always lived in and through culture, and culture experienced through the individual life, the strands are inseparable. Hawthorne was deeply cognizant of how his psychological and vocational conflicts were related to what, as analyst and victim, he understood as a collective regional neurosis. I will speak of *Seven Gables* as an exorcism, but psychologically it might better qualify as a work of self-therapy, and one whose cost, in the end, would arguably rival its benefits.

A Genealogy of New England Morals

[Man is] also the generator of the greatest and most disastrous of maladies, of which humanity has not to this day been cured: his sickness of

> himself, brought on by the violent severance from his animal past, by
> his sudden leap and fall into new layers and conditions of existence, led
> by his declaration of war against the old instincts that had hitherto been
> the foundation of his power, his joy, and his awesomeness.
>
> —Nietzsche, *The Genealogy of Morals*

"The May-pole of Merry Mount" is anthropologist Hawthorne's myth of New England origins. On one level the tale is about secular hedonism and religious austerity ("jollity and gloom") contending for dominance in the emerging New England (9:54); on another, that of the nuptial pair Edith and Edgar, about the growth of the soul; and on a third, about the beginnings of civilization in the passage from the pleasure principle to the reality principle. The tale fictionalizes the idea that Freud and others would later theorize about: that culturally, as biologically, ontogeny recapitulates phylogeny, as the development of the individual replicates that of the race. But the levels of the tale are not neatly parallel; they interpenetrate one another, and in doing so they problematize an allegory already complicated by ambiguity, ambivalence, density of allusion, and a rhetoric of entrapment that invites readers to align themselves with the sunshine and flowers of Merry Mount only to find them deprecated almost immediately as fond illusions. Between the maypole and the whipping post, moreover, the story offers no middle ground. The "grisly saints" bid to "darken all the clime, and make it a land of clouded visages, of hard toil, and sermon and psalm, forever"; the "gay sinners" bid to trivialize it (9:62). Those are the two alternatives.

The narrative shift from Merry Mount as community to Edith and Edgar seems, if not to evade the problem of history, then at least to redistribute the allegorical weight of the tale from the sociocultural to the moral and psychological. Through the fable of the lovers, the story ranges itself with other Hawthornean narratives of the soul's journey from an innocence that is ignorance to a sober awareness of life's difficulties. Morally and spiritually, Edith and Edgar's lapse from paradise gives promise of being a fortunate one; like Adam and Eve in *Paradise Lost* (Book XII, ll. 648–49), they leave their Eden to go "heavenward, supporting each other along the difficult path which it was their lot to tread, and never wasted one regretful thought on the vanities of Merry Mount" (9:67). Within the tale as moral apologue, history recedes, the "dark Puritans" stand as emblems of "the sternest cares of life" (9:5), and the ethos of Puritanism itself, as Lawrence Buell says, becomes "associated with something like adult reality and Merry Mountism" with "a childish indulgence that the mature person has outgrown."[9]

Nonetheless, the historical dimension of the tale is too prominent to be allegorized away, and we can never forget that Edith and Edgar will pass their temporal lives in a world presided over by John Endicott, "the severest Puritan of all who laid the rock-foundation of New England" (9:66). The levels of the plot—historical, moral and spiritual, anthropological—thus confound one another. Endicott's conquest of Merry Mount reenacts the mythic origin of all civilization, but the event is not an auspicious or even a representative one: *this* civilization will be exceptionally marked by discontents. A communal neurosis—hostile to pleasure, to the senses, and to art—has been implanted in New England life at the very outset, so that the archetypal growth of the soul is forced to occur within culture-specific conditions deeply inhospitable to it.

This *con-founding* of New England is Hawthorne's unifying theme in "Merry Mount." Incisive as he is about the problem, however, Hawthorne cannot escape the binary opposition between "a wild philosophy of pleasure" (9:203) and a morbid denial of it. He seems to be hovering around, but unable productively to grasp, two concepts later formulated by Herbert Marcuse in his critique of Freud in *Eros and Civilization*: (1) "*surplus-repression*," or the "*additional* controls" that a particular society institutes "over and above those indispensable for civilized human association," and (2) the "*performance principle*," or the dominant form that the reality principle assumes at a given historical moment.[10] On one side, he portrays the Puritans as "most dismal wretches" who scourge and mutilate social offenders and divest the New World of even the lawful "hereditary pastimes of old England" (9:60); on the other, he presents them as embodiments of the reality principle who live closer to "the sober truths of life" than the gay Merry Mounters (9:60). His Puritans thus symbolize both necessary and ultimately desirable social and psychological repression and *un*necessary and *un*desirable surplus repression—the latter imposed on behalf of a historically constructed vision of reality that will be transmitted to their descendants as a matrix of cultural being.

In going beyond his historical sources to emphasize Puritan severity— "Further penalties, such as branding and the cropping of ears, shall be thought of hereafter" (9:64), Endicott tells his lieutenant—Hawthorne illustrates how surplus repression leads to a rechanneling of erotic energies into sadism. In *The Scarlet Letter* the Puritan women who revile Hester in the marketplace are punitive in proportion to their ugliness and inferably their sexual frustration; and in "Main-street" the constable who flogs a bare-breasted Quaker woman through Salem at the behest of Major Hawthorne has "a smile upon his lips" (11:70).[11] The paradox of repression in "Merry Mount," as Nietzsche would argue of Western civilization generally in *The Genealogy of Morals*, is that while the curtailment of natural instincts "provides the soil for the growth of what is later called man's *soul*," it also generates a "sublimated cruelty resulting from the cooping of his animal nature."[12] A simple act like Endicott's cropping of Edgar's "love-lock and long glossy curls" (9:66) is a token of the fury turned against beauty and pleasure, the fury becoming the substitute pleasure.

To suggest that Hawthorne understood these things is not to say that he escaped their hold. "Man," Nietzsche remarked, "has looked for so long with an evil eye upon his natural inclinations that they have finally become inseparable from 'bad conscience'" (Nietzsche 228). In "Merry Mount," "bad conscience"—Hawthorne's residual distrust of pleasure and the senses even as he is powerfully drawn toward them—shows itself in the animal imagery he adapts from "Comus" to disparage the revels of the community as descents into bestiality. The Merry Mounters are not genuine innocents, they are adults childishly playing at innocence; but since the story includes no pleasures that are *not* childish (sanctified courtship leading to marital love excepted), Hawthorne's portrayal has the effect of banishing most "natural inclinations"—"the old mirth of Merry England" as well as "the wilder glee of this fresh forest" (9:57)—from the New England-to-be. Q. D. Leavis finds Hawthorne "subtler and wiser than Milton" in recognizing the "disaster" that follows from the unmediated clash of "two partial truths or qualified goods,"[13] yet Hawthorne may be more Miltonic than Leavis allows. By accepting "the moral gloom of the world" as an incontestable fact (9:68), he goes far toward identifying a historically generated "performance principle" (the Puritan view of reality as somber, toilsome, and care-ridden) with reality itself. He has not introjected Puritan beliefs as such; rather, he has imbibed the New England ethos and naturalized its coordinates of experience even as he rejects the theology that shaped them and the social practices they produce.

"The May-pole of Merry Mount" is a relatively early work, accomplished as art but lacking what Giles Gunn calls "a normative perspective outside of culture from which and by means of which to criticize the products created within it."[14] Although Hawthorne can "think across culture" to the extent that he recognizes and deplores its repressions,[15] he is still enmeshed in its core assumptions about life. Without a vocabulary for cultural analysis or a broad comparativist view of history, he can *feel the desirability* but not *conceive the possibility* of a minimally repressive society in which the life of the senses would be shorn of inherited guilt. Beneath the overt levels of the tale—those on which the writer is in command of his materials—the "problem of New England" in "The May-pole of Merry Mount" is the problem of Hawthorne *thinking* about New England.

Recentering the New England Past

> So stern was the energy of his aspect, that the whole man, visage, frame, and soul, seemed wrought of iron, gifted with life and thought, yet all of one substance with his head-piece and breast-plate. It was the Puritan of Puritans; it was Endicott himself!
>
> —Hawthorne, "The May-pole of Merry Mount"

...the most rigid of any of the magistrates.

—Caleb Snow on John Endicott, *History of Boston* (1825)

In an 1833 oration delivered in Salem, "The Importance of Illustrating New-England History By a Series of Romances like the Waverley Novels," Rufus Choate argued for the power of fiction to animate the barebones "facts, the lessons, of history" and infuse them into consciousness of the people. Choate warned, however, that as "no age is heroic of which the whole truth is recorded," the wise romancer will cultivate only "the useful truth" and allow the rest "to putrefy or be burned."[16] The larger question for Choate, as Lawrence Buell observed of antebellum historical writers generally, was what to do with a Puritan ancestry, a source of regional pride and proclaimed national preeminence insofar as the Puritan resistance to tyranny was taken to prefigure the American Revolution, but a cause, too, for discomfort, even shame, since these ardent champions of liberty were also vigorous persecutors.[17]

The campaign to purge the New England legacy of Puritan punitiveness began much earlier, in 1769, with the boosterism of Plymouth elders seeking to raise the fortunes of a town that social, economic, and political history had made a regional backwater. In *Imagining New England*, Joseph A. Conforti shows how, accelerating in the 1790s with Jeremy Belknap's *American Biography, or An Historical Account of Those Persons who Have Been Distinguished in America* (1794, 1798) and again in 1820 with Daniel Webster's bicentennial address in Plymouth, New Englanders seized on the historical neologism "Pilgrims" and glorified the legacy of Plymouth in order to create "a narrative of republican beginnings unencumbered by the Puritan record of intolerance."[18] As Plymouth waxed in New England's and later in America's mythmaking, Massachusetts Bay waned, or at least was subsumed to "a powerful discourse of Plymouth-republican origins" that served, in Conforti's phrase, "to Pilgrimize the Puritans"[19] and, in Choate's, to disseminate a "useful truth."

In dramatizing the story of Merry Mount, Hawthorne reverses the thrust of recent historiography on both counts; he Puritanizes the Pilgrims and excavates precisely the kind of material Choate sought to bury. Far from being a cradle of American liberty, Plymouth in "The May-pole of Merry Mount" is alluded to only as a nearby "settlement of Puritans" (9:60), and its agent in routing the Merry Mounters is the Salemite John Endicott, whose community Edith and Edgar, as progenitors of New England, will presumably join. The identic locus of New England has been reclaimed for Massachusetts Bay and its founding village, Salem, an "anti-Plymouth" associated with liberty (the Puritans fled from tyrannical king and church) but also with intolerance and repression.

Hawthorne makes this double legacy his subject in the Salem tale "Endicott and the Red Cross," which Michael Davitt Bell calls an account of "the symbolic birth of the American character."[20] In a moment of New England crisis, John Endicott ("for ever honored be" his name!) steps forth to cut the symbol of England, and of Royal tyranny, "from New England's banner, the first omen of the deliverance which our fathers consummated" nearly a century and a half later (9:441). The story opens and closes with filiopietist orthodoxy; most of the rest is open heterodoxy—a litany of Puritan persecutions and punishments, among them a scarlet *A* affixed to the gown of a beautiful young adulteress. "Was it not for liberty to worship God according to our conscience" that we came to this land, Endicott proclaims to the crowd. "Call you this liberty of conscience?" replies a "Wanton Gospeller," whose offense is to read scripture other than as the ministers and magistrates see fit (9:439, 435).

Bell takes the story as a balanced historical representation of the two faces of Endicott (liberator and persecutor) as they epitomize the mixed character of Puritan New England. He concedes the depicted "loss of certain kinds of passion, gaiety, and humor" associated with Old England, but he finds Hawthorne "willing to accept this intolerance as a necessary concomitant to the heroic act of self-definition in separating from England."[21] Why should intolerance be "necessary"? and how far into the American future must its spirit extend, if not as outright persecution, then as chilling social disapproval? The celebration of Endicott in the story is formulaic and conventional, the depiction of Puritan severity forceful and subversive. The Wanton Gospeller has a point. Hawthorne underscores it when, contravening historical evidence that showed Endicott incited by Roger Williams,[22] he portrays Williams as a voice of wise moderation but also as "an elderly gentleman" (the actual Williams was in his thirties) sadly ineffectual against Endicott (9:436). Hawthorne is not fictionalizing history but recasting it as founding myth. Williams's tolerant Puritanism, which might have fathered a more generous America, is presented as already in retreat before the righteousness of Endicott, whose triumph is complete and whose character will imprint itself upon the region. Not Plymouth and Bradford, not even Boston and Winthrop, were the epicenters of early New England history for Hawthorne. Salem and Endicott were, and their chief legacy, which persisted long after the occasions for zeal had passed, was bigotry and repression.

An Iron Cage Called Liberty

> [Hegemony] is a whole body of practices and expectations, over the whole of living: our senses and assignments of energy, our shaping perceptions of ourselves and our world. It is a lived system of meanings and values ... [that] constitutes a sense of reality for most people in the society, a sense of absolute because experienced reality beyond which it is very difficult for most members of the society to move, in most areas of their lives.
>
> —Raymond Williams, *Marxism and Literature*

Though typical of much New England writing in its eulogy of the founders, "Endicott and Red Cross" is typical of Hawthorne's treatment of the past chiefly in its emphasis on Puritan repression. Frederick C. Crews only modestly exaggerates when he says that "the finding and punishment of sin were *all* that [Hawthorne] found noteworthy in the Puritan character."[23] As a youth, Hawthorne had no Mary Moody Emerson or Lyman Beecher to serve as a conduit between Puritan piety and coolly mercantile times. Nor did regional history come to him through Hathorne legends told by the fireside; he was raised by practical Mannings. Even Michael J. Colacurcio, who makes the strongest case for Hawthorne as historian, concedes that "Hawthorne's natal mind and early sympathies were formed at a considerable distance from the various Calvinisms of his remote Puritan ancestors," which he "would have to recover rather than transcend."[24] He never did recover them if recovery involved empathy for the lives of deeply spiritual persons unlike himself. Hawthorne's Puritans are legalists—people of conscience, works, and narrow social conformity, not pietists whose life centers upon the felt presence or absence of grace. When Hawthorne does portray living faith, it nearly always takes the form of fanaticism or religious melancholy, as with the Quaker Catherine and Tobias Pearson in "The Gentle Boy." Hawthorne *read* his way into the knowledge of Puritanism that gives his tales their authority on contextual matters but that otherwise seems hardly to have occupied his mind.

It was as a hegemonic organization of social and cultural life—a pervasive somberness "with hardly a single thread of rose-color or gold" in its tapestry, as he wrote in "Main-street" (11:78)—that the inheritance of Puritanism most vitally affected Hawthorne. "No, they are not gay," Henry James has the visiting European Felix Young report of his duty-burdened New England cousins of Hawthorne's time (the 1840s): "They are sober; they are even severe. They are of a pensive cast; they take things hard.... It is not the epicurean temperament."[25] Set fifty years earlier, Harriet Beecher Stowe's *The Minister's Wooing* illustrates how the narrow theological intensity of New England acts to "produce rather strength and purity than enjoyment" even in the healthy-minded Mary Scudder, and how in the "thoughtful, earnest, deep-natured" Mrs. Marvyn—a woman of "eager and hungry mind" and latent aesthetic sensibility—it makes for religious melancholia, starvation of the intellect and the senses, and "a habitual shame-facedness" about emotions even within the family.[26] In this last respect, Stowe might almost have been describing the emotional tenor of Hawthorne's early family life. His widely remarked shyness and reserve were in keeping with the spirit of his reclusive mother and older sister, whose eccentricities were only aggravated forms of the regional inhibition Hawthorne complained of to Howells. The "peculiarities" that Frederick C. Crews identifies in Hawthorne are nearly all variations on common New England qualities; they include his "fear of passion; his tendency to reduce historical issues to a psychomachia between impulse and inhibition;...his association of art with [a] guilty role; his clinical coldness, which works at cross-purposes with his endorsements of affection and community; his yearning toward a Phoebe- or Hilda-like blandness to swallow up his morbidity; and, as a result of all this, his profound loneliness and premature world-weariness."[27]

If Hawthorne suffered *from* the New England temper, he suffered still more *under* it. The collective portrait in his early letters, in the semiautobiographical Oberon stories, and in Horatio Bridge's reminiscences of his young manhood is of an indolent would-be artist guiltless about shedding New England theology— he loathed compulsory Sunday chapel at Bowdoin with its "red hot Calvinist sermon from the President, or some other dealer in fire and brimstone" (15:59)—but internalizing its work ethic, or at least reluctantly conceding its fitness and necessity. In "Passages from a Relinquished Work," he projected a version of himself into his nameless protagonist, "a youth of gay and happy temperament, with an incorrigible levity of spirit, of no vicious propensities, sensible enough, but wayward and fanciful," who chafes under his clerical guard-ian's insistence that he adopt "a particular profession" rather than live modestly on an inherited "competence" (as Hawthorne lived at home), "keeping aloof from the regular business of life" (10:407): "This would have been a dangerous resolution, any where in the world; it was fatal in New-England. There is a gross-ness in the conceptions of my countrymen; they will not conceive that any good thing may consist with what they call idleness.... The principle is excellent, in its general influence, but most miserable in its effect on the few that violate it" (10:407).

While there was no figurative clerical guardian in his early life, Hawthorne evidently did feel the real or fancied criticism of Salem's establishment, and like his storyteller, who grants the "excellence" of the principle invoked against him, he incorporated it as an accusatory "sense of triviality, a conviction that serious masculinity was reserved for the 'man of affairs.'"[28] "Idler" would remain his half-ironic epithet for himself through "The Custom-House," and even late in life, long after achievement and publicity had made him a literary personage and Franklin Pierce had made him a consul, he had doubts whether he had writ-ten enough and whether it all amounted to anything against the labors of his contemporaries. The "chief duty" that Emerson assigns the American scholar— "self-trust" in the face of sneers from "so-called 'practical men'" and against "the self-accusation, the faint heart, the frequent uncertainty and loss of time" that come from the scholar's absorption of cultural norms (*CWE* 1:59, 62)—is the duty Hawthorne imposes on his artist of the beautiful, who "must keep faith in himself, while the incredulous world assails him with its utter disbelief" (10:454). It was not a lesson he could steadfastly heed. "The bane of your life has been self-distrust," Bridge wrote him in December 1836. "I wish to God I could impart to you a little of my own brass," he added the following February: "But you will never have confidence enough in yourself though you will have fame" (*PRNH* 73, 74).

"Confidence" involved sloughing off the perceived opinion of Salem and envisioning a new identity for himself and a cultural milieu capable of support-ing it. "Main-street" (1849), written just before *The Scarlet Letter*, is Hawthorne's attempt to do precisely that: to take command of New England history by remythologizing it and adapting its new configuration to his ambitions as a writer. Rufus Choate had likened historical romance to a "showman's box" pic-turing "genuine specimens,—real living men and women of every class and calling in society, as it was then constituted," who "talk and act in character."[29] "Main-street" realizes Choate's idea through the device of an impresario with a crank-mechanism that anticipates the latter-day slide projector. Endicott, Winthrop, Morton of Merry Mount, and Anne Hutchinson all make their expected appearance, as do the familiar Puritan punishments and scenes from the witch trials. More surprising are the glowing sketches of founder Roger Conant and of the early settlers' faith, which "burned like a lamp within their hearts, enriching every thing around them with its radiance" (11:58). The evo-cation of Puritan piety, however, turns out to be a prelude and foil to its loss: "All was well, so long as their lamps were freshly kindled at the heavenly flame. After a while, however, whether in their time or their children's, these lamps began to burn more dimly, or with a less genuine luster; and then it might be seen, how hard, cold, and confined, was their system,—how like an iron cage was that which they called Liberty!" (11:58). Long before Perry Miller described "Declension in a Bible Commonwealth,"[30] Hawthorne was mapping the constriction of Puritan life, initially lit by faith and leavened with remnants of the Old English merriment, into a narrower, gloomier practice "sinister to the intellect and sinister to the heart." "Nor, it may be," he continues, "have we even yet thrown off all the unfavorable influences which, among many good ones, were bequeathed to us by our Puritan forefathers" (11:67–68).

Writing ostensibly of "the pastness of the past," Hawthorne is more intimately concerned with its "presence" in the form of "miserable distortions of the moral nature" (11:67) that continue to warp New England character. In one of its chief modern forms, Yankee philistinism, Puritanism displays itself in "Main-street" in the interjections of "an acidulous-looking gentleman in blue glasses," who, like the scoffing Peter Hovenden in "The Artist of the Beautiful," "make[s] it a point to see things precisely as they are" and carps at the paint-and-pasteboard absur-dity of the showman's effects (11:54). By incorporating this withered figure into his sketch, Hawthorne caricatures and disarms an imagined part of his New England audience. But the skeptic's contempt for artifice and imagination also reflects Hawthorne's own chronic doubts about the romancer's activity. "New England" is within him as well as around him; it may even be *more* within him.

As it unfolds, "Main-street" works toward an accommodation of author and audience predicated on a common deliverance from the legacy of the past. After collapsing the eighteenth century into the single tableau of the Great Snow of 1717 (to the neglect of the Revolutionary period so prominent in New England historiography), Hawthorne's showman hurries onward, toward the present. The "dreary monotony" of the past, so like "one of our actual New England winters, which leaves so large a blank—so melancholy a death-spot—in lives so brief that they ought to be all summer-time" (11:81), will now be exchanged for the warmth and variety of present-day life, and the stylizations of romance for a more contemporary and broadly appealing realism. Hawthorne and his audience will meet on the shared ground of post-Puritan middle-class experience.

But the crank of the showman's mechanism breaks; "the scene will not move"; and the representations of the present and future, which were to have been "far better than [those of] the past" (11:81), are never shown. The failure is telling. However he may have wished to, Hawthorne in 1849 was unprepared to take leave of the past as a setting and of romance as a fictional form. It may be that he still felt bound by talent and temperament to historical subjects (though in Concord he had avoided them); or that returning to Salem revived the "Salem" in him and undid the emancipating work of the Manse years; or that, unsure of himself as a writer, he hesitated to try his hand at close mimesis; or simply that he was already immersed in the projected volume that would group "Main-street" and other historical sketches with "The Scarlet Letter." In any case, given the thrust of "Main-street" toward a realist's art, *The Scarlet Letter* seems (save in its forest scenes) a return to an old milieu and an old literary practice. The book that properly follows from "Main-street" is *The House of the Seven Gables*.

Exorcising Salem

> Since the symbolic transformation involves a sloughing off, you may expect to find some variant of killing in the work.... So we get a "scapegoat," the "representative" or "vessel" of certain unwanted evils, the sacrificial animal upon whose back the burden of these evils is ritualistically loaded.
>
> —Kenneth Burke, *The Philosophy of Literary Form*

Beyond its status as a fictional text with an announced intention "to connect a by-gone time to the ... Present" (2:2), *The House of the Seven Gables* is a symbolic action that aims to *disconnect* present from past and redirect writer Hawthorne and New England collectively from the gloom of history to what "Main-street" calls "the sunshine of the present" (11:81). Brenda Wineapple describes the book as "a kind of exorcism."[31] Its objects are several. First among them is the Pyncheon character. With his Bible in one hand and "iron sword-hilt" in the other, Colonel Pyncheon is emblematic of the 1640s Puritan ruling class, just as Judge Pyncheon with his guise of benevolence and sultry, dog-day smile is emblematic of the 1840s Whig ruling class. The donnée of Hawthorne's contemporary plot—Judge Pyncheon's effort to extract a secret from Clifford—is an implausible contrivance. The book's real quarrel with the judge is less for what he does than what he *is*, or what over the course of history he and his kind culturally represent. Most immediately, the judge is Salem clergyman-politician Charles W. Upham, who assured Hawthorne he "would never need fear removal under a Whig administration" (16:280), then proceeded to do whatever he could to oust him; "that smooth, smiling, oily man of God!" Sophia Hawthorne sneered (in Mellow 295). Yet Upham himself was only a type of the New Englander whom Hawthorne chronically felt beleaguered by and abashed before. Judge Pyncheon is a surrogate for the generations of New England males from Endicott through Upham who Hawthorne felt had exerted a baleful influence upon regional character and, directly in person or indirectly through the spirit of place, upon himself.

The chief action of Judge Pyncheon is his persecution of Clifford, both in the past (his complicity in Clifford's wrongful conviction) and in the present. But the antipathy between the cousins precedes their uncle's death and is a function of their very natures: Clifford the aesthete, Jaffrey the hard materialist. Clifford, Hawthorne writes, "felt that native and original horror of the excellent Judge, which is proper to a weak, delicate, and apprehensive character, in the face of massive strength" (2:172). And later: "That strong and ponderous man had been Clifford's nightmare. There had been no free breath to be drawn, within the sphere of so malevolent an influence" (2:313). Clark C. Griffith notes the repetition of "words like *iron, energy, massive, hard, [and] granite*" in reference to the Pyncheon character.[32] These or similar words appear in Hawthorne's description of John Endicott and also, in less sinister form, of blacksmith Robert Danforth in "The Artist of the Beautiful," a "man of main strength" whose "hard, brute force darkens and confuses the spiritual element" in Owen Warland and "would drive [him] mad" with frequent contact (10:453–54). Danforth is extroverted and good-natured, "a kindly figure" like Hawthorne's recollected blacksmith-grandfather, Richard Manning (5:122); even so, solid, obtuse masculinity discomfits the lover of the beautiful by making his aims and achievements seem insubstantial; he feels unmanned, or un-Manninged.

Criminalizing Colonel Pyncheon and then Jaffrey enables Hawthorne to objectify his aversion in palpable form and make the judge into what Kenneth Burke calls "a 'suppurating device' (that brings the evil 'to a head')" and allows it to be confronted, openly discredited, and expelled.[33] Beneath the level of plot, which focuses on Pyncheon aristocracy, ruthlessness and greed, the problem of Pyncheonism for Hawthorne is the cultural circumstance of an artist-nature like Clifford (or himself) being inherently "at cross-purposes with the [New England] world" and finding his "existence a strangeness, a solitude, and a torment" (2:149). With Jaffrey's death, this circumstance is symbolically removed. "The weight is gone," Clifford tells Hepzibah: "it is gone off this weary old world, and we may be as light-hearted as little Phoebe herself!" (2:250). If Hawthorne, too, seems to exult in the judge's death in the gleefully arch "Governor Pyncheon," it is because Clifford's hatred and feeling of liberation are embodiments of his own.

Beyond delivering Clifford, Hawthorne must also deliver himself *from* Clifford. In "Fragments from the Journal of a Solitary Man," Oberon had worried about the fitness of his stance of aesthetic idler when youth passed into middle age. Now middle-aged himself, Hawthorne saw other faults; the aesthete was effete, parasitic, and given to a hedonism that tended to coarsen and grow selfish and petulant with time. Hawthorne never overcame his youthful ambivalence toward aestheticism, even in Europe in the presence of civilized models like poet Leigh Hunt and multitalented sculptor William Wetmore Story; the former lacked backbone, the latter earnestness of purpose. Elizabeth Peabody reports that "Mr. Hawthorne used to say that he inherited the granite that was in this ancestor," a sea captain described by one of his peers as "the sternest man that ever walked a deck!" (*NHW* 1:182). As Peabody tells it, Hawthorne seems to have been proud of the inheritance.

In *Seven Gables* Hawthorne loathes and fears the specter of John Endicott, updated in Judge Pyncheon, but he also follows Endicott in looking askance at the aesthetic and regarding it as corrosive of the moral. "Not to speak it harshly or scornfully"—which Hawthorne proceeds immediately to do—"it seemed Clifford's nature to be a Sybarite" (2:108). The worst side of the sensualist's "love and necessity for the Beautiful" (2:109) is his instinctive recoil at the ugly or grotesque. Clifford can hardly bear to look at Hepzibah, who lives selflessly for him. "He owed her nothing" in return for all she "had silently given," Hawthorne writes: "A nature like Clifford's can contract no debts of that sort" (2:109).

Hawthorne could portray Clifford's fastidiousness so keenly because to a marked extent he shared it.[34] However he may prize her goodness, Hepzibah repels the aesthete in him, too, both as writer and as man. Unless it was allied to delicacy, grace, or fine intelligence, female plainness offended Hawthorne, even in his own fitfully attractive young daughter, Una. Hawthorne dissects Clifford, he *is* Clifford, and he chastises and seeks to expel the element of

Clifford in himself, unable to imagine an aestheticism that is *not* selfish, effeminate, hedonistic, and enervating. As New England artist, the connoisseurly and the moral are at odds within him, as they are within another mixed product of the region, Henry James's Rowland Mallet in *Roderick Hudson*. Mallet manages the outward problem of New England by uprooting himself and living in Rome; he manages the inward problem by combining his love of the beautiful with an "uncomfortably sensitive conscience," an absolute probity, and a want of the sybarite's "simple, sensuous, confident relish of pleasure."[35] Hawthorne is a Mallet of an earlier generation who lacks the worldliness to distance himself from his cultural situation, assess the competing tendencies in his nature, and achieve some sort of working reconciliation. Instead, the aesthete in him protests against the overbearing New England fathers while the residual Puritan joins the fathers in disparaging the aesthete as an amoral voluptuary. Hawthorne must kill off Judge Pyncheon *and* he must curb Clifford, or "Clifford*ism*," which he does by making a salutary moral instrument of Clifford's suffering. Had Clifford not been victimized in youth but lived to cultivate "his taste to its utmost perfectibility," his aestheticism might over time "have completely eaten out or filed away his affections." "May not" his thirty years in prison, Hawthorne asks, "have had a redeeming drop of mercy, at bottom?" (2:112).

The paradox Hawthorne develops through Clifford is that while the artist must be relieved of the burden of Puritan hegemony in order to thrive, he must also retain healthy and regulative ties to a world still (to its credit) imbued with Puritan rigor. Hawthorne resolves the issue by metonymically substituting one artist (Holgrave) for another (Clifford) and incorporating him, through marriage to Phoebe, into a reconstituted New England. Virtually overnight, Phoebe arrests the dry rot of the old house, rids it of dust and grime, and brightens its shadowy physical and metaphysical corners with her own sunshine. She exorcises the past without leaving a bewildering moral vacancy. Conservative herself, and therefore a vehicle for the organic continuity of tradition, she frees New England of Puritanic gloom while regrounding it neo-Puritanically in a gentler, more feminized but hardly less exacting conscientiousness. "So fresh...and yet so orderly and obedient to common rules" (2:68), Phoebe is a cheerful, detheologized version of her ancestors in whom "the stern old stuff of Puritanism" (2:76) lives on in the form of a comfortable adherence to usages, naturalized for her as the beneficent reign of "law" and haloed with an aura of spirituality. The Puritan with his Bible and sword has been replaced by the angel in the house with her dust-rag and smile, and the substitution has been achieved without compromising the integrity and cosmic trust that Hawthorne values most in the old religion and would preserve.

Transcending Transcendentalism

"But if Mr. Holgrave is a lawless person!" remonstrated Phoebe, a part
of whose essence it was to keep within the limits of law.
"Oh," said Hepzibah carelessly... —"I suppose he has a law of his own."
—Hawthorne, *The House of the Seven Gables*

Phoebe's lawfulness is essential to Hawthorne, for even as he rebels against
Puritan hegemony he is cognizant of the void created by the dismantling of tradition. Whether individually as an Emersonian disemburdening of convention
or institutionally as a reordering of social arrangements, the radical exorcism of
the past seemed to Hawthorne a perilous undertaking that needed itself to be
exorcised or otherwise contained.

Holgrave is Hawthorne's sanscullotish reformer, by descent because he is a
dispossessed Maule, by conviction because he is one of the alienated young who
have absorbed the spirit of 1840s Transcendentalism and harkened to its call to
build a new world. The sketch of Holgrave moving about from place to place,
profession to profession, yet always carrying "his conscience with him" and
maintaining a core of "identity" (2:177) recalls Emerson's "sturdy lad from New
Hampshire or Vermont, who in turn tries all the professions, who *teams it, farms
it, peddles*, keeps a school, preaches, edits a newspaper, goes to Congress,... and
so forth, in successive years, and always, like a cat, falls on his feet" (*CWE* 2:43).[36]
Like Emerson himself, who claimed to "unsettle all things" and urged his contemporaries to "clear [them]selves of every usage which has not its roots in
[their] own mind" (*CWE* 1:188, 156), Holgrave "seemed to unsettle everything... by his lack of reverence for what was fixed; unless, at a moment's warning,
it could establish its right to hold its ground" (2:177).

Although Hawthorne had little sympathy with Transcendental reform, he
uses its iconoclastic spirit in *Seven Gables* as a ground-clearing instrument to
sweep away the detritus of history, much as the Unitarianism from which
Transcendentalism sprang swept away the vestiges of Calvinist orthodoxy.
Delusive in itself, Transcendentalism had value for Hawthorne in inspiring the
young with a deconstructive fervor that rattled the mind-set, if not the societal
pillars, of New England. As Transcendental reformer, Holgrave is thus another
"suppurating device." He brings the quarrel with the "odious and abominable
Past" (2:184) to a rhetorical head—"We read in Dead Men's books! We laugh at
Dead Men's jokes, and cry at Dead Men's pathos!" (2:183)—then is himself, as
radical, neutralized and brought happily within a renovated version of the social
system. Rhetorically, this is accomplished through the authority of the narrator's
"patchwork" theory of social change (2:180), which overrides Holgrave's apocalyptic one; dramatically, it is achieved through Holgrave's recantation and

submission to Phoebe. The self-reliant Emersonian with "a law of his own" and a "deep consciousness of inner strength" abruptly comes to see himself as wandering "all astray" and in need of the stabilizing "poise" of Phoebe to constrain his own "oscillating tendency" (2:85, 180, 302, 307).

Holgrave's about-face is a replaying of Hawthorne's own in "The Old Manse" when, after a forest overnight of speculative freedom with Ellery Channing, he finds it "sweet... to return within the system of human society" and the benign "institutions that had grown out of the heart of mankind" (10:25, 26). The solution he offers in both works to the challenge of reform is a species of interior redecoration in which the structures of society are renovated from within by the transformative power of love. In the chapter "Phoebe's Good-Bye," Holgrave, a man who "love[s] nothing mouldy" and would burn all old houses (2:184), comes to feel that "moonlight, and the sentiment in man's heart responsive to it, is the greatest of renovators and reformers," all others "no better than moonshine" (2:214). "How good, and beautiful," and "young" is the world, he exclaims, "with nothing really rotten or age-worn in it!" (2:214). It is a small step from Holgrave's newfound veneration for the venerable to his pronouncement that houses should be built in stone so that each generation might remake "the interior, to suit its own taste and convenience," while the exterior maintains the "permanence... essential to the happiness" of social life (2:314–15).

Exorcised symbolically through the death of Judge Pyncheon and ideologically through Holgrave's critique of the past, the Puritan tradition survives in salutary form (radical exorcism having itself been exorcised) in Holgrave's marriage to Phoebe. With "a church-going conscience" (2:154) and a dutiful habit of prayer, Phoebe has just enough religion to maintain the core beliefs needed to keep chaos at bay. In truth, Hawthorne writes, Phoebe is "a Religion in herself, warm, simple, true, with a substance that could walk on earth, and a spirit capable of Heaven" (2:116). Domestic woman is the new Incarnation, happily joining body and immortal soul, the commonplace and the ideal, and she is the *only* incarnation that the secular world of the book seems to require.

Holgrave's late conversion—his wish to "conform [himself] to laws, and the peaceful practice of society" (2:307)—is hastily managed by Hawthorne, with scarcely a hint of psychological plausibility beyond an infatuated lover's homage to his beloved. Its importance is to signal Holgrave's, and through him Hawthorne's, eagerness to join a new domestic, forward-looking New England relieved of its sins and sin-infatuation, shorn of its bullying philistinism, and yet preserving, as Phoebe does in lightened form, the marrow of Puritan rectitude. As in "The May-pole of Merry Mount" and "Endicott and Red Cross," Hawthorne is writing regional myth, but in *Seven Gables* it is a comic myth of rebirth and reconciliation (save for the scapegoated Judge Pyncheon): of past with present, Pyncheon with Maule, and author with middle-class, middlebrow audience.

Exorcism as Self-Excision

> We see young men who owe us a new world, so readily and lavishly
> they promise, but they never acquit the debt; they die young and dodge
> the account: or if they live, they lose themselves in the crowd.
>
> —Emerson, "Experience"

The five days of rain following the death of Judge Pyncheon cleanse the New
England world of *Seven Gables*. The genial sunshine that seems to bless the house
and the blooming of Alice's posies amount to a cultural resurrection, the return
of the sunshine and flowers of Merry Mount that promised to "beautify" New
England before the shadow of Puritanism "darken[ed] all the clime, and [made]
it a land of clouded visages" (9:62). Hawthorne has not repudiated the reality
principle associated with the Puritans' vision; rather, he and New England seem
to have emerged on the thither side of it, as if the long Puritan hegemony constituted an epoch in the development of culture analogous to the sin- and gloom-
ridden phase of psychic life through which individuals had to pass in their moral
growth. The affirmation that "Merry Mount" could make for Edith and Edgar
only with respect to their passage heavenward is made for Phoebe and Holgrave
within temporal life itself. Their heaven, for now, is earth.

"'Pretty good business!' quoth the sagacious Dixey," as Holgrave, Phoebe, and
the others head off to Judge Pyncheon's country house, which they inherit, along
with the judge's tainted fortune (2:319). The windfall is gratuitous, except as a
fairy-tale gift to the reader and an added authorial blessing on the nuptial couple.
What the book is truly celebrating is the installment of healthy, law-abiding
domesticity of the kind Hawthorne believed he had found in his marriage to
Sophia, whom he sometimes called "Phoebe." He professed to be pleased with
the finished book (it delighted Sophia) and to consider it "a more natural and
healthy product of [his] mind" than *The Scarlet Letter* (16:421). As he wrote in
"Main-street," "the blame" for his darker writings rested on "the somber spirit of
our forefathers, who wove their web of life with hardly a single thread of rose-
color or gold, and not on me, who have a tropic love of sunshine, and would
gladly gild the world with it, if I knew where to find so much" (11:78). In *Seven
Gables* he found enough to gild a New England corner of it.

"An artist worth his salt is permanently separated from ordinary reality,"
Nietzsche remarked: "On the other hand, we all know that the constant unreal-
ness of his innermost being will sometimes fill him with despair, and that he will
then attempt what is strictly forbidden him, to be like other men" (Nietzsche
235). Midway through *Seven Gables* Hawthorne wonders what might become of
Holgrave, whom he takes as "the representative of many compeers in his native
land" (2:181). In 1840s America, with "qualities" such as his, "some of the

world's prizes [seemed] within his reach" (2:181). He is one of Emerson's "young men who owe us a new world" (*CWE* 3:30). Will he provide it? In notable ways, Holgrave's marriage plays off that of the "village uncle," who renounces his vocation as artist to marry "a frank, simple, kind hearted, sensible and mirthful girl" remarkably like Phoebe, one who similarly never "shocked a taste" (9:316). Holgrave will not become a coarse rustic like the village uncle; he will become a country squire with a life of an ampler sort, but his artist days will be behind him—the world owing its aesthetic impulse as well as its reformist one "to men ill at ease" (2:306). Late in the narrative Phoebe doubts whether she has "scope enough to make [Holgrave] happy" (2:306). She does, because Holgrave will contract his own to fit hers. Phoebe's domain is "the well-worn path of ordinary life" (2:142). There Holgrave will live, having chosen, like the village uncle, what Nietzsche would say is "strictly forbidden him, to be like other men."

Through Holgrave's engagement, Hawthorne is rendering his own feeling of deliverance through Sophia Peabody; Holgrave's words, "You are my only possibility of happiness," echo a courtship letter of Hawthorne's (2:306, 15:305). Yet even as he celebrates Phoebe as domestic angel and augury of an emergent New England, Hawthorne registers a surreptitious protest, as if aware that in exorcising Puritan gloom with household sunshine he were *excising* a part of himself. With her natural aversion to "mystery" and her "horror" at "all extravagance" (2:218, 166), Phoebe narrowly delimits the province of the real, and Holgrave, for the sake of happiness, stability, and social integration, consents to live within those limits. The rapidity and completeness of his transformation astound Phoebe ("how wonderfully your ideas have changed!" [2:315]), as they have readers. The note of unlikelihood is quickly subsumed into the epithalamic mood of the ending, but it lingers as a hint of bogusness, even of rueful parody. Millicent Bell finds "more pessimism and irony than we have supposed" in Holgrave's submission to a new cultural order scarcely more hospitable to the artist's values and vocation than the old one had been. "At what cost," Bell wonders, has Holgrave's assimilation to the modern and bourgeois been achieved?[37]

So Hawthorne may have wondered about his own domestic bargain as he labored to "pour some setting sunshine" over the ending of his book (16:376). Disagreeable as it was to him, his Salem self had the virtue of unity: the inner man and his writings were one. Beginning in the Manse period, his self split in two—the intuitions of the writer *against* the conventionalisms of the family man. The conclusion to *Seven Gables* seems a triumph of the latter. The convenient but ill-managed quality of Holgrave's conversion—and the fact that Hawthorne, acknowledging as much, let it pass—testify not only to his difficulty in bringing his themes to a satisfactory resolution, but also, perhaps, to a conscious or unconscious wish that acute readers should feel the ending's humbug and take it for the expedient it is. Even as he aligned himself with Holgrave and Phoebe, Hawthorne gauged the consequences of doing so and felt the spuriousness of presenting Holgrave's normalization as an unqualified triumph.

Purged by the death of Judge Pyncheon, the House of the Seven Gables seems "the residence of the stubborn old Puritan, Integrity, who, dying in some forgotten chamber, had left a blessing in all its rooms and chambers, the efficacy of which was to be seen in the religion, honesty, moderate competence, or upright poverty, and solid happiness, of his descendants, to this day" (2:285–86). Formerly a scene of horrors, the house has come to symbolize the worthiest in New England tradition and a link between present and past. Hawthorne's "organic conservatism" points naturally toward Holgrave and Phoebe remaining in the house and sacralizing it through the freshness of love. Why, then, does Hawthorne have them leave it?

In the end, I think, Hawthorne's recoil against Salem overrode both the logic of his fictional themes and the thrust of his ideology. "The farther I get from it," Clifford says of the house, "the more does the joy, the lightsome freshness, the heart-leap, the intellectual dance, the youth, in short—yes, my youth, my youth!—come back to me" (2:262). So Hawthorne felt of Salem. "I detest this town so much that I hate to go into the streets, or to have the people see me," he wrote Horatio Bridge in February 1850, shortly after finishing *The Scarlet Letter*: "Anywhere else, I shall at once be entirely another man" (16:312–13). Indeed he would, though not nearly so much as he liked to think. Having worked to exorcise "Salem" and ratify a pact like Holgrave's with sunny domesticity, it is questionable whether the other man he sought to become would be a deeper, more authentic, or more self-contented one.

A Citizen of Nowhere Else

> After freeing himself from Salem, Hawthorne never found any permanent rest, anywhere.
>
> —Julian Hawthorne, *Nathaniel Hawthorne and His Wife*

As he sets out with Phoebe to begin a new life, Holgrave sees nothing but happiness ahead. Nearly nine years after his honeymoon idyll at the Manse, how did Hawthorne assess a life that was no longer in the making but, so far as he could foresee (an English consulship was nowhere on the horizon), definingly made? Julian notes that "the two or three years" after Hawthorne came to Lenox "comprised his period of greatest literary activity" (*NHW* 1:358). Thanks to the efforts of James T. Fields, they were certainly his period of greatest success. Beyond encouraging Hawthorne to write, actively promoting him, and reprinting his earlier works, Fields, as Richard H. Brodhead says, "converted Hawthorne's work into an *oeuvre*," consolidating "the volumes that Hawthorne produced in straggling fashion…into a visible body" that helped create "the identity 'Hawthorne.'"[38] Spurred by the new "demand" for his work, Hawthorne wrote with greater "facility" than ever (16:462), but writing had become a job; as he told his sister Ebe, he "hate[d] the thought of [it], except from necessity" (16:402). As necessity increased with the birth of his daughter Rose in May 1851, so did his feeling of life closing in; "with each new child," James R. Mellow notes, "Hawthorne turned more reflective and sometimes a bit somber" (Mellow 353). Even success brought its negatives insofar as it demystified the satisfactions of fame. "The 'bubble reputation' is as much a bubble in literature as in war," Hawthorne told Horatio Bridge in March 1851, "and I should be not one whit happier if mine were world-wide and time-long, than I was when nobody but yourself had faith in me" (16:407).

Although Hawthorne had every reason to feel content in 1851–52, readers like Brenda Wineapple and Thomas R. Mitchell seem right in suggesting "a weary, middle-aged discontent."[39] For Mitchell, the friendship and literary example of Melville, a writer whose trajectory in 1851 seemed spectacularly upward, would have reinforced Hawthorne's feeling that he himself "had few years of creative work ahead" and "lacked the enthusiasm and energy of youth."[40] Between the letters of complaint to Ebe and Bridge (March 11 and 15, 1851) is one to Evert Duyckinck (March 14) written from Melville's Arrowhead, where Melville had made his guest "snug and comfortable" (15:404). If, for Melville, visits to Lenox were an escape from stifling domesticity to brandy, cigars, and "ontological heroics" (*WHM* 14:196), for Hawthorne, visiting or hosting Melville may have been the same.

Julian speaks of Lenox as "one of those places where a man might be supposed to write because the beauty around him wooed him to expression" (*NHW* 1:431). Nonetheless, Hawthorne did "not feel at home" there (16:465). The climate in the Berkshires bothered him; he had colds; he missed the seacoast; he quarreled with his landlords; and he came to dislike his cramped red cottage, "certainly the most inconvenient and wretched little hovel that I ever put my head in" (16:454). Ebe blamed Sophia for the move from Lenox—"it is so much like the Peabodys never to be settled. If Nathaniel buys a place, she will have some excuse for leaving it in a year or two" (*EMH* 70)—but in fact no residence would ever satisfy Hawthorne for long.

About the marriage, one can only speculate. As a newlywed at the Old Manse, Hawthorne had felt reborn, but as parenthood, responsibility, and age took their toll, along with the probable waning of his sexual life during and after Sophia's pregnancy of 1850–51, a part of him seems to have chafed at the domestic happiness he had wished for and received. Holgrave and Phoebe make an attractive couple riding off to their nuptials, but can Holgrave be faithful to Holgrave and Phoebe to Phoebe without compromise and dissimulation? For Hawthorne, Sophia's constitutional optimism amounted to an invitation, almost a command, to veil a nature already given to veils. "Such an unviolated sanctuary as was his nature," Sophia told Annie Fields shortly after Hawthorne's death in 1864, "I his inmost wife never conceived nor knew."[41]

T. Walter Herbert's portrait of the marriage as a "battlefield of souls" is sensationalized and often rings untrue.[42] The invisible but probably more significant struggle was within each partner as each grew conscious, or strove to remain *un*conscious, of the self-abridgments and self-betrayals attached to the life they had made together. Sophia curtailed her art and a good deal of her sociability, Hawthorne his footlooseness, physical and intellectual. Fictively, his resentments took the form of a semicovert hostility toward the Sophia-based Phoebe and later Hilda, objects of an effusive authorial praise interlaced with qualifications, disparagements, and sometimes (especially in *The Marble Faun*) near-gibes. His repetition of "little" with Phoebe and his wearisome emphasis on her conformity to "ordinary rules" (2:305), her intolerance of whatever departs from them, and her limited appreciation of depth, mystery, and suffering even after her supposed development during the course of the book—all betray an impatience indicative of Hawthorne's own as the horizons of life contracted after the Manse years. The marriage that gave promise of embodying a felicitous middle way between Puritanism and Merry Mount, the oppressively moral and the blithely hedonistic, turned out to be a decorous adulteration of both, with neither the depth and earnestness of the Puritan's way nor the playful sensuousness of the Merry Mounter's. Instead, he found to his mild chagrin, life had simply grown bourgeois.

6

Sisters Act

Our objects, as you know, are to insure a more natural union between intellectual and manual labor than now exists; to combine the thinker and the worker, as far as possible, in the same individual; to guarantee the highest mental freedom, by providing all with labor, adapted to their tastes and talents, and securing to them the fruits of their industry; to do away with the necessity of menial services, by opening the benefits of education and the profits of labor to all; and thus to prepare a society of liberal, intelligent, and cultivated persons, whose relations with each other would permit a more simple and wholesome life, than can be led amidst the pressures of our competitive institutions.

—George Ripley to Ralph Waldo Emerson
(November 9, 1840), on Brook Farm

In abolishing private property we deprive the human love of aggression of one of its instruments, certainly a strong one, though certainly not the strongest; but we have in no way altered the differences in power and influence which are misused by aggressiveness, nor have we altered anything in its nature.

—Freud, *Civilization and Its Discontents*

Going Forward, Looking Back

The ancient manners were giving way.
> —Emerson, *"Historic Notes of Life and Letters in New England"*

He talked a lot about the past, and I gathered that he wanted to recover something, some idea of himself, perhaps.

—Fitzgerald, *The Great Gatsby*

In chapter 14 of *The Blithedale Romance*, "Eliot's Pulpit," Hawthorne prefaces the book's pivotal debate on gender, sexuality, and feminist reform with narrator Miles Coverdale's self-conscious invocation of the Pilgrims, "whose high enterprise, as we flattered ourselves, we had taken up and, and, and were carrying… onward and aloft, to a point which they never dreamed of attaining" (3:117). Where *The Scarlet Letter* opens in the shadow of the prison door and with an announced skepticism toward any projected utopia, *Blithedale* begins as a neo-Puritan errand into the wilderness undertaken to establish "the life of Paradise anew" (3:9). Like *Walden*, the record of another such errand, the book is at once a dramatized experiment-in-progress and a report on the experiment's results. While *Walden*, however, presents itself as a chronicle of success—life has not "proved to be mean"[1]—*Blithedale*, as though marking a terminus for American Renaissance hopes, confesses its founders' hopes "exploded" (3:9). The morning atmosphere of the early to middle 1840s has given way to midcentury's prosaic afternoon.

The rueful "sigh" Coverdale heaves as he begins his narrative is not wholly a function of hindsight (3:9). From the outset of his adventure, Coverdale is sensible of the paradoxes involved in combining intellectual and physical labor, of living cooperatively within a competitive market society, of redefining gender roles even as women are assigned to the kitchen, laundry, and sewing room and men to the fields, of disavowing class distinctions while retaining the tastes of gentility, and of enjoying a pristine relation to nature while pitching manure. Still earlier, Coverdale sees the fate of the enterprise portended in the freshly fallen snow as it receives "the impress of somebody's patched boot or overshoe" (3:11). As A. N. Kaul says, "the main characters of the story" bring to Blithedale "the outwardly repudiated social values and attitudes" of the world they flee.[2] They also bring the sexual and aggressive impulses of human nature.

Despite his awareness of the community's quixoticism and ultimate failure, Coverdale is deeply attached to the memory of it, as though whatever life he may have passionately lived occurred within the span of those summer months. The nostalgia in the book is not Coverdale's alone. Even as he worked more industriously than ever, Hawthorne, like Coverdale, seems to have felt that inwardly his life had "come to rather an idle pass" (3:247). Having arrived at age forty-seven as an established author and a financially solvent man among men, he found success wanting and, as Thomas R. Mitchell says, "began to look backward—not just to his summer at Brook Farm but to what he would call... 'the summertime of life' that had 'passed away,'"[3] especially his years in Concord. By May 2, 1852, when he sent the *Blithedale* manuscript to E. P. Whipple, he had already arranged to purchase Bronson Alcott's Concord house. Having imaginatively returned to Brook Farm / Concord in his new romance, he would now return in fact.

A Knot of Dreamers

I wish, at least, you would help me to choose a name. I have put "Hollingsworth," on the title-page, but that is not irrevocable....Here are others—"Blithedale,"—well enough, but with no positive merit or suitability. "Miles Coverdale's Three Friends";—this title comprehends the book but rather clumsily. "The Veiled Lady"—too melodramatic;

and besides, I do not wish to give prominence to that feature of the
Romance.... "The Blithedale Romance"—that would do, in lack of a
better.

—Hawthorne to E. P. Whipple (May 2, 1852)

At one point or another Hawthorne thought of titling his book after each of its
four major characters. His final choice may signify an evasion of choice, as
Richard H. Brodhead says,[4] but as the Blithedale community quickly resolves
itself into Coverdale and his three friends (the larger community being peripheral,
its members nameless except for Silas Foster), his title may be taken to suggest
the set of relationships among what he oxymoronically calls "A Knot of Dreamers"
(ch. 3). A knot may be a cluster or group; it may be a tangle; or, as Coverdale will
later claim, it may be a problem presented for his personal solution. Dreamers
may be idealists, but they may also be fantasizers spinning out fictions about
themselves and others. *Blithedale's* image of a "knot of dreamers" functions like
The Scarlet Letter's prison door; it is a threshold symbol announcing the impending
conflict between utopian idealism and human imperfection.

The lines of the story are evident early on. In "A Knot of Dreamers" Zenobia
glowingly voices her admiration for Hollingsworth ("what a man he is!") despite
the fact that she "could never tolerate a philanthropist, before." "Neither can
I now!" Coverdale replies, promptly baring his hostility toward a rival who as
lecturer has "deeply" moved Zenobia, whose "perfectly developed figure" he has
been picturing in a fig leaf (3:21–22, 17). The significance of the exchange is
underscored by what immediately preceded it, Coverdale's rendering of the
"generous" impulse of Blithedale's founders, who sought to replace the economic
competitiveness of society "with familiar love" (3:19). Structurally, through juxtaposition, the chapter anticipates Freud's argument against a later knot of
dreamers (communists) in *Civilization and Its Discontents*: "If we do away with
personal rights over material wealth, there still remains prerogative in the field of
sexual relationships, which is bound to become the source of the strongest
dislike and the most violent hostility among men who in other respects are
on an equal footing."[5]

In "The Supper-Table" the knot is tightened with the entrance of Hollingsworth
escorting a bedraggled Priscilla, who falls on her knees before Zenobia with a
look of adoration and mute beseechment. As Zenobia draws back, Hollingsworth
"positively frown[s] at her," "stern and reproachful"; with "that inauspicious
meaning in his glance," Coverdale interjects, Hollingsworth "began his influence
upon her life" (3:28). The scene is a miniature of the story ahead, down to
Zenobia's capitulation before Hollingsworth and Coverdale's position as marginalized observer. Hawthorne will complicate his plot, flesh out his characters,
and endow them with ideas, histories, and archetypal resonances, but the core of

his action lies here, in the circumstance of these would-be millennialists subject to sexual impulses they as yet barely recognize.

The backdrop for *Blithedale*'s drama of contention is an ontological void. In no romance of Hawthorne's are God, moral law, and Providential design so thoroughly absent. Although Hollingsworth is shown praying, none of the book's characters are governed by religion; history appears as a "chaos of human struggle" (3:246); and the narrative voice, secular and ironic, is unsoftened by the familiar Hawthornean pieties. Beneath its overt themes, *Blithedale* is a study of human beings left to themselves in a world left to itself. As Priscilla peers through the "uncurtained" kitchen windows that first night, "the sense of vast, undefined space, pressing from the outside against the black panes…, was fearful to her.… The house probably seemed to her adrift on the great ocean of the night" (3:36). Men and women huddled together before a fire against "the awfulness that really exists in [the] limitless extent" outside (3:36): this is *Blithedale*'s image for the human position in the universe.[6]

At another dinner table in a different cultural milieu, Virginia Woolf's Mrs. Ramsay lights the evening candles and uses her social genius to compose a group of discordant individuals into something like a harmonious community—an "island" of precarious order and stability making "common cause against [the] fluidity" of the darkness outside.[7] This is what civilization is for Woolf: a stay against entropy created and maintained through unremitting human effort lest the darkness in the world and the darkness in the self plunge things into chaos. When Mrs. Ramsay leaves the room, and later when she dies, "a sort of disintegration set[s] in."[8] There is no Mrs. Ramsay in *The Blithedale Romance*, no Phoebe to create a modest housewifely facsimile of order, and no social institutions to ensure stability or impose restraint. There are only the jostlings of strong- or weak-willed individuals with their baggage of history, their identic myths, and their aggressive or passive-aggressive agendas. These are the knot of dreamers "whose present bivouâc was considerably farther into the waste of chaos than any mortal army of crusaders had ever marched before" (3:52). In other words, these are the vanguard of the modern.

Pandora's Box

> Prometheus is the archetype-hero of the performance principle. And in the world of Prometheus, Pandora, the female principle, sexuality and pleasure, appear as curse—disruptive, destructive.… The beauty of the woman, and the happiness she promises[,] are fatal in the work-world of civilization.
>
> —Herbert Marcuse, *Eros and Civilization*

In this prolonged interview [between the serpent and Eve], the unprej-
udiced reader must be impressed with the courage, the dignity, and the
lofty ambition of the woman.

—Elizabeth Cady Stanton, commentary on Genesis 3:1–24,
The Woman's Bible (1895)

Soon after Zenobia welcomes him to Blithedale with "a fine, frank, mellow voice," a "soft and warm" (though not demurely small) hand, and "a glimpse of white shoulder" (3:14, 15), Coverdale offers a description of her. Like Hester, Zenobia is tall, dark-haired, regal, and voluptuous in a way that sets her off from the delicate mid-nineteenth-century feminine ideal. The physical difference is also a difference of character and bearing. Zenobia's "free, careless, generous modes of expression" (3:16) testify to the vitalizing energies of sex suppressed by official culture. Coverdale enlarges on how delightful it is to meet a woman who is truly a woman—"not," he says, "that I would convey the idea of especial gentleness, grace, modesty, and shyness, but of a certain warm and rich characteristic, which seems, for the most part, to have been refined away out of the feminine system" (3:17).

Coverdale's attitude toward Zenobia will pass through several phases, but his ongoing ambivalence toward her and woman generally is contained in these words "refined away," which may mean sifted and cleansed of impurities or, anti-thetically, deprived of nutriment and vigor. Is "natural" womanhood desirable—refinement yielding an insipid, if culturally valued product, as white sugar and white bread have been valued—or is the natural crude and unusable for pur-poses of civilization, like unrefined petroleum, unrefined gold, or the kindly but unrefined Silas Foster? As emblematized by the hothouse flower in her hair, Zenobia is both a woman of nature, luxuriantly sexual, and a woman of culture, elegantly artificial. Nonetheless, Coverdale's first impression is correct: Zenobia is extraordinary for her physical vitality.

Two readings of history, grounded in two notions of the relationship between body and spirit, collide here. In one, humanity, in becoming civilized, is seen as having severed itself from the sources of pleasure and must recorporealize itself or emotionally wither. In the other, civilization is viewed as a process of *decor-porealization* in which the matter is transmuted into spirit and sensual pleasure into the satisfactions of culture, or at least the proprieties of middle-class life.

Nina Baym sees the myth of sublimation as "diabolic" in its "crude equation... between spirit and lack of body," resulting in an "abnormal" eroticism "in which young, frail, immature girls [like Priscilla] become objects of sexual interest while fully sexed adult women [like Zenobia] are experienced as frightening, corrupt, or repellent."[9] Abnormal for whom? not for a large segment of Anglo-American Victorian culture. In *The Scarlet Letter*, though "ladylike" in the "an-tique" sense of having majesty or state, Hester belongs morally as well as materially to a "coarser" age whose physicality time has winnowed into the "delicate, evanescent, and indescribable grace" of nineteenth-century woman (1:53). Is this progress or debilitation? Hawthorne is equivocal, mirroring a culture for which "nervousness" in both sexes (but especially in women) was regarded at once as a malady and as a token of evolutionary superiority. Jaffrey Pyncheon in *The House of the Seven Gables* is ethically no whit better than the bluff, beefy colonel of Puritan days, but to the extent that his complexion is "sallow" rather than "ruddy" and his temperament marked by a "quicker mobility" and a "keener vivacity," he illustrates what the book proposes as "the great system of human progress, which, with every ascending footstep, as it diminishes the necessity for animal force, may be destined gradually to spiritualize us by refining away our grosser attributes of body" (2:121). Jaffrey's problem, like that of "most other men"—grossness for Hawthorne was an almost exclusively male quality, until he met British dowagers—is that he has not evolved *enough* and could use a "century or two more of such refinement" to relieve him of his "remarkable degree of fundamental development" (2:121).

Zenobia and Hester are magnificently physical women, but as such are they auguries of a regenerating new naturalism or throwbacks to an old anarchic naturalism? In a latter-day inversion of Freud, Marilyn French mounts a critique of Western culture whose terms are remarkably similar to Hawthorne's. Like Freud, French identifies the male with civilization, the female with nature; but where Freud saw civilization as a bulwark against nature, French sees it, in its dominant Western form, as a life-denying impediment to nature. "The masculine principle" for French is impatient with earth and hostile to its rhythm of birth, growth, decay, and death; "it aims to construct something [an idea, an institution, a movement, a dynasty] in the world and within time that will enable the individual to transcend" the cyclicality of nature and achieve "a sort of immortality."[10] The feminine principle is twofold. In its "outlaw" aspect it is aligned with nature, celebrates pleasure (especially sexuality), and accepts the finality of death; in its "inlaw" aspect it is a creation of and handmaiden to the patriarchy, for which it serves "as a moral touchstone...lifting man from his essential bestiality" within the forms and purposes of male-dominated civilization (French 25).

In *Blithedale*, Zenobia is a representative of the outlaw feminine, Priscilla of the inlaw feminine, and Hollingsworth of the transcendent masculine. This is the cultural framework in which the romance takes place, but with what assignments of value? Within patriarchal ideology, the function of the hero is to raise benighted man from brutishness to civilization, as Hollingsworth would raise criminals; within feminist ideology, the function of the heroine is to provide a vital corrective to civilization's goal-directed sublimations. What is *Blithedale*'s "ideology"?

In likening its outlaw woman, Zenobia, to Pandora and Eve, Coverdale anticipates the divided attitude the book will take toward her as an instrument of
potential liberation and potential havoc. Highly sexed though she is, Zenobia as
Pandora/Eve is not narrowly identified with nature or the body. Her claims are
for a full and free participation in life and an expression of the total human personality, intellectual and aesthetic as well as romantic/erotic. The tree whose
fruit Eve samples is the tree of knowledge; Pandora's motive is curiosity. The
weakness of both women in patriarchal myth—in feminist myth it is their
strength—is that they wish to know more than they are permitted to know. They
break through the male-imposed confines of their situation and in doing so,
according to myth, bring disaster upon the world. Feminist countermyth might
see it otherwise. As Elizabeth Cady Stanton reads Genesis, the tempter "roused in
the woman that intense thirst for knowledge that the simple pleasures of picking
flowers and talking to Adam could not satisfy."[11] Eve rebels in order to become
adult and fully human.

Like other Hawthorne males (and Hawthorne himself), Coverdale is at once
entranced by female sexuality and discomfited by it, or by the feelings of pruri-
ence it awakens in him. "Assuredly, Zenobia could not have intended it—the
fault must have been entirely in my imagination," Coverdale says as an innuendo
of Zenobia's prompts him to imagine her "fine, perfectly developed figure, in
Eve's earliest garment" (3:17). It is troubling for Coverdale to confront his sexual
feelings, still more to think they might have been deliberately provoked by a
respectable woman. Even so, his attitude toward Zenobia remains admiring
until, during his illness, his sensitized intuition hints that she "has lived, and
loved" (3:47). He does not mentally accuse Zenobia of unchastity, simply of
having been "a wife" (3:47). His word "lived" is as significant as "loved"; indeed,
the two are entwined, since female nonvirginity for Coverdale (and Hawthorne)
is at once a physical and a metaphysical condition. As the latter, it involves a
worldliness that is unbecoming, even hazardous for women in their role as repos-
itories of morality, redeemers of men, and pillars of a religiosity that supports an
otherwise shaky cosmic optimism. In Hawthorne's fiction, as in his marriage,
women serve men and the interests of civilization through what they are *not*
allowed to know, think, be, and do.

Zenobia is a Pandora who has opened the proscribed box or an Eve who has
eaten the apple. "She made no scruple of oversetting all human institutions,"
especially those involving "the relation between the sexes," a "startled" Coverdale
says (3:44). Her ideas are the lesser part of her radicalism. "In her person," Irving
Howe remarks, "is realized the threat to traditional modes of life which the
others merely talk about."[12] Far more than Hester, who outwardly conforms,
Zenobia "step[s] out of the common path"—with success, too, for "the world"
grudgingly concedes "the sphere of ordinary womanhood" to be "narrower than

her development required" (3:190). Through Zenobia, Hawthorne enlarges on the feminist critique adumbrated in "Another View of Hester"; he dramatizes the rebellious womanhood that Hester can display only in moments; yet beyond these things, and beyond gender itself, he plays out an impulse to reorder social arrangements to conduce to human freedom and self-realization. Zenobia as Pandora is the protagonist of *Blithedale*—of its plot because as agent or object she is the initiator of its sexual tensions, and of its social theme because she, not the sketchily drawn Blithedale community, is the vehicle for its most generous hopes for the future.

Eliot's Pulpit

> The business of the political novelist, as Hawthorne pioneers it in *The Blithedale Romance*, is…to uncover the play of passion taking place through and under the play of public ideas, and more specifically to bare the mechanisms by which the energies of sexuality, voice, and political conviction transform themselves into one another.
>
> —Richard H. Brodhead, *The School of Hawthorne*

> With the intellect I always have, always shall, overcome; but that is not half of the work. The life! the life! O, my God! shall the life never be sweet?"
>
> —Margaret Fuller, *Memoirs of Margaret Fuller Ossoli*

In "Eliot's Pulpit" issues of feminism, sexuality, and social prophecy come to a head. Outwardly a symposium of ideas, inwardly, as Brodhead says, a drama of their entanglement with private motives and myths, the chapter is also Hawthorne's colloquy with himself on gender matters as inflected by his intellectual and personal relationship with Margaret Fuller. In his previous romances, narrative intrusions had established a framework of value against which the text might struggle, even rebel, but from whose confines it could never wholly escape. In "Eliot's Pulpit" there is neither an omniscient narrative voice nor a reliable dramatic one. Coverdale, whose relationship to Hawthorne is unstable throughout the text, plays an especially multifarious role in this chapter—by turns, observer, commentator, agent provocateur, authorial surrogate, and invested participant, in this last function no more authoritative than any of the other characters. Hawthorne is not simply letting his dramatis personae play out their natures; the positions they take, even when obviously rooted in character and situation, are nearly always refractions of some thought or attitude of his own. It is as if he were standing outside himself and staging a monodrama. Dialogues sometimes work toward a resolution. That this one does not, except in terms of the power relationships among its speakers, illustrates what Paul John

Eakin calls the "debilitating dependencies" that mold and are molded by group interactions, even ostensibly intellectual ones.[13]

Because "Eliot's Pulpit" is a dense, resonant chapter, I would like to explore it under successive headings and as it appears in conversation with Fuller's writing and example, the latter especially as Hawthorne witnessed it during her ten-day visit to the Old Manse in July 1844. Despite Hawthorne's prefatory claim that *Blithedale*'s "characters...are entirely fictitious" (3:2), contemporary readers quickly recognized Fuller in Zenobia, an association Hawthorne coyly invites by having Priscilla convey a letter of Fuller's to the bedridden Coverdale and even assume (partly because of her clairvoyant gifts, partly because she is the half sister of Zenobia/Fuller) something of Fuller's aspect. Feminism for Hawthorne centered on Fuller, who signified to him not a collection of writings or a set of ideas but a circumstanced "case": the writings emerged from the life; the life reflected back upon the writings.

1. "...the injustice which the world did to women, and equally to itself, by not allow-ing them...their natural utterance in public" (3:120). Zenobia's words echo a main argument in *Woman in the Nineteenth Century* directed against the contemporary notion of separate spheres determined by nature, man's sphere being the public world, woman's the home. Fuller herself pays homage to this idea when she allows that even in a reformed society "a large proportion of women" would still "delight to make the nest soft and warm. Nature would take care of that" (*WNC* 175). Fuller had strong maternal feelings of her own, and, visiting Concord in the summer of 1844, she was literally surrounded by newborns—Emerson's son Edward, her sister Ellen and Ellery Channing's daughter Greta (named after her-self), and, her favorite, the Hawthornes' Una, "a most beautiful child" in whom she delighted.[14] Her concern in *Woman* is with women like herself who have other talents and ambitions and/or who by choice or circumstance do not marry.

Hawthorne would not have given Zenobia's words the textual power he did if he did not sympathize with her grievance, yet the thrust of his public and private statements is toward a rejection of public woman on the ground of unseemli-ness. As he wrote in the early sketch "Mrs. Hutchinson" (and to some degree would always believe), "the display of woman's naked mind to the gaze of the world" constitutes "a sort of impropriety" scarcely less objectionable than the display of her naked body.[15] On this subject, Hawthorne practiced what he preached. Although Sophia was a talented writer, "after their marriage," Thomas Woodson notes, Hawthorne "never permitted her to seek public outlets, pur-portedly because of his prejudice against women of letters" (15:31). Sophia shared the prejudice herself. Years before she met Hawthorne she was furious with her sister Elizabeth for circulating her Cuba journal: "I feel as if the nation were feeling my pulse.... If I were stuck up bodily upon a pole & carried about the streets I could not feel more *exposed*."[16] Objecting to Fuller's "speech...from the throne" (*WNC*)), Sophia remarked that even before her marriage she felt "that each woman could make her own sphere quietly" and that "it was always a shock to [her] to have women mount the rostrum" (*NHW* 1:257). The definition Hollingsworth gives of woman's "office"—that of "the Sympathizer, the unreserved, unquestioning Believer," the helpmate who supports self-doubting man by saying of his work, "'It is well done!'" (3:122)—is the one Sophia defined for herself and took pride in. As Julian put it, "She believed in [Hawthorne's] inspiration; and her office was to promote, as far as in her lay, the favorableness of the conditions under which it should manifest itself" (*NHW* 1:40). Hollingsworth's belief that "the heart of true womanhood knows where its own sphere is, and never seeks to stray beyond it!" (3:123) is also Sophia's: "Home, I think, is the great arena for women, and there, I am sure, she can wield a power which no king or conqueror can cope with" (*NHW* 1:257).

In *Woman* Fuller identifies the condition for woman's inner freedom as "self-impulse," the decision to live not for husband and family's sake but "*first* for God's sake," that is to say, for her own sake as a God-infused being (*WNC* 176). Hollingsworth calls this self-dependent woman a "monster" (3:123). Although the scene aligns readers with Coverdale in protesting this "outrageous affirmation of...masculine egotism" (3:123), in substance Hollingsworth's position could pass for Hawthorne's, certainly for his wife's. "I did not like the tone of it," Sophia wrote her mother of *Woman*, "& did not agree with her at all about the change in woman's outward circumstances."[17] Hollingsworth sees feminist agitation as the refuge of those who have "missed women's peculiar happiness" (Sophia's view as well) or who are "really neither man nor woman" (3:123; v. *NHW* 1:257), a subtle dig at Fuller as pilloried by hostile contemporaries. Hollingsworth's abusiveness belongs to his character and situation, but when Coverdale observes that "Hollingsworth had boldly uttered what he, and millions of despots like him, really felt" (3:123), his words extend to men like Hawthorne as well.

What is remarkable about "Eliot's Pulpit" is how it scrambles, even inverts, Hawthorne family pronouncements about gender. While Hollingsworth's views, which resemble Hawthorne's and Sophia's, are made to seem harsh, bigoted, and overbearing, Zenobia's on public woman, which are *not* Hawthorne's, appear as reasonable, socially productive, and just. Hawthorne the artist is creating drama from ideas, yet can a writer so thoroughly detach himself from his typical opinions as to elicit sympathy for what he privately condemns, antipathy for what he professedly believes? "Eliot's Pulpit" suggests that the radical division within Hawthorne's nature is not simply a conflict of ideas and values but of moods or levels of being. Like most of us, Hawthorne had a magnanimous self and a pettish self. A man of acute perception, pragmatic good sense, principled fairness, and (toward his friends) extraordinary loyalty and generosity, he was also a man of conventions, prejudices, irritabilities, and moral and philosophical trip wires, the most sensitive of which related to sex and to woman's nature and role. In "Eliot's Pulpit" he seems, initially at least, to be writing from his worthier self and subjecting his lesser to clear-eyed criticism.

2. "*[Women] are not natural reformers, but become such by the pressure of exceptional misfortune. I could measure Zenobia's inward trouble, by the animosity with which she now took up the general quarrel of woman against man*" (3:121). In saying this, Coverdale has the advantage of special knowledge, having overheard Zenobia's conversation with Westervelt on the wood-path; his view, however, is consonant with Hawthorne's elsewhere. In speculating on the roots of feminist reform, Hawthorne was extrapolating from the life and work of Fuller as he understood them. Zenobia's entanglement with Westervelt draws closely upon Fuller's sketch "Mariana" from *Summer on the Lakes, 1843* (1844), in which an ardent, intellectual young woman gives herself to a shallow, unfeeling man in whom "a whole province of her being" finds nothing answerable[18]—in *Blithedale's* words, "finds that the real womanhood, within her, has no corresponding part in him" (3:103). The question left hanging in both texts is whether, "with a heart capable of the highest Eros,"[19] a woman like Mariana or Zenobia could have found satisfaction in avenues *other* than love.

This was a matter Fuller agonized over for herself. To those who knew her well, as Hawthorne did from her Concord visits of 1842 and 1844, Mariana's frustrations of mind, heart, and vocation were a projection of Fuller's own. Within the decorous New England world of the late 1830s and early 1840s, Fuller stood out, in Emerson's words, as a "foreigner" whose intensities "foreboded rash and painful crises."[20] Where others saw in Fuller "unemployed" powers—"She had no room for utterance, no sphere adequate," James Freeman Clarke lamented (*MMFO* 1:135)—Hawthorne also saw diverted powers. Fuller's peculiar but representative tragedy, as he came to formulate it, was that of a nature frustrated in the culturally authorized path of marriage, denied or unable to find fulfillment in other paths—as Zenobia says, "the pen is not for woman. Her power is too natural and immediate"; Fuller agreed (3:120; *WNC* 115)—and consequently thrown back upon itself in eccentricity and defiance.

As Hawthorne read "Mariana" and *Woman in the Nineteenth Century* with Fuller's visit to the Manse freshly in mind, he must have felt as Coverdale would after hearing Zenobia on the wood-path. He had been granted a privileged glimpse of the private life and could view the obverse side of the public pronouncement. The period May through July 1844 was an especially trying one for Fuller, whose "almost daily entries" in her journal, her editors note, "show her struggle to reconcile 'deep yearnings of the heart' with the wounding and disappointing reality of insufficient love" (*MFJ* 38). Her most recent involvement may have been with William Clarke, brother of her friends James Freeman and Sarah Clarke, who had served as her guide in the Midwest (*MJF* 43–50).[21] In any case, Fuller felt herself "left a 'lady in waiting,' wanting a 'worthy' relationship, coping with the pain of this disappointing one, and determined to renounce love and be alone rather than be in an imperfect one" (*MFJ* 48). This was more easily said than done. "O I need some help. No I need a full a godlike embrace from some sufficient love" (*MFJ* 71), she wrote on July 4, less than a week before arriving at the Old Manse. Her firm resolve, her literary work, and the kindness of friends like the Hawthornes did help, and presently she was "able to take the superior views of life, and my place in it." "But," she added, "I know the deep yearnings of the heart & the bafflings of time will again be felt, & then I shall long for some dear hand to hold" (*MFJ* 92).

Fuller often confided in male friends, and it would have been surprising if she did not confide in Hawthorne, whom she found "mild, deep, and large" and, except for his habitual reserve, potentially more "a brother to me than... ever any man before" (*MFJ* 85, 108). Clarke writes of "conversations, in which, impelled by the strong instinct of utterance, she would state, in words of tragical pathos, her own needs and longings,—her demands on life,—her conflicts with self, with nature, with the limitations of circumstances, with insoluble problems, with an unattainable desire" (*MMFO* 1:108). Hawthorne probably heard or intuited such things as well. It was one thing to assert, as Fuller did in *Woman*, that "the legitimacy of freedom" for contemporary women must be established by "the power of continence" (*WNC* 118–19); it was quite another, as Hawthorne would have observed, to live with its exactions.

If the example of Fuller made Hawthorne keenly sensitive to the tragedy of gifted women and the injustice done them, it also disposed him to rationalize their feminism as a product of private trials. As Zenobia vows to "lift up [her] own voice, in behalf of woman's wider liberty" (3:120), Coverdale smiles knowingly. We dislike him for his smirk, yet insofar as we, too, have overheard Zenobia and Westervelt,[22] we are obliged to concede its element of psychological truth.

3. *"Poor child!... She is the type of womanhood, such as man has spent centuries in making it"* (3:122). Zenobia is referring to Priscilla the "gentle parasite" (3:123), who would happily submit to man's protective strength. If Zenobia resembles Fuller's Minerva (the active, intellectual, masculine side of androgynous female nature), Priscilla as clairvoyant is the extreme of the "feminine" side, or "Muse," as characterized by an "unimpeded clearness of the intuitive powers" (*WNC* 116). In defining woman's essential nature as "electrical in movement, intuitive in function, [and] spiritual in tendency" (*WNC* 115), Fuller reinscribes the contemporary gender ideal but with two important differences: she sees the requirements of the social moment giving "preference" to Minerva (*WNC* 118), and she distinguishes the Muse as sibylline prophetess from her much-diminished

alter ego, Victorian culture's angel in the house, or Marilyn French's "inlaw woman."

Coverdale pays homage to an idealized form of inlaw woman when he counters Zenobia's feminism with a professed feminism of his own: an adulation of Madonna-woman as a repository of "tenderness" and of "the religious sentiment in its utmost depth and purity" (3:122, 121). Zenobia scorns such spineless adoration, not only because it desexualizes woman but also because it demeans man, who "is never content, unless he can degrade himself by stooping towards what he loves" (3:122). To justify and reinforce their exclusion of women from public life, Zenobia implies, men have gilded women's cage by assigning them the role of spiritual redeemer and in so doing have externalized many of their own better qualities. As a critique of nineteenth-century gender ideology, Zenobia's words are trenchant, yet like so much in "Eliot's Pulpit" they tell against Hawthorne himself, who shared the substance of Coverdale's view and even, in his courtship letters, its elevated rhetoric. As Julian said, Hawthorne "believed, and was delighted to believe, in the higher purity and (as it were) angelic wisdom of [Sophia's] feminine nature," which he regarded as the crown of feminine nature generally (*NHW* 1:42).

The stances of Coverdale and Hollingsworth are extreme projections of the self-contradiction within Hawthorne and within patriarchal ideology itself, which nominally pedestalized women even as it practically subordinated them. Zenobia's contempt for the attitudes of both men is Hawthorne's, yet so, paradoxically, are the attitudes themselves. In this single chapter, Hawthorne has managed to separate out the strands in his conception of women, externalize them in his dramatic characters, and let them contend with each other, observing their interplay as if the contention itself were the chief object of interest, the ideas themselves being epiphenomena of character.

4. "'Women almost invariably behave thus!' thought I. 'What does the fact mean? Is it their nature? Or is it, at last, the result of ages of compelled degradation? And, in either case, will it be possible ever to redeem them?'" (3:124). Coverdale is responding to Zenobia's abject surrender to Hollingsworth and his own "ill-luck" in finding himself an object of scant interest to both women after "freely conced[ing] all their claims" (3:124). By "redeem" Coverdale means "deliver from social and psychological bondage." The irony is that woman, conventionally portrayed as man's deliverer, is seen here as requiring deliverance herself—deliverance *from* man. Measuring Zenobia by Fuller's standard of self-impulse, Coverdale pronounces her, personally and as a representative of her sex, a Minerva manqué.

In the end, is Hawthorne, through Coverdale, challenging women to rise to Fuller's ideal or, with a show of ruefulness, taking secret satisfaction in their failure to do so? Years later in Rome, after hearing stories about Fuller and Angelo Ossoli, he would exult in what he took to be Fuller's disintegration: "And, by and by, this rude old potency [in her nature] bestirred itself, and undid all her labor [at self-creation] in the twinkling of an eye. On the whole, I do not know but I like her the better for it... because she proved herself a very woman, after all, and fell as the weakest of her sisters might" (14:157). There is no more devastating passage in all of Hawthorne's notebooks. Having fictionalized Fuller's submission in Zenobia's, Hawthorne seems to have felt vindicated to find life imitating art.

Zenobia's surrender brings the dialogue in "Eliot's Pulpit" to an abrupt close. Whatever the social and political right of the matter, psychologically, given Zenobia's character, self-impulse has shown itself an unrealizable ideal. The questions for feminist reform, and for *Blithedale* as a would-be prophetic or conservative text, are whether nature or culture is at fault and, if culture, what might be done about it.

Spheres of Influence

> The events are purely mental.... Three persons of essentially different characters and purposes, are placed together; the law of spiritual influence, the magnetism of soul on soul begins to operate; and the processes of thought and emotions are then presented in perfect logical order to their inevitable catastrophe.
>
> —E. P. Whipple, unsigned review of *The Blithedale Romance*

Friends of Fuller often described her effect on people as magnetic. To be intimate with Fuller was to be brought within her gravitational field and exposed to the force of her personality. James Freeman Clarke spoke of "the magnetism by which she drew [her friends] toward herself," Emerson of the young women who gathered around her as "quite reduced... to satellites" (*MMFO* 1:75, 280). Both men were appealing to the language of animal magnetism, or mesmerism, a phenomenon widely popular in the later 1830s and 1840s whether as a stage entertainment, a medical treatment (Fuller and Sophia Hawthorne both consulted mesmerists for headaches), or a science or pseudoscience that seemed to enlarge the realm of natural laws and blur the boundaries between the material and the spiritual.

Aside from lending an aura of romance to his realistic materials, mesmerism supplied Hawthorne with a figurative language for exploring the psychodynamics of his characters' relationships and of human relationships generally. In this latter respect, it reached beyond individual psychology to a theory of motivation, and beyond that to suppositions about the processes and ends of natural life and their connection to spiritual life. The cosmological pretensions originally attached to mesmerism—its notion of an all-pervasive "universal fluid"[23]— were of scant interest to Hawthorne except as they evoked the prospect of empty materialism. What intrigued him was mesmeric possession as an extreme in-stance of, and a ruling metaphor for, the play of dominations that seemed at work in human interactions, which he signified in *Blithedale* through the motifs of magnetism and "spheres of influence."

Rooted in the body (sexuality), magnetism in *Blithedale* is a charismatic power that radiates outward through the entire personality with a force that var-ies in individuals from the weak to the spellbinding. Zenobia and Hollingsworth have powerful magnetism. Coverdale calls Hollingsworth's a species of "necromancy" in its hold on Zenobia and Priscilla (3:124), but he feels it, too, as Hollingsworth tries to enlist him in his reformist cause. Coverdale himself has but "a feeble degree of magnetism," as he says apropos of Priscilla's tepid response to his offered hand (3:168); he has still less when illness wastes his physical substance and temporarily endows him with the powers of a "mesmerical clairvoyant" receiving the impress of others (3:47). "The spheres of our companions have, at such periods," he writes, "a vastly greater influence upon our own, than when robust health gives us a repellent and self-defensive energy" (3:46).

Coverdale's "spheres" are not the contemporary domains of gender performance; as Richard H. Brodhead observes, they are "fields of force—zones of charged energies that repel or attract one another, and that interpenetrate one another in such a way that the force of the weaker field gets captured by and reorganized on the lines of the stronger."[24] Emerson used gravitational imagery for the anxiety he sometimes felt about being "warped" by a book "clean out of [his] own orbit, and made a satellite instead of a system" (*CWE* 1:56). For Emerson, persons, too, had to be cultivated judiciously and kept at a safe dis-tance, "lest" in "talk[ing] to them and study[ing] their visions" one should "lose [one's] own" (*CWE* 2:126). The instinctive tendency of the self is to resist incor-poration—Coverdale retires to his hermitage for just this purpose, to reconsoli-date his beleaguered "individuality" (3:89)—but at times the self can be so overmastered as to acquiesce in or even will its submission. The notion survives in the double meaning of the word "enthralled": to be charmed, as by a lover; to be held in or reduced to servitude.

In *Blithedale* enthrallment is less a matter of conquest from without than of influence establishing itself within. Such influence may be benign, as Zenobia claims when she imagines Coverdale "strengthened and enobled" by coming "within the sphere of a strong and noble nature" like Hollingsworth's (3:68). But also, and more frequently, the influence may constitute a kind of psychic imperi-alism in which one person mentally colonizes another. Beginning, it may be, with physical touch, the process ends in the mental subjugation of the weaker by the stronger. Coverdale recognizes this when, rejecting Hollingsworth's plea to join him in his lifework, he says, "Had I but touched his extended hand, Hollingsworth's magnetism would perhaps have penetrated me with his own conception of all these matters" (3:134). In Henry James's *The Bostonians*, Olive Chancellor seeks to secure Verena Tarrant for herself by having Verena come to see things "sincerely and with conviction, in the light in which" Olive herself "see[s] them."[25] This is what the characters in *Blithedale* are continually trying to do: bring others under their dominion by making them see themselves and the world as the colonizer sees them. In rebuffing Hollingsworth, Coverdale asserts "his right" to see things "through his own optics, instead of" Hollingsworth's (3:135).

Hollingsworth's challenge can be met because it is forthright and identifiable; others can be more insinuating. After conversing with Westervelt on the wood-path, Coverdale finds himself "possessed by a mood of disbelief in moral beauty or heroism, and a conviction of the folly of attempting to benefit the world" (3:101). Viewing the world for a time through Westervelt's "optics," Coverdale looks disparagingly upon Hollingsworth, Zenobia, and even Priscilla, who now seems to him only a "poor little seamstress" (3:100). Westervelt's hand had touched his sleeve (3:95), a token of the subtler contamination Coverdale comes to feel "in regard to all life's better purposes" (3:101). He shakes off the influence (not as completely or permanently as he thinks) by recognizing it as such and discounting its infectious cynicism. "There are some spheres," he reflects, "the contact with which inevitably degrades the high, debases the pure, deforms the beautiful" (3:101).

The gothic paraphernalia surrounding Westervelt, whose serpent-like walking stick recalls the devil figure's in "Young Goodman Brown," is one of the less felicitous features of *Blithedale*, but philosophically the character himself is important. "Altogether earthy, worldly, made for time and its gross objects" (3:241), Westervelt is not an old-fashioned devil of malignancy but a newfangled one of scoffing materialism whose crime is to deny humanity its uplifting, if tenuous idealism. His discourse on "psychological phenomena" (3:200) in the village hall is "eloquent, ingenious, plausible, with a delusive show of spirituality, yet really imbued throughout with a cold and dead materialism" (3:200). The claims of mesmerism cited by a blue-spectacled man in the audience—claims of "the miraculous power of one human being over the will and passions of another"; of "human character" being "but soft wax in [the mesmerist's] hands; and guilt, or virtue, only the forms into which he should see fit to mould it"; and of "the religious sentiment" amounting to no more than "a flame" for the mesmerist to "blow up" or "utterly extinguish," at his pleasure (3:198)—are not contested by Coverdale; they are met, rather, with "horror and disgust" and dispatched with the quasi-logic Hawthorne often uses to banish uncomfortable thoughts: "If these things were to be believed, the individual soul was virtually annihilated, and all that is sweet and pure, in our present life, debased, and ... the idea of man's eternal responsibility was made ridiculous, and immortality rendered, at once, impossible, and not worth acceptance" (3:198). The scene ends with

Hollingsworth's rescue of Priscilla from Westervelt, ostensibly a proof of the capacity of love and the spirit to override materialism. In fact, Hollingsworth merely proves himself the stronger force as he trains on Priscilla "the whole power of his great, stern, yet tender soul" (3:203). One man's magnetism overrides another's.[26]

While performances like Westervelt's were a fraud, Hawthorne could not so easily dismiss the implications of magnetism about the materiality of psychic processes, and therefore about the materiality of life itself. "The miraculous power of one human being over the will and passions of another" is precisely what human interactions in *Blithedale* attest to. To advance their interests or agenda or simply from bitterness or frustration, its characters work to implant their vision in one another. (1) Westervelt, who wishes to reclaim Priscilla, convinces Zenobia that Priscilla will "plague" her "in more ways than one" (3:104). (2) Adopting Westervelt's view of the matter, Zenobia tries to thwart her imagined rival by fashioning the story of "The Silvery Veil," at once threatening Priscilla and encouraging the hesitant Theodore/Coverdale to woo her himself. (3) Coverdale does so, but spurned by Priscilla in his tepid advances, he twists the knife by forcing her to confront her secret feelings about Zenobia, then from "petty malice" fans the flames of sexual jealousy by remarking "how pleasantly and happily Zenobia and Hollingsworth are walking together!" (3:126). (4) Slighted as well by a haughty Zenobia in the boardinghouse, Coverdale takes revenge by hovering about Priscilla's connection to Hollingsworth, thereby aggravating the suspicion planted in Zenobia's mind by Westervelt. (5) In the judgment scene at Eliot's pulpit, devastated by Hollingsworth's rejection of her, Zenobia becomes majestic and, blending truth, half-truth, and passionate denunciation, imposes on Hollingsworth her own bitter view of his transgressions. Though she later recants her words to Coverdale, they have hit their mark: Hollingsworth's "faith in himself is shaken" (3:219), he comes to see himself as Zenobia paints him, and he departs a broken man. (6) Later still, from a "bitter and revengeful emotion, as if flinging a poisoned arrow at Hollingsworth's heart" (3:243), Coverdale compounds Hollingsworth's feeling of guilt by taunting him about his aborted reform project and, implicitly, his responsibility for Zenobia's death. In each of these instances a character tries to capture or wound another by making his or her own self-interested view of things prevail, usually with great success.

Richard H. Millington calls *Blithedale* "a counternovel to *The House of the Seven Gables*" in its inversion of its predecessor's sentimentality: "The forms of feeling and behavior that had seemed the resources of middle-class culture in the earlier book ... all become in *Blithedale* either masks for acts of self-aggrandizement and predation or defenses against awareness."[27] This is a terrifying, nihilistic, Westerveltian vision, as Hawthorne knows. Westervelt can work his way so effectually into Coverdale because his "cold skepticism" toward "spiritual aspirations" appeals to a strain in Coverdale's "own nature" (3:101–2). In dialogue with Westervelt, Coverdale is in dialogue with a hated and feared part of himself. So, in writing *Blithedale*, is Hawthorne, who evades the implications of his action, a chaotic play of interest and power, by deflecting them away from psychological realism to melodrama. Through the demonized figure of Westervelt, he is able to caricature and denounce soul-impugning materialism even as his characters' behavior bears continuing witness to it. "What delusion can be more lamentable and mischievous, than to mistake the physical and material for the spiritual?" (15:589), Hawthorne wrote Sophia Peabody in October 1841, hoping to dissuade her from continuing mesmeric treatments. Yet how to tell the two apart or lay claim to the spiritual at all when behavior seems explicable by purely naturalistic motives? In a phrase describing the action of *Blithedale*—"the magnetism of soul on soul begins to operate"—reviewer E. P. Whipple inadvertently touches on the problem at the core of the book.[28] "Magnetism" and "operate" suggest the determinisms of materialistic psychology, while "of soul on soul" retains the traditional notion of immaterial, immortal spirit. That Whipple could join the two ideas with no sense of oxymoron is a mark of how well Hawthorne has managed to obscure his book's inner division, even perhaps from himself.

Romancing

> The essential difference between novel and romance lies in the conception of characterization. The romancer does not attempt to create "real people" so much as stylized figures which expand into psychological archetypes.
>
> —Northrop Frye, *Anatomy of Criticism*

> …you are born at the same time with a lot of other people, all mixed up with them, like trying to, having to, move your arms and legs with strings only the same strings are hitched to all the other arms and legs and the others all trying and they don't know why either except that the strings are all in each other's way like five or six people all trying to make a rug on the same loom only each one wants to weave his own pattern into the rug.
>
> —William Faulkner, *Absalom, Absalom!*

In "Zenobia's Legend," fresh from her meeting with Westervelt on the wood-path, Zenobia rehearses her later betrayal of Priscilla by casting a silvery veil over her, symbolizing her bondage. The irony is that Zenobia herself is under a veil. The "Magician" of her story has told a "lady" that "in love, in worldly fortune, in all [her] pursuit of happiness," a pale, gentle maiden "is doomed to fling a blight over [her] prospects" (3:115). The lady is swayed by his view and acts upon it, as Zenobia herself will. Psychologically, this is the significance in *Blithedale* of "casting a veil" over someone. The process of colonizing is not a matter of impulse or short-term calculation; it involves assigning another person an ongoing part and weaving him or her into the tapestry of one's self-mythology.

The dominant weaver in *Blithedale* is, of course, Coverdale. As he peers from his window in the Boston hotel, Coverdale feels "perplexed and annoyed... not to be able to resolve [the] combination of human interests" he observes "into well-defined elements" (3:150). This is what the romancer does; he weaves narratives to bring the chaos of life to interpretive order. In this sense, "romancing" is not an exclusively literary activity but a way of patterning experience even as it unfolds, of assigning meaning to it, and, if the romancer is also a participant in events, of positioning himself advantageously within them and justifying his enacted role.

In chapter 9, "Hollingsworth, Zenobia, Priscilla," Coverdale presents his friends as "indices of a problem which it was my business to solve" (3:69). The preceding chapter had ended with Zenobia and Hollingsworth scoffing at Coverdale and with Hollingsworth in evident possession of both women. Feeling himself "at best but a secondary or tertiary personage" with the others (3:70), Coverdale adopts the stance of interpreter as the most gratifying one available to him. It allows him to imagine he has chosen his exclusion, it confers on him a detached "choral" status, and it enables him to appear judicious while making radically biased pronouncements on the others. Even as he claims to speak from love of Hollingsworth, Coverdale proceeds to fabricate a myth of revenge, self-justification, and fantasized triumph. In Coverdale's "romance," Priscilla vis-à-vis Hollingsworth "is as perilously situated as the maiden whom, in the old classical myths, the people used to expose to a dragon" (3:91). At this point, Coverdale has little reason to believe that Priscilla "thought [Hollingsworth] beautiful" other than that he himself "often thought him so" (3:71), still less to suppose that Hollingsworth, intent on his project, returns or even notices her interest. Least of all has he ground for making a "dragon" of Hollingsworth, who has shown more tenderness and generosity toward the weak than he himself has. "If I had any duty whatever, in reference to Hollingsworth" (3:71), Coverdale begins the line of rationalization that will carry him to the climax of his fantasy, with himself as rescuer of the endangered maiden. As it turns out, the would-be knight-errant is grossly errant: he mistakes the dragon (it is Westervelt), flatters his own capacity for action, and misassigns the role of the hero, which will belong to Hollingsworth. Further, in imagining Zenobia and Priscilla contending over Hollingsworth, and in meddling with them as if this were indeed the case, Coverdale, who likes to think of himself as "aloof from the possibility of personal concernment" (3:97), helps bring about the "catastrophe" he claims to have anticipated (3:72).

A first-person romance may be inherently problematic since any narrator who is distinctively characterized is likely become a reflexive center of interest, drawing the reader away from the outward reference of the story to the conditions of its telling. Is *Blithedale* truly a romance or a psychological novel about a romancer who self-interestedly shapes facts and lacunae into myth? In chapter 9 Coverdale raises the question himself when he acknowledges "the kind of error into which my mode of observation was calculated to lead me" (3:71). And yet, he adds, let his darkened, invidious account of Hollingsworth stand "both for its truth and its exaggeration," its objectivity and its warped subjectivity (3:71). Coverdale's words invite us to watch him closely, gauge the nature and extent of his distortions, discern the motives behind them, determine *his* elusive character, and make out, so far as we can, the "real" Hollingsworth independent of Coverdale's presentation of him. Hawthorne, it seems, would have us consider the activity of life-romancing as the romancer tries to negotiate experience by constructing a fiction and passing it off as truth. In this, Coverdale as narrator is attempting to do to his readers what *Blithedale*'s characters do to each other: bring them within his sphere of influence, make them see through his optics, cast a veil over them. The difference is that Coverdale makes a book out of his myth while the others do not.

It is not simply Coverdale who would have us doubly engage the text; Hawthorne would as well. "Read my story as a psychological novel about an unreliable narrator," he seems to say, "*and* as a romance about the characters he brings to life." Within *Blithedale* as novel, Zenobia is a distinct individual and, as Henry James said, Hawthorne's "nearest approach... to the complete creation of a person" (James 106); within *Blithedale* as romance, she is an archetype of "the high-spirited Woman, bruising herself against the narrow limitations of her sex" (3:2). The book's other characters also expand into archetypes: Hollingsworth into "the self-concentrated Philanthropist," Priscilla into "the weakly Maiden, whose tremulous nerves endow her with Sibylline attributes," and Coverdale into "the Minor Poet, beginning life with strenuous aspirations" (3:2–3). From the outset, the questions with *Blithedale* are, first, what unifying action Hawthorne will shape from the disparate but representative figures announced in its preface and, second, what archetypal significance he will find in it.

As the book developed, he was able to find very little significance of the kind he wanted (archetypal) and too much of a kind he didn't want (naturalistic). Through its first fifteen chapters *Blithedale* is the most vibrant of Hawthorne's fictions, largely because it is the most dramatic and immediate. That it subsequently falls into disarray may be owing to his want of staying power as a writer. Yet *Blithedale* may also be impaired by another factor, Hawthorne's ambivalence toward the psychologism responsible for much of the book's early success. His realist's technique has led him—aesthetically, to good effect; morally, to his deep unease—to a realist's understanding of behavior and something like a realist's associated metaphysics. The subtle malice in Zenobia's treatment of Priscilla, for example, needs no transcendent layer of reference to enrich its meaning; it is complete in itself, both in its local context and as it models the artistic mimesis of life-experience. It scarcely matters whether Zenobia is a unique individual or a type of the energetic, highly sexed woman jostling with her pallid but threatening rival; in either case, her relationship to Priscilla, like all the relationships in *Blithedale*, resolves itself into a naked play of interests and aggressions occurring wholly on the level of the naturalistic. The characters love; they project futures; they try to enlist one another in their life-scripts; they struggle and suffer; intentionally or not, they inflict harm—and there it ends. Their lives have no significance beyond themselves, or, if they do resonate, it is only as illustrations of societal forces within a kind of turbid and purposeless *comédie humaine*.

As early as chapter 9, Hawthorne seems to have felt that his experiment in human nature could not be left as a tale of soulless strivings and contentions, as if these comprised the sum of human life. Coverdale's "romance" of a monomaniacal Hollingsworth wreaking havoc on the community arises from his own sexual jealousy and feelings of exclusion, but it also served Hawthorne's requirements. It delivered him from a novelistic continuity he had never been able to sustain and from a novelistic approach to morality he found abhorrent, if probably true. To escape the "merely psychological," Hawthorne needed to import Good and Evil into *Blithedale*'s world, and for that he needed an identifiable sinner.

"Hollingsworth: A Romance"

> I have put "Hollingsworth" on the title page . . . as presenting the original
> figure about which the rest of the book clustered itself.
>
> —Hawthorne to E. P. Whipple (May 2, 1852)

Writing of Henry James's novels, Richard Poirier describes the "felt tension between dramatic and allegorical impulses" that arises from "using characters to illustrate ideas while at the same time investing them with a dramatic and personal vitality that breaks the bounds of any assigned representational function."[29] With Hollingsworth, Hawthorne's "original" focus in *Blithedale* (16:536), the reverse occurs. More through what we are told than what we are given to see, a charismatic, many-sided character is made to illustrate "the process by which godlike benevolence has been debased into all-devouring egotism" (3:71). At least some of the reductiveness in Hollingsworth's portrait may be ascribed to Coverdale's sexual envy as it infects his telling, yet Coverdale's hostility toward reformers is substantially Hawthorne's own, dating back to the 1830s. Hawthorne may be allowed his convictions; the problem in *Blithedale* is an aesthetic one of an excess of vituperation to visible cause.

Hollingsworth receives the treatment he does partly because he is *Blithedale's* conscripted sinner. "After all the evil that he did...," Coverdale moralizes, in preparation for the fit "retribution" to be laid upon Hollingsworth (3:243). Just what evil *did* he do? Zenobia, in white heat, makes several accusations, some just, others doubtful:

1. Hollingsworth "aimed a death-blow" at the Blithedale community by turning it into an instrument for his purpose (3:218). Yes, he did, in ultimate intention, but not, so far as we see, even in incipient action.
2. Hollingsworth discarded Coverdale as a friend because Coverdale refused to join him in his enterprise. True.
3. Hollingsworth took Zenobia into his plan "as long as there was hope of [her] being available," then cast her "aside again, a broken tool!" (3:218). Zenobia's implication is that Hollingsworth spurns her because she has been disinherited. The probable truth is that he does so because of her betrayal of Priscilla to Westervelt. Zenobia acknowledges her guilt openly: "You [Priscilla] stood between me and an end which I desired. I wanted a clear path" (3:220). Hollingsworth's "judgment" of Zenobia is a decision to sever relations with someone who has acted treacherously (3:215).
4. Hollingsworth means to "sacrifice" Priscilla, presumably by marrying her for her newly acquired fortune (3:218). This is also questionable. Hollingsworth has been Priscilla's protector since first escorting her to Blithedale. By forcing him into the further role of gallant rescuer, Zenobia brings about precisely the outcome she seeks to prevent.

Later, when Coverdale "bitterly" exclaims, "Hollingsworth has a heart of ice!...He is a wretch!" Zenobia springs to his defense: "Presume not to estimate a man like Hollingsworth! It was my fault, all along, and none of his. I see it now!" (3:225). So far as Hollingsworth's behavior toward herself is concerned, she is right. But it suits Coverdale, who has lost both women, to pile his frustration onto Hollingsworth and subsequently to blame him for Zenobia's death. A man of acute conscience, Hollingsworth comes to accuse himself of murder, like Reuben Bourne after Roger Malvin's death (3:243). Coverdale does nothing to help the situation. He has found his scapegoat and brought his story to interpretive coherence. By vilifying Hollingsworth and acceding in his "just" punishment, he has wrung a kind of moral symmetry from the murky events he half ignorantly recounts.

It may have been Hawthorne's first intent to write an antireformist book, "Hollingsworth: A Romance." That he continued to find "Hollingsworth" "the best [title] that has occurred to me" (16:536) suggests a remarkable miscomprehension of what he wrote or else a form of denial. "It is evident on every page," Philip Rahv observes, "that the only genuine relationship is that of Coverdale to Zenobia,"[30] as we are made to feel in the aftermath of the judgment scene when Zenobia and Coverdale are left alone. Having created Zenobia, Hawthorne found Hollingsworth fading back into the status of a thematic abstraction— hence the dramatic underdevelopment of his story. Yet as in *The Scarlet Letter*, whose most "genuine relationship" is between the narrator and Hester, Hawthorne needed the framework of sin to rein in his fascination with his heroine and interpose itself against the "natural" life she represented. Except as Coverdale applies it to Hollingsworth, "evil" is not a word pertinent to *Blithedale*, whose characters act from self-interested motives that have little to do with wickedness. "But I never wished you harm" (3:220), Zenobia tells Priscilla. No one in *Blithedale*, not even Westervelt, wishes anyone harm other than from momentary vexation or as others appear obstacles to one's designs. With the phrase "all the evil that he did," *Blithedale*'s jumble of motives and behaviors crystallizes into a cause-and-effect pattern of moral law. Even more than Westervelt, Hollingsworth as evildoer is Hawthorne's vehicle for warding off the book's nihilism and funneling its vision of human relations gone awry into a single originary source, whose punishment sets the moral world aright.

It is significant in this context that Hollingsworth should be a prison reformer. Although the word "sin" is generally absent from *Blithedale*,[31] as James McIntosh notes, it does appear in Coverdale's remarks on Hollingsworth's reform project, "a scheme for the reformation of the wicked by methods moral, intellectual, and industrial, by the sympathy of pure, humble, and yet exalted minds, and by opening to his pupils the possibility of a worthier life than that which had become their fate" (3:131). To modern readers, such a program of rehabilitation seems enlightened, meritorious, and considerably less quixotic than the utopian community itself, but in *Blithedale* it comes in for harsh criticism, partly from Coverdale's fastidiousness ("A loathsomeness that was to be forever in my daily work!") but also from his residually theological identification of criminality with "a great, black ugliness of sin" (3:134). For Coverdale, criminals are not simply people who have committed a crime; they are "the wicked," whether corrupt by nature or corrupted by the inward ramifications of their acts. As he says elsewhere in disparagement, Hollingsworth should have tested his theory "by perpetrating some huge sin, in his proper person, and examining the condition of his higher instincts, afterwards" (3:36).

Hawthorne's intention to trace Hollingsworth's descent into egotism, monomania, and incipient madness does not require contempt for his enterprise itself. Why should an appeal to criminals' "higher instincts" be treated with scorn, and in a manner, moreover, that seems to underwrite the scorn? Although

Hollingsworth is not a cynical materialist—witness his loathing for Fourier (3:53)—he is something Hawthorne found almost equally insidious. He is an environmentalist, a romantic meliorist, a man who believes, as the mesmerists do, that human character is malleable, though in his case to be molded through patience and intelligence for a redemptive purpose. However laudable the end, such faith amounts to the rejection of a key Hawthornean belief, the identic *definitiveness* of sin. For Hollingsworth, sin—or rather, crime; he would deny the equivalence of the two—is not, as Hawthorne says with Hester, "a new birth" (1:80) whose consequences are lifelong; it is something that may with guidance and effort be set behind. Without being an unbeliever—in his habit of prayer and genuine kindness, he is the book's only practical Christian—Hollingsworth is, by Hawthorne's measure, a de facto naturalist in his assumptions about good and evil. If Hollingsworth is right about crime, Hawthorne himself is wrong— wrong in his moral psychology and what it implies about the cosmic order, and wrong, moreover, in his career-long practice as a romancer. It is not enough that Hollingsworth be defeated and punished; like Hester, he must be brought to accede to his punishment and admit the reality of sin and the necessity of lifelong penitence.

Blithedale Pastoral, Blithedale Pasture

Et in Arcadia ego

—Latin motto, used for a painting by Guercino (1618),
later by Nicholas Poussin

The manuscript Hawthorne sent to E. P. Whipple early in May 1852 ended with "Blithedale Pasture," in which Coverdale moralizes on Zenobia's death. The chapter is concerned with the meaning of that death, with the meaning of death itself, and with the import of the life that Zenobia's suicide presents for reflection. Zenobia's own proffered moral—"that the whole universe, her own sex and yours, and Providence, or Destiny, to boot, make common cause against the woman who swerves one hair's breadth out of the beaten track" (3:224)—has more bitterness than truth to it. Zenobia is punished for her behavior toward Priscilla, and punished only by being spurned by Hollingsworth; the universe, destiny, and the combined sexes enter in only insofar as society has delimited Zenobia's possibilities and disposed her to identify happiness with romantic love. When Westervelt vents his exasperation at the waste of a triumphant life ahead, Coverdale answers in the voice of gender convention: "In all this,... there would have been nothing to satisfy her heart" (3:240). Yet Coverdale grudgingly allows Westervelt's view its "share of truth" (3:241), which he elaborates in a plea for reform that echoes Margaret Fuller's in "Mariana." "It is nonsense, and a miserable wrong—the result, like so many others, of masculine egotism," he says, "that the success or failure of woman's existence should be made to depend wholly on the affections, and on one species of affection; while man has such a multitude of other chances, that this seems but an incident" (3:241).

Why must Zenobia die? Less for her sins or for society's than for her creator's fears and tenuously held beliefs. The pastoral Hawthorne stages at Blithedale is his climactic experiment in romantic naturalism, or the trustworthiness of human impulses left to themselves in a secular world. What Hester could realize only in a flight from the community and a happiness à deux with her lover becomes with Zenobia the prospect of free human development within a reconstituted community. Both heroines cast off from traditional society and, in doing so, wander in a wilderness in which truth and error are difficult to distinguish and the promptings of desire have no regulatory social or moral check. More victims than transgressors, they are nonetheless brought back within the pale. As Hester is made to bow to the exigencies of moral law, Zenobia bows to the conventions of social law, allowing that the woman who "swerves one hair's breadth" from them "goes all astray, and never sees the world in its true aspect, afterwards!" (3:224).

Zenobia had already lived and died in Hawthorne's imagination by the time the *Memoirs of Margaret Fuller Ossoli* appeared (also in 1852), but in James Freeman Clarke's account of Fuller, Hawthorne would have recognized many of the anxieties he had explored through Zenobia and originally been led to ponder from his observation of Fuller. "Margaret's life *had an aim*, and she was, therefore, essentially a moral person" (*MMFO* 1:132), Clarke asserted, by which he turns out to mean close to the contrary: that Fuller's morality, rooted in an impulse toward "self-culture" (*MMFO* 1:132), was an egocentric one that set her against established society and Immutable Law. As Clarke sees it, "the good and the evil which flow from this great idea of self-development she fully realized" (*MMFO* 1:133). The evil appeared first "only in a certain superciliousness of tone toward 'the vulgar herd'... and in an idolatrous hero-worship of genius and power," but with time it expressed itself in a "desire for universal experience"—a Goethean omnivorousness dangerous for anyone in midcentury New England but positively damning for a woman—"and an unwillingness to see that... a perfected development here must often be renounced" (*MMFO* 1:133–34). Clarke's implication is that the pursuit of full selfhood not only entails egotism and pride but may also become entangled with urgencies of the body. The lesson he draws from "the pathos and tragedy" of Fuller's life (*MMFO* 1:134) extends beyond Fuller to a critique of the romantic ideal of self-culture.[32] He signals the idea by prefacing his memoir with an epigraph from Fuller's beloved Goethe:

> There are not a few instances of that conflict, known also to the fathers,
> of the spirit with the flesh, the inner with the outer man, of the freedom
> of the will with the necessity of nature, the pleasure of the individual
> with the conventions of society, of the emergency of the case with the
> despotism of the rule. (*MMFO* 1:60)

Years later in Rome, moralizing on her career, Hawthorne presents Fuller much as Clarke does, as "a woman anxious to try all things, and fill up her experience in all directions" (14:155). He sees Fuller's "total collapse" as the predictable result of her effort to "make herself the greatest, wisest, best woman of the age" despite the "rude old potency" that lay deep in her nature (14:156, 157). Here, as in antebellum notions of female (im)propriety, breadth of experience, freethinking, iconoclastic behavior, and sexual ardor are so entwined that it is hard to say which is the primal cause and which the effects. In his portrait of Zenobia, Hawthorne conflates all of these things. "The hardihood of her philosophy" (3:44), her indifference to conventions, "the freedom of her deportment" (3:47), and her verbal and physical eroticism combine to produce an impression that Zenobia has lived too much and knows more than is proper for a woman to know and for anyone of either sex to advert to in public.

Fuller's real-life "collapse" and Zenobia's fictive one testify to what Hawthorne saw as the destabilizing consequences of romantic naturalism. To locate the ends of life in the growth of the human personality, irrespective of convention and moral restraint, was to unleash psychic impulses that made for anarchy. It was to leave the self exposed to the demands of sexuality, apparent even in the mood swings and secret thoughts of Priscilla; it was to reduce personal relations to a lawless play of dominations and submissions; and it was to define humanity's position in the universe as that of the Blithedale farmhouse early in the book, an island of flickering light and warmth "adrift on the great ocean of the night" (3:36).

Still, there is Zenobia, queenly to the last. "She gave me her hand," Coverdale writes of his final moments with her, "with the same free, whole-souled gesture as on the first afternoon of our acquaintance; and being greatly moved, I thought of no better method of expressing my deep sympathy than to carry it to my lips" (3:227). With that gesture, *Blithedale* comes full circle and its brief against romantic naturalism dissolves temporarily in sheer admiration for Zenobia, only to be followed by disaster. "The dark lady is a rebel and an emancipator," Philip Rahv observes, "but precisely for this reason Hawthorne feels the compulsion to destroy her. *He thus converts the principle of life, of experience, into a principle of death.*"[33] Hawthorne would not have seen it that way. For him, Zenobia's "principle of life" (natural vitality) was itself "the principle of death." Regardless of other considerations, to stake oneself on life in nature was to accept the fact of annihilation. Before the late addition of "Miles Coverdale's Confession," *Blithedale* had ended thus:

> How much Nature seems to love us! And how readily, nevertheless, without a sigh or a complaint, she converts us to a meaner purpose.... While Zenobia lived, Nature was proud of her, and directed all eyes upon that radiant presence, as her fairest handiwork. Zenobia perished. Will not Nature shed a tear? Ah, no! She adopts the calamity at once into her system, and is just as well pleased, for aught we can see, with the tuft of ranker vegetation that grew out of Zenobia's heart, as with all the beauty which has bequeathed us no earthly representative, except in this crop of weeds. It is because the spirit is inestimable, that the lifeless body is so little valued. (3:244)

"...the lifeless body is so little valued." Intentionally or not, there is irony here, for everything that most delighted Coverdale in Zenobia emanated from that body with its hunger for life in *this* world.

Loving Priscilla

> ...yet, do not grieve;
> She cannot fade, though thou hast not thy bliss,
> Forever wilt thou love, and she be fair.
>
> —Keats, "Ode on a Grecian Urn"

Left alone with Zenobia after the judgment scene, Coverdale finds an "analogy" between her situation of rejection and his own (3:222). When he kisses her hand, it is with something more than "deep sympathy" (3:227), but his relation to her, as he knows, is that of a courtier to a queen. Priscilla also has moments of haughtiness, but she is not beyond Coverdale's reach. In the boardinghouse it is "Priscilla's beauty, not Zenobia's," that arrests Coverdale (3:169), and elsewhere in the narrative there are sufficient hints of his interest that his closing confession of love does not come as a complete surprise, though it does throw readers back upon events to revaluate them.

What does it mean that Coverdale should love Priscilla, or profess to? "The Veiled Lady" was the least appealing of the titles Hawthorne considered for *Blithedale* because (so he said) he did "not wish to give prominence to that feature of the Romance" (16:536). Nonetheless, his book begins and ends with the Veiled Lady / Priscilla, and although Coverdale claims that the "pretensions" of the Veiled Lady "have little to do with the present narrative" (3:6), thematically they have a great deal to do with it, especially *as* pretensions. Richard H. Brodhead sees the Veiled Lady as "the representation of 'woman'" in nineteenth-century "domestic ideology," veiled in public because she belongs to the private sphere, and attenuated in physique because culture views "'woman' as something separate from or opposed to bodily life and force," therefore spiritual.[34] In "Zenobia's Legend" the Veiled Lady complains to Theodore of being "a sad and lonely prisoner, in a bondage which is worse to me than death" (3:112–13). Figuratively, she is lamenting her imposed sequestration from the world. In asking Theodore to deliver her through an act of faith, symbolized by a kiss, she is seeking to trade her physical and experiential virginity for fulfillment in the normative role of wife and mother. This is Priscilla's goal as well. In "Eliot's Pulpit" she responds disapprovingly to Coverdale's exaltation of women as spiritual guardians of humanity. What she wants is ordinary domestic happiness with a protector like Hollingsworth. Female ethereality is a male construct serving male needs and male purposes.

In the boardinghouse scene Zenobia asks Coverdale why "it never occurred to [him] to fall in love with Priscilla" (3:170). Coverdale *has* fallen in love with Priscilla, or intermittently likes to think he has; but aside from a well-grounded fear of rejection, he hesitates to commit himself because he distrusts his idealized image of her. Zenobia plants an early suspicion—"She is neither more nor less...than a seamstress from the city"—and proceeds to deliver a pithy deconstruction of nineteenth-century gender mythology: "and so, as she has hardly any physique a poet, like Mr. Miles Coverdale, may be allowed to think her spiritual!" (2:33). Westervelt's words to Coverdale—"Some philosophers choose to glorify this habit of body by terming it spiritual" (3:95)—build upon Zenobia's, but they register on Coverdale only because he has misgivings of his own. From the first, Priscilla's "wan, almost sickly hue" struck him as attributable to the straitened circumstances of her life (3:27), and as her days at Blithedale revive her health and animal spirits, she comes to seem what in fact she probably is, a sprightly, if delicate, girl on the verge of womanhood. From the detached perspective of his "hermitage," and tainted by Westervelt's cynicism, Coverdale realizes that if he cares for Priscilla, it is not "for her realities—poor little seamstress, as Zenobia rightly called her!—but for the fancy-work with which I have idly decked her out!" (3:100). His doubts inhibit him and, unable to make an unreserved gesture of faith, he courts Priscilla with a tepidness that is self-defeating. As the Veiled Lady prophesies of Theodore, he is doomed to be haunted by the thought of a missed happiness, but with an added uncertainty about whether it *would* have been happiness. "Pity that she must fade so soon! These delicate and puny maidens always do" (3:226), Zenobia says of Priscilla, spitefully but with an air of truth.

As it rounds out the narrator's history, "Miles Coverdale's Confession" is largely gratuitous. Coverdale's nostalgia and ennui are visible from the start, and even his feelings for Priscilla can be inferred from the body of the text. We cannot know what led Hawthorne to add the chapter—it may have been a suggestion from Whipple (3:xix)—but we can note its effect, which is to shift the book's attention and symbolic allegiance from Zenobia to Priscilla, that is, from nature to spirit. If, as Brodhead says, "the whole impetus of the Veiled Lady plot is to resuscitate in the figure of Priscilla a locus of absolute spiritual value" and thereby "avert the deepest implications" of the story (Brodhead 110–11), the function of the epilogue is to underscore that commitment against what Hawthorne may have considered the powerful attraction of Zenobia even in death. Loath as he was to propel "such a shrinking damsel" as Priscilla "into the vanguard and make her the standard-bearer" (16: 536), this is what he elected to do.

Whomever Coverdale loves, the dominant note at the beginning and end of *Blithedale* is one of bittersweet retrospect. Though scarcely forty, Coverdale feels life behind him and the most he can do, or take pleasure in doing, is "rake away the ashes from the embers in [his] memory, and blow them up with a sigh" (3:9). In this, like Keats's time-frozen lover, he differs from Hawthorne, who married his Priscilla and entered the world of conventional domesticity. As he peers out his hotel window at a family across the courtyard, Coverdale wonders why "more than one of these families [need] to be in existence," since they are all "so much alike" (3:150). To seem redundant, middle-class marriage needn't be a cauldron of hatred and frustration; it need only be ordinary, confining, predictable, and dull. Hawthorne spares Coverdale any such disillusion by leaving his idealization of Priscilla intact and having him live a bachelor fixated on his arcadian summer of the past.

Nostalgia seems the only even mildly positive value educible from *Blithedale*, none of whose characters find happiness for themselves or augur a happier social future. Beneath its particulars of plot and theme—Zenobia and feminism; Hollingsworth and prison reform; the Veiled Lady, Westervelt, and mesmerism; Coverdale's vacillations; the utopian community itself—what holds *Blithedale* together are its roots in a divided mind resolved to test the possibilities of a natural life liberated from the past, from social institutions, and from the New England obsession with sin. On all counts, the experiment fails, as Hawthorne knew it would. *Blithedale* confirms for the present and future what "The Prison Door" had claimed from the collective experience of the past: that would-be Utopias do need cemeteries and do need prisons, if only in the form of mental ones in which the guilt-ridden incarcerate themselves. The remarkable thing is that despite its social and psychological pessimism, *Blithedale* remains, as Henry James says, "the lightest, the brightest, the liveliest" of Hawthorne's long fictions (James 105). Whatever Hawthorne the philosopher and moralist may have believed, his delight as man and artist was in the vital energies of life, which in *Blithedale* center on Zenobia. To paraphrase the Romantics on Milton,

Hawthorne in midcareer was a budding novelist and therefore of the naturalist's party without knowing it.

After Zenobia there was nothing left to do with romantic naturalism, and after Phoebe and Priscilla (the practical and spiritual faces of the feminine ideal), no further explorations to be made of gender ideology. As a writer of romance (if *Blithedale* indeed *is* a romance), Hawthorne seems to have reached a dead end. Even Julian stumbles when it comes to imagining the direction his father's career might have taken if a combination of circumstances hadn't intervened to send him abroad (*NHW* 1:474). After his prodigious labors of 1849–52, which included children's books and the Pierce biography, Hawthorne must have been exhausted. He was settled in Concord now, at the house he renamed The Wayside, but the town in its abolitionist fervor was less congenial to him than it had been a decade earlier. The consulship was a godsend. A life that had narrowed and seemed without prospect of adventure or surprise suddenly opened out in an anticipation of new scenes, new acquaintances, new experiences, and possibly a new vision and new literary practice. On March 26, 1853, he sailed for Liverpool.

St. Giles, London, ca. 1850

Francis Bennoch, age 33, 1857

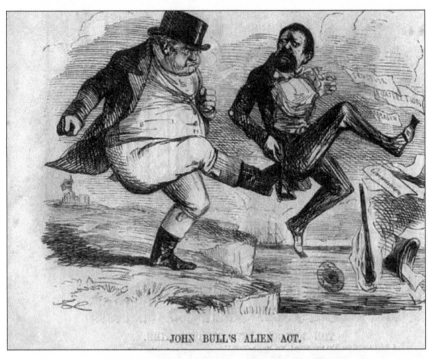

"John Bull's Alien Act." Political cartoon by John Leech.

Delia Bacon, age 42, 1853

Roman Forum, ca. 1850

St. Peter's Plaza, Rome, 1850

Faun of Praxiteles (ca. 130 AD), Capitol Museum, Rome

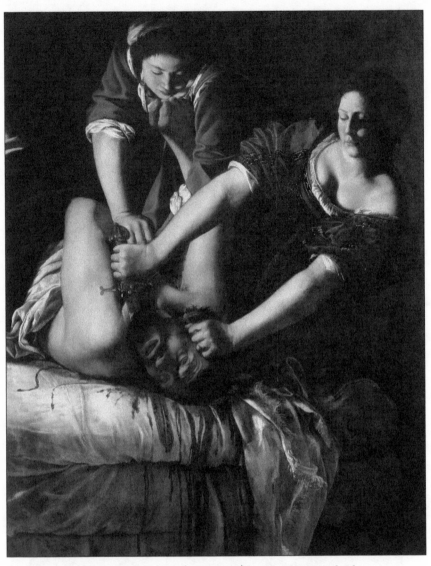

Judith Slaying Holofernes (ca. 1611-12) by Artemisia Gentileschi

The Transfiguration (ca. 1516-1520) by Raphael

Photographic portrait by Matthew Brady, ca. 1860–5

In the Belly of the Beast

It is human life; it is this material world; it is a grim and heavy reality.
I have never had the same sense of being surrounded by materialisms,
and hemmed with the grossness of this earthly life, anywhere else.

—Hawthorne on London, *The English Notebooks* (1857)

Our Old Home, Our New Homelessness

He began to feel the deep yearning which a sensitive American—his
mind full of English thoughts, his imagination of English poetry, his
heart of English character and feeling—cannot fail to be influenced by,
the yearning of the blood within his veins for that from which it has
been estranged.

—Hawthorne, "Etherege," *The American Claimant Manuscripts* (1861)

Like most twenty-year exiles, he has lost his native country without
finding another; but then it is as well to recognize the truth, that an
individual country is by no means essential to one's comfort.

—Hawthorne, on expatriate sculptor Hiram Powers, *The French and
Italian Notebooks* (1858)

Meeting Hawthorne in Concord in September 1852, English traveler Henry A.
Bright recalled that "he spoke of England, and how he longed to see it, and how
deeply he and all New Englanders felt towards it."[1] Within a year, thanks to
Franklin Pierce, Hawthorne, then forty-nine, would be settled as consul in
Liverpool, and Bright, twenty-three-year-old son of a shipping magnate, would
be his closest companion and most enterprising local sponsor. Hawthorne originally planned to spend no more than five years in Europe, including a year in
Italy. As it turned out, he would not see America for seven and a half years. He
arrived in England in July 1853, departed for France and Italy in January 1858,
and returned to England in June 1859, where he remained for another full year.
When he finally set sail for America in June 1860, Hawthorne was not the provincial he had been in leaving it; nor, resettling in Concord, did he abandon hope
of seeing England again. Indeed, partly because of American politics, partly

because England had affected him deeply, he did not come home eagerly. As he more than once remarked in notebook entries and letters, had he not had family to consider, he might not have come home at all.[2]

Culturally, England did not challenge Hawthorne as dramatically as Italy would, yet precisely because it was, through his reading, more familiar to him and more congenial to elements of his character, its influence worked more subtly. There were no visible crises, no fits of petulance or exasperation as there would be in Rome, only a gradual weaning away from American insularity and prejudice and a progressive acclimatization both physical (an animal pleasure in English food; a qualified affection for English weather) and moral. Without intending or fully recognizing it, Hawthorne distanced himself from one country without becoming, like Washington Irving, an enthusiast of another. On the contrary, far from sentimentalizing England and the English, Hawthorne could be critical, even at times acerbic, as English reviewers of *Our Old Home* were stung to note. As his son Julian observed, "one is apt to be a more severe critic of one's blood relations than of strangers," and "Hawthorne's attitude toward England," in part at least, "was that of a descendant jealous of his ancestor's honor" (*NHW* 2:170). More intimately, it was that of a man who sees what another milieu might have made of him and who is both drawn to and repelled by this foreign secret sharer in his own nature.

Since even Hawthorneans may have only slight familiarity with Hawthorne's English sojourn, it is useful briefly to outline Hawthorne's English experience and suggest its significance. Incisive as his observations frequently are, what Hawthorne made of England, objectively, may be of less import for Hawthorne studies than what England called forth in him—first shallowly, as it tapped his traveler's expectations and inbred republican feelings about aristocracy, then with increasing seriousness as the example of England posed moral and meta-physical questions that cut to the heart of his implicit worldview. At issue is the character of a New England idealist's encounter with what he regarded as the ponderously "real." In the end, the question of England in its manifold "material-isms" became for Hawthorne a question of the physical and spiritual nature of human beings and the (dis)order of the universe they inhabited.

Within a year, probably much sooner, Hawthorne was "sick and weary" of the "damnable annoyances" of his office, "what with brutal shipmasters, drunken sailors, vagrant Yankees, mad people, sick people, and dead people," he told publisher William D. Ticknor, his chief American correspondent during this period (17:247, 248). "Some persons," he imagined, "would console themselves with the dignity of the office, the public and private dinners, and the excellent opportunity of playing the great man on a small scale; but this is to me a greater bore than all the rest: so that you see I have nothing to comfort myself with but the emoluments" (17:248).

The emoluments were substantial. From the first, with "ordinary luck," Hawthorne hoped to "bag from $5000 to $7000 clear per annum" if he lived frugally (17:119), savings that Ticknor would invest for him. After the scrimping and borrowing of the preceding several years, he was delighted to find himself living comfortably in the present, but he was also thinking of the future, having two daughters to apportion and a son to educate. James T. Fields had made of Hawthorne a modest success, but he knew he could not depend on the flow of his creativity or the public's continuing taste for his work, and when the writing ceased, or ceased to sell, so would the income. He worried about a bill introduced in Congress in 1854 to curb consular fees and limit salaries to $7,500, out of which official expenses were to be paid. The bill eventually passed, but its application was delayed until the next congressional session, by which time, Hawthorne estimated, he "shall have got together about as much money as there is any use in having" (17:338).

Aside from the irksomeness of his consular duties, Hawthorne hated Liverpool, "the most detestable place as a residence that ever my lot was cast in" (17:119). The large stucco house he first rented at Rock Ferry, a middle-class suburb across the Mersey from Liverpool, was comfortable, even elegant, but between the rent, household upkeep, and serving staff, it was also expensive, and the family left it after less than two years. They went on to lead what Hawthorne called "a strange, vagabond, gypsy sort of life" (22:149). They took rooms in Mrs. Blodget's boardinghouse in Liverpool, patronized by American sea captains; in other assorted boardinghouses, lodging houses, and hotels; in Leamington Spa (on three occasions); in Manchester (for the 1857 Arts Exhibition); in London, in Redcar (Yorkshire), and in Bath; in his friend Francis Bennoch's house in Blackheath, near London, while the Bennochs summered on the continent in 1856; and in the unfashionable seaside resort of Southport, within commuting distance of the consulate. Some of the moves had to do with travel, others with Sophia's health (the English climate was hard on her lungs), and still others with Hawthorne's by now chronic restlessness.

During his first two years in England, Hawthorne confined himself closely to Liverpool and its environs; he did not visit London until September 1855, nearly twenty-six months after arriving in England. His shyness also limited opportunities for observation. Even in Liverpool, he tended to sequester himself from society; one of the advantages of Rock Ferry was that its distance from Liverpool would "render it impossible for me to go to parties, or to give parties myself, and will keep me out of a good deal of nonsense" (17:19). When requests did come, he often tried to escape them. Responding to a Liverpool socialite's invitation to a fancy ball, he acknowledged "his folly and absurdity in declining an invitation which any other man would go down on his knees to get," but he likened himself to "an owl or a bat," who, "when invited to take a pleasure trip in the sunshine,..."

feels it fitter for himself to stay in his dusky hole than to go blinking about among other people's enjoyments. The truth is," he added—the shame of confession apparently being preferable to the trial of social intercourse—"Mr. H has all his life been under a spell, from which it is now too late to free himself" (17:175). Like Hester's scarlet *A*, Hawthorne's shyness became a cultivated badge of isolation, a defensive noli me tangere. Chancing to spy Tennyson in a room at the Manchester Arts Exhibition, Hawthorne commented on the poet's "shy and secluded habits" and was "indescribably sensible of a morbid painfulness in him, a something not to be meddled with" (12:52). Hawthorne might as easily have been referring to himself. The two men, only yards apart, never met.

To the extent that Hawthorne did enter the social world, it was largely thanks to Francis Bennoch, a London businessman and minor poet to whom, Hawthorne said, "I owed most in England" (5:340). In later years, Bennoch grew pompous in celebrating his intimacy with Hawthorne; in fact, Bennoch was never more than a genial factotum, though a crucial one. "Bounteous" as Bennoch was in "his plans for making [Hawthorne's] time pass pleasantly" (21:424), it is reasonable to "wonder," with Thomas Woodson, "whether without [his] combination of awed idolatry and aggressive management Hawthorne would ever have made his way" (17:38). Until Hawthorne called upon Bennoch at his office during his second visit to London in March 1856, his social and professional acquaintance was largely comprised of middle-class burghers, or worse. Within his limited reach, Bennoch opened up social and literary London to Hawthorne, leading him "to many scenes of life, in town, camp, and country, which I could never have found out for myself" (5:340–41). The high points were a civic dinner sponsored by the Lord Mayor of London and a literary breakfast given by Richard Monckton Milnes, at which Hawthorne met writers (the Brownings included) and men of "high rank," all of whose manners he "liked greatly" (22:83).

Hawthorne's English years are the best-documented and least-addressed phase of his career. The want of interest is chiefly due to the want of finished literary work aside from the sketches worked up from journal materials, published in the *Atlantic Monthly* beginning in October 1860, and collected, with additions, in *Our Old Home* (1863). Although Hawthorne had no great enthusiasm for the volume, Henry James considered it "the best written" of all his works (James 118), and editor Woodson is egregiously wrong in labeling it "a dark and limping counterpart to Washington Irving's *Sketch-Book*" (17:3). Irving's essays are facile and sentimental; Hawthorne's, when they heed his own injunction to render "impressions" and "states of mind produced by interesting and remarkable objects" rather than simply the objects themselves (5:259), are detailed, reflective, and bracingly candid.

Intellectually indolent and socially reserved, Hawthorne might seem lacking in the qualifications of a penetrating observer, yet he was one, far more so than

Emerson in *English Traits* (1856). What Hawthorne had in happy abundance and Emerson lacked (except for his opening chapter, "First Visit to England," one would hardly know that Emerson had ever left America's shores or taken his senses with him) were the novelist's gifts of keen perception and vivid expression. England and the English come to life in *The English Notebooks* and *Our Old Home* through the mind and sensibility of an observer who, though rarely of a conceptualizing bent, is alert to the provocations of experience as they ramify outward to the root coordinates of life, from the psychology of individuals and types through matters of social organization and national character to questions of history, human nature, and the governance (or nongovernance) of Creation.

By mid-1856, the tone of Hawthorne's journal softens as he grows more comfortable with London, lets down his cultural defenses, and expands his familiarity with English society and English types. Aside from characteristic qualities of temperament and tone—a wry, self-deprecating irony capable of cutting to the bone—three circumstances helped condition Hawthorne's stance toward England.

1. He was a republican, with what he felt "ought to be the natural hatred of men—and the particular hatred of Americans—to an Aristocracy" (12:475). He was also, however, a man of taste, with a liking for comfort and an appreciation of those outward graces that even Matthew Arnold conceded to his upper-class "barbarians."[3] In his projected English romance, he resolved to do justice to the "grand, beautiful, and noble characteristics" of aristocracy (12:475) even as he recognized that the system itself must and should pass. On the other side, he was impaired by a fastidiousness that made him recoil from the coarseness and degradation of the English lower classes and despair of any foreseeable change in their condition. His ideology, in short, was at odds with his sensibility.

2. He was a provincial, unacquainted with extraliterary culture, who combined the delicacy of the nascent connoisseur with what his son Julian called "the arrogant, uneasy, Puritan conscience, which would not let him unrestrainedly enjoy a rose unless he could feel convinced that both the rose and he deserved it" (*NHW* 2:143). Henry James's account of Americans' "habit of looking askance at foreign institutions—of keeping one eye, as it were, on the American personality, while with the other they contemplate these objects" (James 121)—is an apt characterization of some of Hawthorne's earlier notebooks, in which (usually to their detriment) English villages are compared to New England villages, English girls to American girls, the English lower classes to the American lower classes, and English officials to American officials. Privately, he took pleasure in the British difficulties at Sebastopol as a much needed comeuppance for a nation cocksure of itself and contemptuous of

America (21:138). As he settled into England, he gradually outgrew his aggressive-defensive stance, and although he never adopted an English frame of reference, he gave promise of developing into a Jamesian cosmopolite able to "pick and choose and assimilate" the best of foreign culture while retaining the "unprecedented spiritual lightness and vigour" that James considered the distinctive property of the American.[4] "All past affairs, all home-conclusions, all people I have known in America, and meet again here," he wrote after seeing longtime American acquaintance George Bradford, "are strangely compelled to undergo a new trial," because, "being free from my old surroundings and the inevitable prejudices of home, I decide upon them absolutely" (21:115). (Bradford did not profit from the revaluation.)

   3. He was a romancer, an idealist in life as well as in literature, who held to the reality of the spiritual above the material and who found in middle-class England a nation of happy materialists. Emerson also noted this quality: "Man in England submits to be a product of political economy"; he is "materialist, economical, mercantile."[5] Emerson's materialists are in the tradition of Locke and Adam Smith—*homo economicus;* Hawthorne's are in the tradition of that figure of truth and caricature, John Bull, an eating, drinking, extroverted, and wholly unintellectual man cozily at home in his earthy world and insensible that here or hereafter there could be any better one.[6]

   Even more than the fact of aristocracy or of English condescension toward America, it was this earthbound complacency that most deeply unsettled Hawthorne. Mildly chiding Emerson for crediting the English with "all the qualities that they value, or pride themselves upon," Hawthorne admitted to erring himself (if error it was) in the opposite direction from "a certain malevolence and hostility in my own breast" (17:540). Arnold believed that Hawthorne's view of the English was owing to his frequent "contact with the British Philistine; and the British Philistine is a trying personage."[7] Arnold is right about Hawthorne's first two years in England, yet even after visits to London enlarged the diplomat's social and cultural acquaintance, it was still the bluff, hearty John Bull that impressed him, for better and worse, as the essential Englishman.

   A month before leaving England for the Continent, Hawthorne summed up his four and a half years' experience in a pronouncement on foggy, mud-befouled December London: "It is human life; it is this material world; it is a grim and heavy reality. I have never had the same sense of being surrounded by materialisms, and hemmed with the grossness of this earthly life, anywhere else" (22:433). England, especially London, was the actual as distinct from the ideal; it was the body as distinct from the soul; it was, as Hawthorne never tired of saying, beef and ale. What he does *not* say at such moments is that he himself became a fond consumer of these commodities, taking pleasure in physical life, even in the appalling Liverpool slums, and venturing happily into city or country taverns to order a chop, drink a pint of ale, and smoke a cigar. Beyond merely observing John Bull, Hawthorne acquired many of his habits and tastes. His quarrel with the English was in part a lover's quarrel with those aspects of his own nature that embraced the material, enjoyed Hogarth and Dickens, preferred Dutch painting to Italian, and professed an admiration for the novels of Anthony Trollope to the prejudice of his own (18:229).

Despite frequent grumbling, the problem for Hawthorne was not that he disliked England and the English but that he liked them too much and found himself comfortably sliding into their ways. To a New England romancer tinged with puritan asceticism as sublimated by midcentury sentimentality— a vocabulary of the spirit severed from traditional religiosity and, for that reason, all the more invested in its genteel idealism—the beef-and-ale solidity of the English character raised disturbing questions. If Trollope was right about literature and experience, if London with its "grossness of . . . earthly life" was indeed a fit image of the human, then Hawthorne would have to revise his beliefs, behavior, literary practice, and very conception of reality. Julian notes that his father could maintain a "respectful and intelligent curiosity" toward Italy because "he had no personal stake" in the matter (*NHW* 2:170); with England, he had a deep personal stake. Though grounded in observation, his "John Bull" was an exaggerated portrait that allowed him simultaneously to indulge and denigrate a version of his own disposition toward the earthy and material. "John Bull" was an alter ego, a somewhat coarse but cheerful and well-meaning English Hyde to his own self-consciously thin-blooded American Jekyll. Amid the omnipresent materialisms of England, Hawthorne felt himself in a world of counterromance. He was in the belly of the beast. He was in his own belly and discovering, to his seriocomic chagrin, that he was more than half liking it.

Pilgrimages

I longed to wander over the scenes of renowned achievement—to tread, as it were, in the footsteps of antiquity, to loiter about the ruined castle, to meditate on the falling tower, to escape, in short, from the commonplace realities of the present and lose myself among the shadowy grandeurs of the past.

—Washington Irving, *The Sketch Book of Geoffrey Crayon, Gent.* (1819–1820)

Its aspect disappointed me; but so does everything.

—Hawthorne on Sir Walter Scott's Abbotsford, *The English Notebooks* (May 10, 1856)

For an antebellum American nurtured on literature, to journey to England was to undertake a pilgrimage. Irving set the tone, established the expectation, and served as the ancestral norm against which experience played itself out, whether sentimentally or ironically. The "accumulated treasures of age" that drew Geoffrey Crayon to Europe had a mixed effect on pilgrim Hawthorne, for whom Crayon's "charms of storied and poetic association" were almost invariably dissolved by the encounter with material fact.[8] Viewing Stonehenge, "a cluster of large gray stones…forming no very picturesque or noteworthy spectacle," Hawthorne "knew that the reality was going to dwindle woefully within my ideal; as every-thing else does" (22:52). Disillusionment was the keynote of nearly all his English pilgrimages. Only Gothic cathedrals exceeded expectation. Their recesses drew one ever deeper with "vast revelations and shadowy conceal-ments" (5:265); they seemed "the greatest work man has yet achieved" (21:223). Indeed, because they *were* so rich, so unfathomable, and so conducive to exalted ideas of human capacity, they threw into relief the shallow, ritualized religion they harbored. English cathedrals aspired and *in*spired; English worship plod-ded along worn paths.

Were Hawthorne's disappointments the failure of England as a nation or a culture or were they testimonies to the deflationary power of the real as it inev-itably confounds romantic expectations? Visiting Shakespeare's birthplace, Hawthorne found it "woefully shabby and dingy, coarsely built, and such as the most poetical imagination would find it difficult to idealize"; he was "conscious of not the slightest emotion while viewing it, nor any quickening of the imagi-nation" (5:97; v. 22:26). Burns's cottage was "even more unsatisfactory," a "poor, mean dwelling," unfit for any civilized inhabitant, that all but divested Burns of his poetic halo (21:268, 270). Scott's Abbotsford was most disillu-sioning of all because of Scott's prominence in Hawthorne's literary pantheon. The house—"but a villa, after all; no castle, nor even a large manor house"—left no "simple and great impression"; it seemed "a plaything" and prompted Hawthorne to reflect "that Scott could not have been really a wise man, nor an earnest one, nor one that grasped the truth of life" (22:22, 26, 22, 26). Leaving Abbotsford, Hawthorne felt "remorse" for having come at all (22:27); his count of enchanted objects had diminished by one. Toward the end of his life Hawthorne returned to Scott and "read aloud the whole of [his] novels" (*NHW* 2:9). The disenchantment was with the man and his milieu, not with his imag-ined world. The latter could survive and continue to enthrall, if it were safely cordoned off from reality.

After a second visit to Abbotsford, Hawthorne expressed his loathing for the practice of "making pilgrimage to the shrines of departed men," which "seldom or never produces (in me, at least) the right feeling" (22:331). The exception was a journey he made alone, on his fifty-first birthday, to Samuel Johnson's

Lichfield, then the following day, in "one of the few purely sentimental pilgrimages that I ever undertook" (5:133), to nearby Uttoxeter, scene of Johnson's belated penance for a youthful act of disobedience to his bookseller father. Hawthorne "knew and loved" Johnson chiefly through Boswell—that is to say, "as a man, a talker, and a humorist" rather than as a writer (5:122)—and it was *as* a man *to* a man that he uncharacteristically "set [his] foot on the worn steps, and laid [his] hand on the wall of the house, because Johnson's hand and foot might have been in those same places" (21:222).

With his sturdy common sense and "muddy imperfection" of spirit (5:122), Johnson seemed to Hawthorne quintessentially English: "he meddled only with the surface of life, and never cared to penetrate farther than to plough-share depth" (5:122). In the extraordinary moment of his penance, however—"as beautiful and touching an incident as can be cited out of any human life" (21:227)—the proud, obstinate Johnson was drawn to the marketplace as magnetically as Dimmesdale to the scaffold, and in as powerful a testimony to the imperativeness of conscience. The gesture validated everything Hawthorne held sacred but seldom saw confirmed outside of literature, and yet it seemed to have no reality except for literary people like himself. He found it "strange and stupid" that no monument or inscription commemorated the incident and that present-day inhabitants of "the absurd little town" knew "nothing" of the moment in their history that "sanctifie[d]" the town "to the heart of a stranger from three thousand miles over the sea!" (21:227, 229). Moral and spiritual life survived its situational moment only as inscribed in art and perpetuated in the imaginations of those who live in art—of the "solitary child" (now a middle-aged pilgrim) who had stood "on tiptoe to pull down books from no very lofty shelf" and who achieved through impressionable reading a "sort of intimacy" with writers and their heightened world that marked him forever (5:122).

So far as he was, or sought to be, a romancer, Hawthorne was always that child, nursing his idealism in a bluff material world whose negations echoed within him in tones of skepticism, self-deprecation, and irony. In working up his notebook entries into the *Our Old Home* chapter "Lichfield and Uttoxeter," Hawthorne makes literary capital of the discordance between poetry and fact. For the sake of "picturesque arrangement and full impressiveness," he sets the penitent Johnson at "the very nucleus of the crowd—the midmost man of the market-place—a central image of Memory and Remorse, contrasting with, and overpowering the sultry materialism around him" (5:134). At the same time, practical sense tells him that Johnson's penance probably took place unnoticed "in the corner" of the church-door where his father "might very conveniently have located his stall" (5:134). Fitness "absolutely require[s] that Johnson shall not have his penance in a corner, ever so little retired" (5:134); he must stand front and center and his contrition must be an object of public wonder: "I am resolved, therefore, that the true site of Dr. Johnson's penance was in the middle of the market-place" (5:134).

"The true site": what *is* true, the outward circumstance or the kernel of meaning the romancer distills from it in contravention of fact? By "fitness" Hawthorne seems to mean something like the adequacy of life to the demands the imagination makes of it. In "Lichfield and Uttoxeter" life proves meagerly *un*fit as the chapter oscillates wildly between wishful idealism and skeptical realism, Don Quixote and Sancho Panza.

The Gothic cathedral in Lichfield strikes Hawthorne as "the object best worth gazing at in the whole world," a marvel of "uncomprehended beauty…, of which I could appropriate only the minutest portion" (5:125). It simultaneously humbles and exalts, showing Hawthorne "how earthly" he is but also "whisper[ing] deeply of immortality" (5:125). Yet the mood of elevation quickly wanes, and Hawthorne begins "to lose the vision of a spiritual or ideal edifice behind the time-worn and weather-stained front of the actual structure" (5:125–26). The decayed carvings of angels, saints, martyrs, and kings "perversely" take on "the appearance of a sugar-image, after a child has been holding it in his mouth" (5:126). Even the aesthetics of the cathedral seem questionable now that Hawthorne finds himself in "the wrong mood" and without the "childlike simplicity" required to feel its spell. Upon entering the cathedral, he had observed choristers, mostly young boys, "with voices inexpressibly sweet and clear," dressed in long white robes that made them seem "like cherubs" (5:128, 129). "All at once, however," one of the choristers removes "his white gown, transforming himself before my eyes into a common-place youth" in "modern" dress of a "decidedly provincial cut" (5:129). "This absurd little incident," Hawthorne confesses, "had a sinister effect in putting me at odds with the proper influences of the Cathedral, nor could I quite recover a suitable frame during my stay there" (5:129). Having glimpsed the performance from backstage, Hawthorne can no longer yield to its illusion. Like the atmospherics of literary romance, idealizations in life depend on mystification and are vulnerable to the sudden and thorough deflations wrought by hard fact.

In "Lichfield and Uttoxeter," the chief deflationary force is the monolithic figure of Johnson himself, whose robust English "sagacity" operates as a counter to Hawthorne's New England "yeast" and "native propensities towards Fairy Land" (5:122). Johnson's spell acts on Hawthorne as Westervelt's does on Coverdale on the wood-path near Blithedale, save that Johnson's materialism is corporeal, blunt, and seemingly incontrovertible whereas Westervelt's is intellectual, sinister, and specious. The effect, nonetheless, is much the same; both insinuate themselves into the idealist's mind and plant the claims of the materially real. "After coming so far to indulge a solemn and high emotion, and standing now on the very spot where my pious errand should have been consummated,"

Hawthorne slips (as he says the reader "may be scandalized to learn") into a local pub for a dinner of "bacon and greens, some mutton-chops," and "a gooseberry pudding," along with "a pitcher of foaming ale" (5:135). "Dr. Johnson would have forgiven me," he adds wryly,

> for nobody had a heartier faith in beef and mutton than himself. And as regards my lack of sentiment in eating my dinner, it was the best thing I had done that day. A sensible man had better not let himself be betrayed into these attempts to realize the things which he has dreamed about, and which, when they cease to be purely ideal in his mind, will have lost the truest of their truth, the loftiest and profoundest part of their power over his sympathies. (5:135)

Nothing could be more Johnsonian in spirit, save perhaps kicking a stone in Lichfield cathedral as Johnson had kicked a stone to refute Berkeley's idealism. If the ideal seems to reassert itself in the phrase "the truest of their truth," Hawthorne deflates it with an additional one, "Such were a few of the reflections which I mingled with my ale" (5:136), and the pendulum swings back toward Johnsonian materiality. What began as a "purely sentimental pilgrimage" ends in the deconstruction of a pilgrimage, and it is only when Uttoxeter market lies safely behind him that Hawthorne can again make it "holy to [his] contemplation" (5:138).

Geoffrey Crayon's pilgrimages largely succeed—live up to their billing—because Irving has Crayon feel what his bookish imaginings predispose him to feel. Hawthorne's sound common sense and impatience with humbug (the Johnson in him) preclude his playing to audience expectations and gilding reality. The truth was that English literary shrines were commonly a disappointment. The lesson they taught, for any honest pilgrim, was simple and emphatic: poetry is one thing, actuality another. If you have built castles in the air, keep them there; they have no business on solid earth.

John Bull and His Consort

> National character is necessarily a construct, an artifice. Whoever defines or identifies it is at best selecting, sifting, suppressing, in the search for what is taken to be representative.
>
> —Paul Langford, *Englishness Identified*

> John Bull cannot make himself fine, whatever he may put on. He is a rough animal, and incapable of high polish, and his female is well adapted to him.
>
> —Hawthorne, *The English Notebooks* (August 25, 1855)

In his preface to *Our Old Home,* Hawthorne claims to "have very little to say about the deeper traits of national character" (5:3). In fact, the nature of the English—what they look like, how they conduct themselves, whether or not they qualify as gentlemen or ladies, what, how, and how much they eat and drink, whether or not they *have* "deeper traits" or are simply the well-adjusted animals they appear to be—obsesses him. From the first, he is alert to "English hospitality," but he wonders whether their "warmth of heart" is "genuine" (21:6). After four and a half years, he will conclude that it is, but he will still feel a gulf of mind and sensibility between England and New England. Personally, Hawthorne liked most of the Englishmen he came to know, more so "with the progress of the acquaintance" (5:4), but he cannot be said to have respected many of them (17:380). "The English character," he wrote in *Our Old Home,* "is by no means a very lofty one; they seem to have a great deal of earth and grimy dust clinging about them" (5:224).

Although "the decades after 1848" that coincided with Hawthorne's residence in England constitute "the full flowering of English thinking on the national character,"[9] the quality that the English found most distinctive about themselves, their love of liberty, would not have impressed an American, who had a good deal more of it. Cartoons in *Punch* typically represent the Englishman as thick-bodied with short legs and a large paunch, yet precisely because this caricature was so familiar and its features allowed their modicum of truth, it rarely appeared in discussions of the national character, then or later. Paul Langford's chapter on "Physicality" in *Englishness Identified* focuses almost exclusively on the Englishman's athleticism, with secondary remarks on his love of red meat.[10] Americans viewed English physicality quite differently. "Heavy fellows, steeped in beer and flesh pots, they are hard of hearing and dim of sight,"[11] Emerson wrote of the English. The physical seemed to Emerson a fitting index of the intellectual and moral, as it did to Hawthorne. In *The House of the Seven Gables* Hawthorne imagines "the great system of human progress" slowly "spiritualiz[ing] us by refining away our grosser attributes of body" (2:121). In England, he found a race that seemed locked in the mid-eighteenth century. An early dinner at the Liverpool town hall strikes the note of the journals. The rooms themselves were sumptuous; "as to the company, they had a kind of roughness ... :—elderly John Bulls—and there is hardly a less beautiful object than the elderly John Bull, with his large body, protruding paunch, short legs, and mottled, double-chinned, irregular-featured aspect. They are men of the world, at home in society, easy in their manners, but without refinement; nor are they what one thinks of, under the appelation [*sic*] of gentleman" (21:17).

"Gentleman" is prophetic: during his first years in England, Hawthorne will be obsessed with determining who is and who is not a "gentleman." "Englishmen," he remarks, "are apt to look like anything but gentlemen, even when they most unquestionably are so;—men of birth, rank, wealth, station having the aspect of…jolly country tavern-keepers, as much as anything. Neither is there any degree of elegance of manner; but, after a while, you feel and acknowledge that they are really gentlemen" (21:161). An MP Hawthorne meets at a large Liverpool dinner (its guest of honor, no less) reminds him on first sight of an "intelligent mechanic" such as he might encounter in America, "the usual English homeliness, and unpolished surface" overlaying what turns out to be "earnestness of purpose, and fullness of common-sense" but no distinction of intellect (21:162, 163). The proprietor of Smithills Hall, an English country house, could have stepped out of *Tom Jones*: a former MP and "a good specimen enough of the old English country gentleman, not highly polished, pretty sensible, loving his land and his trees, and his dogs and his game, doing a little justice-business," and in general filling his position quite well enough (21:294). Even the thirty-year-old Lord Stanley, heir to "an illustrious house" (22:203) and later to become a high-ranking cabinet minister, has the appearance of "a salesman in a dry-goods establishment, or belonging to some other genteel line of business," until Hawthorne learns who he is and comes to discern "a gentle dignity and half imperceptible reserve" that modifies, but does not entirely efface, his original impression (22:202).

Hawthorne was not a snob for rank as such, but he was for "gentlemanliness," which he associated with refinement of sensibility and a courteous, undemonstrative decorum. Melville qualifies as a gentleman in his eyes; Englishmen he meets privately or in his official capacity, though competent, kindhearted, and thoroughly respectable, are often pointedly identified as *not* being gentlemen. It may be that Hawthorne's public position gave him a new consciousness of status or that Britons' own distinctions of class and culture invited a reflexive judgment of *them* such as he would not have made of persons in egalitarian America. For the most part, however, Hawthorne was repulsed by the "roughness and uncouthness" he found even "in the most cultivated" of Englishmen (21:75). Racially, the Englishman seemed to start at a disadvantage, being made of "homely material," and it was only through "high rank, or remarkable intellect, or both" that a gentleman might be made of him (21:83). The Marquess of Lansdowne struck him as one who "would have been a very common-place man in the common ranks of life" and whom high rank had notably improved (22:83). But the process of elevation needed to work upon developable material. The lower classes were condemned to brutishness by generations of inbreeding. "Stubbed, sturdy figures, round, coarse faces, stubnoses—the most evident specimens of the brown bread of human nature," Hawthorne observed of a group of "plebian" schoolgirls on holiday, with nothing of Henry Higgins's faith that tutelage might "make a lady out of any one of them" (21:288). "Culture," in Raymond Williams's Arnoldian sense of a training bearing "close relations with the idea of human perfection,"[12] was not, in Hawthorne's view, exclusively a matter of nurture and education. "The sturdy Anglo-Saxon nature," he wrote flatly in *Our Old Home*, "does not refine itself short of the third generation" (5:320).

An Englishman seemed most himself to Hawthorne when he was eating or drinking, which he did "so heartily, and on the whole so wisely—trusting so entirely that there is no harm in good beef and mutton—and a reasonable quantity of good liquor"—that it was a "satisfaction" to see him at it (21:417). In the final chapter of *Our Old Home*, "Civic Banquets," Hawthorne eulogizes English feasting—"the consummate flower of civilization and refinement"—in language bordering on high burlesque. He professes to wonder how Englishmen will accommodate themselves to a heaven "from which the earthly institution of Dinner shall be excluded" (5:310). Although his tone is genial, his misgivings on the subject are real, if intermittent. Eating—the gratification of animal appetite—would always be an equivocal act for Hawthorne, enjoyed in fact but seldom in principle, except when made sacramental by the presence of his wife. There was nothing sacramental in what he saw in the second-class refreshment room at the Manchester Arts Exhibition: "John Bull and his female . . . in full gulp and guzzle, swallowing vast quantities of cold boiled beef, thoroughly moistened with porter or bitter ale; and very good meat and drink it is," Hawthorne noted, having evidently sampled them himself (22:367). The most elegant civic banquets, associated with "Church and State, and grown so majestic with long hereditary customs and ceremonies" (5:310), achieved, for the English, a sort of mystical quality, "a dreamlike development of spiritual happiness" conjured up "out of the very perfection of that lower bliss" (5:312). Such a dinner qualified as a consummate work of art; indeed, it seemed latter-day England's most characteristic work of art. In passages like this, Hawthorne is at once celebratory, mock-celebratory, and self-mocking. He envies the English their unfallen simplicity in pleasure-taking and partakes of it insofar as he can (his English residence having given him temporary license), but he cannot wholly approve of their gusto for the physical or, as his irony suggests, of his own.

Highly developed as a stomach, the Englishman seems atrophied as a soul. Emerson cited the national "torpidity on the side of religion" and, with a Puritan's contempt for ecclesiastical forms, decried English worship as "a quotation" and the English church as "a doll."[13] Hawthorne agrees in substance, but he grounds his remarks in direct observation, drawn from a visit at Smithills Hall: "I should like to know how much true religious feeling is indicated by this regular observance of religious rites. . . . [T]he Englishman goes from prayer to pleasure, and is a worldly man in all respects till morning prayer-time comes about again. If an American is an infidel, he knows it; but an Englishman is often so without suspecting it" (21:298). Even in the grand cathedrals, or especially in them, English religion seems to Hawthorne a matter of empty ritual. The sermons are "cold and commonplace," with no inwardness; "the magnificence of the setting quite dazzles out what we Puritans look upon as the jewel of the whole affair" (5:226, 227).

The gift of the English being for material life, they were most successful when they remained within its limits. The phrase "English genius" struck Hawthorne as close to oxymoronic. In his hypersensitivity, Tennyson was "altogether as un-English as possible" (22:353). Even Nelson, England's consummate hero, "was unlike his countrymen in the qualities" of poetry, imagination, and nervous excitability that distinguished him (22:353). Nelson "was a man of genius," Hawthorne added in *Our Old Home*, "and genius in an Englishman ... is usually a symptom of a lack of balance.... An ordinary Englishman is the healthiest and wholesomest of human beings; an extraordinary one is almost always, in one way or another, a sick man" (5:232). If, as Melville said, "all mortal greatness is but disease" (*WHM* 5:74), the English were most commendable when they were *not* great but simply jolly, sensible creatures untroubled by profound thought: "If you make an Englishman smart, (unless he be a very exceptional one, of whom I have seen a few), you make him a monster; his best aspect is that of ponderous respectability" (5:319). At times Hawthorne grew weary of such stodginess; he claimed to have found more progressive talk among the American sea captains at Mrs. Blodget's boardinghouse than anywhere else in England (21:343), but progressivism was not what he sought out or valued in the English. Meeting a Manchester newspaper editor who had known Emerson, read Thoreau, and could talk of Margaret Fuller, Hawthorne found "this vein of literary taste" unpromising in a Briton. "The illiberals, the conservatives, the men who despise and hate new things and new thoughts," he went on, almost perversely, "are the best worth knowing": "The best thing a man, born in this island, can do, is to eat his beef and mutton, and drink his port and porter, and take things as they are, and think thoughts that shall be so beef-ish, mutton-ish, port-ish, and porter-ish, that they shall be matters material rather than intellectual" (22:38).

In brief, Hawthorne "patronized" John Bull in every sense of the word: he did not want his typical Englishman to be anything other than what he was. In *Our Old Home* he engages in chauvinistic nose-pulling—writing chiefly for an American audience, he means to puncture what Henry James would call "that quiet and comfortable sense of the absolute, as regards its own position in the world, which reigns supreme" in the British mind (James 121)—but his notebook entries on English character are equally critical, though rarely without affection and even a sort of bemused envy. A materialism so complacent and self-complete, so devoid of American restlessness and New England morbidity, had an appeal of its own, both aesthetically as a phenomenon and personally as an antidote to Salem-bred austerities.

Hawthorne's empathy with the English ended abruptly when it came to sex; for this displaced American Puritan, the Victorians were not Victorian enough.

The English seemed to Hawthorne a physical people who had tamed themselves to a rough decency among the upper and middle orders and who, as a society, dealt with indecency in the lower orders largely by ignoring it and otherwise containing its potentially disruptive occasions, like the carnivalesque Greenwich Fair Hawthorne attended in the year before it was officially banned. One of his earliest impressions in England was of "a coarseness, a freedom, an—I don't know what"—among lower-class women "that was purely English," American women having almost universally "something ladylike and delicate" about them (21:8). For all their apparent chaos, gender relations in English slums some- times seemed to Hawthorne governed by "laws of intercourse which were never violated" and "which perhaps had as deep a foundation in natural fitness as the code of the drawing room" (5:283–84). Such confidence dissolved, however, whenever he encountered the Molly Seagrim–like (his allusion) roughness of English women, overtly physical among the lower classes and restrained in their betters "only by a merciless rigor on the part of society" (5:284). From a dis- tance, purely as a national phenomenon, Henry James could delight in the mix of magnificence and vulgarity of a hypersexualized figure like his Millicent Henning (from *The Princess Casamassima*); Hawthorne, in life, would have felt the first, recoiled from the second, and been disconcerted by their conjunction, still more by his fascination with it.

Hawthorne was no innocent with regard to lower-class sexuality, having wit- nessed it in frontier areas of New England as well as in Boston. Liverpool and London were nonetheless a revelation, but what shocked him most was the moral indifference (or worse) on the part of men he considered gentlemen. The demeanor of Lord Lansdowne, "a kind old man," prompted Hawthorne to con- jecture that the English aristocracy was "generally... kind, and of [a] beautiful deportment" worthy of Americans' emulation, until Henry Bright informed him that this "respectable" old man, "as I innocently considered him, is a most disrep- utable character" and by rumor "the original of Thackeray's Lord Steyne" (22:84, 87). The relationship between manners and morals, the winning and the chaste, would bedevil Americans in Europe throughout the nineteenth century. In a nation (America) in which middle-class sexual mores were hegemonic among respectable people, there was no equivalent to the liberties openly allowed or assumed by the English upper class or to the casualness with which such matters might be discussed. Even Francis Bennoch came in for criticism on this score. Describing a British acquaintance (known to Hawthorne) who had "seduced innumerable women" and fathered "an infinity" of bastards, "Bennoch exempli- fied the grossness of the English nature in the careless and unhorrified way in which he told these things" (21:424). Philanthropists aside, Hawthorne wrote in *Our Old Home,* "Englishmen of station and respectability... have neither any faith in the feminine purity of the lower orders of their countrywomen, nor the slightest value for it, allowing its possible existence" (5:241). Still less, as Bennoch's example suggested, did they reverence their own purity in thought and word, however conventional they might be in deed. "The subject cannot well be discussed in these pages," Hawthorne instructed his American audience,

> but I offer it as a serious conviction from what I have been able to observe, that England of to-day is the unscrupulous old England of Tom Jones and Joseph Andrews, Humphrey Clinker and Roderick Random; and in our refined era, just as in that more free-spoken epoch, this singular people has a certain contempt for any fine-strained purity, any special squeamishness, as they consider it, on the part of an ingenuous youth. They appear to look upon it as a suspicious phenomenon in the masculine character. (5:241)

Hawthorne's recoil at sexual looseness was characteristic. Because sex was seldom merely sex for him but was entwined with ideals of woman's ethereal nature, to make light of purity, in reference to *any* class, was to call into question the reality of the moral order and therefore of the spiritual order. So-and-so's "infinity" of bastards and the casual attitude taken toward them were more than an affront to virtue; they were a challenge to belief. Bennoch could hardly have imagined what trip wires his light gossiping had touched.

Because of all he invested in female nature, other manifestations of coarse English womanhood disturbed Hawthorne even when they were not associated with sexuality. "John Bull" seemed an apt name for so beefy a physical and moral specimen as the Englishman. Hawthorne had no comparable epithet for English women (although at least once he refers to "the female Bull" [5:240]), but what was tolerably Hogarthian to him in the male was horrific in the female. Emerson also remarked on the "disadvantage" of body type that inclined Englishwomen toward stockiness rather than grace,[14] but for Emerson this was a physiological and aesthetic misfortune, not the moral damnation it came close to representing for Hawthorne. By virtue of their appearance and manner, Englishwomen amounted to a positive refutation, indeed a hideous travesty, of any notion of female ethereality. Except, perhaps, for the vitriolic passage on Margaret Fuller in *The French and Italian Notebooks*, Hawthorne's writings offer nothing so brutal as his notebook characterization of English women. Two early impressions merit quoting at length, if only for their extraordinary animus. That of September 24, 1853:

> The women of England are capable of being more atrociously ugly than any other human beings; and I have not as yet seen one whom we should

distinguish as beautiful in America. They are very apt to be dowdy. Ladies often look like cooks and housemaids, both in figure and complexion;—at least, to a superficial observer, although a closer inspection shows a kind of dignity, resulting from their quiet good opinion of themselves and consciousness of their position in society....As a general rule, they are not very desirable objects in youth, and, in many instances, become perfectly grotesque after middle-age;—so massive, not seemingly with pure fat, but with solid beef, making an awful ponderosity of frame. You think of them as composed of sirloins, and with broad and thick steaks on their immense rears....Nothing of the gossamer about them; they are elephantine, and create awe and respect by the muchness of their personalities. Then as to their faces, they are stern, not always positively forbidding, yet calmly terrible, not merely by their breadth and weight of feature, but because they show so much self-reliance, such acquaintance with the world, its trials, troubles, dangers, and such internal means of defence;—...they seem like seventy-four gun ships in time of peace;—you know that you are in no danger from them, but cannot help thinking how perilous would be their attack, if pugnaciously inclined,—and how hopeless the attempt to injure them. Really they are not women at all;—not that they are masculine, either, though more formidable than any man I ever saw. (21:41–42)

And a year later (September 16, 1854):

I have heard a good deal of the tenacity with which English women retain their personal charms to a late period of life; but my experience is, that an English lady of forty or fifty is apt to become the most hideous animal that ever pretended to human shape. No caricature could do justice to some of their figures and features; so puffed out, so huge, so without limit, with such hanging dewlaps, and all manner of fleshly abomination—dressed, too, in a way to show all these points to the worst advantage, and walking about with entire self-satisfaction, unconscious of the wrong they are doing to one's idea of womanhood. They are gross, gross, gross. Who would not shrink from such a mother! Who would not abhor such a wife! I really pitied the respectable elderly gentlemen whom I saw walking about with such atrocities hanging on their arms—the grim, red-faced monsters! Surely, a man would be justified in murdering them—in taking a sharp knife and cutting away their mountainous flesh, until he had brought them into reasonable shape, as a sculptor seeks for the beautiful form of woman in a shapeless block of marble. The husband must feel that something alien has grown over and incrusted the slender creature whom he married, and that he is horribly wronged by having all this flabby flesh imposed upon him as his wife. "Flesh of his flesh," indeed!...Nor is it possible to conceive of any delicacy and grace of soul existing within; or if there be such, the creature ought to be killed, in order to release the spirit so vilely imprisoned....American women, of all ranks, when past their prime, generally look thin, worn, care-begone, as if they may have led a life of much trouble and few enjoyments; but English women look as if they had fed upon the fat of meat, and made themselves gross and earthy in all sorts of ways. As a point of taste, I prefer my own countrywomen; though it is a pity that we must choose between a greasy animal and an anxious skeleton. (21:133–34)

It is remarkable that Ticknor and Fields allowed an only slightly tempered version of these remarks to be published in *Our Old Home*.

Le Connoisseur Malgré Lui

> I am making some progress as a connoisseur, and have got so far as to be able to distinguish the broader differences of style; as, for example, between Rubens and Rembrandt.
>
> —Hawthorne, *The English Notebooks* (August 16, 1857)

If there was a golden mean between the material and the spiritual, the hearty, corpulent Englishman or -woman and the nervous, angular American, it seemed realized in the elderly British poet Leigh Hunt, born of self-exiled American parents and impressing Hawthorne, when he visited him outside of London, as "thoroughly American, and of the best type" (5:274). Like some of Henry James's expatriates, Hunt combined an American freedom of view with a European "fineness, subtlety, and grace" (5:273); he appeared to come out, as it were, on the *other* side of civilization, with manners "so obedient to some rule so subtile that the nicest observer could not detect the application of it" (5:272). Hunt seemed not to have "an English trait in him from head to foot, morally, intellectually, or physically. Beef, ale, or stout, brandy, or port-wine, entered not at all into his composition" (5:273). Yet neither did he resemble Hawthorne's countrymen. His ways owed nothing to national character or social convention, still less to a self-conscious flouting of their norms; they were "soft," "agreeable," "exceedingly appreciative of whatever was passing" around him, exquisite in penetration and tact, and uniquely his own (5:272).

Hunt is central to Hawthorne's thinking about national character and the evolution of the race because he represents a type that seems worthy of beau ideal status but is conspicuously denied it. Anticipating James, Hawthorne's sister Elizabeth remarked (apropos of *Our Old Home*) that "the mind of a cultivated American must necessarily be fed upon the best that other nations can supply, and so is likely to share in the qualities of all" (in *NHW* 2:234). Hunt displays this high eclecticism par excellence, and to Hawthorne he augurs "perhaps what our future intellectual advancement may make general among us" (5:273–74). Yet despite liking Hunt enormously, Hawthorne has reservations about him and utters his prophecy "a little reluctantly" (5:273). He sees Hunt as made for comfort, leisure, beautiful surroundings, and the society of appreciative women; his flaw is "a lack of grit" (5:273). Hunt is like Clifford of *The House of the Seven Gables,* enlarged and tempered by Europe and shorn of his worst selfishness but still, for all that, an enervated aesthete. He is "a light, mildly joyous nature, gentle, graceful, yet seldom attaining to that deepest grace which results from power; for beauty, like Woman, dallies with the gentle, but yields its consummate favor only to the strong" (5:275). Confronted with the choice, beauty or strength, Hawthorne opts for strength. Measuring Hunt's felicitously refined temperament against his own New England one, he says (gently dismissing both Hunt and the Hunt-type), "But I am of somewhat sterner stuff and tougher fibre than Leigh Hunt" (21:386).

Hunt was a countertype to John Bull and another possible alter ego for Hawthorne; he was the gentleman-as-connoisseur Hawthorne felt he might become as he surprised himself by developing a taste for painting during his frequent visits to the Great Exhibition in Manchester in 1857. As he weighed the merits of this persona, Hawthorne circled around two questions that figured prominently in nineteenth-century discussions of culture. The first concerned the relationship between the aesthetic and the moral. The idea of connoisseurship was titillating to Hawthorne the New Englander, for it verged on the sumptuously equivocal, if not the expressly forbidden. On one side, he was naïvely proud of his "progress as a connoisseur." Having noticed "some of [the painters'] defects from the first," he could feel himself "mounting a few steps higher" and beginning to appreciate some of their "beauties" (22:359). But was the game worth the candle? "Taste seems to be a department of moral sense," he wrote in the aborted English romance "The Ancestral Footstep," "and yet it is so little identical with it, and so little implies conscience, that some of the worst men in the world have been the most refined" (12:74). While the Scottish Common Sense philosophy he had imbibed in college argued for the congruence of the aesthetic and the moral senses, the lessons of history and observation—of Nero, for example, "a monster" for "all his elegant tastes, his love of the beautiful, [and] his artist nature" (14:295)—taught otherwise.

The second question involved two overlapping but potentially rival meanings of "culture": (1) a process of inner development; and (2) the acquisition and appreciation of agreed-upon products of art and thought.[15] Although Hawthorne approached museums reluctantly, like a child snatched away from play, after repeated visits he came to take pleasure in the consciousness of his developing sense of taste. But was it a genuine development or simply an initiation into a freemasonry whose standards were arcane, hermetic, self-perpetuating, and self-serving? As he found himself "recognizing more and more the merit of the acknowledged Masters in the art," he wondered whether this was a sign of true refinement or evidence of his acceptance of "the wrong principles which may have been laid down by the connoisseurs" (22:361). He would ask this question again in Italy, repeatedly. It amused him to think that on returning to America he would "doubtless...pass for a man of taste" (22:375); it must have amused him, too, to phrase it like that ("pass for"), an acknowledgment at once of the modesty of his accomplishments, the rudimentary state of Americans' refinement, and the likelihood that he had learned enough of the connoisseur's idiom to be taken for the real thing.

The Manchester experiment ended much as later aesthetic ones would, with Hawthorne's temporary exhaustion with the galleries, abetted in this case by Sophia's bronchial discomfort in sooty Manchester. The place the family removed to was new, prosperous, familiar, and thoroughly philistine. "'Genteel' is the word for it" (22:371), Hawthorne wrote of Leamington Spa. Indeed, so well did "genteel" fit Leamington that Hawthorne makes it an ironic epithet, as if he were characterizing not only the town but also, with self-deprecating irony, his way of inhabiting it. "Genteel" may also be a dismissive pun; the genteel is not the truly "gentleman-like" but an insipid bourgeois counterfeit of it. In this sense, Hawthorne's choice of Leamington (where the family had previously resided) seems virtually a choice of identity. After the arduousness of acquiring culture at the Manchester Exhibition, Hawthorne relaxes his ideal of connoisseurship, forgoes civilized being in the manner of Leigh Hunt, and settles for living anonymously in a "small, neat house, in a circle of just such houses," in "this prettiest, cheerfullest, cleanest of English towns" (22:385). It seemed, for a time, enough to be comfortable—but only for a time. Within two months, Hawthorne found himself "getting tired" of genteel Leamington (18:124) and looking forward to Italy, where the process of civilizing himself would begin again. Like Melville oscillating between the symbolic poles of land (material comfort) and sea (spiritual aspiration), Hawthorne oscillated between the identities of sedate philistinism and would-be connoisseurship, John Bull and Leigh Hunt, alternately pursuing each, wearying of each, and never discovering a stable middle way.

The Unthinkable

> We are not concerned with the very poor. They are unthinkable, and
> only to be approached by the statistician or the poet.
>
> —E. M. Forster, *Howards End*

The twelve chapters of *Our Old Home* have no obvious arrangement, either by date of composition and magazine publication or by the chronology of Hawthorne's English experience, but at least some of them seem artfully positioned for thematic effect. The chapter "Up the Thames" ends with Hawthorne's extended portrait of Leigh Hunt; the succeeding chapter, "Outside Glimpses of English Poverty," begins with his going "designedly astray among precincts that reminded [him] of some of Dickens's grimiest pages" (5:277). On the further side, "Outside Glimpses" is flanked by the sumptuous feasting of "Civic Banquets." The contrasting chapters, on rich and poor, elegant and degraded, recall Melville's fictive diptych "The Paradise of Bachelors and the Tartarus of Maids." They sermonize by structural juxtaposition.

Early on in Liverpool, Hawthorne began taking daily walks through the city, "preferring the darker and dingier streets, inhabited by the poorer classes," which he found "very picturesque in their way"—the gin shops; filthy, ragged, sickly looking people; "men haggard, drunken, care-worn, hopeless, but with a kind of patience"; mothers openly nursing infants: "there is a bustle, a sense of being in the midst of life, and of having got hold of something real, which I do not find in the better streets of the city" (21:18, 19). "The real," virtually synonymous for Hawthorne with the earthy and *un*genteel, both attracted and repelled him, the former because he had excluded so much of it from his life and work, the latter because in dangerously thrilling ways it challenged the beliefs on which that life and work rested.

In one of his first walks around Liverpool, Hawthorne comes upon a poor Irish family by the ferry house, a father ("gray-haired and gray-bearded, clad in an old drab over-coat"), a mother ("pale, with a thin, anxious, winkled face"), and their three young daughters, none above nine years old, all "quite pretty, with delicate faces": "They all looked very shabby, but yet had a decency about them" (21:51). Unasked, Hawthorne gives one of the girls a sixpence, regretting later that it had not been more; the parents thank him and say "they had been traveling a long distance, and had nothing to live upon, but what they picked up on the road" (21:51). "There is not much that can be caught in the description of this scene," Hawthorne writes, "but it made me understand, better than before, how poor people feel, wandering about in such destitute circumstances, and how they suffer, and yet how they know a life not quite miserable, after all; and how family love goes along with them.... Somehow or other, I got into the interior of this poor family, and understand, through sympathy, more of them than I can tell" (21:51–52). Such compassion for the pathos and dignity of desperate humanity is uncommon in *The English Notebooks*. Even in this entry, Hawthorne admits to having assimilated "some of the English indifference as to beggars and poor people" (21:52). Hawthorne is not natively callous; rather, like Melville's lawyer-narrator in "Bartleby, the Scrivener," he understands that "to a sensitive being, pity is not seldom pain. And when at last it is perceived that such pity cannot lead to effectual succor, common sense bids the soul be rid of it" (*WHM* 9:29). Hawthorne feels a version of what the modern city-dweller sometimes feels walking past the homeless living in cardboard boxes on the streets: one can't help all of them; one can't substantially and permanently help *any* of them; so in self-defense one develops an emotional carapace. When Hawthorne thought he might be able to influence social change, he tried to do so, as when he urged reform of the brutal conditions in the American merchant marine in his correspondence with Secretary of State Lewis Cass and Senator Charles Sumner; but English poverty, though appalling, was beyond his remedy or palliation. When "two companies of working people" show up at his Rock Park door "asking assistance—being out of work, and with no resource other than charity," Hawthorne is affected by their "meekness" and feels the injustice of their plight. Whether he also contributed to their relief he does not say (21:157).

Even sympathy had its limits, however. At times, Hawthorne could be squeamish, recoiling at the filth and brutishness of the poor as his aesthete Clifford recoils at the homeliness of Hepzibah, insensible to whatever moral worth might lie beneath the repugnant appearance. The "multitudinousness and continual motion" of slum life reminded him of the wriggling of "maggots in cheese" or of "devilish-looking insects scampering to-and-fro" beneath an overturned log (21:26; 5:282). It must be remembered that Hawthorne saw England in the years between the failed Chartist movement and the Reform Bill of 1867, a period during which, as J. Dover Wilson observed, "the great mass of people were in a condition of ignorance, squalor, and brutality which in our happier age"—Wilson was writing in 1932, the depths of the Depression—"it is almost impossible to imagine."[16] Conditions for most workingmen had improved somewhat since the 1830s, but not for all; the "proletariat...had been stratified," G. M. Young observes, and there remained "a vast, untouchable underworld."[17] It was this underworld that drew Hawthorne's attention, as both a social phenomenon and a disquieting manifestation of the human.

"I think I have never seen a populace before coming to England," Hawthorne remarked in one of his earliest observations of English life (21:8). By "populace" he meant a large, hereditary, and upwardly *immobile* lower class, such as seemed not (yet) to exist in America. Hawthorne is aware of class inequities and the "insolence of riches and prosperity" (21:156), but his stance toward them is divided. Returning with Henry Bright from watching skaters at two private estates, he marvels at "how comfortable Englishmen know how to make them-selves" in their snug, neat, well-guarded seclusion, "appropriated to the same family for generation after generation"; they truly fashion "a home." Yet having lately seen the poor queue up for soup tickets, he goes on to wonder "whether anybody is entitled to a home, in so full a sense, in this world" (21:156). His moral sense is at odds with his aesthetic sense (which includes his pleasure in well-groomed surroundings, ease, and abundance), the one inclining him toward republican sympathy, the other toward an association with the moneyed classes and a corresponding *dis*sociation from the poor. Watching a group of uniformed workhouse girls debark from the ferry, he finds no trace "of beauty, or scarcely of intelligence, in so much as one individual" but only "mean, coarse, vulgar fea-tures and figures, betraying unmistakably a low origin, and ignorant and brutal parents. They did not appear wicked, but only stupid, animal, and soulless. It must require many generations of better life to elicit a soul in them" (21:19).

"Elicit a soul in them." What can the phrase mean? When Hawthorne took his son Julian to the zoological gardens in Regents Park, he was discomfited by the monkeys, which bore enough of a resemblance to human beings to seem a malicious parody of "the master-piece of creation" (21:315). The British under-class affected him in a similar way. Did Leigh Hunt and the filthy, ragged men and "inconceivably sluttish women" who haunted the gin shops share the same spiritual essence? (5:278). Were the latter recognizably human at all? In the shapes of careworn women sitting on their "doorsteps, nursing their unwashed babies," the "fairest spectacle" in human life was degraded into "the foulest"; and "yet motherhood, in these dark abodes, is strangely identical with what we have all known it to be in the happiest homes.... It was the very same creature whose tender torments make the rapture of our young days" (5:283). The "sameness" was what disturbed him, for in such a maternal relationship in such an environ-ment there was no aura of the spiritual, only the instinct of brute mammalian life. Just as "it might...be supposed that Satan," not God, "had perpetrated monkeys" in order to ridicule human presumption (21:315), so it might be imag-ined that some diabolical agency had planted the maternal instinct in filthy and often vice-ridden women for the purpose of flouting notions of motherhood's sacredness. The women Hawthorne observed in the worst slums were similar enough to his own mother and to the mother of his children for him to infer from their example that life processes across all classes were at bottom merely biological and that while social amelioration was surely imperative and just, the superstructure of ideology that sublimated the naturalistic into the spiritual was a civilized illusion. Shorn of mystification, to "elicit a soul" meant practically to raise the underclass to health, solvency, and middle-class decorum. This, as

Young says, was the fundamental "aim" of "Victorian reform": "the steady diffusion of culture and comfort downwards and outwards in widening circles."[18] Materially and mentally, this was a laudable, if difficult enterprise; spiritually, however, what could such "diffusion" mean other than enlisting the populace in the genteel fictions with which middle-class society concealed or gilded its physiological origins and operations?

Such skepticism may have been the devil's voice speaking, but the grittiness of English poverty had the effect of stripping away many of Hawthorne's professed beliefs and laying bare the chronic suspicions he harbored beneath them. "Unless your faith be deep-rooted and of most vigorous growth," he warned his readers in *Our Old Home*, "it is the safer way not to turn aside into this region so suggestive of miserable doubt" (5:286). Hawthorne's own faith was neither, yet he compulsively revisited this dangerous region, physically, then in thought, as if obliged on both levels to peer into the abyss.

With its harrowing account of street life, "Outside Glimpses of English Poverty" is Hawthorne's closest approach to a sociology with its associated suppositions about historical agency and teleology. As an observer of social phenomena, Hawthorne grasped the relationship between economic bankruptcy and "moral bankruptcy,"[19] or the dynamic by means of which poverty and hopelessness erode the higher impulses and produce an apathy that in turn accelerates the downward spiral toward dissolution. "Along with disastrous circumstances, pinching need, [and] adversity so lengthened out as to constitute the rule of life," he writes, "there comes a certain chill depression of the spirits which seems especially to shudder at cold water" (5:278). The poor are unwashed and unkempt—at once a symbol, a symptom, a consequence, and an aggravating cause of their moral squalor. Wandering their teeming streets, where so much of their life takes place (their rooms being squalid and unwholesome), Hawthorne marvels at the prodigality of nature in bringing forth such a superfluity of beings and leaving them alone to struggle for life: "It might almost make a man doubt the existence of his own soul, to observe how Nature has flung these little wretches into the street and left them there, so evidently regarding them as nothing worth, and how all mankind acquiesce in the great mother's estimate of her offspring" (5:281–82). Was Malthus right about the harsh, inexorable laws that regulate life? And if he was (and Darwin would be), did atheistic materialism follow? Was it only the poor who seemed or were "soulless," or did their spiritual condition impugn all humanity's? "For, if they are to have no immortality," Hawthorne writes of the degraded poor, "what superior claim can I assert for mine? ... Until these slime-clogged nostrils can be made capable of inhaling celestial air, I know not how the purest and most intellectual of us can reasonably expect ever to taste a breath of it. The whole question of eternity is staked here. If a single one of these helpless little ones be lost, the world is lost!" (5:282).

Hawthorne is not exaggerating, or at least not much. Beyond comprising a social horror, English poverty insinuated a metaphysical one, the indifference of laissez-faire capitalism seeming to mirror, or even issue from, the indifference of a laissez-faire universe. If there is a crisis episode in *Our Old Home,* it is Hawthorne's notebook-based account of a tour of the West Derby workhouse, a cradle-to-coffin systemization of the problem of the poor. The sketch is an anatomy of the workings of the institution, a clean, orderly, but sterile antithesis to the disorder of the streets; it is a test of well-intentioned paternalistic efforts at remedying the worst social evils. For Hawthorne, the visit also turns out to be a personal trial in which he must demonstrate what sort of human being he is and what he genuinely believes about society, human nature, the course of history, and God's universe. Early in the tour, Hawthorne and his group are taken to the "hot and vaporous" laundry room, where they are "forced to inhale the strange element [of pauper-life] into [their] inmost being" (5:299). "What an intimate brotherhood is this in which we dwell," Hawthorne moralizes, "do what we may to put an artificial remoteness between the high creature and the low one!" (5:299). A remoteness, however, is precisely what Hawthorne tries to maintain as the tour proceeds. In the children's ward, he relates that "a singular incommodity befel one member of our party" when a child of indeterminate sex— "sickly, wretched, humor-eaten,... the offspring of unspeakable sin and sorrow" stretching back perhaps several generations—"took an unaccountable fancy to the gentleman just hinted at," a man of great "reserve" and "afflicted with a peculiar distaste for whatever was ugly" (5:300). As the child sidles nearer the man as if expecting to be caressed, Hawthorne presents the moment as a moral Judgment Day: "It was as if God had promised the poor child this favor on behalf of that individual, and he was bound to fulfil the contract, or else no longer call himself a man among men" (5:300). Like Bartleby for Melville's lawyer-narrator, the child seems to have been "billeted upon [the gentleman] for some mysterious purpose of an all-wise Providence" (*WHM* 9:37). Hawthorne "watche[s] the struggle in [the gentleman's] mind with a good deal of interest" and commends him for performing "an heroic act," one that "effected more than he dreamed of toward his final salvation, when he [takes] up the loathsome child and caress[es] it as tenderly as if he had been its father" (5:301). In "Bartleby" the lesson forced on the narrator is Christ's "injunction... 'that ye love one another'": we are truly our brother's keeper (*WHM* 9:36). This is the lesson *Our Old Home* draws, along with another: by virtue of this fraternal connection, we are all implicated in the aggregated sins of the world and are bound to help relieve them:

> No doubt, the child's mission in reference to our friend was to remind him
> that he was responsible, in his degree, for all the sufferings and misde-
> meanors of the world in which he lived, and was not entitled to look upon

a particle of its dark calamity, as if it were none of his concern; the offspring
of a brother's iniquity being his own blood-relation, and the guilt, likewise,
a burthen on him, unless he expiated it by better deeds. (5:301)

Generous as they are, Hawthorne's words are written for the occasion and
are quite different from those he recorded privately just after his visit. In the
published sketch, he neglects to say that the fastidious gentleman was himself
and that his reaction to the child was considerably less laudable. He is
appalled, he writes in his notebook, that the child should "choose [him] to be
its father!" and take hold of two of his fingers "(luckily the glove was on)." "I
wish I had not touched the imp," the passage concludes, "and yet I never
should have forgiven myself if I had repelled its advances" (21:413). Duty
and conscience, not wisdom and sympathy, actuate him. He is ashamed *not* to
do what circumstances call upon him to do; there is no moralizing about
human complicity.

"Bartleby" ascends from its narrator's moment of epiphany to the deep and
universal sense of the tragic represented by its closing "Ah, Bartleby! Ah
humanity!" (*WHM* 9:45). "Outside Glimpses" *de*scends from its comparable
moment. No sooner does one trial end than another begins, this one openly
involving Hawthorne in propria persona. In the next ward, he comes upon "a
baby, which, beyond all reach of comparison, was the most horrible object that
ever afflicted my sight," yet was not without "a premature intelligence" that
seemed to arraign passersby for "the deadly wrong of its existence" (5:303).
Hawthorne's distress is not for the afflicted child, who will likely die in a few
days; it is for himself: the child "pollut[es] my moral being with the sense of
something grievously amiss in the entire conditions of humanity" (5:302–3).
He is relieved to learn that the child came from "unhealthy [that is, syphilitic]
parents. Ah yes! There was the mischief" (5:303), he exclaims, seizing on the
fact as if it were sufficient to right the universe again. Sexual transgression
becomes the lightning rod that enables Hawthorne to divert his sense of the
"grievously amiss" (cosmic malfeasance, indifference, or absence) and ground
misery in human vice. Insofar as questions of theodicy continue to assert themselves—why has God *made* syphilis? why has he allowed innocents to suffer for
their parents' sin?—Hawthorne brushes them aside with platitude: God "has
imposed" on us (humanity in general) "the necessity to suffer in soul and body
till this dark and dreadful wrong be righted" (5:304). He himself does not suffer
for long, passing on to other matters and to other areas of the establishment after
settling the issue in his own mind. The notebook original, however, continues:
"Did God make this child? Has it a soul capable of immortality?—of immortal
bliss? I am afraid not. At all events, it is quite beyond my conception and understanding" (21:414).

If God did not make this child, who or what did? The ghastly facts of natural life unhinge Hawthorne because they seem inexplicable within any conception of a benign, superintending Providence. "Depressed by the sight of so much misery, and uninventive of remedies for the evils that force themselves on my perception," Hawthorne can only wish for a "new Deluge" that would dispose of the problem as one might dispose of unwanted kittens: "So far as these children are concerned, it would be a blessing to the human race... if every one of them could be drowned to-night" (5:304; v. 21:415). He promptly retracts such a solution as "certainly beyond the scope of man's discretionary rights" (5:305). He does not *believe* the terrible thing the moment provokes him to say; nonetheless, he does *feel* it, not as a literal wish but as the reflex of a pained sensibility wanting to be spared further sight of the offending cause. A social problem resistant to human intervention has shaded into a metaphysical problem, and the extremity of his response is a measure of how thoroughly his structure of belief has been challenged.

The balance of Hawthorne's visit is uneventful but dreary. Some of the males, taught a trade, have hope of bettering themselves; the females have virtually none. They will become domestic servants in the "meanest" of households, where they will "fare scantily, endure harsh treatment, lead shifting and precarious lives, and finally drop into the slough of evil, through which, in their best estate, they do but pick their slimy way on stepping-stones" (5:305). The workhouse episode ends formulaically with the utopian prophecy (absent from the notebook) of a future beyond acquisitive materialism and therefore beyond the "need of almshouses" (5:306), but nothing in Hawthorne's social analysis gives basis for hope that such a happy development is even remotely on the horizon. On the contrary, the underclass will perpetuate itself indefinitely. Efficiently organized and kindly run, the workhouse is an instrument for turning out standardized, marginally decent human products, less raucous but also less variegated than those of the street, which turns out its own products with appalling fecundity.

What oppressed Hawthorne most about the English class system was the mechanical regularity with which, from bottom to top, it replicated itself. In "Outside Glimpses," Hawthorne passes artfully, by seeming association, from the workhouse to a group of lower-class weddings performed en masse at Manchester Cathedral during the Easter holiday, when the usual clergyman's fee was waived. "They were my acquaintances of the poor streets, or persons in a precisely similar condition of life, and were now come to their marriage-ceremony in just such garbs as I had always seen them," the men in tattered or grimy workman's coats, the women in ragged dresses beneath shabby shawls (5:307). There was "nothing virgin-like in the brides, nor hopeful or energetic in the bridegrooms"; all seemed to labor under the "strange miscalculation of supposing that they could lessen the sum" of their "individual misery" by joining it with another's (5:307). Hawthorne's account is unsparingly dour. If there was anything of joy, color, or humble dignity in the Manchester proceedings, or any intuition on his own part of the beauty and mystery of life even in rags, he fails to record it in notebook or chapter. He observes the ceremony with grim omniscience, as if the course of these lives were foreordained, then lays the scene "away in memory as one of the saddest sights I ever looked upon" (5:308).

To complete his chapter on poverty and class, Hawthorne juxtaposes these weddings against another he later chanced to see at the same cathedral, an upper-class marriage performed by a bishop and four subsidiary clergymen. "The bridegroom's mien had a sort of careless and kindly English pride; the bride floated along in her white drapery" (5:308). The couple drive off "to live on their abundance in one of those stately and delightful English homes…; and all this fair property seemed more exclusively and inalienably their own, because of its descent through many forefathers, each of whom had added an improvement or a charm, and thus transmitted it with a stronger stamp of rightful possession to the heir" (5:309). Property begets property; poverty, poverty. Hawthorne ends "Outside Glimpses" on a quasi-Jacobin/Marxist note, questioning the legitimacy of a system that "gives one married pair" so much of a home and a multitude of others little or no home at all (5:309). He wonders whether working-class patience may wear thin and the wealthy may confront a moral crisis, if not a revolutionary *dies irae*. The chapter has been structured to culminate in this question, but its late-emerging focus on class division serves the additional purpose of allowing Hawthorne to evade the philosophical issues the workhouse visit has raised and left dangling. *The Scarlet Letter* softens its tragic ending with the prophecy of a "new truth" that will be disclosed "when the world should have grown ripe for it, in Heaven's own time" (1:263). In "Outside Glimpses," Providential teleology is notably absent, and the inequities of poverty and class are left to "the gentlemen of England" to face by themselves as they can (5:309).

National Indentures

> Each of us, when separated, having one side only, like a flat fish, is but
> the indenture of a man, and he is always looking for his other half.
>
> —Plato, *Symposium*

"Outside Glimpses" is so wrenching a chapter that it seems astonishing that Hawthorne should follow it with the celebration of conspicuous consumption in "Civic Banquets"; it is as if Melville positioned "The Paradise of Bachelors" after, not before, "The Tartarus of Maids." Perhaps Hawthorne's publishers felt that a marketable book could not end on such a dire note. And yet the evasions of *Our Old Home* seem characteristically Hawthorne's own. He had no solution to class injustice, nor was he a reformer by temperament or conviction; still less was he a disturber of cosmic peace. The ruminations that English poverty forced on him were not willingly entertained or pressed to intellectual or social conclusions. Hawthorne observes candidly; he reflects; he hazards possibilities; then he turns to other things. Rarely in the notebooks does he pursue any thought to finality; as a skeptic and an ironist, he distrusted finality. He enjoyed the process of reflection more than the definite results of it.

There is also a certain fitness to Hawthorne's concluding *Our Old Home* with "Civic Banquets." Ultimately, the belly of the beast *was* a belly. It was the love of physical comfort and a corresponding aversion to physical, moral, and intellectual *dis*comfort that made the aristocratic Englishman, as Arnold said, a barbarian, the middle-class Englishman a philistine, and the lower-class Englishman a near-brute. The evils of class and laissez-faire capitalism were not created by the English character, but they were, Hawthorne felt, tinctured and upheld by it; a more spiritual, idealistic people might have managed their material life better.

Nonetheless, there was much in England and the English for an American to admire, even to envy, down to their beef-and-ale heartiness and open materialism. London, especially, came to delight him, and he left it with a sad expectation of the barrenness awaiting him at home. "If it were not for my children," he told William D. Ticknor in April 1856, "I question whether I would ever see America again" (17:481). Return he did, however, with a bereft feeling that instead of incorporating England into his being, he had been wrenched away from a vital and happy part of himself. After Bennoch and his circle, Wayside neighbors Waldo Emerson and Bronson Alcott seemed dry, rarefied company, and even the Saturday Club, which included the genial Holmes and Lowell, wanted the jolly earthiness Hawthorne recalled of English gatherings. "I spend a monotonous life, seldom quitting my own hill-side, and trying earnestly to take root there," he told Henry Bright on December 17, 1860. "I find, however, that I staid abroad a little too long, and as a consequence, have lost my home-feelings for the present, if not forever" (18:356).

"Homelessness" would be his condition for the remaining few years of his life. It was also, he came to feel, the condition of the original and ideal Anglo-American character, which had lost its wholeness in the geographical separation between peoples and later in their political and cultural separation. So far as yearnings for "our old home" took the form of an ambition for title or a nostalgia for an idealized England known from books, they were unhealthy and anachronistic. On the level of character, however, England and America, in Hawthorne's view, were not rivals or antitheses so much as divided halves of a unitary being, like the divided selves in Plato's *Symposium* endlessly seeking their complementary other from a "desire" of "reuniting our original nature, making one of two, and healing the state of man."[20] This is the thought Hawthorne developed in the unfinished English romance "Etherege" when he imagined a kind of national cross-migration:

> ...it would be good for the whole people of England, now, if it could at once be transported to America, where its fatness, its sleepiness, its too great beefiness, its preponderant animal character, would be rectified by a different air and soil; and equally good, on the other hand, for the whole American people to be transported back to the original island, where their nervousness might be weighted with heavier influences, where their little women might grow bigger, where their thin, dry men might get a burthen of flesh, and good stomachs; where their children might, with the air, draw in a reverence for age, forms, and usage. (12:193)

As he came to terms with his English experience, Hawthorne grew to feel that materiality, in moderation, was not at all a bad thing. During the course of his residence, he himself "had renewed [his] fibre with English beef and replenished [his] blood with English ale" (5:218). Morally as well as physically, he had grown stouter, earthier, less angular, and more seasoned. He believed his countrymen might profitably do the same.

8

Indian Summer

Plants commonly soon cease to grow for the year unless they have a fall growth—which is a kind of 2nd spring. In the feelings of the man too the year is already past & he looks forward to the coming winter.... The period of youth is past.... But there is an aftermath in early autumn—& some spring flowers bloom again—followed by an Indian summer of finer atmosphere & of a pensive beauty. May my life not be destitute of its Indian summer.

—Thoreau, *Journal* (September 8, 1851)

You certainly grow richer and deeper at every step of your advance. I shall be glad to think that I, too, may improve—that, for instance there may be something ruddier, warmer, and more genial, in my later fruitage. It is good for the moral nature of an American to live in England, among a more simple and natural people than ourselves. Ale is an excellent moral nutriment; so is English mutton; and perhaps the effect of both will be visible in my next romance.

—Hawthorne to Longfellow (May 11, 1855)

Maskenfreiheit

Maskenfreiheit, the freedom conferred by masks.

—John Updike, *Self-Consciousness*

After less than six months in England, settled comfortably in Rock Ferry, Hawthorne writes of being "happier, this Christmas, than ever before,—by our fireside, and with my wife and children about me. More content to enjoy what I had; less anxious for anything beyond it, in this life." Salem seems securely behind him, and he has come to see the "blank" of its years as the "preparation" to which he owes the comparative fullness of this "declining half of life" (21:148). His happiness makes it especially "strange" that he should be troubled by "a singular dream" that has recurred throughout his first year in England:

It is, that I am still at college—or, sometimes, even in school—and there is a sense that I have been there unconscionably long, and have quite failed to make such progress in life as my contemporaries have; and I seem to meet them with a feeling of shame and depression that broods over me, when I think of it, even at this moment. This dream, recurring all through these twenty or thirty years, must be one of the effects of that heavy seclusion in which I shut myself up, for twelve years, after leaving college, when everybody moved onward and left me behind. How strange that it should come now, when I may call myself famous, and prosperous!—when I am happy, too!—still, that same dream. (21:148–49)

The past, Hawthorne was finding, was not dead. It was, however, being overlaid by new manners and practices that worked their way inward to tincture all but his deepest self. It might be supposed, Bryan Homer dryly remarks, that Hawthorne's habitual "reticence" would not "have been the best foundation for...the necessarily public life of a consul in a thriving, rambunctious English port such as Liverpool."[1] In fact, despite socially reclusive ways, Hawthorne seems to have adapted remarkably well to the demands of his office, both at the consulate and at the endless civic dinners in which his position gave him a prominent place. He even came to enjoy what at first seemed "the most awful part of [his] official duty," the obligation "of making dinner-speeches" (21:135). After some initial trepidation (and made "pot-valiant with champagne"), he carried off an early speech with surprising aplomb and afterward felt "as if I should like to rise again; it is something like being under fire,—a sort of excitement, not exactly pleasure, but more piquant than most pleasures" (21:136).

Hawthorne could shed his shyness because he knew he was playing a role and came to regard it, in John Updike's words, "with a certain amusement, as something of an imposture."[2] A "sense of illusion still pursues me," he wrote in "Consular Experiences," the prefatory chapter of *Our Old Home*: "There is some mistake in the matter. I have been writing about another man's consular experiences, with which, through some mysterious medium of transmitted ideas, I find myself intimately acquainted, but in which I could not possibly have had a personal interest" (5:38). Just as years earlier "the life of the Custom-House" came to lie behind him "like a dream" (1:44), so his consular life seemed "a dream altogether" (5:38), as it partly did even at the time. "My real self," he remarks, "had lain, as regarded my proper mode of being and acting, in a state of suspended animation" (5:38).

What *was* Hawthorne's "real self"? Did he still think of himself as a writer? In "The Custom-House" he claims to have fretted about the loss of his literary gift and to have welcomed his political "decapitation" as a blessing in disguise, though in fact he did everything he could to prevent it. In his new position he was similarly ambivalent as he followed the progress of the congressional bill that would limit consular salaries and fees and make it impossible for him to continue in office. "It would seem to be a desirable thing enough that I should have had sufficient income to live comfortably upon, for the rest of my life, without the necessity of labor," he wrote Horatio Bridge in March 1855, expecting the bill to take effect imminently (it did not), "but, on the other hand, I might have sunk prematurely into intellectual sluggishness—which now there will be no danger of my doing" (17:322). In truth, as with his surveyorship, his letters show him eager to remain in office, whatever the literary cost.

Indeed, reminders of the writer and the man he used to be were not always welcome. Looking over *Mosses from an Old Manse* in April 1854 for a proposed new edition to be published by Ticknor and Fields, Hawthorne felt distant from the author, professing not "entirely [to] comprehend [his] own meaning in some of these blasted allegories," though recalling he "always had a meaning—or, at least, thought" he had. "I am a good deal changed since those times," he added, "and to tell the truth, my past self is not very much to my taste, as I see myself in the book" (17:201).

By his second year in England he had begun to molt. "Whether that I had renewed my fibre with English beef and replenished my blood with English ale, or whatever were the cause," he adapted to the English climate, growing tolerant of its dank, foggy winters and enamored of its summers (5:217). The beef and ale worked so transformatively that when he called upon Francis Bennoch in London in March 1856, twenty-seven months after their first meeting, Bennoch, he reports, "did not at first recognize me, so much stouter have I grown during my English residence;—a new man, as he says" (21:423).

As the "new man" assimilated English ways, his New England asperities softened and he relaxed into the comparative mellowness of his nascent John Bull. Hawthorne was not trying to fit in so much as to *blend* in and become the chameleon-like figure he imagined years ago in "Sights from a Steeple," a seer who penetrates empathetically into the life around him while himself remaining unseen. What the narrator in "Sights" achieves by removing himself from the crowd, Hawthorne achieved by losing himself in the crowd. To be among so many people and observe them so keenly (they being oblivious of him) was at once the ultimate invisibility, the ultimate immersion in common life, and the ultimate stabilization of identity: he was a recording consciousness, pure and simple. In London especially, Terence Martin observes, he had an exhilarated sense "of being at the center of human activity."[3] "As nowhere else in the world," he said, he experienced there a kind of homeless "home-feeling" in relation to humanity: "that mysterious yearning—the magnetism of millions of hearts operating upon one—which impels every man's individuality to mingle itself with the immensest mass of human life within his scope" (5:215, 214–15). By "stepping aside [from his life] for a moment," the subject of his early sketch "Wakefield" loses "his place" in the order of things and becomes "the Outcast of the Universe" (9:140); by stepping aside from *his* life, Hawthorne felt incorporated into the universe.

He walked nearly everywhere, often without plan. As Julian reported, he "enjoyed the vague and irresponsible wandering even more than the deliberate and pre-meditated sight-seeing" (*NHW* 2:71). He enjoyed it most when he wandered alone, without family. He would have agreed with Samuel Johnson that "it is not in the shewy evolutions of buildings, but in the multiplicity of human habitations which are crouded together, that the wonderful immensity of London consists."[4] Piccadilly, Regent Street, and the newer, "aristocratic-looking edifices" of the West End attracted him little (21:310); he preferred the "dingy, smoky, midmost haunt[s] of men" on "Fleet-street, and Ludgate-street, and along Cheapside" (22:450), often circling back as if by magnetism to St. Paul's, "the central spot of all the world" (5:214). His first solitary walk set the tone. He "plunged headlong into London, and wandered about all day, without any particular object in view, but only to lose myself, for the sake of finding myself unexpectedly among things that I have always read and dreamed about" (21:306). Literally, Hawthorne means lose his way, then chance upon some fabled landmark, but his biblical "lose myself, for the sake of finding myself" aptly suggests the sloughing of one identity for the purpose of discovering another.

The Trollopizing of Nathaniel Hawthorne

> A consulship in a bustling town will give [Hawthorne] the cheerful reality, the healthy air of every-day life which is his only want.
>
> —Mary Russell Mitford to James T. Fields (1853)

At nearly a thousand pages in the Centenary edition, Hawthorne's *English Notebooks* are more than 70 percent longer than either his *American* or his *French and Italian Notebooks*. In his prefatory note to *Our Old Home*, Hawthorne claims that the materials worked up into its twelve sketches were originally "intended for the side-scenes, and back-grounds, and exterior adornment, of a work of fiction" (5:3–4). This seems unlikely, his editors note, given the character of most of the entries, especially after 1853 (21:717).

In the quantity of time they demanded to no definite literary end, the notebooks seem to have been an end in themselves. Nina Baym sees their lengthy travel accounts as Hawthorne's laborious substitute for a camera,[5] but no photographs could have worked to deepen and consolidate his impressions as writing did. Description was not always easy for him. Sensitive to detail but wanting a technical vocabulary, Hawthorne had difficulty articulating the differences he noted between cathedrals in Lincoln, York, Lichfield, Peterborough, Shrewsbury, and other places. English scenery also resisted description; except for tourist regions like the Lake Country, it was a pleasing but undramatic landscape that needed to be appreciated during leisurely strolls, not glimpsed from a passing train and set to paper (22:372). Persons were more salient and Hawthorne is often at his liveliest with them, but when he is writing with active curiosity he can be engaging whatever he turns his attention to.

Beyond serving as a record of experience, the notebooks were an outlet for a writer who was not otherwise writing, and as such they were both a gratifying creative activity and a confirmation of vocation, though it was no longer a romancer's vocation. In *The House of the Seven Gables* and *The Blithedale Romance* he had experimented with realism, only to be drawn back to romance by something like a failure of aesthetic or philosophical nerve. Now, residing in a country of realists, Hawthorne became one himself. Except for brief passages on the "bloody footstep" at Smithills Hall, virtually nothing in the English notebooks testifies to a continuing interest in literary romance. He told Longfellow to anticipate "the effect" of English mutton and English ale "in [his] next romance" (17:341), holding to the genre itself but promising to give it a new solidity. His hopes, as it turned out, would outrun his practice, but his allegiance was clear. In a letter to James T. Fields, written from Leamington Spa in February 1860, just as *The Marble Faun* was about to go to press, he voiced his reservations about the book and the character of his writing generally:

> It is odd...that my own individual taste is for quite another class of works than those which I myself am able to write. If I were to meet with such books as mine, by another writer, I don't believe I should be able to get through them. Have you ever read the novels of Anthony Trollope? The precisely suit my taste; solid and substantial, written on the strength of beef and through the inspiration of ale, and just as real as if some giant had hewn a great lump out of the earth and put it under a glass case, with all its inhabitants going about their daily business, and not suspecting they were made a show of. (18:229)

What is strangest is not that Hawthorne should admire Trollope but that he should do so enviously. What had he been doing in the more than 1,500 printed pages of his English and his French and Italian notebooks if not hewing out great lumps of earth? He believed that "it need[ed] an English residence to make [Trollope's books] thoroughly comprehensible" (18:229–30). Perhaps it also needed a residence in England to write them. If so, he should have been well prepared to do so when, after four and a half years he left England for the Continent in January 1858, settled in Rome, and began work upon an English fiction the following spring.

Mimesis

And the whole power, whether of painter or poet, to describe rightly what we call an ideal thing, depends upon its being thus, to him, not an ideal, but a *real* thing.

—John Ruskin, *Modern Painters*

If Hawthorne's development in England consisted primarily of rooting himself more firmly in earth, it also included what he considered the very *un*-English process of refining his aesthetic taste. He came to Europe knowing little about nonliterary culture, and the multitude of things to *be* known, whether historically in the British Museum or pictorially in the art galleries, oppressed him. It was not culture itself he found tedious so much as the labor of acquiring it. After an initial feeling of utter demoralization (to be repeated with each new encounter), he was pleased to discover in himself a sort of aesthetic tropism pointing him toward the light. "It is of no use for me to criticise pictures, or to try to describe them," he wrote after visiting the National Gallery in March 1856, "but I have an idea that I might get up a taste, with some little attention to the subject" (21:439).

Getting up a taste was what the Hawthornes proposed when they took lodgings in Manchester during the summer of 1857 to attend the great Arts Exhibition in preparation for their residence in Italy. Belated consular business required Hawthorne to commute to Liverpool several times, but he attended the exhibition as faithfully as he could, entering with Sophia and sometimes the children but frequently wandering off by himself to view the paintings at his own pace and without the necessity of discussing them with anyone. Initially he "was unquiet, from a hopelessness of being able fully to enjoy" the exhibition; "the sight of a great many pictures together" dispirited him, like "having innumerable books open before you at once" when you can study only one at a time (22:342). He took the idea of viewing seriously and doubted that many in the crowd of spectators (himself included) "got the kind of enjoyment" the exhibition was meant to produce (22:343). Gradually, however, enjoyment did come, first of a simple sort ("Positively, I do begin to receive some pleasure from looking at pictures, but, as yet, it has nothing to do with any technical merit, nor do I think I shall ever get so far as that" [22:354]), then with growing confidence in his taste, if humility about his knowledge.

Beyond exposing Hawthorne to art, the Manchester exhibition invited him to meditate more deeply on his own art, specifically on the problem of aesthetic realism and idealism he had pondered throughout his career and addressed in his literary prefaces. So far as it represented materiality and found its fictional expression in Trollope, England *was* realism. Landscapes aside, English painting for Hawthorne derived from Hogarth, and English painters were ill advised to attempt "anything high, heroic, and ideal" (22:345) since they wanted the faculty to achieve it: "they are strong in homeliness and ugliness; weak in their efforts at the beautiful" (22:345–46). Realism had its merits (fidelity to surfaces) but also its limitations (literalism). The Pre-Raphaelites, who interested him, seemed almost perverse in "willfully...abjur[ing] all beauty"; their claim to attention came from "the thought and feeling" that went into their work and made it "disclose a deeper value the longer you look" (22:347). Even so, imitating nature as minutely as they did ("they almost paint separate hairs"), Holman Hunt and others of the school were "stiff and unnatural," the higher truth to nature requiring an element of "enchantment" that "keep[s] the object from pressing so boldly and harshly upon the spectator's eyeballs" (22:347).

In reflections like these, Hawthorne was thinking simultaneously about art, the relationship of art to life, and, within life itself, the relationship between the actual and the ideal. Considerations of genre, or mode of representation, were seldom exclusively aesthetic for Hawthorne; mimesis was entwined with metaphysics: what, if anything, beyond the materiality of things, was real? Residence in England seemed to prompt a version of that question almost daily, except among the English, who sensibly never concerned themselves with such things.

Without explicitly framing the issue as such, Hawthorne looked to art for an incarnation he did not find in life: the spiritual *within* the material or at least, through the virtuosity of craft, suggested *by* the material. Even before he went abroad, the Dutch Masters, whom he had praised in *The Blithedale Romance*, were the painters most to his liking. The Manchester exhibition confirmed this. The Dutch seemed to him "the most wonderful set of men that ever handled a brush" (22:356). In their almost microscopic realism, they "accomplish all they aim at" and yet somehow manage to "get at the soul of common things, and so make them types and interpreters of the spiritual world" (22:356). This was an art he could respect and even aspire to produce, a union of Trollope's faithfulness to appearances with his own efforts at "a broader and higher truth" (22:347): realism *and* romance; the material *and* the ideal, a new form of fiction that seemed (this was before George Eliot) without precedent.

How difficult such an achievement was is suggested by Julian's description of his aesthetics as a vexed paradox: "The art [in Manchester] seemed to him artifice; he wished the picture to be as good as nature in the first place, and then as much better as selection and arrangement could make it" (*NHW* 2:142). What he really wanted was that nature should be better. Its defect was that it was too natural, or, as he liked to say of America's aboriginal landscapes in comparison to England's cultivated ones, too "ragged" (21:348). As to the Dutch painters, Julian added, "he was inclined to ascribe great merit to [them], on account of the minute perfection of their technique," while at the same time he "disapproved of them" for applying themselves to "undignified subjects" (*NHW* 2:142). The "life-like representations of cabbages, onions, turnips, cauliflowers, and peas; such perfect realities of brass kettles and kitchen crockery" (22:356) that earned Hawthorne's artistic admiration did not satisfy his soul. Nor, despite the pleasure he took in them, did Trollope's novels.

Between Trollope's kind of work and his own, or aside from both altogether, was an artist who intrigued and perplexed him—Turner. The license Hawthorne claimed for romance in deviating from palpable reality, Turner claimed by departing from everything palpable at all, and yet he could not be called a rarefied idealist. Even in his first dismissive response—"As for Turner, I care no more for his light-colored pictures than for so much lacquered ware, or painted gingerbread"—Hawthorne was sensible that the "fault" or "deficiency" was his own, to be remedied only by an equivocal process of "sophisticating" himself (22:346–47), or adopting esoteric standards. "If [pictorial genius] exists only for connoisseurs," he remarked, "it is a very suspicious affair" (22:444). And yet, he came to feel, the connoisseurs may be right. Viewing Turner's paintings less than four months later at Marlborough House, he grudgingly found them "tantalizing," though the ideal standpoint for looking at them eluded him: "At a certain distance, you discern what appears to be a grand and beautiful picture, which you shall admire and enjoy infinitely if you can get within the range of distinct vision. You come nearer, and find only blotches of color, and dabs of the brush, meaning nothing when you look closely, and meaning a mystery at the point where the painter intended to station you" (22:444).

Turner disturbed Hawthorne enough to make him want to solve the mystery, determining "to buy Ruskin's pamphlet at my next visit, and look at [the paintings] through his eyes" (22:445). Nine years earlier he had read an early edition of Ruskin's *Modern Painters*.[6] If he recalled Ruskin now or read him again, he would likely have been even more disconcerted. In his Manse notebook he had described reflections in water as mirroring objects with the utmost distinctness yet "arrayed in ideal beauty, which satisfie[s] the spirit incomparably more than the actual scene" and seems "the real thing which Nature imperfectly images to our grosser sense" (8:360). Hawthorne felt suggestions of this ideality in Turner's landscapes, some of which "were, indeed, full of imaginative beauty, and of the better truth etherealized out of the prosaic truth of Nature; only it was impossible actually to see it" (22:444). Where Hawthorne's mimesis distills and elevates the real in order to grasp its spiritual essence, Turner's seems to beckon only to withhold, shrouding the real in "beautiful dream-land" mists in order to mystify (22:444). Ruskin would have told him this was exactly the point. Turner's reflections were *intended* to balk expectations of mirroring, literal or spiritual, and to show "in the reflection" not a refinement of reality but "a mockery" of it.[7] Turner's water images "have all character," Ruskin remarked,

> and are evidently reflections of something definite and determinate; but yet they are all uncertain and inexplicable.... [W]e cannot penetrate or interpret; we are not allowed to go down to them, and we repose as we should in nature, upon the luster of the level surface. It is in this power of saying everything, and yet of saying nothing too plainly, that the perfection of art here, as in all other cases, consists.[8]

For Hawthorne, a spiritualism that says everything and nothing was as unsatisfying as materialism, which it practically amounted to. Although he found "something wonderful...in Turner's lights, and mists and yeasty waves," the realist in him wished that the "pictures looked in the least like what they typify" (22:357), while the idealist wanted their "playing colour and palpitating shade" (Ruskin's words) to be more than nebulous "images of something."[9] The function of art being to "interpret life" (22:346), of what value was idealization if it baffled interpretation and threw us back on the opaque surfaces art existed to transcend? The aesthetic rendering of material objects had to be faithfully done, and it had to be illustrative of definite and *usable* moral or spiritual truth. Turner was more unsettling than a pictorial materialist because he *seemed* a spiritualist yet one whose divine order, like Emerson's, was without a recognizable human face.

Had he known their work, Hawthorne might have found provocation in contemporary American painters. Hudson River artists like Thomas Cole and Frederic Church were romancers of the kind he had sought to be beginning with *The House of the Seven Gables*—materialists in their attention to detail, idealists in their composition and wrought effect. Also suggestive might have been Luminists like Fitz Hugh Lane and Martin Johnson Heade, for whom objects could "not rationally be allowed to lose their tactile identity" but in whose work "ultra-clarity" was complemented by "dazzling light emanating from a different core, enveloping detail in atmosphere" and suggesting the transcendent.[10] The Luminists were like New World Turners ballasted by Yankee common sense. An innovative aesthetic discourse was circulating in America, and had Hawthorne availed himself of it he might have been led beyond the binary of realism and romance in which he had long been fixed. England had tipped his character toward realism, but it had not changed the terms in which he approached aesthetic matters. At the end of his English residence, though wishing to incorporate mutton and ale into his new writing, he had little more than the old oppositions to work with.

Footsteps, Forward and Back

> What does haunt late works are the author's previous works; he is burdensomely aware that he has been cast, unlike his ingénue self, as an author who writes in a certain way, with the inexorable consistency of his own handwriting.
>
> —John Updike, "Late Works," *Due Considerations*

Beyond furnishing material for a potential romance, Hawthorne's English experience seemed to call out for interpretation through the medium of fiction, though by the time he came to begin such a work in the spring of 1858 his thoughts about European life had already been complicated by his months in France and Italy. Henry James spoke of his own fictions as originating in a donnée, often an anecdote or bit of dinner table conversation that suggested to him the germ of a story. "The American Claimant Manuscripts," as the Centenary editors call them—"The Ancestral Footstep," begun on April Fools Day, 1858, and the two later drafts, "Etherege" and "Grimshawe," probably written in 1861 just prior to and during the early months of the Civil War (12:502)—had two données, conceived independently but almost contemporaneously. The first involved a story Hawthorne was told at Smithills Hall, "one of the oldest residences in England" (21:291), about a bloody footstep imprinted on the flagstone floor by a nonconformist clergymen accused of heresy and later burned at the stake in Queen Mary's time (21:160, 291–93). "Of course, it is all humbug," Hawthorne scoffed, adding that "the legend is a good one" (21:293) and perhaps seeing it as the kind of gothic fragment his imagination could turn to account. The second donnée, recorded five days later, involved Americans' "fancy for connecting themselves with English property and lineage" (21:140) such as Hawthorne knew it from consular experiences. "In my Romance," he wrote, as if the project were already fixed in his mind,

> the original emigrant to America may have carried away with him a family-secret, whereby it was in his power (had he so chosen) to have brought about the ruin of the family. This secret he transmits to his American progeny, by whom it is inherited throughout all the intervening generations. At last, the hero of the Romance comes to England, and finds that, by means of this secret, he still has it in his power to procure the downfall of the family. (21:162).

Although Hawthorne poked fun at Americans' dreams "of a great English inheritance" (21:231), he himself was not without ancestral pretensions to wealth and position. He told William D. Ticknor that, "according to family tradition," his emigrant ancestor "was a person of some standing in the world, and brought fifty servants with him" (17:319), and in *The House of the Seven Gables* the Pyncheons' ducal ambitions had drawn on Manning family claims to vast tracts of land in Maine. In *Seven Gables* he had explored the themes of dispossession, dark family secrets, hidden documents, and a grievance nurtured through generations and dispelled when the ancient wrong is righted. The claimant manuscripts will owe much to *Seven Gables*, a kinship Hawthorne oddly failed to see or at least never acknowledged.

From the outset, the problem with the manuscripts was the uncertain connection between their two données. The claimant material pointed ahead toward a fictionalization of the contrasts between England and America, a chief subject in the English notebooks and later in *Our Old Home*, and toward a mode of representation strongly realistic; the legend of the bloody footstep pointed backward toward the themes of *Seven Gables* and the plot contrivances of gothic romance. At issue during these watershed months of 1858 was the kind of writer Hawthorne would become in the next phase of his career. As the claimant theme took shape in his mind, he considered grounding it in quasi-fact by having his hero, then called Middleton, tell the story to himself, "in a friendly way, at the Consulate, as many people have communicated quite as wild pretensions to English genealogies" (12:52). The book, he wrote, "shall be offered, half seriously, as the account of the fortunes that he met with in his search for his hereditary home" (12:87).

The opening paragraph of "The Ancestral Footstep" suggests the direction the work might have taken. Read out of context, its authorship hidden, it might almost be ascribed to Henry James, who, ignorant of Hawthorne's manuscript, wrote his own Hawthornesque version of the claimant story in "A Passionate Pilgrim" (1871):

> He had now been searching long in those rich portions of England, where he would most have wished to find the object of his pursuit; and many scenes which he would willingly have identified with that mentioned in the ancient, time-yellowed record which he bore about with him. It is to be observed that, undertaken at first as the amusement of a grown man's play-day, it had become more and more real to him with every step of the way that he followed it up.... In all his life, including its earliest and happiest days, he had never known such a spring and zest as now filled his veins, and gave lightsomeness to his limbs; this spirit gave to the beautiful country which he trod a still richer beauty than it had

ever born; and he sought his ancient home in it as if he had found his
way into Paradise, and were endeavoring to trace out the signs of
Eve's bridal bower, the birth-place of the human race and all its glorious
possibilities of happiness and high performance. (12:3)

In Jamesian fashion, Hawthorne begins in medias res and situates the reader
in the protagonist's consciousness with a mixture of sympathetic identification
and ironic distance. The protagonist is unnamed; no characterizing background
is given beyond the suggestion of an idyllic childhood (to be drastically reversed
in "Etherege" and "Grimshawe"); his errand is hinted at but unspecified; he is
shown to be predisposed toward a happily romantic view of its object; and the
growing intensity of his pursuit, at first a diversion, now an exhilarating quest, is
presented with an irony more smiling than dark yet with forebodings of a comeuppance (or worse) ahead. The familiar American theme of a Paradise to be
found or made in the New World is inverted: *this* passionate pilgrim, like James's
Clement Searle, will seek his Paradise in Europe.

While hazy about the particulars of his plot, Hawthorne began "The Ancestral
Footstep" with a clear sense of his theme. Middleton is the descendant of an emigrant who, whether sinning, sinned against, or both, fled to America and left to
his posterity a dim legend about English claims, which Middleton, "carrying
with him certain ancient documents," sets out to investigate (12:11). Though
disenchanted with the rough-and-tumble of American politics (he had briefly
been a congressman), Middleton is a good republican who scorns the prospect
of an English title and is wealthy enough not to covet England lands. What
attracts him to the family estate once he arrives in England is what attracted
Hawthorne to rural England, the feeling of peace and stability attaching to it, so
different from "the turbulent life from which he had escaped across the sea"
(12:33). "To connect himself with the life of old England" would be to rejoin the
broken thread of his ancestry (12:38) and thereby, in a vague spiritual way, to
become settled, at home in the world, historically rooted, and self-complete. As
an American "disconnected with [England] so long, alien from its habits of
thought and life, [and] reverencing none of the things which Englishmen
reverenced," Middleton is aware of the presumption of intruding upon his
English kin and "disturb[ing] them in the life that belonged to them" (12:42).
Yet even as he reasons thus, his footsteps carry him "with a sort of shame" toward
what he has discovered is his ancestral home (12:42).

Through Middleton, Hawthorne is dramatizing what in *Our Old Home* he
would deprecate as the American's sympathy for the old and outworn as it
expresses itself in "a blind, pathetic tendency to wander back again" (5:19). So
conceived, "The Ancestral Footstep" was to be a fictive sermon on the folly of
nostalgia, all the more complex for the strain of nostalgia in Hawthorne himself.

Middleton does turn out to be the rightful heir, but in the end, consistent with Hawthorne's ideological convictions, he "rejects both [title and estate], feeling that it is better to take a virgin soil, than to try to make the old name grow in a soil that had been darkened with so much blood and misfortune as this" (12:11).

Middleton's decision is swayed by a young woman named Alice whom he meets and falls in love with, a figure of mysterious background, nationality, and relation to the English principals of the plot. Alice is quite sure that Middleton has no business staying in England: "Your lot is in another land. You have seen the birthplace of your forefathers, and have gratified your natural yearning for it; now return, and cast your lot with your own people" (12:56). "The American who comes hither, and persuades himself he is one with Englishmen," she tells Middleton, "makes a great mistake," or, if not, "is not worthy of his own country, and the higher development that awaits it" (12:72). Along with the seductions of English wealth and title, Alice belittles Irvingesque "ideas of the past, the associations of poetry, [and] the loveliness of an age-long home" as incommensurate with "the higher impulses of our nature" and "the chance of acting upon the unmoulded future of America" (12:72).

Alice is the spokeswoman for a prophetic nationalism that waned in Hawthorne during his years in England, partly from distance, partly because of the political news emanating from home. In the face of America's darkening present and uncertain future, "The Ancestral Footstep" sets out to reaffirm an ideal America transferred from history to the imagination. Coincidentally or not, "Middleton" and "Alice" are the names of Cooper's hero and heroine in *The Last of the Mohicans,* progenitors of the new, post-Colonial America that would emerge in the decades ahead. Hawthorne's Middleton and Alice are also progenitors, carrying the process a step further toward to a *cultural* postcolonialism weaned from longings for "our old home." Wedded, Middleton and Alice return to America as "the Adam and Eve of a new epoch [Hawthorne told himself in a note], and the fitting missionaries of a new social faith, of which, there must be continual hints through the book" (12:58). There are no suggestions that the America they return to may be on the brink of dissolution.

Like *The Marble Faun,* which also ends with its wedded pair returning from crime-blackened Europe to America, "The Ancestral Footstep" is the autumnal expression of an American of "the earlier and simpler type" (as Henry James called Hawthorne) before "the war-cloud...dropped a permanent shadow" on him (James 112, 136). It may also be an aging man's fantasy of living life again, differently. Though not one of Hawthorne's dark heroines, Middleton's Alice may be something better—an intelligent, free-spirited young woman, not beautiful but "very piquant" (12:35) and in all respects more than the equal of the hero. With Alice, Hawthorne departs from the division of womanhood into opposing types, the alluring but dangerous and the ethereal but confining. While only a sketch in an unfinished work, Alice gives promise of being Hawthorne's first "modern" woman, free at once from residual Puritanism and from Victorian ideals of "true womanhood." Indeed, Alice is made to mock the latter with a vivacity that shows Hawthorne ready to mock it. "I have heard," she tells Middleton, "that your country-women are a far more delicate and fragile race than Englishwomen; pale, feeble, hot-house plants, unfit for the wear and tear of life, without energy or character, or any slightest degree of physical strength to base it upon" (12:71). When Middleton rallies to defend American woman-hood—"slight in aspect, slender in frame, as you suggest, but yet capable of bringing forth stalwart men"—Alice counters him with a wit reminiscent of Zenobia's: "I think I see one of these paragons now, in a Bloomer, I think you call it, swaggering along with a Bowie knife at her girdle, smoking a cigar, no doubt, and tippling sherry cobblers and mint-juleps" (12:71).

In character and vocation—as first conceived, she is a sculptress who for-merly lived in Rome—Alice is modeled upon Louisa Lander, a young Salem-born sculptress whom the Hawthornes befriended early in their Roman residence and who undertook to model a bust of Hawthorne even as he, during conversations in her studio, took "a similar freedom with her moral likeness" (14:78). Hawthorne was fascinated with the "position" of "a young woman, living in almost perfect independence, thousands of miles from her New England home, going fearlessly about these mysterious streets, by night as well as by day, with no household ties, no rule or law but that within her; yet acting with quiet-ness and simplicity, and keeping, after all, within a homely line of right" (14:78). He would use a version of these words in *The Marble Faun* with Hilda, whose situation (but not whose character) is based upon Lander's. Hawthorne may or may not have fallen in love with Lander—possibly he himself couldn't have said—but almost certainly, as T. Walter Herbert argues, he "saw in [her] a 'delightful freedom' that he himself yearned to regain."[11] Lander seemed the wife he would have wanted if he were twenty-five years younger and the world stretched before him. Through Middleton's marriage he enacted a fantasy of life recommenced, just as through the couple's return to America he enacted the fan-tasy of a nation whose future was "unmoulded" (12:72).

Hawthorne's idyll with Lander ended abruptly when Roman gossip charged that she had posed nude (or worse) for a fellow artist, upon which Hawthorne, as "guardian of the sanctity of his domestic circle" (18:158), coldly cut his ties with her. Herbert sees Hawthorne reacting with "guilty alarm" to forestall potential rumors about his own repeated sittings with her, often à deux.[12] This may be, but the stiffness of his letter to her may also suggest feelings of deep betrayal and sexual jeal-ousy. He had invested himself in an ideal image of Lander, and as their relationship developed he could assure himself of his own purity of heart only by assuming her purity of body; even a whiff of sexual impropriety was enough to unnerve him.

Hawthorne's productive work on "The Ancestral Footstep" coincided with his friendship with Lander, who left for America in April 1858, for a stay of six months. That same April Hawthorne saw a copy of Praxiteles' faun and in July he began what would become *The Marble Faun* (15:xxi–xxii); the last dated entry for "The Ancestral Footstep" is May 15, 1858. Residing now in Italy, he probably found the legend of the faun taking greater hold of his imagination than the bloody footstep; its theme of the development of the soul, moreover, was familiar territory. Rumors about Lander's behavior came to his attention in October 1858, too late to account for his abandoning one manuscript for another, but they can help explain why, on returning to the claimant material in "Etherege" and "Grimshawe" in 1861, the fetching Alice/Lander was replaced by a demure, self-effacing child-then-woman named Elsie. The fantasy of a new life with a new woman in a young America went the way of Louisa Lander's reputation, which never recovered from the allegations of her American artist-friends in Rome.

Even without the complications of Lander, "The Ancestral Footstep" would likely have self-destructed from the internal tension between its serious thematic content (the claimant material, realistically presented) and its gothic apparatus, the bloody footstep whose import Hawthorne could never settle and whose elaboration drew him into ever more tortuous byways of plot. If Hawthorne never found "the true key-note of this Romance," as he said, it was partly because he wanted it to *be* "a Romance, grim, grotesque, [and] quaint," and at the same time "have so much of the hues of life that the reader should sometimes think it was intended for a picture" (12:58). He might as well have tried to join Frans Hals and El Greco, with a touch of Hogarth thrown in. "It must be a humorous work, or nothing" (12:58), he wrote on May 11, 1858, an intention he would compromise the very next day when he began to transform the current heir of the estate, Eldredge (etymologically, "old ruler") from "a commonplace old English country-gentleman," and thereby a subject for representative social commentary, into a sinister Italian-bred Catholic who returns to England with nothing of the Englishman left in him (12:53, 60–61). It meant one thing for Middleton to renounce aristocracy because of its social inequity and historical anachronism and quite another for him to be entangled in plot machinations from *The Mysteries of Udolpho*.

If "The Ancestral Footstep" begins like "A Passionate Pilgrim" or perhaps *The Ambassadors*, it develops in a way closer to James's *The American*. The moral climax of James's novel is Christopher Newman's decision not to deploy a secret knowledge he has obtained to avenge himself on an aristocratic family he feels has "cruelly wronged" him. Newman, James later wrote in his preface to the novel, "would arrive at his just vindication and then would fail of all triumphantly and all vulgarly enjoying it.... He wouldn't 'forgive'...; he would simply turn, at the supreme moment, away, the bitterness of his personal loss yielding to the very force of his aversion."[13] This restraint would be Newman's triumph and that of the morally superior "new man" the American at his best represents. Aesthetically, it would also be James's triumph in that it resisted conventional expectations of a dramatic denouement and climaxed instead in the purely *moral* action of Newman's renunciation.

In returning to his book after thirty years, James felt he had not been sufficiently true to his original impulse. He had sacrificed probability of character and situation to flamboyance, making Newman's "performed outrage so much more showy, dramatically speaking, than sound" (*The American* xix). He explained his lapse by citing the beguilements of "romance," a genre in which the writer, "for the fun of it," "insidiously…cut[s] the cable" tying fiction to reality and presents "experience…exempt from the conditions that we usually know to attach to it" (*The American* xviii, xvii). Plot and theme, James felt in retrospect, worked against each other in *The American* to the extent that readers undervalued Newman's grand decision because the author attached "too scant an importance to its fashion of coming about" (*The American* xix). The element of romance diminished the book by lending it the aspect of a literary *jeu* that neither author nor audience could take with full seriousness.

The reference to *The American* is pertinent because something of a like sort happened with "The Ancestral Footstep." The story straddles genres; it straddles tendencies within Hawthorne toward realism and idealism; and it straddles the divide between an established literary practice and a prospective new one. From the outset, Hawthorne saw Middleton's quest as precipitating a strange and terrible catastrophe. Initially, this took the form of Eldredge accidentally shooting and killing himself in the act of butting Middleton with a gun, after which Middleton resigns his claim in guilt and disgust. Improbable from the start, such a resolution becomes more so as Hawthorne invests it with obscure hints of fatality. Middleton's "mere presence" on the scene somehow lays bare "a buried secret that immediately assumed life and activity, the moment that it was above ground again" (12:13, 18). Even Alice joins in advancing the myth: "It was foreordained that you should shed this man's blood…by digging into that old pit of pestilence" and "set[ting] the contagion loose again" (12:23).

What this foreordination might consist in, Hawthorne is at a loss to explain. In *The House of the Seven Gables*, suggestions of historical nemesis had been underlain by a more convincing form of agency, the generational reappearance of the Pyncheon character. No such agency operates in "The Ancestral Footstep," since the Italianate Eldredge is wholly unlike the perpetrators of the original crime. The evil initially linked to the English class system comes instead to center in a stock gothic villain, and what began as a thoughtful exploration of transatlantic contrasts is lost in the windings of an increasingly intricate, lurid, and unbelievable plot. Like James, Hawthorne has been led away from his impelling theme by the temptations of romance. The only "fatality" that properly belongs to the story comes from Middleton's naïve and misguided tampering with Old World affairs. Hawthorne, however, wants a mysteriously reactivated evil, and such an evil he will have, hazy though he is about what it signifies and how it might be embodied in an efficient narrative action.

If Hawthorne appears fixed within the mental traces of *The House of the Seven Gables*, he also seems captive to his long-standing belief that life, viewed realistically, is too meager to serve the purposes of imaginative literature and too finite and material to satisfy the longings of the soul. It is not enough that Middleton should weigh the aristocratic English past against the republican American future and choose the latter for social and ethical reasons; the story must have an aura of the supernatural, like the halos affixed to otherwise terrestrial figures in medieval art to certify they are saints. The medieval artist worked from belief or at least for an audience that required a show of belief; Hawthorne does not. His halos have symbolic *status* but no symbolic *referent*; they are mystifications that mystify nothing.

Much of the rest of "The Ancestral Footstep" manuscript consists of plot speculations that exfoliate wildly on all sides as the romantic donnée of the bloody footstep comes to overwhelm the realistic donnée of the claimant. Visiting Kenilworth Castle in September 1857, Hawthorne observed how its crumbling walls were held in place by the trees and vines that had sprouted in them and continually ate into their substance. "Thus an abuse has strangely grown into a use" (22:378), he commented, likening the foliage to English traditions and institutions as they upheld cultural practices whose generating principle had long ago atrophied. Less benignly, the analogy applies to Hawthornean romance. A genre created to frame and elevate content has persisted long after the content has become stale and its associated devices formulaic; a use has grown into an abuse. Hawthorne had hoped to incorporate mutton and ale into his new romance, enlivening it and, in English fashion, *materializing* it. Success would have given a fresh direction to his writing. In its early sections "The Ancestral Footstep" is remarkably promising, but as it develops it deviates from its forward impulse, steps backward toward "Salem"—its later drafts, "Etherege" and "Grimshawe," would physically open in Salem—and devolves into gothic fantasy. What Hawthorne said of Kenilworth's supportive trees holds true for his own late, anachronistic use of romance: "Hawthorn, however, next to ivy, is the great ornament and comforter, of these desolate ruins" (22:378).

No Country for Old Men

> America is a good land for young people, but not for those who are past their prime. It is impossible to grow old comfortably there . . . .
>
> —Hawthorne to Longfellow (August 30, 1854)

In returning Middleton and Alice to America, Hawthorne suppressed what troubled him most about his country, the "miserable confusion" of its political life as it lurched toward the cataclysm of the Civil War (18:227). Had he been without family to consider, he might have remained in England, in or near London. "Why don't you come over?—being now a man of leisure, and with nothing to keep you in America," he wrote Longfellow, a widower, in 1854 (17:250). Five years later, after an exhausting residence in Rome, he found England genially suited to his slower metabolism as America would not have been. As he would write in *Our Old Home*, "I have frequently observed, in Old English towns, that Old-Age come forth more cheerfully and genially into the sunshine, than among ourselves, where the rush, stir, bustle, and irreverent energy of youth are so preponderant, that the poor forlorn grandsires begin to doubt whether they have a right to breathe in such a world any longer, and so hide their silvery heads in solitude" (5:165).

The abolitionist Concord of 1860 to which Hawthorne returned "was a very different place" to him, Julian remarked, "from the Concord of 1853" (*NHW* 2:11). Against the background of changing times, his own want of change made his "political views...unwelcome and suspicious" to his neighbors, or so he felt.[14] Aside from the partisan political climate, there was no *Maskenfreiheit* for Hawthorne in Concord. People knew him too well; he knew himself too well, as if his old American identity were lying in wait for him, ready to mock the after-dinner speechmaker as a fraud. In his alienation he quickly resumed "his old reclusive habits" (Mellow 539). "Time is burying my English life," he wrote Francis Bennoch on December 17, 1860, "throwing month after month upon it, as a sexton throws shovelsfull of earth into a grave." The metaphor is telling: he felt buried alive in Concord. "I lose England without gaining America," he told Bennoch, "for I have not really begun to feel at home here" (18:352).

It may have been nostalgia for England that led Hawthorne to return to the claimant manuscript early in 1861. Beyond helping him distill his English experience, "Etherege," his second effort at a bloody footstep romance, was a vehicle through which he might refresh that experience and perhaps recover or shore up the English side of him he believed he had lost.

"Etherege" begins in a dusty, spider-ridden house by a graveyard in Salem and takes nearly fifty pages and twenty years to bring its title character to England to search for his ancestral home. Why Hawthorne felt the need to give Middleton-now-Etherege a bizarre childhood is a mystery. As a setting, Salem is represented by little more than the household of Etherege's guardian and is given no symbolic resonance. Its choice may be romancer Hawthorne's effort to tap into the sources of his art or else, through Etherege's journey from Salem origins to the English countryside, to trace a much-displaced version of his personal journey. Although Etherege is still a youngish man, Hawthorne gives him his own yearning for rest amid the serenely beautiful English countryside with its associated "habits of life

and thought" (12:147). Etherege's feelings of "ancient peace," generational continuity, and the effect of old family dwellings in "giving length, fullness, body,
substance, to this thin and frail matter of human life" echo a refrain in the English
notebooks, along with the idea that Americans live in "poor tents of a day, inns
of a night" destined to pass from family to family and thwart hopes of a quasi-
immortality through lineage and inheritance: "Posterity! An American can have
none" (12:186).

The theme of republican ambivalence toward aristocracy is more fully articu-
lated in "Etherege" than in "The Ancestral Footstep," but it is also more disas-
trously obscured by a labyrinthine, overpopulated plot. What eluded Hawthorne
to the point of despair was, still, the relationship between the claimant material
and its historical antecedents in the bloody footstep. "How can it appear," he
asked himself, "as if dead men's business, that had been buried with them, came
to life again, and had to be finished now? Truly this is hard;—here's the rub; and
yet without it, the story is meager and barren" (12:198). There, indeed, was the
rub. A realistic story set in the present and focused on themes of class and
national character appeared to Hawthorne no adequate story at all either in
dramatic interest or depth of theme. He saw clearly enough that "if [he] could
get rid of any great crime on the part of the family, it would be better" (12:199),
but he could not bring himself to do so—"crime," as always, being the condition
of literary meaning for him. Instead, he multiplied characters and plot lines, hoping he might discover his theme as he went along ("What, what, what! How,
how, how!" [12:198]; "twon't do" [12:198, 219, 220]).

"Etherege" fails for the same reason that its title character fails: both return
home—Etherege to America, Hawthorne to romance—without having incorporated the "heavier influences" of English life needed to temper American nervousness (12:193). Just as the bloody footstep poisons Etherege's relationship
to England, so Hawthorne's obsession with it poisons his. He loses the perspi-
cacity and humor of the English notebooks; he loses his material English self.
The footstep becomes a synecdochical idée fixe, as if the apparatus of romance as
a genre and vision hinged upon it. Even after he abandoning the claimant material
entirely, he imported the footstep into his later unfinished romance "Septimius
Felton," although it has nothing to do with his main subject, Septimius's quest
for the "elixir of life."

A man at odds with himself, his town, his country, and his times, weakened by
declining health, and frustrated in the activity on which his living (in all senses)
depends, runs the risk of falling into misanthropy or despair. In a quiet, inward
way, this may have happened with Hawthorne. "Of all the trials, this is the heavi-
est to me,—to see you so apathetic, so indifferent, so hopeless, so unstrung,"
Sophia wrote him on July 27, 1861, about the time of the claimant manuscripts.[15]
The most significant change from "Etherege" to "Grimshawe," the last of the three

manuscripts, is the alteration in the old guardian's character. Through most of "Etherege," the doctor who raises Edward (Ned) Etherege, though eccentric, is "kindly, but shy," educated, "agreeable," and American-born (12:90, 91). After 130 pages of text Hawthorne can still describe him as "an old humorous bachelor" (12:222). Two pages later, however, for no assignable reason, he changes his mind: "Perhaps the doctor himself might be an English misanthrope, who has a spite against his family.... Make his character very weird indeed, and envelope it in dread and mystery, with as much of the grotesque as can be wrought into it" (12:224). So reconceived, "Doctor Grim," as his wards Elsie and Ned (renamed Redclyffe) call him, dominates the succeeding "Grimshawe" manuscript for close to a hundred pages and so influences the remaining ones that even after the doctor's death the claimant theme pales in cultural significance.

In his late tale "The Jolly Corner" Henry James has an expatriate American dilettante return to New York, where in the old family house he encounters a ghost who represents his alter ego, the brutalized man he might have become had he stayed in America. In "Grimshawe" Hawthorne invents two such alter egos, the English-born Grimshawe and the American schoolmaster Seymour (later Colcord), each formed by nature in such a way "that one must be hostile to the other" (12:402). "Grimshawe," whose name recalls Fanshawe, is "grim Hawthorne," an extreme projection of his materialist, corporeal self and of the most caustic side of his character. "Seymour"—whose name is also resonant ("see more"), as may be its mutation into Colcord, a variant on airy transcendental Concord—is Hawthorne's effete, moonshiny self, the "mild, shy, gentle, melancholic, exceedingly sensitive, and not very forcible man" (9:7) that readers inferred from *Twice-Told Tales*. Though gifted with "a good deal of intellectual ability," Grimshawe is "very dark on the moral side"—"a grown-up child, with the exception of lost simplicity and innocence, and ripened evil" (12:362). Seymour, in middle age, is his countertype—also "childlike" but in unworldly ways and with "a certain want of substance..., a something of earthly bulk, a too etherealness" (12:387, 393) that makes him contemptible even to the children. Though "as far apart... as the range of human nature would permit [them] to be" (12:402), the two men are linked by a connection to ancient events abroad. Seymour comes from a race characterized by "a nicety of conscience, a nicety of habit, which either was in itself a want of force, or was necessarily connected with it" (12:394–95). The American founder of that race was an emigrant who had suffered so much in England "that always afterwards, on the forest-leaves of this land, his foot left a print of blood wherever it trod" (12:395). And whether by uncanny coincidence, design, or fate, the old doctor has a portrait of that very emigrant hanging on his wall.

What can Hawthorne be up to? James R. Mellow sees the author of the last romances as having "wandered into a hall of mirrors in which fragments of his personal life and pieces of his imaginative fantasies were reflected and repeated in bewildering sequence" (Mellow 546). When Seymour is first introduced, he is trying to calm a Salem mob that has attacked Grimshawe, for which he receives a blow on the head "as unresistingly as if it had been kindly intended" (12:386). Dazedly recovering from his wound, Seymour enjoys the "pleasant dimness and uncertainty" of his condition: "the grossness, the roughness, the too great angularity of the actual is removed from me. It is a state I like very much" (12:387). Hawthorne might as easily have been describing the romancer's stance toward reality. On one side, Hawthorne is the dewy Seymour who prefers to live with ideality; on another, he is the cynical Grimshawe who abuses Seymour for lacking the "beef and ale" that "would have saved" him and his race from "exhal[ing]" (12:394). For all his coarseness and bursts of malignity, Grimshawe is charismatic in his "rude manhood" and "human warmth," while Seymour is capable "only of gentle and mild regard" and prompts no warmth in others (12:393). Seymour is Hawthorne's embodiment (or *dis*embodiment) of the Salem romancer he still harbors within him, disdain him as he might; Grimshawe is his jolly corner representation of the brute materialist he might become if he allowed his "English" side, his physicality and sagacious realism, to reign unchecked. Rather than work to reconcile "America" and "England," idealist and realist, Hawthorne caricatures them and sets them against each other in what amounts morally to mutual annihilation.

How Hawthorne planned to resolve this masochistic psychodrama is unknown. It is hinted (misleadingly) that Grimshawe does away with Seymour. In fact, he sends him off because he considers him "a dangerous fellow" who "would have taken the beef out of" Ned (12:408). (Years later, Seymour resurfaces in England as Colcord, an adjunct to claimant Ned's quest.) In truth, Grimshawe is the dangerous fellow. In answer to Ned's questions about his origins ("Tell me…where I came from, and how you came to have me"), Grimshawe breaks out:

> Whence did you come? Whence did any of us come? Out of the darkness and mystery, out of nothingness, out of a kingdom of shadows; out of dust, clay, impure mud, I think, and to return to it again.… [H]e must be a wiser man than Doctor Grim who can tell you why you, or any other mortal came hither; only, one thing I am well aware of, it was not to be happy. To toil, and moil, and hope, and fear, and to love in a shadowy, doubtful sort of way, and to hate in bitter earnest—that is what you came for! (12:356–57)

Grimshawe is a good man perversely gone astray, and when in a rare moment his better side emerges—as when he praises "Truth; then Courage; then Justice; then Mercy" and begins "doubtfully to speak of man's spiritual nature and its demands, and the emptiness of everything which a sense of these demands did not pervade, and condense and weighten into realities"—he is "transfigured" in the eyes of the children (2:374, 375). But the mood is quickly broken, he "burst[s] into one of his great roars of laughter," and once again he is "the uncouth, wild-bearded, rough, earthy, passionate figure, whom they called Doctor Grim, looking ashamed of himself, and trying to turn the whole matter into a jest" (12:375).

Grimshawe the cynic and closet idealist is the obverse of Hawthorne the idealist and closet cynic, and in endowing him with dramatic power beyond any character in his late fiction (Miriam excepted) Hawthorne is venting the nihilistic suspicions of a lifetime, aggravated by the trials of an aging writer struggling to write and alienated from time and place. Having created Grimshawe, Hawthorne kills him off. He will not center his book on such a figure, yet he does title his manuscript after him and he allows Grimshawe's misanthropy and unbelief to strike the note for the action to come, Redclyffe's quest for his inheritance.

Perhaps the best way to regard the claimant manuscripts is to view them as a geologist might a Pacific island group: interests erupt and subside as they pass over the volcanic hot spot of Hawthorne's imagination, leaving behind islets of plot in various stages of new-formed jaggedness and erosional decay. The constants are the two données of the claimant and the footstep (never brought into sensible relation) and the themes of aristocracy and England versus America. Characters are introduced, then disappear; names are changed for no apparent reason; relationships change; narrative lines are considered, then rejected. After beginning "The Ancestral Footstep" with Middleton's immersion in English life, the drafts deepen in their thematic concern, then lose their way in Etherege/Redclyffe's gloomy childhood and a maze of Radcliffean English horrors.

Mellow believes the late manuscripts fail because Hawthorne despairs of his efforts at realism and "surrender[s] his imagination" to gothic fantasy, only to find that gothicism embroils him in chaos (Mellow 545). In fact, after the impressive opening of "The Ancestral Footstep," Hawthorne never gave realism a sustained try. In 1855 he had looked ahead to "something ruddier, warmer, and more genial, in [his] later fruitage" (17:40) in consequence of his physical and metaphysical English diet. Instead, on returning to America, integration became *dis*-integration, the Englishman in him (Grimshawe) set *against* the Salemite (Seymour), both made repellent. Had he followed his intuition and rid his story of the "great crime" (12:199), the claimant manuscript might have been among his very best works. But by literary and philosophical habit he had lived too long with "crime" and felt aesthetically naked without it. What might have been a signal accomplishment became a signal disaster. The productive Indian summer Hawthorne hoped would follow from his English residence became a winter of literary and personal discontent.

A Fine Bewilderment

The dawn of the American consciousness of the complicated world it
was so persistently to annex is the more touching the more primitive
we make that consciousness; but we must recognize that the latter can
scarcely be interesting to us in proportion as we make it purely primitive. The interest is in its becoming perceptive and responsive, and the
charming, the amusing, the pathetic, the romantic drama is exactly that
process. The process, in our view, must have begun, in order to determine the psychological moment, but there is a fine bewilderment it
must have kept in order not to anticipate the age of satiety.

—Henry James, *William Wetmore Story and His Friends*

The Ambassador from Salem

Removed from familiar surroundings, the traveler [in Italy] saw his formerly unquestioned sense of identity, based on accepted assumptions
and on a specific role in society, fall away, and the problem of who he
was became an important one.

—Paul S. Baker, *The Fortunate Pilgrims: Americans in Italy, 1800–1860*

In a notebook entry for what would develop into *The Ambassadors*, Henry James
recounts an anecdote he heard from a young friend, Jonathan Sturges, about
William Dean Howells, who had been visiting in Paris. Nearing sixty, Howells
seemed sad, James was told. "Virtually in the evening of his life, as it were, it was
all new to him: all, all, all," James remarks. Then the novelist in him sets his imagination to work:

> …it gives me the little idea of the figure of an elderly man who hasn't
> "lived," hasn't at all, in the sense of sensations, passions, impulses, plea-
> sures—and to whom, in the presence of some great human spectacle,
> some great organization for the Immediate, the Agreeable, for curiosity,
> and experiment and perception, for Enjoyment, in a word, becomes, *sur
> la fin*, or toward it, sorrowfully aware.[1]

Although James would not get to his story for some time, it is one he had broached years earlier in *Hawthorne* when he described "this odd, youthful-elderly mind, contending so late in the day with new opportunities for learning old things, and, on the whole, profiting by them so freely and gracefully" (James 118). In *The Ambassadors* Sturges's words on Howells develop into the scene between Lambert Strether and Little Bilham in the sculptor Gloriani's garden in Paris. "Live all you can," Strether tells his companion: "It's a mistake not to.... I haven't done so enough before—and now I'm old; too old at any rate for what I see."[2] James did not speculate on any comparable epiphany for Hawthorne, but had there been one it might well have occurred during his 1858 visit to the Sienese villa of expatriate American sculptor William Wetmore Story, whom he had known in Boston in the early 1840s and befriended again in Italy, and whom James would also befriend, even to becoming, at the family's request, his biographer. Hawthorne thought the area around Siena "much more agreeable" even than that around Florence (14:446), where had had recently summered, and in Story himself he found "the most variously accomplished and brilliant person—the fullest of social life and fire—whom I have ever met" (14:447).

Born in Salem, son of former Supreme Court justice Joseph Story and a distinguished legal scholar himself, Story left the law and America and settled in Rome, where he became the leading light in the colony of American artists. Prosperous, widely acclaimed, happily married with blossoming children, and a delightful host who "bubbled and brimmed over with fun" (14:447), Story, at thirty-nine, must have seemed to Hawthorne, fifteen years older, much that he himself was not and could never be, both individually and as a product of his generation. James described Hawthorne as an American sojourning in Europe rather than a Europeanized American (James 128), a thought that in some form must have struck Hawthorne as he measured the life Story had made for himself as an artist in Italy against his own. That Story seemed finally "not a happy man" (14:445) had to do with his private limitations: with so many "sparkling talents," he had none that approached genius (14:448). It was Story's way of life that appealed so deeply to Hawthorne, outwardly in its circumstances, inwardly in its easy, appreciative mode of being. Story was a Leigh Hunt in the prime of life, amid the most congenial milieu, and with enough manly vigor to keep him from enervation. It was a life and character to be envied.

For all that, James's image of Hawthorne profiting "freely and gracefully" from Old World culture has only a partial truth. If Hawthorne anticipates James's Strether relaxing his New England austerity and yielding to the charm of Europe, he also resembles Strether's provincial friend Waymarsh gnashing his teeth at European artifice, indolence, venality, sexual laxity, and dirt. Indeed, the running tension between "Strether" and "Waymarsh" might be said to define much of *The French and Italian Notebooks*, culturally and intellectually the richest Hawthorne kept but also, in their "fine bewilderment,"[3] the most precariously balanced between an emergent aesthetic naturalism and a residual New England puritanism.

If *The French and Italian Notebooks* are less genial in spirit than *The English Notebooks*, it is partly owing to the fact that, surrounded almost constantly by family, subject to the demands of tourism, and dealing with a people whose language and habits were alien, Hawthorne could rarely unwind. The logistics of guiding a family of five (plus governess Ada Shepard) through the complications of foreign travel and residence could be daunting, or worse—"a bore beyond anything that can be pre-conceived" (14:475). Even in Florence, where he could "absolutely walk on the smooth flags of [the city] for the mere pleasure of walking, and live in its atmosphere for the mere pleasure of living" (14:284), there was little walking and living of the solitary, unencumbered kind he liked to do in England, no sauntering into the equivalent of a local pub to observe or sociably interact with native life or simply settle into himself. Still less was there a Francis Bennoch to ease his way into cultivated Italian society, even if the barriers of language, culture, and sensibility could be overcome. As Richard H. Brodhead observes, "Hawthorne met few Italians and made little effort to understand their ways; and he showed virtually no responsiveness to Italy as another society with its own collective life, forging its own history in the present day."[4] Like other traveling Americans, who "did not visit Italy primarily to meet people but to see things,"[5] Hawthorne took in the sights and frequented the galleries. Evenings he played cards with his family or paid calls on resident Americans, often artists, in whom he found a version of America reflected back to him. Though cosmopolitan by New World standards, men like Story and Florentine sculptor Hiram Powers harbored biases on morality, gender, and sexual propriety shaped by their upbringings in Boston and Cincinnati, nor were they above professional rivalry and catty gossip. In *The Marble Faun* Hawthorne would contrast the freedoms of Rome with their absence in New England, where morality is homogeneous and behavior visible to everyone. In fact, as evidenced in the cruel ostracism of Louisa Lander (Story headed the self-appointed committee that investigated rumors about her), the American artist colony could be every bit as provincial and censorious as Salem philistines. Altogether, even as Italy held out the prospect of free enjoyment, it bound him within a circle of judgment and opinion far more constricting than he had inhabited in England.

Hawthorne's January 1858 visit to France en route to Italy was brief—a scant two weeks—but it strikes the note of his response to the Continent. The life of the senses made its initial appeal to him by way of French cookery. The dishes in his first Paris dinner "were very delicate, and a vast change from the simple English system, with its joints, shoulders, beef-steaks and chops; but I doubt whether English cookery, for the very reason that it is so gross, is not better for man's moral and spiritual nature, than French. In the former case, you know that you are gratifying your coarsest animal needs and propensities, and are duly ashamed of it; but, in dealing with these French delicacies, you delude yourself into the idea that you are cultivating your taste while filling your belly" (14:11). Within a few days he had begun to change his mind, though not without misgivings: "In my opinion, it would require less time to cultivate one's gastronomic tastes, than taste of any other kind; and, on the whole, I am not sure that a man could do a better thing than to afford himself a little discipline in this line.... [Our meal] was all very good, and we respected ourselves far more than if we had gorged a quantity of red roast-beef; but I am not quite sure that we were right" (14:26). That the question of "respecting oneself" should occur at all to Hawthorne, who was never more than a moderate eater, is a token of how deeply the Puritan distrust of sensual pleasure had woven itself into his nature. Soon, nonetheless, he was quietly congratulating himself on having developed a taste in taste: "We dined in the Restaurant de L'Echelle; but already we are getting to be connoisseurs in French cookery, and we found nothing very admirable in the dishes of to-day" (14:34). Food would seldom be a subject in his Italian notebooks, whether because it was less artfully prepared and presented than in France or because Hawthorne had grown used to good dining, yet nearly always in his accounts of sensual pleasure there is a lingering feeling of unease, as though physical enjoyment involved a relaxation of morality, if not worse.

Cuisine aside, Hawthorne's main impression of Paris was of its "splendor," its "unwearying magnificence and beauty," which took him "altogether by surprise" (14:13, 14). "London is paltry, despicable, not to be mentioned in the same day, nor compared even for the purpose of ridiculing it, with Paris," he added: "I never knew what a palace was, till I had a glimpse of the Louvre and the Tuilleries;—never had any idea of a city gratified, till I trod these stately streets" (14:14). The architectural grandeur of the Louvre impressed him even more than its paintings; Notre Dame seemed "the most magnificent Gothic edifice [he] had ever seen"(14:30). Counterbalancing this was "the horrible muddiness ... of all Paris" (14:34), which, apart from unsightliness and inconvenience, struck him almost as a moral affront. Within a week he confessed he was "quite tired of Paris, and never longed for a home so much" (14:34). This would be the pattern of his Continental experience: delight, astonishment, revelation, recoil (often at filth), weariness, then yearnings for home, though having once traversed the cycle Hawthorne might, as with Rome, traverse it again on a level of keener appreciation and deeper disgust. As his initial enthusiasm for a place waned, the Strether in him yielded to the Waymarsh and he grew bored and critical until his energies revived with a change of scene and the cycle recommenced.

Rome

Here [in Rome] I both feel how it all was, and, strange to say, I am also
magnetized with the power that hovers invisibly in this air.... What,
then, is this Rome that will hold sway over mankind, whether or no, in
past and present time?

—Sophia Hawthorne, *Notes in England and Italy*

At present Rome masters him: he has been subdued by the vanquished
Queen of Christendom.... Uncrowned, disheveled, and forlorn, she
yet remembers a spell taught her in the old pagan ages, which takes us
captive, and binds our hearts to her forever.

—unsigned review, "The Author of Adam Bede and Nathaniel
Hawthorne," *North British Review* (August 1860)

Italy overwhelmed and disoriented Hawthorne, awakening in him the aesthete's
sense of beauty and pleasure along with the aesthete's fastidiousness and troubling the moralist and the historian with intimations of chaos that could not be
contained within New World ideas of virtue and Providential design. All told,
Hawthorne spent about seventeen months in Italy, residing in Rome from late
January through May 1858, in or around Florence from June through September,
and in Rome again (after traveling) from mid-October through late May 1859.

Like other Anglo-American tourists, Hawthorne saw Rome as a layered city:
ancient Rome, Catholic medieval and High Renaissance Rome, and contemporary Rome, the last an enclave under papal rule in a still disunited Italy. Although
the short-lived Roman republic of 1849 was barely a decade in the past—he
might have heard tales of the heroic days from William and Emelyn Story, residents at the time and friends of Margaret Fuller's—Hawthorne shows no interest
in Italian politics beyond a gratitude for the French troops that patrol the streets
and keep the populace in order. Partially because he knew it better than Paris but
chiefly for its imperial past, Rome came to symbolize for him the two faces of
Europe, its heights higher than Paris's (he was dazzled by the beauty and opulence of the Italian churches), its depths lower (he was appalled by the filth and
decay of its urban life). Here, more than in London, was the site of Western
human experience. As Sophia said, Rome was "how it all was"—and how it
continued to be.[6]

If for Sophia visiting Italy was the realization of a long-standing dream, for
Hawthorne it was a version of the repressed northerner's venturing into a world
of pleasure and equivocal ease in which "life flowed along in slow movement"
and time was not to be saved but to be "savored."[7] Nathalia Wright observes that
for Henry James (who in this respect was more typical than not) "the southern,
pagan world of Italy" came to represent "the whole early experience of man, as
the northern, Christian, particularly the Anglo-Saxon world represented man's

recent experience."[8] "As he traveled south in any longitude," Wright continues, James professed to be "always struck with 'that most charming of all watchable processes, the gradual soft, the distinctly demoralized, conversion of the soul of Nature,' its return 'from a comparatively grim Theistic faith to the ineradicable principle of Paganism.'"[9]

James's view of North and South is squarely in the tradition of the German Romantics, whose interpretation of European culture became the inscribed Protestant mythology for well over a century. The demarcation was not simply geographical; it was historical (ancient vs. modern), temporal (childhood vs. maturity), ethical (natural vs. spiritual), and religious (pagan or Catholic vs. Protestant). In contrast to the "refined and ennobled sensuality" of the Greeks, A. W. Schlegel wrote, "the stern nature of the North drives man back within himself; and what is lost in the free sportive development of the senses, must, in, noble dispositions, be compensated by earnestness of mind."[10] For Schlegel, "the root of human existence" was religion, and in its absence, as with even the best of the Greeks, humanity "would become a mere surface without any internal substance."[11] Visiting classical ruins, Hawthorne, too, felt, the cultural and moral discontinuity between pagan and Christian civilization, the latter constituting "a deeper life of the human race" than anything suggested by the remains of Rome (14:167). In *The Marble Faun* Kenyon will contend that the "sculptors of the Middle Ages have fitter lessons" for his art than do the ancients; their masterpieces "belong to our Christian civilization; and, being earnest works, they always express something which we do not get from the antique" (4:313). And yet, as Kenyon also says, the earnestness of modernity has its price: "the iron rule in our days, to require an object and a purpose in life ... [,] makes us all parts of a complicated scheme of progress, which can only result in our arrival at a colder and drearier region than we were born into" (4:239). Italy, James felt, was "a refuge from" this "hardness & haste, of the Northern world" and a return to a simpler life, "though it 'wouldn't do' alone" without the North.[12] Hawthorne would have agreed, with greater emphasis on "though."

Apart from its cultural alienness, ancient Rome confounded Hawthorne's sense of time and history. In America, Salem counted as old; in Rome, where the dry climate preserved ruins in an ageless, unendearing whiteness, "the sixteenth century, in which many of the churches and fountains seem to have been built or re-edified, seems close at hand, even like our own days; a thousand years, or the days of the latter empire, is but a modern date; and scarcely interests us; and nothing is really venerable of a more recent epoch than the reign of Constantine" (14:57). Nina Baym characterizes Hawthorne's Rome as "the house of the seven gables writ large: everywhere in the city people carried forward their lives within the shapes bequeathed to them by an ancestry stretching back to the beginning of time."[13] Outwardly, this is true (people living near or within ancient structures); morally, it is not, for there was no organic continuity of life stretching back to antiquity and no transmitted historical consciousness. Rather, every-where Hawthorne felt *dis*continuity, an incongruous juxtaposition of epochs and a cheek-by-jowl coexistence of the "sublime and the ridiculous" (14:88): noble monuments used as public privies; the temple of Minerva occupied by a bakeshop; the Colosseum patrolled by French soldiers, with a Christian shrine at its center and youths gaily running footraces around it.

From his earliest writings, Hawthorne's identity had been bound up with his possession of a deep historical sense. Rome did for him something of what the nineteenth-century unearthing of the fossil record did for believers in the literal truth of Genesis; it vastly expanded human time in ways that challenged assump-tions about the nature of reality. Faced with 2,500 years of civilization in place of the familiar 200, Hawthorne felt called upon to recalibrate the meaning of history or confront its possible absence of meaning. Of all Roman monuments, the Pantheon pleased him most, partly because it managed to bridge pagan, Renaissance, and modern—a Roman temple converted into a Christian church and surrounded by the lively confusion of a neighborhood market—but primarily because its open dome symbolized to him a connection of the present moment to heaven and the eternal that bypassed the conundrums of historical being.

The Marble Faun would be infused with a sense of the annihilating density of Rome. In James's *Roderick Hudson* Rowland Mallet will similarly be oppressed by a Roman "atmosphere so heavily weighted with echoes and memories [that] one grows to believe that there is nothing in one's consciousness that is not fore-doomed to moulder and crumble and become dust for the feet and possible malaria for the lungs, of future generations." Mallet comes to terms with Rome through "a sort of relaxed acceptance of the present, the actual, the sensuous—of life on the terms of the moment."[14] This is the aesthetic naturalism Hawthorne had been drawn to, ambivalently, through much of his career. How he might have met the challenge of Rome had not Una's illness blighted his second term of residence is conjectural, save as he met it fictively in *The Marble Faun*, drafted during that terrible time and rewritten months later in England. The actual Rome remained unfinished business for him. Worn out by Una's and the family's ordeal, he left the city with a rueful sense of relief. As he wrote on May 29, 1859, four days before his scheduled departure,

> I looked at everything as if for the last time; nor do I wish ever to see any
> of these objects again, though no place ever took so strong a hold of my
> being, as Rome, nor ever seemed so close to me, and so strangely
> familiar. I seem to know it better than my birth place, and to have known
> it longer; and though I have been very miserable there, and languid with
> the effects of the atmosphere, and disgusted with a thousand things in

daily life, still I cannot say I hate it—perhaps might fairly own a love for it. But (life being too short for such questionable and troublesome enjoyments) I desire never to set eyes on it again. (14:524)

"The Emptiness of Picture-Galleries"

Of technicalities,—difficulties overcome, harmony of lines, and so forth,—he had no explicit knowledge; they produced their effect upon him, of course, but without his recognizing the manner of it. All that concerned him was the sentiment which the artist had meant to express; the means and method were comparatively unimportant.

—Julian Hawthorne, *Nathaniel Hawthorne and His Wife*

In a moment of moral crisis in *The Marble Faun*, Hilda goes to her beloved picture galleries for relief only to find herself beset for the first time in her life by "that icy Demon of Weariness" that whispers to her the artifice, the insincerity, and even the fraudulence of much of what passes for great art (4:338). What Hilda wants is a "spiritual revelation" (4:339), and in describing how "her perceptive faculty penetrated the canvas like a steel probe, and found but a crust of paint over emptiness" (4:341), Hawthorne is using the occasion to express his own frustrations with art, notably its failure to provide the kind of mediation between matter and spirit, earth and heaven, normally the province of religion. There were *too many* pictures, and singly and collectively they testified to too little, or at least not to what Hawthorne wished them to.

Residence in Rome and Florence revived in intense form the experiment in connoisseurship that began with Hawthorne's attendance at the Great Exhibition in Manchester during the summer of 1857. The results were much the same, exponentially heightened: an anticipatory mix of dread, awe, and resignation to spousal duty; an initial feeling of inundation; a growing interest in and appreciation of artworks (always selective and within the limits of his daily powers of absorption and endurance); a satisfaction in becoming "more fastidious, yet more sensible of beauty where I saw none before" (14:317); an idiosyncratic reflectiveness on particular works; and finally, with satiety, fits of coldness in which the entire enterprise seemed a phenomenal hoax and even beloved works like the Venus de Medici left him indifferent. On art even more than on other subjects, Strether and Waymarsh fought it out, cyclically, to no definite end.

Hawthorne's notebook account of an early visit to the Palazzo Borghese sounds most of the themes of his Italian gallery experience:

The collection is one of the most celebrated in the world, and contains between eight and nine hundred pictures, many of which are esteemed master-pieces. I think I was not in a frame for admiration, today, nor could achieve that free and generous surrender of myself, which I have already said is essential to the proper estimate of anything excellent. Besides, how is it possible to give one's soul, or any considerable part of it, to a single picture, seen for the first time, among a thousand others, all of which set forth their own claims in an equally good light! Furthermore, there is an external weariness and sense of thousand-fold sameness to be overcome, before we can begin to enjoy a gallery of the old Italian masters. There is such a terrible lack of variety in their sub-jects.... These old painters seldom treated their subjects in a homely way; they were above life, or on one side of it; and if they ever touched the heart, it was by the help of the religious sentiment, which we Protestants can not call up, to eke out our profane admiration. I can hardly think they really had the sentiments themselves; for evidently they were just as ready, or more so, to paint a lewd and naked woman, and call her Venus, as to imagine whatever is purest in womanhood, as the mother of their Saviour.... Raphael, and other great painters, have done wonders with sacred subjects; but the greatest wonder is, how they could ever paint them at all, and always they paint from the outside, and not from within.

I was glad, in the very last of the twelve rooms, to come upon some Dutch and Flemish pictures, very few, but very welcome; Rubens, Rembrandt, Vandyke, Paul Potter, Teniers, and others—men of flesh and blood, with warm fists, and human hearts. As compared with them, these mighty Italian masters seem men of polished steel, not human, nor addressing themselves so much to human sympathies as to a formed intellectual taste. (14:110–12)

While Sophia could delight in the ethereality of Fra Angelico and the artifice of Giotto, Hawthorne required of art the qualities he required of literature: it had to be real; it had to be ideal. Because the Dutch Masters were not "above life, or on one side of it," (14:111), but were planted squarely in its midst, their repre-sentations had the authority of perfect verisimilitude. Just as their "earthen jugs...will surely hold water" (14:317), so their paintings held absolute belief within their modest range of subject and emotion. But Hawthorne also wanted art to bear witness (as life did not) to the reality of the transcendent and its immanence in temporal life; and for this, neither Dutch realism nor Italian ideal-ization sufficed. The "religious sentiment" of the earlier Renaissance painters had to be joined to the technical expertise of the later ones—who generally lacked the sincerity of their predecessors precisely because they *were* self-con-scious artists. Italian art improved, Hawthorne felt, then declined almost as a result of that improvement. Coming after the lifelessness of the early artists, Perugino seemed "the first painter" of "genuine merit" rather than mere antiquarian interest. "Probably," Hawthorne speculated, inferring the character of the artist from the impression made by the artwork, "his religion was more genuine than Raphael's, and therefore the Virgin often revealed herself to him in a loftier and sweeter face of divine womanhood than all the genius of Raphael could produce" (14:324). Given a modicum of realism, spirituality, not virtuosity, counted most for Hawthorne, who could dismiss much of the painting of the High Renaissance as a hollow anticlimax. "After Perugino," he writes, "the pictures cease to be interesting; the art has come forward with rapid strides, but the painters and their productions do not take nearly so much hold of the spectator as before. They all paint better than Giotto and Cimabue—in some respects better even than Perugino—but they paint in vain, probably because they were not nearly so much in earnest" (14:371; v. 4:338).

The painting that exemplified the limitations of art for Hawthorne was the one widely accounted "the greatest painting in the world,"[15] Raphael's *Transfiguration*. Based on two episodes from Matthew, the canvas divides into distinct halves, the lower one showing the apostles vainly trying to dispossess a demoniac boy, the upper depicting Christ's ascension flanked by the figures of Moses and Elijah. Jenny Franchot notes that for "American tourists in Italy" Raphael's painting "was a deeply satisfying representation of the transformation of suffering flesh into spirit or, more precisely, of the moment of triumphant doubleness when man and God are simultaneously visible."[16] This is how the picture was taken by Hawthorne's friend George S. Hillard, whose *Six Months in Italy* (1853) was the most popular of contemporary guidebooks. The painting's "twofold action" was necessary, Hillard argued, "to give it completeness": "The spectacle of the transfiguration would have been no more than a splendid vision, but for the connection thus established between the Savior's glorified state, and the sufferings of humanity which were in him to find healing and relief."[17]

What Hillard sees as the painting's brilliant achievement—its "connection" between Christ above and afflicted humanity below—Hawthorne sees as its failure, a *want* of connection: "the upper portion not thinking of the lower, and the lower portion not being aware of the higher" (14:187). The worlds of earth and heaven, matter and spirit, are utterly dissociated. The painting, Hawthorne remarks, "symbolizes...the spiritual shortsightedness of mankind, that, amid the trouble and grief of the lower picture, not a single individual, either of those who seek help or those who would willingly afford it, lifts his eyes to that region one glimpse of which would set everything right. One or two of the disciples point upward, but without really knowing what abundance of help is to be had there" (14:187–88). From a practical standpoint, the victims are in the situation of those in the Greek Laocoön, which Hawthorne saw as "a type of human beings struggling with an inextricable trouble, and entangled in a complication which they can never free themselves from by their own efforts, and out of which Heaven will not help them" (14:138). In Raphael's Christian painting, Heaven, of course, *will* help, but only later, after human time, and only the spectator knows that; the sufferers don't, and even the disciples seem tentative. As Hawthorne reads it, the painting is a miniature of the problem of faith and experience, since within its frozen moment, which stands for any human moment, earthly suffering is perceived as final, with at most two or three hands gesturing upward toward the unseen.

It is a measure of the tension within Hawthorne's demands on art that he should have objected that Raphael's Christ "looks too much like human flesh and blood to be in keeping with the celestial aspect of the figure" (14:187). Raphael, that is, has failed to do for Hawthorne what religion failed to do— convince him simultaneously of the humanity of Christ and of his divinity. Nearly two months later, returning to the question, he finds he wants a *more* human Christ and "wish[es] Raphael had painted the Transfiguration" in the manner of the "Dutch wizards" while "at the same time preserving his breadth and grandeur of design" (14:317). He is still looking to be convinced, but he realizes that art can manage the desired incarnation, and so fulfill its highest mission, only through a minute fidelity to the real as illuminated by a vision of the suprareal. The painting that came closest to this ideal was a fresco by Sodoma of Christ bound to a pillar, which Hawthorne saw in the cathedral in Siena. What impressed him most in the painting was Christ's "loneliness. You feel as if the Savior was deserted, both in Heaven and earth; the despair is in him, which made him say, 'My God, why hast thou forsaken me!' Even in this extremity, however, he is still divine; and Sodoma almost seems to have reconciled the impossibilities of combining an Omnipotent Divinity with a suffering and outraged humanity" (14:492). The significant words are "almost" and "impossibilities." The innocent Christ's suffering is deeply poignant and outrageous to his (and our) humanity; he appeals to the God who authorizes or allows this suffering; his despair at receiving no answer produces a profound existential "loneliness"; and his bearing in the face of that loneliness—the consummate form of a universal human fate—is "divine." But can Christ's pain within the picture and the spectator's in viewing it be reconciled with belief in an omnipotent God? No, such things are "impossibilities." If art is faithful to reality, "a*lmost*" is as near as it can approach to a resolution, and even its "almost" is not intrinsic to the artwork but imported by the viewer's hopeful "imagination," which "completes what the artist merely hints at" (14:492). The greater the viewer's faith, the more affirmative the painting seems. Commenting on the same fresco, Sophia Hawthorne finds none of the despair her husband does; *her* Christ displays "a spirit and a pride so angelic, so superb, that one feels that he submits not through weakness, but through conquering might."[18] Husband and wife project their respective temperaments and beliefs upon mute canvas—Sophia, her "couleur de rose" optimism; Hawthorne, his troubled Pyrrhonism.

The concern with Christ as testator and Savior that recurs in Hawthorne's comments on religious art and occasionally in churches is almost entirely absent elsewhere in the notebooks. Living intimately with the paintings may have prompted, if not genuine religious feelings, then at least an empathetic meditation on them. Even here, Hawthorne's interest is selective. Paintings of the saints, the infant Christ, and the Virgin Mary seldom engage him for long; it is the man-God who reconciles matter and spirit—who as man suffers and who as God forgives—that fascinates him, for only through such a figure can he negotiate the human condition with *its* suffering and felt need for forgiveness. For this reason he is deeply uncomfortable with the severe Christ he sees in the Sistine Chapel:

> In the Last Judgment, the scene of the greater part of the picture lies in the upper sky, the blue of which glows through betwixt the groups of naked figures; and above sits Jesus, not looking in the least like the Savior of the world, but with uplifted arm denouncing eternal misery on those whom he came to save. I fear I am myself among the wicked, for I found myself inevitably taking their part, and asking for at least a little pity, some few regrets, and not such a stern denunciatory spirit on the part of Him who had thought us worth dying for.... It would be a very terrible picture to one who should really see Jesus, the Savior, in that inexorable Judge; but it seems to me very undesirable that he should ever be represented in that aspect, when it is so essential to our religion to believe him infinitely kinder and better towards us than we deserve. At the Last Day, I presume—that is, in all future days, when we see ourselves as we are—man's only inexorable Judge will be himself, and the punishment of his sins will be the perception of them. (14:214–15)

In displacing the judgment and punishment of "the Last Day" to private conscience, Hawthorne essentially psychologizes it. Christ is important to him for bestowing the forgiveness that he, identifying with the plight of the "wicked," is in no position to bestow upon himself. His idea of redemption is therapeutic (deliverance from personal guilt) rather than eschatological (atonement within a divine plan), and it comes only at the last. Until "Time is over" and we "shall know why"—Emily Dickinson's words for an account of things that comes too late [#215])—humanity for Hawthorne is confined to the terrestrial half of Raphael's *Transfiguration*, in which suffering has no apparent reference to anything beyond itself. What W. H. Auden in "Musée des Beaux Arts" calls

suffering's "human position" (thereby implying the possibility of other positions) is, for Hawthorne, its only knowable position. We range ourselves "spiritually" according to how we meet this fact. The painting that moved him most
profoundly, the so-called *Beatrice Cenci* ascribed to Guido Reni, has entirely to
do with this "human position":

> . . . it is the very saddest picture that ever was painted, or conceived;
> there is an unfathomable depth and sorrow in the eyes; the sense of it
> comes to you by a sort of intuition. It is a sorrow that removes her out
> of the sphere of humanity; and yet she looks so innocent, that you feel
> as if it were only this sorrow, with its weight and darkness, that keeps
> her down upon the earth and brings her within our reach at all. She is
> like a fallen angel, fallen, without sin. It is infinitely pitiful to meet her
> eyes, and feel that nothing can be done to help or comfort her; not that
> she appeals to you for help and comfort, but is more conscious than we
> can be that there is none in reserve for her. (14:92–93)

Without allowing for anything transcendent (no help "in reserve for her"),
Hawthorne's account of Beatrice comes close to realizing his ideal of "incarnation," save that the "spiritual" has been resituated wholly within the human.
Beatrice's "transfiguration" is a secular one achieved through the majesty of bot-
tomless sorrow. Like Hunilla in Melville's "The Encantadas," another sinless
victim of human cruelty and divine silence, Hawthorne's Beatrice is a type of
innocence crucified, which may be the only aspect of Christ that Hawthorne
could steadfastly believe in. What Melville said of Hunilla, Hawthorne implies
of Beatrice: "Humanity, thou strong thing, I worship thee, not in the laurelled
victor, but in this vanquished one" (*WHM* 9:157). If Sodoma's Christ is divine
"even in his extremity" (14:492), Guido's Beatrice seems "divine" *through* her
extremity.

Such, of course, is a naturalistic understanding of "divinity"—the metamor-
phosis of clay into "spirit" through profound suffering. If this, indeed, is what
Hawthorne was inclining toward, he would have found himself promptly
checked by a quirk of propinquity. "Close beside Beatrice Cenci," he wrote,
"hangs the Fornarina [ascribed to Raphael], a brunette, with a deep, bright glow
in her face, naked below the navel and well pleased to be so for the sake of your
admiration—ready for any extent of nudity, for love or money,—the brazen trollope that she is. Raphael must have been capable of great sensuality, to have
painted this picture of his own accord and lovingly" (14:93). That Raphael could
paint a *Fornarina* as readily as a *Transfiguration* seemed to Hawthorne a scathing
indictment of the spiritual authenticity of high Italian art (4:337); without
the sublimating glow of religion, which in Raphael's case flickered on and off,

paintings of the female sunk back into a coarse celebration of sex. The juxtaposition of the *Cenci* and the *Fornarina* would have underscored for Hawthorne the extremes within the natural, the one rising almost to the heavenly, the other barely escaping the bestial, and the difference between them only a matter of degree within the slippery slope of character and circumstance. The worst offender for Hawthorne was Titian, whose technical accomplishment made the eroticism of his paintings all the more alluring. Hawthorne's description of "Titian's Magdelene, the one with the golden hair clustering round her naked body" (14:333), is a classic example of the repressed Puritan's lust affair with the erotic. Viewing the painting a few years earlier, George S. Hillard had wondered whether "it would not have been better, on the whole," that such a "dazzling" picture "had never been painted."[19] Hawthorne is delighted it has been painted, before the censor in him steps in to silence admiration:

> This Magdelene is very coarse and sensual, with only an impudent assumption of penitence and religious sentiment, scarcely so deep as the eyelids; but it is a splendid picture, nevertheless, with those naked, lifelike arms, and the hands that press the rich locks about her, and so carefully let those two voluptuous breasts be seen. She a penitent! She would shake off all pretence to it, as easily as she would shake aside that clustering hair and offer her nude front to the next comer. Titian must have been a very good-for-nothing old man. (14:334)

In the presence of a picture like the Magdalene, Hawthorne himself becomes "a very good-for-nothing old man," and one who more than half enjoys being so, though he needs to fib about it. The lightning rod for his sexual anxieties was not Roman behavior except as it reached him through the alleged trespasses of countrywomen like Louisa Lander and Margaret Fuller; it was nudity in art, which discomforted him to the degree that it was realistic. On the nominal ground of anachronism, he objected to full or partial nudity in sculptures of modern-day figures (Washington in a toga?), and on the ground of wearisome repetition to nudity in latter-day treatments of classical subjects. He particularly loathed the flesh-tinted statues of English sculptor John Gibson, whose "lascivious warmth of hue quite demoralizes the chastity of the marble, and makes one feel ashamed to look at the naked limbs in the company of women" (14:157). To admire the human form in art, it was necessary for Hawthorne to desexualize it. The cool whiteness of classical statuary, together with the absence of individuating facial expression, achieved this in ancient artworks, but the innocence of the Greeks was not culturally transportable. A nude became unacceptably "naked" when fashioned by a contemporary, who could not "sculpture nudity with a pure heart," Hawthorne writes (self-revealingly), "if only because he is compelled to steal guilty glimpses at hired models" (4:123). In *The Marble Faun* he makes the liberated Miriam the vehicle for prudish views, which he lifts from his notebook despite their inappropriateness to her dramatic character.

Hawthorne's favorite statue was the Venus de Medici in Florence, which he searched out "with the half-hope, half-fear, that she might stand before me," surprised that he "cared so much" about this "or any possible woman" (14:297). The Venus did not disappoint him: "She is very beautiful; very satisfactory; and has a fresh and new charm about her, unreached by any cast or copy that I have seen" (14:297–98). Setting aside the fact that she *was* a Venus, goddess of love, Hawthorne took the statue as a Platonic type of "all womanhood" and an index of "the high destinies of the human race" within "Nature's plan" (14:297). He was also impressed by the Apollo Belvedere and the Laocöon. In the presence of Greek statuary, Hawthorne became something of a Greek himself, taking pleasure in the forms of the human simply *as* human. Finally, however, the Greeks in their aesthetic naturalism lay on the far side of the great divide between North and South, modern and ancient, Christian and pagan, spiritual and material, and while he admired contemporary productions like Story's *Cleopatra* and Harriet Hosmer's *Zenobia*, he felt that sculpture was a vestigial art, culturally outgrown. There was no returning to the old naturalism and, for Hawthorne, no salutary venturing forward toward a new. Painting dissatisfied him because of its aesthetic failure to represent the Christian promise, sculpture because of its common indifference to it. The galleries of Rome and Florence were a source of great pleasure to him—it was "with a sad reluctance" that he "bid . . . farewell forever" to the Pitti Palace and the Uffizi (14:429)—but they were also "empty" insofar as they failed to satisfy the spiritual cravings they did so much to awaken.

Churchgoing

> [Catholicism] offers a so much richer pasturage and shade to the fancy, has so many cells with so many different kinds of honey, is so indulgent in its multiform appeals to human nature, that Protestantism will always show to Catholic eyes the almshouse physiognomy.
>
> —William James, *The Varieties of Religious Experience*

Leaving the "hideous town of Bolsena" en route to Rome in October 1858, Hawthorne feels, as Holgrave had in *The House of the Seven Gables,* that "all towns should be made capable of purification by fire, or of decay, within each half-century" in order not to accumulate "vermin and noisomeness" or stand in the way of modern improvement (14:481, 482). On a market day in Perugia he felt quite different. "The scene was livelier than any I have seen in Rome," its everyday bustle particularly striking against "the curious and picturesque architecture of the principal streets" dating back centuries (14:259). Presiding over the activity was the majestic "bronze statue of Pope Julius III" that Hawthorne would make use of in *The Marble Faun*. "He seems to have life and observation in him," Hawthorne writes, "and impresses the spectator as if he might rise up from his chair, should any public exigency demand it, and encourage or restrain the people by the dignity and awe of his presence" (14:260). Nowhere in *The French and Italian Notebooks* is Hawthorne more respectful of a traditional society living amid the physical structures of the past and under the paternal eye of the church. He recognizes the thought as such and despairs of doing justice to it: "I wish I could in any way catch and confine within words my idea of the venerableness and stateliness, the air of long-past time subsisting into the present, which remains upon my mind with the recollection of these mediaeval antiquities of Perugia" (14:260).

The buildings alone would be empty shells without the superintending spirit of Pope Julius and the Church. This is the inference Hawthorne draws from the "now dead city" of Assisi, "a sort of stony growth out of the hill-side" that flourished once as "the seat, and birth-place almost, of art" thanks to the "great ecclesiastical garden in which [the flower] was sheltered and fostered" (14:253). Arcadian Italy—the Monte Beni of *The Marble Faun*—could be delightfully picturesque, but whatever vitality of *soul* Italy had for Hawthorne resided in the life of its peasantry and urban populace as nourished by the rituals and traditions of the Church.

Like most Anglo-Americans, Hawthorne arrived in Italy with the stereotypical Protestant prejudices about the venality and corruption of the priesthood and the political machinations of the Vatican. As a reader and practitioner of romance, he was also steeped in the lurid anti-Catholicism of the English gothic and was not above making use of it in his "Etherege" manuscript and *The Marble Faun*. He never entirely shed some of these attitudes or undertook to familiarize himself (beyond casual observation) with Catholic institutions, practices, and beliefs. His engagement with Catholicism—in places serious and half admiring, elsewhere formulaic and manipulative—was essentially threefold: aesthetic, psychological, and spiritual, the last of these relating more to the atmosphere of the Church than to its doctrines and authority.

Hawthorne's first acquaintance with Italian Catholicism came through the cathedrals in Genoa, which "dazzled" him with their magnificence—"this sheen of polished variegated marble, covering every inch of the walls; this glow of brilliant frescoes all over the roof, and up within the domes; these beautiful pictures by great masters, painted for the places which they now occupied, and making an actual portion of the edifice; this wealth of silver, gold, and gems, that adorned the shrines of the saints"—and led him to feel "what a splendid religion it was that reared" them (14:48, 49). St. Peter's impressed him even more ("I never saw nor imagined so bright and splendid an interior as that of this immense church"), accustomed as he was to the gray dimness of English cathedrals (14:55). Light, color, opulence, and ubiquitous decoration made for a feast of the senses to someone nourished on the dry crusts of New England simplicity. In England, the Waymarsh in Hawthorne had complained about the perfunctoriness of the Anglican sermon; in Italy, the Strether temporarily forgot such things before the sheer gorgeousness of the setting.

In *The Minister's Wooing* Harriet Beecher Stowe, literally a daughter of the Puritans as Hilda figuratively is, wonders what difference it would have made for her aesthetically starved New Englanders to have "been born in Italy," beneath (say) "the shadow of the great Duomo in Florence," and to have been exposed to "the wondrous pictures of Raphael and Leonardo da Vinci" and "the Apollo, the Venus."[20] The greatness of the founding Puritans for Stowe lay in their effort to "reconcil[e] the most tremendous facts of sin and evil, present and eternal, with those conceptions of Infinite Power and Benevolence which their own strong and generous natures enabled them so vividly to realize" (*MW* 194). In pondering these matters, however, they and their descendants "divested [them] of all those softening poetries and tender draperies which forms, ceremonies, and rituals had thrown them in other parts and ages of Christendom" (*MW* 194). New England religion was strong, but it was also narrow, unadorned, and cold. Catholicism in Italy awakened Hawthorne to precisely those elements in Christianity that Anglo-American Puritanism had suppressed. Against the physical barrenness of New England's churches and what he considered the spiritual barrenness of Old England's, Hawthorne found the Italian churches warm and replete—brilliant to the eye but filled, too, with Stowe's "softening poetries and tender draperies," qualities that, beauty aside, brought out the emotional (feminine) side of religion as distinct from the rigidly theological (masculine) one.

Stowe eventually transferred her allegiance from New England Congregationalism to Episcopalianism. Hawthorne himself, though resistant to Catholicism by training and conviction, was fascinated by it in the way that republican Americans might be fascinated by aristocracy and monarchy even as they ideologically deplored them. In a sense, Rome (or High Church religion), like England (or High State politics), could seem to ritual-impoverished Americans "our old home." William James shows himself surprisingly responsive to ritual, when, having begun *The Varieties of Religious Experience* by dismissing the "second-hand religious life" of churches and theologies, he comes around to valuing what he calls the outbuildings and "overbeliefs" of religion—ideas, practices, or trappings with which individuals or groups clothe their experience of the divine in order to enrich, clarify, or communalize it.[21] Chief among these vestments are the aesthetic, and against the inward and private thrust of his concept of religion

James expresses admiration for those very things—"an organ and old brasses, marbles and frescoes and stained windows," the liturgy, even the church hierarchy—that his New England predecessors had vehemently opposed (*VRE* 361–62). "Compared with such a noble complexity" as Catholicism's, he writes, "how flat does evangelical Protestantism appear, how bare those isolated religious lives whose boast it is that 'man in the bush God may meet'" (*VRE* 362–63).

For Hawthorne, who never met God anywhere, the appeal of Catholicism lay entirely in some of its outbuildings. The ornamental impressed him first, of course, but as he wandered through churches, magnificent and humble, he was increasingly taken with the obscure side-chapels that allowed solitary worshippers a haven for peaceful communion, so different from the commun*alism* of New England worship and the red-hot sermons he recalled from his youth. Slipping into an ordinary Roman church, he seems almost envious of the Catholic's "blessed convenience" in "finding a cool, quiet, silent, beautiful place of worship in even the hottest and most bustling street, into which they may step, leaving the fret and trouble of the world at the threshold, purifying themselves with a touch of holy water as they enter, and kneeling down to hold communion with some saint, their awful friend; or perhaps confessing all their sins to a priest, laying the whole dark burthen at the foot of the cross, and coming forth in the freshness and elasticity of innocence" (14:195).

Though empathetic, Hawthorne writes as an outsider at once distant from the church's gravitational pull and wistful for its ever-available succor. Mindful of what James would call the "bitter negativity" of Protestantism (*VRE* 362), he wonders whether some of the "inestimable advantages" identified with Catholicism might not truly "belong to Christianity" in general and therefore be "compatible with [the] purified faith" of his own tradition. "Perhaps," he writes privately (he would say nothing of the sort in *The Marble Faun*), "it would be a good time to suggest and institute" changes in American religion: "Protestantism needs a new Apostle to convert it into something positive" (14:195).

Hawthorne's allusion to confession anticipates another of William James's outbuildings. For James, the efficacy of confession is psychological, not sacramental; "it is part of the general system of purgation and cleansing" by which the sin-burdened soul throws off "shams," "exteriorize[s]" its inner "rottenness," and establishes "right relations to [its] deity" (*VRE* 364). "What an institution that is!" Hawthorne exclaims of confession after a visit to St. Peter's: "Man needs it so, that it seems as if God must have ordained it. This popish religion certainly does apply itself most closely and comfortably to human occasions; and I cannot but think that a great many people find their spiritual advantage in it, who would find none at all in our formless mode of worship" (14:59; v. 4:344, 346). In *The Marble Faun* Hawthorne projects his ambivalence into an exchange between Hilda, who marvels "at the exuberance with which [Catholicism] adapts itself to all the demands of human infirmity" (words drawn almost verbatim from his notebook), and Kenyon, who echoes the familiar Anglo-Saxon criticisms of the priesthood and the political Church, also drawn from the notebook (4:368; 14:91).

It is difficult to read Hawthorne's remarks on confession without wondering how he might have reconsidered Dimmesdale, and the psychology of guilt generally, with the spectacle of Catholicism before him. "If he had been a protestant," Hawthorne writes of "a young man" he had seen "standing before a shrine, writhing and wringing his hands in an agony of grief and contrition," "I think he would have shut all that up within his heart, and let it burn there till it seared him" (14:49; v. 4:347). As he observed the faces of communicants leaving the confessional, Hawthorne could hardly have failed to ask whether the laws of conscience he had devoted a career to illustrating were "laws" at all or simply functions of a morbid hyperconsciousness still operative in America centuries after it had been absorbed into the broader, more temperate current of English life. Was what Henry James, speaking of Waymarsh, would call "the sacred rage"[22]—the narrow and intense moralism that balked at pleasure and beauty as well as at vice—simply a form of provincial philistinism with nothing "sacred" about it at all? And was the moral psychology with which he himself understood sin only a de-Puritanized version of this New England malady?

Perhaps, however, New Englanders were right, if extreme. In *The Marble Faun* Hawthorne will have Hilda go to a confessional in St. Peter's to unburden herself of the terrible secret of having witnessed Donatello's and Miriam's crime. "And, ah, what a relief!" he writes: "When the hysteric gasp, the strife between words and sobs, had subsided, what a torture had passed away from her soul! It was all gone; her bosom was as pure now as in her childhood. She was a girl again" (4:358). With these last words—a rendering of Hilda's feelings of renewed innocence—Hawthorne introduces a cautionary note, reflecting the widely held Protestant view that confession absolves sinners of the necessity of coming to terms with their sin and thereby keeps them in a state of moral childhood. It allows them to emerge from the confessional "unburthened, active, elastic, and incited by fresh appetite for the next ensuing sin" (4:411–12) or, in Hilda's case, for the next absolutist moral judgment.[23]

At most, Hawthorne viewed confession as psychotherapy and, unlike William James, was unwilling to call it "spiritual" because of its practical fruits for living. The priest who rebukes Hilda for availing herself of Catholic privileges has good reason for doing so, beyond sectarianism. Hilda is making use of a sacrament without believing in its divine efficacy; she is treating a spiritual rite as if it were a device for self-recovery that enables her to get on with life; in effect, she is blaspheming. Catholic reviewer Orestes Brownson had charged as much about Hawthorne in a comment on *The Scarlet Letter*: "Mr. Hawthorne mistakes the character of confession. He does well to recognize and insist on its necessity; but he is wrong in supposing that its office is simply to disburden the mind by communicating its secrets to another; to restore the sinner to his self-complacency.... Confession is a duty we owe to God, and a means... of restoring us to the favor of God."[24] On the principal point, confession as a duty to God, Hawthorne would not have argued with Brownson, but he would likely have added, in Protestant fashion, that the relation to God is inward and personal, not to be mediated through the intercession of a priest (other than as sympathetic listener) or the mystifying medium of a sacrament.

Ultimately, the effect of Hawthorne's encounter with Catholicism was to catholicize (small *c*) his Protestantism. What attracts him is a transsectarian Christianity symbolized by the Pantheon, under whose open dome—"that great Eye, gazing heavenward" (4:457)—individuals may choose "the particular altar for their devotions" and perform them in the manner that suits them best (14:98), confident that their worship will be acceptable to God. Hawthorne commends Catholicism not for its unity and *community* but for its wisdom in providing peripheral space for a private and latitudinarian "mode of worship," by means of which "a great deal of devout and reverential feeling is kept alive in people's hearts" (14:98). Paradoxically, in short, he praises Catholicism, in one of its subordinate strains, for being *Protestant*. Once a Roman temple, the Pantheon, as its name and history suggest, represents in Hawthorne's mind a religion for all people, all epochs, and all gods, and capable in its openness to the sky and elemental grandeur of design of proclaiming the dignity of the spirit against all the surrounding meanness of actual life, not excluding the smells of the produce market just outside its doors.[25] Like Philip Larkin's wayside church amid "suburb scrub," it is "a serious house on serious earth..., / In whose blent air all our compulsions meet, / Are recognized, and robed as destinies"—a place "proper to grow wise in," whatever denominational name one might attach to that wisdom.[26]

The Comforts of Home

How she pined under this crumbly magnificence [of Rome], as if it were piled all upon her human heart! How she yearned for that native homeland, those familiar sights, those faces she had known always.

—Hilda, in *The Marble Faun*

As he passed one little wooden house after another, with their white clapboards and their green blinds, perhaps he found his thoughts not quite so cloudless as the sky. It is dangerous to have a home; too much is expected of it.

—Julian Hawthorne on his father's return to Concord,
Nathaniel Hawthorne and His Wife

In "My Kinsman, Major Molineux," having journeyed from country to city, simplicity to complexity, innocence to experience, Robin feels nostalgic for the village life he formerly scorned and to which he would now happily return, but instinct tells him he is forever "excluded from his home" (11:223). At her lowest moment, Hilda in *The Marble Faun* also thinks of "her native village, with its great, old elm-trees, and the neat, comfortable houses, scattered along the wide grassy margin of its street, and the white meeting-house, and her mother's very door," icons of a simple New England life that "never brought any strange event" but only "sober week-days, and a solemn Sabbath at the close!" (4:342). She, too, would willingly be delivered from the knowledge thrust upon her. At the close of the book she and Kenyon do return to America, as Hawthorne did soon after completing it. Yet having experienced the breadth and depth of Rome, can Hilda and Kenyon truly return "home"? Can Hawthorne?

Terence Martin notes that Rome for Hawthorne "came to represent... the antithesis of his New England sense of home, all the more forcibly to be resisted because submitting to it would require a radical shift in vision, in faith, in personality."[27] What was the price he paid for resistance? James's Rowland Mallet feels the home-appeal of the New England town even as he prepares to depart for Rome: "here were kindness, comfort, safety, the warning voice of duty, the perfect absence of temptation," even "beauty too" of a modest sort (*RH* 92). Rome was none of these things, but it was "an education to the senses and the imagination" (*RH* 159), it was life in its fullness, and it had to be encountered, whatever the result. Less worldly than Mallet, Hawthorne is like another of *Roderick Hudson*'s characters, the provincial but clear-sighted Mary Garland, who feels "overwhelmed" by Rome, as if "a wall in [her] mind had been knocked down at a stroke" and she faced "an immense new world" that made "the old one, the poor little narrow familiar one" of her past, "seem pitiful" (*RH* 262–63). "It seems to me very frightful to develop" (*RH* 263), she confesses—to be made to come to terms with "an old and complex civilisation" (*RH* 264); yet having begun the process, she is aware there is no turning back or even wishing to: "The charm [of America] is broken; the thread is snapped. I prefer to remain here" (*RH* 272).

After years of expatriation, the thread was snapped for Hawthorne as well. Warming to Rome in the spring of 1858 as the city itself warmed, he admitted "a sort of fascination" that "will make me reluctant to take my final leave of it.... The United States are fit for many excellent purposes," he told William D. Ticknor, "but they are certainly not fit to live in" (18:140). After a long summer and early fall in Florence and elsewhere, Hawthorne looked forward to returning to Rome, but Una's protracted bout with malaria (late October 1858 through April 1859) put an end to whatever development a further residence might have brought. In a pocket diary he recorded the vicissitudes of Una's condition, fully expecting she would die (*NHW* 2:207), as she nearly did. Her illness took its toll on both parents—Sophia (and later Julian) came to regard it as permanently destructive of Hawthorne's health—and all but terminated the visits to galleries, churches, and historical sites, as well as most social calls; even family card games were suspended. From November through February Hawthorne made no entries in his notebook, though he did force himself to work on *The Marble Faun*. Franklin Pierce, visiting Rome in March, proved a godsend during this period, and Hawthorne's grateful tribute to him ("Well; I have found in him, here in Rome, the whole of my early friend, and even better than I used to know him" [14:519]) is among the most deeply felt celebrations of friendship in all of the notebooks. His late tribute to Rome is more rueful, conscious as he was of an opportunity missed and never to be regained:

> I am wearing away listlessly these last precious days of my abode in Rome. Una's illness is disheartening; and by confining my wife, it takes away the energy and enterprise that were the spring of all our enterprises. I am weary of Rome, without having seen and known it as I ought; and I shall be glad to get away from it, though no doubt there will be many yearnings to return hereafter, and many regrets that I did not make better use of the opportunities within my grasp. Still, I have been in Rome long enough to be imbued with its atmosphere, and this is the essential condition of knowing a place; for such knowledge does not consist in having seen every particular object it contains.
>
> At any rate, in the state of mind in which I now stand towards Rome, there is very little advantage to be gained by staying here longer. (14:511–12)

Hawthorne's return to England (first to Redcar, Yorkshire, then once again to Leamington Spa) was made nominally to secure the copyright advantages of transatlantic publication, but in fact Hawthorne was not ready to return home, if "home" it was. "What shall we do in America!" (14:434), he wondered in September 1858, fresh from a visit to the Uffizi. Fleetingly he entertained the idea of Siena as a comfortable place in which to "take root" (14:428); at other times he considered London, America being "a country to boast of, and to get out of, and keep away from," and England being "the only country to live in" (18:161). He dreaded returning to the cramped quarters of The Wayside in Concord. The house could and would be enlarged; the resources for culture and enjoyment in America were another matter. In the end, it was not nostalgia for New England that kept him from settling in Europe, nor even considerations of family; it was the recognition that anywhere else, even in England, he would be an air plant, rootless and in limbo. Living abroad, he wrote toward the end of *The*

Marble Faun, we either "defer the reality of life" or, in belatedly repatriating our-selves, find "that life has shifted its reality to the spot where we have deemed ourselves only temporary residents. Thus, between two countries, we have none at all, or only that little space of either, in which we finally lay down our discon-tented bones. It is wise, therefore, to come back betimes—or never" (4:461).

Hawthorne wrote these words before returning to America; one wonders how he might have amended them as he settled into the heat of a Concord summer, several months after Harpers Ferry. Had he "come back betimes"? David B. Kesterson speaks of the "eclecticism" with which Hawthorne absorbed his Italian experience, "even the unpleasant aspects of Rome, and returned to his Wayside home...a changed man and writer. New England may still have been as much as his heart could hold, but many of his thoughts remained abroad."[28] This is a happy way of phrasing an experience of cultural dislocation that seems, by Julian's account, not to have been happy at all. In Italy he had been wooed to a life of the senses, to the contemplation of a history immeasurably longer and deeper than his family's or region's, and to a vertiginous pleasure in edging away from conventional belief to the brink of the modern. He had gone far toward becoming Strether without leaving the residual, perhaps the essential, Waymarsh in him behind. He had put these developments into *The Marble Faun*, partly to express them but also, and primarily, to try to contain them. He had found, as Mary Garland says, that it was "very frightful to develop." More frightful still, he would find at home, was not to.

On the Crust

So, then, Solidity's a Crust—
The core of fire below.

—Melville, "The Apparition"

Rom(e)ance

We know not how to characterize, in any accordant and compatible terms, the Rome that lies before us.... Everywhere, some fragment of ruin, suggesting the magnificence of a former epoch; everywhere, moreover, a Cross—and nastiness at the foot of it. As the sum of all, there are recollections that kindle the soul, and a gloom and languor that depress it beyond any depth of melancholic sentiment that can be elsewhere known.

—Hawthorne, *The Marble Faun*

The Marble Faun is the same high allegory on the "fortunate fall"... that Hawthorne had written of before in many of his tales and romances.

—James R. Mellow, *Nathaniel Hawthorne in His Times*

Like *The Scarlet Letter,* framed by the prison door and the rosebush, *The Marble Faun* is announced by two threshold symbols. The first is the statue of "a child, clasping a dove to its bosom, but assaulted by a snake"—"a symbol," we are told, for the timeless situation "of the Human Soul, with its choice of Innocence or Evil close at hand" (4:5). The pairing is unusual—Innocence is commonly opposed to Experience, Evil to Good—but it is also prophetic, for in *The Marble Faun* experience will be shown as dangerously entwined with evil yet essential for anyone who would pass beyond the moral condition of childhood. More openly than any of its predecessors, *The Marble Faun* centers upon the question Philip Rahv sees Hawthorne recurrently asking: "Is experience identical with sin?—and if so, is sin the doom of man or his salvation?"[1]

The figure of the dove associates the child with Hilda of the dovecote and with Hawthorne's own dove, Sophia. Through the window of the sculpture gallery, experience is represented by the statue's countersymbol, Rome, with its grotesque juxtapositions of past and present: "washerwomen hang[ing] out their linen to the sun" close to the Roman Forum (4:6); grand piles of ancient debris lying side by side with the "shapeless confusion of modern edifices" (4:6); layers of civilization piled upon one another and compacted, squeezing out the lives and deaths of generations—"a waste-heap of historic rubbish"[2] (Millicent Bell's words) set against the backdrop of the unchanging Alban hills and a featureless blue sky. If "a vague sense of ponderous remembrances; a perception of [the] weight and density in a by-gone life" seems to overwhelm the present and crowd out its petty claims (4:6), it does so chiefly for ruminative visitors like the narrator and his characters, not for Rome's inhabitants, who, as Hawthorne elsewhere observed, are "not in the least troubled by the proximity" of "the sublime and the ridiculous" (14:88, 87). Omnipresent and all-signifying, historical Rome is also widely ignored and *unsignifying*, like Gallows Hill for latter-day Salemites in "Alice Doane's Appeal." Rome means everything and means nothing; practically, the two may come to the same thing.

While the threshold symbols in *The Scarlet Letter* serve as poles within which the conflicts of the story take place, those in *The Marble Faun* seem mutually subversive. In content and representational mode, the statue of the child belongs to the controlling allegorical structure of the book as it develops the theme of the Fall—narratively, Donatello's; theologically, Adam's; mythically, Western culture's; archetypically, everyone's. The Fall through sin or sorrow may or may not prove a "fortunate" one, but by organizing his story around this idea Hawthorne confines it within the boundaries of traditional theodicy. By contrast, Rome looms amorphously over *The Marble Faun* like "the Malaria"—literally, "bad air," whose "peculiar quality of malignancy" Hawthorne noted long before it touched him personally through Una (4:73, 14:53).

Even early readers of *The Marble Faun* were aware of the disjunction Henry James later described between "the streets of Rome, whose literal features the author perpetually sketches, and a vague realm of fancy, in which quite a different verisimilitude prevails" (James 134). Although Hawthorne calls the Italy of his book "a sort of poetic or fairy precinct" (4:3), a full "nine-tenths of [its] chapters" incorporate notebook materials recorded with a realist's eye (14:920).[3] Many of such passages are reproduced almost verbatim, yet because the Rome of the notebooks is already half symbol, they resonate profoundly, sometimes apart from or even against the book's governing frame. Just as a building like Palazzo Cenci, to which Hilda carries the packet Miriam has given her, is both an actual contemporary residence and a site of historic crime, so all Rome seemed to Hawthorne redolent of evils so remote and obscure as to blend into a pervasive spiritual mal-aria.

Within Hawthorne's canon, *The Marble Faun* at once looks backward and forward—backward in its organizing theme, the fall of man, which "Hawthorne's whole career had prepared him to write"; and forward in situating that theme in a milieu that makes for "pervasive anxiety" and radically destabilizes it.[4] In imposing old patterns upon a new habitation, Hawthorne seems to be evading the implications of his European experience. Figured in Rome, however, Europe makes itself felt throughout *The Marble Faun* as an adjective may modify a noun almost to the point of eclipsing its literal reference. By locating his oft-told drama of the soul's growth within the vast physical and historical arena of Rome, Hawthorne opens a host of unsettling questions, some age-old, others proto-modern, that challenge his allegorical structure and threaten to topple it.

Caverns, Again

> It was perceptible that [Donatello] had already had glimpses of strange and subtle matters in those dark caverns, into which all men must descend, if they would know anything beneath the surface and illusive pleasures of existence.
>
> —Hawthorne, *The Marble Faun*

> But such a condition [the pastoral state of idyll] does not occur only before the beginnings of civilization, rather it is the condition which civilization...aims at as its ultimate purpose. Only the idea of this condition and belief in its possible realization can reconcile man to all the evils to which he is subjected in the course of civilization.
>
> —Friedrich Schiller, *On Naïve and Sentimental Poetry*

Kenyon encapsulates the theme of *The Marble Faun* when he tells Hilda, Donatello "perpetrated a great crime; and his remorse, gnawing into his soul, has awakened it, developing a thousand high capabilities, moral and intellectual, which we never should have dreamed of asking for, within the scanty compass of the Donatello whom we knew" (4:460). As a paradigm for the growth of the soul, Donatello is an idea, not a living character. How perfunctorily the "wonderful process" of his development (4:282) engages Hawthorne is evidenced by the merely secondhand attention he bestows on it. Donatello's maturation is presented almost exclusively through Kenyon, with hints from Miriam, an interested party. Donatello himself has little to say about it other than in morbid complaint, and unlike the other characters' states of mind, his is never a subject for sustained authorial analysis.

Indeed, it is the *other* characters whose descents into caverns—of the self, of Rome, of history, of life generally—are Hawthorne's vehicles for thinking most freshly about the question of evil. Miriam descends, or redescends, by entering the Catacomb of Saint Calixtus and surfacing with the model, an embodiment of the hold of her equivocal past. Hilda enters the cavern by witnessing the murder of the model, Kenyon by suffering the disappearance of Hilda.

Hawthorne himself enters it by problematizing what had been a clear and stable moral idea with the ambiguities of Rome. And the reader enters it by participating in a story that visibly resists its narrator's efforts to schematize it.

Just before Kenyon hazards the idea of the fortunate fall, he proposes an alternative meaning for Donatello's story—that beings of his sort, "compounded especially for happiness, have no longer any business on earth, or elsewhere," life having "grown so sadly serious, that such men must change their nature, or else perish" (4:459). The fall, Kenyon implies, may be understood culturally as a passage from innocence to knowledge, simplicity to complexity, joy to earnestness. A charming anachronism, Donatello reminds moderns of the happy "childhood of their race" before "sin, care, and self-consciousness...set the human portion of the world askew" (4:239–40). In fact, sin, care, and self-consciousness are different maladies with different treatments and different prognoses. Morally (sin), Kenyon sees Donatello's progress as a painful but necessary struggle toward complete humanity. Culturally (care and self-consciousness), however, he cannot help wondering whether such a transformation is "worth the heavy price": "A creature of antique healthfulness had vanished from the earth; and, in his stead, there was only one other morbid and remorseful man, among millions that were cast in the same indistinguishable mould" (4:393).

In its concern with the value of civilization, *The Marble Faun* belongs to a tradition of international romanticism that reaches back to Schiller's *On Naïve and Sentimental Poetry* and ahead to Nietzsche's *The Genealogy of Morals*. For Schiller the lapse from nature issued not from sin but from the evolution of consciousness, a process enacted both culturally in the passage from the Greeks to the moderns and individually in the maturation of the child into the adult. Like children, Schiller argued, the Greeks were at one with nature and perfect within the limits of their finite being, as Donatello seems "the more perfect" for his "very deficiency" of full humanity (4:78). "Once man has passed into the state of civilization," the "*sensuous* harmony in him is withdrawn, and he can now express himself only as a *moral* unity, i.e., as striving after unity."[5] He has begun an arduous journey that can never be completed within the course of a life or, by the race, within a cultural epoch, and that leaves the individual restless, dissatisfied, and doubtful (like Kenyon) whether the gift of consciousness has been worth the sacrifice of pleasure. "We all of us, as we grow older,...lose somewhat of our proximity to Nature," Kenyon says: "It is the price we pay for experience" (4:250).

Kenyon enjoys a glimpse of the childhood of the race when he visits Donatello at Monte Beni in the Tuscan hills, which "he could have imagined...a veritable Arcadia" and Donatello himself a "genial wine-god in his very person" (4:237). The appearance is delusive. Like its "Sunshine," a delicate "wine of the Golden Age" (4:224), the pleasures of Monte Beni are short-lived, untransportable, and "perhaps better appreciated in the memory than by present consciousness" (4:223). In this it resembles the fancied Golden Age itself. As Kenyon comes to know it better, the countryside around Monte Beni turns out "not really the paradise it looked to be, at a casual glance" (4:295), and Donatello's race, though "pleasant and kindly" in youth, is found to have "deficiencies both of intellect and heart" that with age leave it "sensual, addicted to gross pleasures, heavy, unsympathizing, and insulated within the narrow range of a surly selfishness" (4:233, 235). In the end, it is not sunshine Kenyon chooses to celebrate but "the shade of pensive beauty which Eden won from [Adam's] expulsion" (4:276). Like Schiller, he regards a preconscious paradise as a paradise well lost; the "path" of modernity is that "along which man in general, the individual as well as the race, must pass" (Schiller 112).

The literary genre that treats of arcadia is idyll. The Monte Beni scenes contain elements of idyll; the conceit of the Faun is pure idyll. For Schiller, the salutary function of idyll is not elegiac—bemoaning the loss of a happiness that never truly existed and would not have been adequate if it had—but prophetic. By depicting a happy, harmonious world "set *before the beginnings of civilization*," idyll awakens the desire for a more complete happiness in the *future* of civilization, beyond the alienation of modern individual and collective life (Schiller 149).

In its stages of development, Schiller's teleological journey of the race corresponds to Hawthorne's moral and psychological journey through the cavern of the self. As child-become-adult, Donatello rehearses the familiar Hawthornean progress of the soul; as faun-become-modern, he illustrates Schiller's cultural progress from the simple to the civilized. For Kenyon at Monte Beni, the strands converge as Donatello's development recapitulates the development of the race. In the bust Kenyon molds of Donatello, "the features of the antique Faun" are preserved "but now illuminated with a higher meaning, such as the old marble never bore" (4:274). Under Kenyon's hand, especially in a bust he later makes with Donatello's full history in mind, the faun of precivilized idyll becomes, personally, a man of "growing intellectual power and moral sense" (4:380) and, culturally, the augury of a future perfection beyond civilized "care." The actual Donatello never completes this passage but remains fixed in the gloomy midregion of confusion and guilt. Might "morbid and remorseful" modern man (4:393) complete the passage? Did Hawthorne feel he himself had completed it as he worked on his book?

Geographically, the structure of *The Marble Faun* (Rome to Tuscany, then back to Rome) mirrors Hawthorne's residence in Italy, with his extended summer in Florence flanked by two longer stays in Rome. Lea Newman sees the Florence months, in which Hawthorne planned *The Marble Faun*, as a "creative resurgence."[6] Actually, as he told James T. Fields, Hawthorne found "this Italian atmosphere" less "favorable to the close toil of composition" than to dreaming (18:151). Like a New England summer, Florence was made for enjoyment, not for labor, and after his years in the consulship, the demands of family travel, and the miseries of a winter in Rome, Hawthorne was delighted simply to *be*. Sophia reported that in Florence she found him "again as in the first summer in Concord at the Old Manse" (18:152), the idyll of the honeymoon months returning to him, autumnally mellowed. The Villa Montauto (his model for Monte Beni) was indeed arcadian, and in his leisure and modest affluence he fashioned something of the life he admired in William Wetmore Story. He had cause to feel he had arrived at the cavern's depths. For this reason, his summation of his Florentine experience seems surprisingly tepid: "This summer will look like a happy one in our children's retrospect, and also, no doubt, in the years that remain to ourselves; and, in truth, though shadowed with certain glooms and despondencies, I have found it, on the whole a peaceful and not uncheerful one" (14:437). The most Hawthorne can say of these months is "not uncheerful." Positive happiness belongs primarily to his children; even that is an appearance ("will look like") to be cherished in "retrospect." If Florence revived a degree of the ease and pleasure of his first Manse summer, it did so with a bittersweet awareness that they were transient, arrived too late in life, and were at odds with the decorums that now hemmed him in. What Richard H. Millington calls the "quality of unhappiness" evident in *The Marble Faun*—the "expressions of reluctance, fatigue, and restlessness that appear in lulls in the novel"[7]—derives from more than an imputed flagging of creative powers; it reflects an aging man's awareness of dwindling time and opportunity amid the sensuous beauty of a sun-dappled world. Having reached the depths of the cavern, Hawthorne found himself too wearied by the journey or too burdened by discoveries along the way to delight in its perfect sunshine and flowers.

Hawthorne's feelings toward arcadia are on display in the four chapters of *The Marble Faun* set in the Villa Borghese. The sylvan grounds of the villa are a fit setting for Donatello the faun, yet like literary idyll they are not an expression of pristine nature but a commingling of nature and art "that seems to have been projected out of a poet's mind" (4:72). "Here, as it seemed," Hawthorne writes, "had the Golden Age come back again, within the precincts of this sunny glade; thawing mankind out of their cold formalities; releasing them from irksome restraint; mingling them together in such childlike gaiety, that new flowers... sprang up beneath their footsteps" (4:88). The scene recalls the floral festivities of "The May-Pole of Merry Mount," even to hints of a self-conscious revelry worked up for the occasion. Like the Merry Mounters, who fled to the New World "to act out their latest day-dream" (9:59), the "motley throng of rioters" in the Villa Borghese (4:89) are peasants and plebeians enjoying a brief interlude from workaday reality, whose claims the narrator, like a dour Endicott descending on Merry Mount, intrudes to assert. The ring of wild dancers, he writes, resembled figures on

> the front and sides of a sarcophagus, where...a festive procession mocks the ashes and white bones that are treasured up, within. You might take it for a marriage-pageant; but, after a while, if you look attentively at these merry-makers, following them from end to end of the marble coffin, you doubt whether their gay movement is leading them to a happy close. A youth has suddenly fallen in the dance; a chariot is overturned and broken, flinging the charioteer headlong on the ground; a maiden seems to have grown faint or weary, and is drooping on the bosom of a friend. Always, some tragic incident is shadowed forth, or thrust sidelong into the spectacle; and when once it has caught your eye, you can look no more at the festal portions of the scene, except with reference to this one slightly suggested doom and sorrow. (4:88–89)

As if on cue, the revelry is brought to a sudden halt by the appearance of Miriam's model. Like the Puritans in Merry Mount, the model symbolizes the dominion of patriarchal structures that rein in humanity's impulse toward freedom, spontaneity, and joy.[8] As "the spell" of delight is "broken," the merrymakers return to "the weary common-place of daily life," and what "just an instant before" had been "Arcadia" reverts to time-burdened Rome, "where the crimes and calamities of ages, the many battles, blood recklessly poured out, and deaths of myriads, have corrupted all the soil" (4:90).

The weight of history that darkens Rome is paralleled by the obscure private history that overshadows Miriam. Frolicking in the villa as a nymph to Donatello's faun, Miriam wonders, "Is the past so indestructible?—the future so immitigable? Is the dark dream, in which I walk, of such solid, stony substance, that there can be no escape out of its dungeon?" (4:83). The same questions might be asked by humanity about *its* postlapsarian dungeon. For Miriam, fixed in gloom, the only deliverance seems a retrograde one: "If her soul was apt to lurk in the darkness of a cavern," Hawthorne writes, she could at least momentarily "sport madly in the sunshine before the cavern's mouth" (4:83). Her playacting is shared by the company of musicians and dancers decked out in costume and "gone mad with jollity" (4:87), but only for a brief moment. There can be no permanent regress for the individual or the race.

Can there be *progress*? When Miriam beseeches the model to leave her free to create a new life, she speaks for all Adam's descendants petitioning God, society, and conscience to relieve them of the imposition of history since the Fall. Like Hester in the forest exhorting Dimmesdale—"Hast thou exhausted possibility in the failure of this one trial?" (1:198)—Miriam in the Villa Borghese maintains that "the human spirit does not perish of a single wound, nor exhaust itself in a single trial of life" (4:96). To the model's claim of fatality, Miriam replies, "You mistake your own will for iron necessity" (4:96)—"you" referring to the model singly but also as a representative of the religious and political establishment, which has naturalized its worldview into what it takes to be inexorable law.

The model for Miriam is what Moby Dick is for Ahab, the "agent" or "principal" of those forces that oppress humanity and whose overthrow would constitute an epochal liberation (*WHM* 5:164). For the individual and the culture both, the route to the paradise *beyond* civilization may not be through a gradual evolution but through a radical act of *re*volution. "The mind of man," M. H. Abrams writes of the more visionary Romantics, "possesses within itself the power, if it will but recognize and avail itself of the power," to create "a new heaven and new earth, by means of a total revolution of consciousness."[9] Such a revolution may originate or express itself in political action (in Hawthorne's time, the republican and nationalistic movements of 1848) or, on the level of the individual, in a gesture of emancipating defiance. More than *The Scarlet* Letter or even *The Blithedale Romance*, *The Marble Faun* is potentially an apocalyptic text. What if Miriam's model were to be slain?

Curtius's Chasm

> But however this may be, this blackness [in Hawthorne] it is that fur-
> nishes the infinite obscure of his back-ground,—that back-ground,
> against which Shakespeare plays his grandest conceits.
>
> —Melville, "Hawthorne and His Mosses"

> Why is life so tragic; so like a little strip of pavement over an abyss.
>
> —Virginia Woolf, *Diary, Volume Two: 1920–1924*

In the chapter titled "On the Edge of a Precipice," which ends with Donatello hurling Miriam's model off a physical precipice and himself off a moral one, the characters reflect on the story of Curtius, the Roman hero who rode his horse into a chasm made by an earthquake in order, as he believed, to save the city. For Miriam the story suggests the chasm into which "every person takes a peep ... in moments of gloom and despondency":

> The chasm was merely one of the orifices of that pit of blackness that
> lies beneath us, everywhere. The firmest substance of human happiness
> is but a thin crust spread over it, with just reality enough to bear up the
> illusive stage-scenery amid which we tread. It needs no earthquake to

open the chasm. A footstep, a little heavier than ordinary, will serve; and we must step very daintily, not to break through the crust, at any moment. By-and-by, we inevitably sink! (4:161–62)

Predictably, Hilda resists Miriam's moral. For Hilda, life is a matter of ethical choice and "there is no chasm, nor any hideous emptiness under our feet, except what the evil within us digs" and what "good thoughts and deeds" are able to "bridge" and help "fill...up" (4:162). Rome "sank...of no original necessity," she adds, "but because of the preponderance of evil to good among its citizens" (4:162). Miriam's answer—"Well, Hilda, it came to the same thing at last" (4:162)—is startling in its despair but also for its grasp of how a moral issue can shade into an ontological one.

It seems more than coincidental that Hawthorne should have Miriam say "blackness," the word Melville had used for the backdrop of Hawthorne's writings in "Hawthorne and His Mosses" (*WHM* 9:244). F. O. Matthiessen's observation that evil for Hawthorne was a matter of sin in the human heart, for Melville of "titanic uncontrollable forces which seem to dwarf man altogether,"[10] breaks down with *The Marble Faun*, in which the aggregate crimes of pagan, Renaissance, and modern Rome take on a quasi-metaphysical character. For Melville and Miriam both, "blackness" refers to the flaw in the nature of things laid bare in a clear-eyed survey of them. When Miriam describes Curtius's chasm as opening to everyone in "moments of deepest insight," Hilda objects that she "never peeped into it" (4:161). She will, Miriam replies. She and Kenyon both presently do, and Hawthorne avails himself of their experience to portray the vacuity of life as it appears in moments of dejection when psychic energies wane and pieties ring hollow. Although Hilda recoils at Miriam's claim of a "hideous emptiness under our feet" (4:162), she, too, comes to know the hard interrogatory skepticism that dissolves blithe illusions. Hilda's (temporary) disenchantment belongs to her character and situation, but it gathers weight from the length and eloquence of the narrator's rendering of it, much of it borrowed from Hawthorne's notebook.

Hilda looks to deliver herself from her condition by thinking of a beloved painting, Sodoma's fresco of a bound Christ "deserted both in Heaven and earth" (as Hilda feels herself to be) and seeming to ask, "Why has Thou forsaken me?" (4:339). This is the nadir, for Hilda and the narrator both; Hawthorne will not let such a moment stand. "Even in his extremity," he writes, Sodoma's Christ "is still divine"; he "is rescued from [despair], we know not how—by nothing less than miracle—by a celestial majesty and beauty, and some quality of which these are the outward garniture" (4:339–40). The passage draws closely on two notebook entries of October 1858, the second of which presents Christ's suffering as *ir*reconcilable with "Omnipotent Divinity" (14:492). Even in the published text,

Hawthorne concedes that art "cannot comfort the heart in affliction; it grows dim when the shadow is upon us" (4:340). The "emptiness" in the chapter title is not, significantly, "of *the* Picture-Galleries" (particular museums Hilda visits) but of "Picture-Galleries," or art generally, whose idealizations speak only to those inclined by conviction and mood to look sympathetically on them.

Edging close to and retreating from abysses of thought is a recurrent rhythm in Hawthorne's work, but nowhere is it as frequent and characteristic as in *The Marble Faun*. Hilda's experience in the museums is undergone by Kenyon during Hilda's disappearance. The title of chapter 43, "The Extinction of a Lamp," refers literally to the lamp of the Virgin that Hilda tends, emotionally to Kenyon's list-lessness in her absence, and figuratively to his loss of her guiding illumination, without which he wanders "in darkness and astray" (4:409). Like Hilda with her paintings, Kenyon finds himself apathetic toward his favorite statues except for the Laocoön, which, far from consoling him, merges his private grief with the general human condition. "In its immortal agony," the statue "impresses Kenyon as a type of the long, fierce struggle of Man, involved in the knotted entangle-ments of Errour and Evil, those two snakes, which (if no Divine help intervene) will be sure to strangle him and his children, in the end" (4:391). The phrase "*Errour and Evil*" plays off the book's threshold "*Innocence or Evil*" so directly as all but to displace it. Innocence is no longer an alternative. Fixed in marble, the Laocoön's "horror of a moment" seems to Kenyon an embodiment of "the Fate of interminable ages" (4:391). There is irony in the phase "if no Divine help intervene" (4:391) since according to myth it was a god (Poseidon) who *sent* the snakes. Hawthorne's notebook original is even stronger; the victims are "entan-gled in a complication which they can never free themselves from by their own efforts, and out of which Heaven *will* not help them" (14:138; my emphasis), words that Sophia, editing the notebook years after Hawthorne's death, conven-tionalized into "Heaven alone can help them" (14:925).

Hawthorne drafted *The Marble Faun* during the months of Una's illness, and as he witnessed her protracted suffering he must have felt himself and his family undergoing a torment much like Laocoön's. Sophia's health broke several times; even Hawthorne fell sick—for the first time since boyhood, he said. A year before Una's near-death, Harriet Beecher Stowe lost a teen-aged son in a swimming accident on the Connecticut River. In *The Minister's Wooing*, written soon afterward, Stowe has Mrs. Marvyn, who receives word that her son has died at sea, protest bitterly at the scheme of "Divine Government": "To me there is no goodness, no justice, no mercy in anything."[11] Sophia came to take the prospect of Una's death more acquiescently: "Why should I doubt the goodness of God? Let Him take her, if He see best.... I will not fight against Him any more" (*NHW* 2:210). Did she imagine her previous efforts to save Una as fighting God? Did Hawthorne, his? And did he acquiesce as she did in "Divine Government"?

T. Walter Herbert sees broad evidence of Una's "collapse...in the dispersed narrative and descriptive fragments" of *The Marble Faun*.[12] Hawthorne's entry on the Laocoön precedes Una's illness and is a symptom of his general disorientation induced by Rome; but as Rome was the site and its air the imputed cause of Una's suffering, his private distress during the fall and winter of 1858–59 entwined itself with his moral and intellectual bewilderments to provoke a questioning even more intense than that incited by his mother's death a decade earlier. Kenyon's anxiety over Hilda leads him to a comprehensive brooding on Rome, history, and God. Kenyon wishes to believe in a divinity that "keep[s] a little area and atmosphere about" innocents like Hilda (4:413). The violent history of Rome, however, teaches him that "the ways of Providence are utterly inscrutable." Innocents have often cried out for divine help "all in vain; so that, though Providence is infinitely good and wise (and perhaps for that very reason), it may be half an eternity before the great circle of its scheme shall bring us the superabundant recompense for all these sorrows!" (4:413). Without arraigning Providence, Kenyon is obliged to admit its visible disengagement from human affairs, both microcosmically in the fate of individuals and macrocosmically in the grand procession of events. With its centuries of "barbarism and civilization, alternating with one another, like actors that have pre-arranged their parts" (4:410), Rome seems to confute any notion of divine superintendence or even of immanent historical design.

In late sections of *The Marble Faun*, Kenyon's despair merges with that of the narrator to call forth a dormant sermon-in-the-waiting. From Rome's "tokens of...infinite misfortune on an imperial scale," Hawthorne writes, one ought to learn patience and humility, "but it is in vain that you seek this shrub of bitter-sweetness among the [Roman] plants": "Your own life is as nothing...; but still you demand, none the less earnestly, a gleam of sunshine, instead of a speck of shadow, on the step or two that will bring you to your quiet rest" (4:410). Millicent Bell ascribes Hawthorne's words to a nihilism about history,[13] but their root may go deeper, to philosophy. Almost casually, with a single unobtrusive phrase ("the step or two that will bring you to your quiet rest"), Hawthorne grants a finality to life he could barely contemplate at his mother's deathbed. Age, weariness, and the overbearing presence of Rome have forced him to think the unthinkable, but not without a bitter outcry at what he sees as human fate:

> How exceedingly absurd! All men, from the date of the earliest obelisk—and of the whole world, moreover, since that far epoch, and before—have made a similar demand, and seldom had their wish. If they had it, what are they the better, now? But, even while you taunt yourself with this sad lesson, your heart cries out obstreperously for its

small share of earthly happiness, and will not be appeased by the myriads of dead hopes that lie crushed into the soil of Rome. (4:410–11)

It is no great leap from Hawthorne's mid-Victorian "absurd" to Albert Camus's
modernist one; each arises from the gap between what Camus calls "the human
need and the unreasonable silence of the world."[14] Alongside *The Marble Faun*'s
allegory of the Fall of Man as embodied in Donatello are the falls of Miriam,
Kenyon, Hilda, and the narrator into an existential sense of humanity's position
in a purposeless universe. In this ostensibly most conservative of his romances,
Hawthorne stands on the cusp of the modern and in the depths of his disillusion
almost makes a decisive turn toward the future. "How wonderful," he exclaims in
a moment unprecedented in his work, "that this our narrow foothold of the
Present should hold its own so constantly, and, while every moment changing,
should still be like a rock betwixt the encountering tides of the long Past and the
infinite To-come!" (4:411). To live appreciatively in the flux of time, unbur-
dened by the past and requiring nothing of eternity, may not be quite the exis-
tentialism of a Camus, but it is surely akin to the aesthetic naturalism of Walter
Pater. The passage is the outburst of a moment, signaling a direction Hawthorne
may or may not choose to take.

Striking through the Mask

> She failed not to bring out the moral, that woman must strike through
> her own heart to reach a human life, whatever were the motives that
> impelled her.
>
> —Hawthorne on Miriam's paintings, *The Marble Faun*

> If man will strike, strike through the mask! How can the prisoner reach
> outside except by thrusting through the wall?
>
> —Ahab in Melville, *Moby-Dick*

Fresh from William Wetmore Story's Roman studio, Hawthorne described Story's
Cleopatra as "a terribly dangerous woman, quiet enough for the moment, but very
likely to spring upon you like a tigress" (14:177). Openly borrowed from Story's,
Kenyon's Cleopatra—"fierce, voluptuous, passionate, tender, wicked, terrible, and
full of poisonous and voluptuous enchantment" (4:127)—is a woman defeated
but not done for, poised between submission to patriarchal Law (Octavius) and an
impulsive female rebellion that bids to thrust her and the Western world into terra
incognita. "'What a woman is this!' exclaimed Miriam," marveling at the gendered
"truth" in Kenyon's commingling of "all those seemingly discordant elements"
(4:127) and recognizing in Cleopatra a soul sister to herself.

Although Kenyon can sculpt a Cleopatra, he is wary of intimately knowing one, and his attitude toward the ardent, freethinking Miriam is a mixture of admiration and personal and intellectual caution. Like Zenobia in *The Blithedale Romance*, Miriam has "too much life and strength, without a purpose for one or the other" (4:280), and too intense a hunger for life to be contained within the bounds of conventional femininity. Milton R. Stern notes that "Hawthorne almost always calls Miriam a woman and Hilda a girl,"[15] or sometimes a maiden. Whatever her sexual status, Miriam is not maiden*ly* and therefore, within Hawthorne's taxonomy of the female, not safe. From the outset she is surrounded with hints about a Jewish or African lineage and a vague "odour of guilt, and a scent of blood" (4:20, 22, 97), associations typical of the "atmospheric effects, insinuations, and rumors" through which, as Philip Rahv says, Hawthorne seeks to compromise his dark heroines without (save with Hester) directly accusing them of anything.[16] Miriam's real nonvirginity is figurative: she has lived more widely and thought more boldly than becomes a woman. Kenyon has knowledge of experience; like Hawthorne with Sophia, what he reveres in a woman is *inex*-perience, which he equates with noncontamination. "This is a perplexed and troubled world!" he tells Hilda: "It soothes me inexpressibly to think of you in your tower...so high above us all" (4:112). By contrast, Miriam scorns such prisonlike elevation; her demand, in Rahv's words, is for "the right of the person-ality to that self-knowledge and self-development which only the process of experience can provide."[17]

Like Hester and Zenobia, Miriam is saddled with a prehistory that blights her prospect for happiness and compels her either to submit to life-denying con-straints or defy them and become a lawbreaker. Well before she participates with Donatello in killing the model, Miriam kills him several times over in the dis-placements of art. In her paintings, she is Judith slaying Holofernes, Jael slaying Sisera—Old Testament heroines delivering their race from oppression. To these figures Hawthorne adds Salome receiving the head of John the Baptist, symbol-ically decapitating the misogynistic, sin-obsessed Christian tradition at its fount. The violence of Miriam's women is not simply vengeful or reactive; it is *proactive* and performed from an instinct on the artist's part that "woman must strike through her own heart to reach a human life" (4:44) and thereby win her way to—Miriam is unsure what. The act of violence, in her case, precedes and will enable the ideological meaning later given to it.

Exploring the galleries of Florence and Rome, Hawthorne had occasion to see the kind of painting he attributes to Miriam; scenes of Judith and Holofernes were especially common in Baroque Italian art. The painter most famously asso-ciated with the subject, both in her own time and today though not in the 1850s, was Artemisia Gentileschi (1593–1652/53), whose "name," as art historian Judith W. Mann remarks, "conjures up art that is dramatic, populated with uncompromisingly direct visualization of forceful women and integrally related to the events of her life."[18] A native of Rome and the daughter of Caravaggist painter Orazio Gentileschi, Artemisia was sent in her teens to study with her father's friend Agostino Tassi, who raped her. Her father brought charges, and the ensuing trial, complete with lies, insinuations, and torture-by-thumbscrews for Artemisia, resulted in Tassi's conviction (with nominal punishment) and Artemisia's vindication but not in her moral whitewashing. From then on, if not from her earliest painting of a distressed Susanna leeringly spied upon by the Elders, "Artemisia's fame balanced," as Elizabeth Cropper says, "on [the] knife-edge between" the esteemed and the "scandalous."[19]

    In an art world dominated by religious idealism, Artemisia's distinction was to turn the style of Caravaggian realism to themes of female victimization, rebellion, and erotic self-display. Among her best-known paintings are figures of women raped or abused by men (Susanna, Bathsheba, Lucretia, Danäe), women violently avenging themselves upon men (Judith with Holofernes—at least five paintings; Jael with Sisera), and sensuous nudes, pagan or Christian (Cleopatra, Venus, The Penitent Magdalen). R. Ward Bissell argues that in publicly "depriv[ing Artemisia] of some of the 'virtues' which women were supposed to have," her lurid past "left her freer than she otherwise might have been to develop an art unfettered by traditional expectations."[20] The same might be said about Miriam, both in fleeing an unspecified family horror and settling in Rome and, especially, after her moral rejection by Hilda; as she bitterly exclaims, "Hilda has set me free!" (4:287). The remarkable quality in Artemisia's versions of Judith and Holofernes is their vitality. Caravaggio's treatment of the scene features Holofernes's agony but presents Judith with the calm formality of a still life; Artemisia's, as one art historian put it, "is a visualization of how such a grisly deed could actually be accomplished,"[21] and with the deliberateness, moreover, of a political assassination rather than a crime of revenge.

    For a romancer like Hawthorne, Artemisia Gentileschi would have been almost too good to be true, down to her name. Artemis was the goddess of chastity and of the moon; she was also the goddess of the hunt, who, catching the hunter Actaeon as he chanced to see her bathing nude, turned him into a stag and watched as his hounds devoured him. "Gentileschi" suggests genteel, or ladylike, but in the older sense of majestic or statuesque, as Hawthorne calls Hester "lady-like" (1:53). In the Pitti Palace in Florence Hawthorne saw the "admirable" (14:314) Judith and Holofernes by Cristofano Allori, a friend and associate of Artemisia's who "stood godfather to her son christened Cristofano."[22] "A face of great beauty and depth," Hawthorne wrote of the painting, whose Judith "clutches the head of Holofernes by the hair in a way that startles the spectator" (14:314–15). Allori's Judith would have particularly struck Hawthorne for her dark-haired regalness, reminiscent of his own dark heroines. A version of

Artemisia's Judith was housed in the Uffizi, which Hawthorne came to know quite well, but if he did see the painting and learned something of her career through Sophia's books on Italian art, as David R. Mayer argues, there is no record of it beyond his acquaintance with her surname.[23]

Whether or not Artemisia was an influence upon Miriam, her life suggests the kind of history—violated innocence, scandal, flight (Artemisia left Rome soon after the trial), paintings done from "a manifest need to exorcise her own demon,"[24] and the transformation of stain and anger into a source of creative power—that a fiction writer might well invent for a female artist from the paintings he saw in the Italian galleries. For Hawthorne, the issues raised by such a body of work would have included the relationship of fantasy to art, the connections of both to dream on one side and action on the other, and the degree of guilt attaching to all of these things on a spectrum of moral accountability. Years earlier he had explored this subject in "Fancy's Show Box," but beyond that sketch's questions of morality—are we guilty for what we dream, what we fantasize, and what we project into art, or only for deeds as they may actualize these things?—he now saw subtler questions of psychology: do artistic displacements of desire serve as safety valves, relieving the pressure to act, or do they predispose behavior by envisioning scenarios, objectifying patterns of response, and blurring the distinction between fancy and fact? Having slain figures of patriarchy in her art, Miriam cannot be sure whether by a look or an involuntary surfacing of emotion she has helped to do so in reality. Reviewing the night's events, she "seemed dreamily to remember falling on her knees; but, in her whole recollection of that wild moment, she beheld herself as in a dim show, and could not well distinguish what was done and suffered; no, not even whether she were really an actor and sufferer in the scene" (4:171). "In dreams," she tells Donatello (and herself) after the murder, "the conscience sleeps, and we often stain ourselves with guilt of which we should be incapable in our waking moments. The deed you seemed to do, last night, was no more than such a dream; there was as little substance in what you fancied yourself doing" (4:199–200).

The extent of Miriam's guilt is as indeterminate as any moral situation in Hawthorne's writing. "Did you not mean that he should die?" Donatello asks Miriam, with more ambiguity than he knows (4:173). "Mean" as semiconsciously desire or as actionally intend? Earlier that evening at the Fountain of Trevi, Miriam had rebuffed Donatello's "Bid me drown him!" (4:148), yet as she listens to Donatello and Hilda after the model's death she is swayed by their view that she assented to Donatello's act (4:174). Is a spontaneous look— of "hatred, triumph, vengeance, and...joy at some unhoped for relief" (4:210)—tantamount to complicity in a deed?

Because this is the kind of question that characteristically engaged Hawthorne, it is surprising how little he attends to it. He quickly accepts Miriam's tacit concession of guilt and proceeds to treat her as if she were guilty. His interest is not in the casuistry of her performed deed but in the direction of her thoughts as they unfold in the wake of it. At first, like other Hawthornean lawbreakers, she and Donatello feel "an ecstatic sense of freedom" (4:176) as the figure of oppression is removed. Typically, such moments of license in Hawthorne are followed by revulsion, as the self reacts in horror at what it has become. In *The Marble Faun*, however, "the foremost result of a broken law" (4:176) is not psychic release so much as ideological release. The murder propels Miriam and Donatello ahead to "a new sphere, a special law, [that] had been created for them alone" (4:174), as if they were the Adam and Eve of a postdecalogic age. "Forget it! Cast it all behind you" (4:176), Miriam tells Donatello, as Hester had told Dimmesdale in the forest. Where Hester had seen herself and Dimmesdale as free despite their crime, Miriam sees herself and Donatello as free *because* of theirs: "The deed has done its office" (4:176). The "office" of the scarlet letter (1:66) had been to constrain Hester within established ideas of sin and repentance; the "office" of the murder, as Miriam has it, is to empower her and Donatello to transcend such ideas.

"The work of the hero," Joseph Campbell writes, "is to slay the tenacious aspect of the father (dragon, tester, ogre, king) and release from its ban the vital energies that feed the universe."[25] In *The Marble Faun* the price of such release is both less and more than an actual human life. "When Donatello kills the wretch who malignantly dogs the steps of Miriam," reviewer E. P. Whipple observed, "all readers think that Donatello committed no sin at all" because Hawthorne has dehumanized the model and "made him an allegorical representation of one of the most fiendish forms of unmixed evil."[26] Indeed, even as Hawthorne dwells on the culpability of Miriam and Donatello, he goes far toward celebrating their act by having Kenyon avow that, measured by its motives and circumstances, he "know[s] not well how to distinguish it from much that the world calls heroism" (4:384).

In striking through the mask, Miriam cannot overthrow patriarchal morality and power—the model is only their symbol; he is not their source—but she can overthrow their sovereignty within herself. In the Villa Borghese she had bowed abjectly before the model. Killing him is a liberating act that realizes in fact what she began in fantasy with her paintings. Even before the crime, Hawthorne has Miriam indict conventional morality as the refuge of those lacking strength and imagination to gauge actions in their living context. Beatrice Cenci's "sin," she tells Hilda, "may not have been so great; perhaps it was no sin at all, but the best virtue possible in the circumstances. If she viewed it as a sin, it may have been because her nature was too feeble for the fate imposed on her" (4:66). Her words look ahead to Nietzsche's in *Twilight of the Idols*: "Morality, insofar as it *condemns* for its own sake, and *not* out of regard for the concerns, considerations, and contrivances of life, is a specific error with which one ought to have no pity—an *idiosyncrasy of degenerates* which has caused immeasurable harm."[27]

Miriam is a latter-day Beatrice Cenci whose nature is not in the least "feeble" or "degenerate." After slaying the model she carries herself with the kind of "triumphant self-assertion" Nietzsche saw as the fount of "all truly noble morality."[28] Not so, Donatello. "Alas, it was a sad mistake" to involve a weak or undeveloped nature in a crime, Miriam thinks: "He might have had a kind of bliss in the consequences of this deed, had he been impelled to it by a kind of love strong enough to survive the frenzy of that terrible moment; *mighty enough to make its own law, and justify itself against the natural remorse*" (4:199; my emphasis). Hester acts upon just such a law in the forest scene; Miriam, building upon her own deed, makes a revolutionary ideology of it.

Beyond Good and Evil?

It is not remorse!

—Miriam in *The Marble Faun*

"Under what conditions did man construct the value judgments *good* and *evil*?" Nietzsche asks in *The Genealogy of Morals*.[29] Under what conditions, Hawthorne asks in *The Marble Faun*, might woman *de*construct "good" and "evil" and create new value judgments responsive to the needs and circumstances of actual living? Having brought himself to the point of such a question, Hawthorne spends the balance of his narrative trying to contain the character who prompts it, as previously he had tried to contain Hester and Zenobia.

The effort begins early, even before the murder, as if Hawthorne were forearming himself and his audience against Miriam's appeal. In contrast to the iconographic tradition of the "femme forte"—the martial, heroic woman exemplified by figures like Judith, Jael, Cleopatra, and Zenobia, whose statue by Harriet Hosmer Hawthorne found "very noble and remarkable" (14:509)[30]—Miriam's Jael is given the aspect of "a vulgar murderess" and her Salome an air of remorse (4:43, 44). Reinforcing the narrator's political scorn for the paintings ("woman, acting the part of a revengeful mischief against man" [4:44]), Miriam the artist is thus made her own moral accuser.[31] Her sketches of domestic life, "productions of a beautiful imagination," depict the realm of nineteenth-century womanhood in a spirit that shows her admirably capable of inhabiting it, did she not feel tragically excluded from its blessings (4:46). This is the conservative Hawthorne viewing Miriam as Coverdale viewed Zenobia and as he and Sophia viewed Margaret Fuller, as a woman whose public rebelliousness stemmed from private deprivations. Ambivalent as always, however, Hawthorne twists the argument until it turns back on itself in partial negation. Miriam's sketches, we are told, are an outsider's rendering of what "an actual acquaintance" with domestic life would reveal as "hard and dusty" (4:46). But this is not the final word, either. Though idealized, the icon represents "a truer and lovelier picture" of woman's life than the reality (4:46), just as years earlier the reflection of overhanging trees in the Concord River had seemed truer and lovelier than the trees themselves. Illusions make for culturally useful beliefs that must be upheld—and, for candor's sake, must also be discredited. Hawthorne is still fighting the battle between the realist and the idealist, no closer than ever to reconciling their claims yet willing now to make the battle an open subject.

"A spirit who wants great things, who also wants the means to them, is necessarily a skeptic," Nietzsche wrote: "Freedom from all kinds of convictions, to be able to see freely, is part of strength."[32] Skepticism of this kind is not a scoffing at morality but a rejection of absolutes, such as Miriam implies when she revaluates Beatrice Cenci's parricide and finds it, in this particular case, a virtue (4:66). When Hilda, echoing Hawthorne in his notebook (14:93), says of Beatrice, "She is a fallen angel, fallen, and yet sinless," Miriam pointedly reminds her of "the deed for which she suffered" (4:66). Hilda is taken aback; she "had quite forgotten Beatrice's history" and was thinking only of her expression in the Guido Reni painting (4:66). Her confusion is Hawthorne's own: how can Beatrice's air of innocence be squared with the fact of her crime? Hilda responds with typical severity ("Her doom is just" [4:66]), Hawthorne, through his narrator, with denial: "It was the intimate consciousness of her *father's sin* that threw its shadow over her" (4:205; my emphasis). Neither Hilda nor Hawthorne can allow that Beatrice was a murderess *and*, by circumstances, sinless. Nor can Hawthorne allow that Miriam might be both without launching himself into a chartless moral world, at whose threshold his action locates him.

Hawthorne never grapples with Miriam intellectually. Though by far the most compelling character in *The Marble Faun*, she is the one given least attention in its second half, for long sections of which she is sent offstage. When she does appear, it is in the sexually degraded role of spurned and desperate lover. Early in the narrative she had dismissed the masculinist idea "that Nature has made women especially prone to throw their whole being into what is technically called Love.... When women have other objects in life, they are not apt to fall in love" (4:121). Now, like Hester and Zenobia, she is made to show herself a man's woman. "Have I not shocked you, many times," she asks Kenyon after the murder, "by my betrayal of woman's cause, my lack of feminine modesty, my reckless, passionate, most indecorous avowal, that I live only in the life of one who perhaps scorns and shudders at me?" (4:286). Shock has indeed been Kenyon's reaction, compounded by amazement at Miriam's devotion to a love-object whom she had formerly scorned and who, "intellectually, seemed far beneath her" (4:280). Thomas R. Mitchell associates Miriam's passion for Donatello with Margaret Fuller's for Angelo Ossoli, whom Hawthorne (on no personal acquaintance) dismissed as "this boor, this hymen without the intellectual spark" (14:155).[33] Sexual jealousy aside, Hawthorne seems to have been genuinely dismayed by the behavior of this queenly apostle of female "self-dependence" (*WNC* 39). Fuller's term is echoed by Kenyon, who "could not but marvel at the subjection into which this proud and self-dependent woman had willfully flung herself" (4:283). Zenobia had similarly collapsed before Hollingsworth, but he was a man equal to her in charisma and superior in strength of purpose; Donatello is never more than a man-in-the-making.

Hawthorne ascribes Miriam's subjection to the tie, "closer than a marriage-bond" (4:174), that joins the criminals together; "cemented with blood," it "would corrupt and grow more noisome, forever and forever, but bind them none the less strictly for that!" (4:175). There is material here for a Dantesque exploration of psychological damnation—the downward spiral of the complicit—but nothing of the sort occurs. Instead, what Hawthorne shows is the extraordinary sense of responsibility Miriam comes to feel as it delivers her from the morbid egocentrism of her prior life. For Kenyon, Miriam is a Titania grotesquely smitten by a clown with faun's ears. Morally, this is irrelevant. The obligations inherent in the relationship between herself as instigator (if such she was) and Donatello as actor are irrespective of the actor's worth, and it is deeply to her credit that she ignores her own safety and happiness (she, after all, has *done* nothing and is free to live her life) and chooses to "bend and adapt [her] whole nature to do [Donatello] good" (4:282). Having thrown off traditional morality, Miriam has not become lawless; she has risen to a demanding, self-sacrificial law of her own.

In telling Kenyon she feels "neither regret nor penitence" (4:280), Miriam potentially becomes the heroine of a journey beyond socially constituted good and evil, just as Hester does when she demurs at Dimmesdale's "Is this not better...?" on the scaffold (1:254). The moments amount to a kind of test—not for the women, who know what they want, but for the author, who is forced to declare what *he* wants. In the end, Hawthorne will not let his heroines' impenitence stand. Just as Hester is returned to Boston and made to take up the scarlet letter, so, with no attention to the course of her development, Miriam is brought belatedly to acknowledge "an evil deed" (4:429). The last we see of her is in the "kneeling" figure of a "female penitent" in the Pantheon (4:459).

The explicit vindication of law takes place in the marketplace scene in Perugia, which speaks to audience hopes for a romantic union while maintaining an unmitigated sternness of judgment. Beneath the bronze statue of Pope Julius III, Kenyon performs what amounts to a Protestant marriage ceremony, complete with a tendentious sermon on "the mysterious process, by which our earthly life instructs us for another state of being" (4:321). At Monte Beni, Kenyon had urged Donatello to look for peace in "good deeds to mankind" (4:267), in effect a doctrine of atonement and purification through works. In Perugia he enlarges on the idea but with the codicil that the process is never-ending and happiness neither to be sought nor expected. It is ironic that Kenyon should pontificate under the watchful eye of the bronze Julius. A pope may receive confession and bestow absolution; the debt to God and conscience is thereby paid, the sin is consigned to the past, and the cleansed sinner may take up life anew. A Hawthornean sinner is never accorded this privilege. As Kenyon presents it, the aim of repentance is not to relieve the self of past sin but to *bind* it to that sin as the inescapable reference point for present and future experience. The most that Miriam and Donatello may hope for is "a severe and painful life" of unending moral restitution (4:322).

In his late "Postscript" to the romance, Hawthorne denies his lovers even that: Donatello languishes in prison; Miriam languishes in his absence. Miriam's notion that a deed once done and mentally reckoned with "has no existence any more" (4:176) is a heresy that must be decisively routed. Just as Hawthorne forbids Hester's and Dimmesdale's dust to mingle, so he forbids Miriam's and Donatello's lives to mingle, even under the harsh conditions laid down by Kenyon. Sin is sin, forever, *The Marble Faun* insists, and although it can be educative and in this respect productive of good, no degree of worldly happiness can be allowed to issue from it without calling its reality into question.

Like the iconoclasm of Hester in the forest, the proto-Nietzscheanism of Miriam is Hawthorne's glimpse of a potentially renovating morality ahead. His years in Europe had challenged his moral provincialism and encouraged him to think beyond Hester to a still more liberated and liberating heroine. Rome, however, proved too much for him, and in recoil he returned self-protectively to certitudes he knew were not at all certain any longer. Against the fearful *weightlessness* of human life that Roman history seemed everywhere to teach, he held the more desperately to the weight of sin, always the foundation, in his mind, of universal order. To transcend "good and evil," as Miriam sought to do, was to cast off what little defense culture provided against perceptible chaos. The risk was not worth the taking.

Excremental Virtue

I cannot praise a fugitive and cloistered virtue.

—Milton, *"Areopagitica"*

I should like to have you call it "Saint Hilda's Shrine."

—Hawthorne to William D. Ticknor (December 1, 1859)

As Kenyon and Miriam reflect on the figure of the faun in the book's opening scene—"He is not supernatural, but just on the verge of Nature, and yet within it," Miriam says—Hilda responds, "shrinking a little": "It perplexes me. . .; neither do I quite like to think about it" (4:13). Inquisitive by nature, Kenyon and Miriam find thought expansive; not so Hilda, for whom the pun "shrinking" is strikingly apt. Unconventional ideas trouble Hilda and prompt her to contract into a tight coil of disapproval as she wards them off. Perplexity for Kenyon is an invitation to ponder a question, for Hilda to dismiss it. "I do not love to think... that this dull stone" will outlast "any picture, in spite of the spiritual life that ought to give it immortality" (4:150), she says in Trajan's forum, as if pained sensibilities had a veto power over what could and could not be mentally entertained. "It grieves me to hear you speak thus" (4:162), she says of Miriam's "pit of blackness" (4:161). And elsewhere, also to Miriam: "you grieve me to speak contemptuously" of the "daintiness" of Guido Reni's Michael treading on Satan (4:139).

Writing to British critic Henry F. Chorley, who had associated Hilda with Phoebe in *The House of the Seven Gables*, Sophia Hawthorne began her playful but earnest remonstrance, "I am very much grieved that..." (18:238). Hilda's verbal tic may have originated at home, like her doves, her love of ethereal painters like Fra Angelico, her status as a copyist, and the rigid dualism that leads her to feel that right and wrong are polar opposites and that any "dreadful mixture" of the two, were it possible, would be "almost more shocking" (another Hilda word) "than pure evil" (4:384). Kenyon, who knows better, in most cases either silently acquiesces to Hilda or retracts his heterodoxies to please her. Elizabeth Peabody identified Hilda's morality with Sophia's and placed Hawthorne in Kenyonesque relationship to it, adding that it was Sophia's "agonized and stunned" reaction to "moral evil" that constituted "her supreme charm to Hawthorne's imagination" (*NHW* 1:248).

Such a charm did not translate well into fiction. Not only do readers commonly fail to share the narrator's enthusiasm for Hilda,[34] the text itself is also divided between fulsome praise and periodic eruptions of hostility and contempt. The notion of Hilda's "white, shining purity" as, in Kenyon's words, "a thing apart" (4:287) seems offensive, and if it corresponds to Hawthorne's view of Sophia, then the fact that the author has *made* it offensive is doubly significant. His temporary choice of the title "Saint Hilda's Shrine" was not insincere or ironic; the ironies are buried in the text itself, and they grow more pointed as events transform a naïf's half-endearing unworldliness into a woman's culpable deficiencies of empathy and moral imagination. That Hilda could not bear "a feather's weight of sin" (4:128), as Miriam says, is of little consequence until she is called upon to do so, vicariously, and fails to rise to Miriam's desperate appeal for help: "Have I deceived you? Then cast me off! Have I wronged you personally?

Then forgive me, if you can. But, have I sinned against God and man, and deeply sinned? Then be more my friend than ever, for I need you more!" (4:208). "Do not bewilder me thus, Miriam!" (4:208), Hilda answers with utter self-regard.

The effect of Hilda's righteousness is to excommunicate Miriam from the moral community and banish her to the wilderness of the untried. Ostensibly the most Christian of the book's characters, this trimmer of the Virgin's lamp has nothing of Mary's proverbial mercy; her virtues are the masculine Old Testament ones of justice and severity. Adequate as an angel, perhaps, Hilda is wanting "as a human creature" (4:66, 209), and her modest bearing is the garment of an inordinate spiritual pride. No "daughter of the Puritans," as Hilda likes to call herself (4:362), could possibly believe that God set her "in an evil world" with "only a white robe, and bid her wear it back to Him, as white as when she put it on" (4:208). Is Hilda claiming exemption from Original Sin? Her words echo Milton's "Areopagitica," which Hawthorne almost certainly knew from his Salem reading (*HR* 312):

> Assuredly we bring not innocence into the world, we bring impurity much rather: that which purifies us is trial, and trial is by what is contrary. That virtue therefore which is but a youngling in the contemplation of evil, and knows not the utmost that vice promises to her followers, and rejects it, is but a blank virtue, not a pure; her whiteness is but an excremental whiteness.[35]

Hawthorne appeals to the spirit of Milton when he has Miriam disparage the fastidiousness of Guido Reni's Michael as he stomps victoriously on Satan in a painting Hilda greatly admires. "No, No!" Miriam exclaims: "I could have told Guido better. A full third of the Archangel's feathers should have been torn from his wings; the rest all ruffled, till they looked like Satan's own! His sword should be streaming with blood, and perhaps broken half-way to the hilt; his armour crushed, his breast gory; a bleeding gash on his brow, cutting right across the stern scowl of battle!" (4:184). Kenyon is impressed and would have Miriam "paint the picture of man's struggle against sin, according to your own idea! I think it will be a master-piece" (4:184). The counterimage to Miriam's bloodied and tested Michael is the sketch Hawthorne has a gallery artist draw of Hilda as if "gazing, with sad and earnest horrour, at a blood-spot which she seemed just then to have discovered on her robe" (4:330). The title of the sketch, "Innocence, dying of a Blood-stain!" (4:330), is ambiguous: innocence may refer to moral ignorance, Hilda's innocence having died with her knowledge of Miriam's crime, or it may be a personification of Hilda herself, figuratively slain by her encounter with evil. In the first case, Hilda would have embarked on a journey through

Hawthorne's cavern, possibly to reach a higher innocence at the cavern's depths; in the second, she would have quailed at the discovery that a journey was to be made. The "suspense" in the portrait of Hilda involves how she will negotiate her journey.

Hilda tells Miriam that she will "keep [her] secret, and die of it; unless God sends me some relief by methods which are now beyond my power to imagine" (4:212). She does neither; instead, she makes use of Catholic confession to free herself of a burden she can no longer bear. Leaving the confessional, she feels like "a new creature" (4:365), but it is the relief neither of spiritual absolution (in which as a Protestant she does not believe) nor of psychological understanding (which she makes no effort to attain). Her return to being "a girl again"—"Hilda, of the dove-cote" (4:358)—is hardly a triumph except to herself. Miriam's crime has given a heart-knowledge of despondency, gloom, apathy, and guilt, "almost as if she herself had participated" in the crime itself (4:329), but instead of pressing forward through the cavern's depths, she has retreated to its entrance, in denial. This is the narrator's own assessment of her—she "had an elastic faculty for throwing off such recollections as would be too painful for endurance," and against whose "return" she "practiced a subtle watchfulness"—and it would be a harsh one were it not tempered by a sympathetic understanding of the needs of such individuals, "whose delicate organization requires a peculiar safeguard" (4:382).

Although the narrator argues perfunctorily for Hilda's development—she "returned to her customary occupations with a fresh love for them, and a deeper look into the heart of things" (4:375)—the absolutism of her moral views remains constant to the last; even Kenyon calls her "a terribly severe judge" (4:384). Merely to discuss the past reopens the "prison-door" of suppressed knowledge and darkens "the pure air and white radiance of her soul" (4:385). Kenyon is respectful of her vulnerability without bowing to all her opinions, yet when Hilda herself expresses a "painful doubt" about her behavior toward Miriam (4:385), the narrator out-Kenyons Kenyon and half absolves her even of this: "we do not unhesitatingly adopt Hilda's present view" of "the delinquencies...she fancied" (4:386). His intervention is both gratuitous and puzzling, since Hilda's regret is well founded, to her moral credit, and evidence of the softening Hawthorne otherwise claims has taken place. Two Hawthornes seem to be at work here: the idealist, who celebrates Hilda and treats her moral innocence as sacred and inviolable, and the realist, who views it as a priggish, self-protective, and self-impairing illusion. The issue is no longer what will become of Hilda—morally, she will end up close to where she began. It is what, after seven years in Europe, will become of Hawthorne as he takes the measure of Hilda and the moral vision she represents.

Transformation?

> I had quite forgotten that the title, "Transformation," was one of my
> suggestions; but I am very glad it was so, because, in condemning it, I
> shall criticize nobody but myself.
>
> —Hawthorne to Smith, Elder & Company, London (February 3, 1860)

Hawthorne repeatedly voiced his dislike for the English title of *The Marble Faun*, *Transformation*, which, he told James T. Fields, "gives me the idea of Harlequin in a pantomime" (18:230). In one respect the image is appropriate, since *The Marble Faun* prepares for its dénouement with a scene at the Roman carnival, much as *The Scarlet Letter* had done with the festivities of New England Election Day and *The Blithedale Romance* with a community masquerade. In each case Hawthorne dramatically brightens his story with a penultimate moment of freedom and pleasure before necessity asserts itself and the characters proceed to their joyless fates. *The Marble Faun* originally ended with the betrothal of Kenyon and Hilda and their prospective return to America; the fates of Miriam and Donatello were left uncertain and Hilda's "hopeful soul" could imagine the best for them (4:462). The "Postscript" added to the second English printing withdraws even this faint promise. The reality of Donatello's "transformation," or progress through the Hawthornean cavern—in Kenyon's words, "he has traveled in a circle, as all things heavenly and earthly do, and now comes back to his original self, with an inestimable treasure of improvement won from the experience of pain" (4:434)—is compromised by his morbid insistence on seeking judicial punishment and by the authorities' severity in meting it out (4:433). As to the other characters' transformations, they, too, fail to survive the book's ending. Kenyon and Hilda have put aside the difficult lessons of experience; Miriam has become a penitent. *Whose* transformation?

Kenyon's apostasy is particularly disturbing because it is performed knowingly, with an awareness of its cowardice. "Oh, Hilda, guide me home!" he asks of a woman who self-confessedly has "no such wisdom as you fancy in me" (4:461). "Home" is the straitened life of a New England village; it is the refuge of quasi-innocence. Living with "neither pole-star above, nor light of cottage-windows here below" (4:460), Kenyon abandons the search for the former to grasp the solace of the latter. His choice is testimony to how, in Hawthorne's world, speculation is dangerous *especially* for the strong—the weak, like Hilda, being averse to it or shielded by natural repellents. "Neither Kenyon's proposal nor Hilda's response," Richard H. Millington observes, "has anything to do with love."[36] Kenyon seeks an anchor, Hilda a bulwark, and both of them find what they think they need in the other.

Although Hawthorne is not Kenyon, there is no hint of irony in the epithalamic ending of *The Marble Faun*. Richard H. Brodhead sees the book as Hawthorne's attempt "to reinvigorate the obsessions that had energized his early writing."[37] The question is why he should have wanted to do so. Europe had enlarged him by suggesting alternative ways of living, rival measures of value, and capacious new contexts for thinking about history. His notebook reflections on Italy fill *The Marble Faun*, but for the most part they lie aside from its theme of the growth of the soul, a survival from the Salem past. The most significant "transformation" in *The Marble Faun* is the one Hawthorne *almost* undergoes as he peers more profoundly than ever before into "that pit of blackness that lies beneath us, everywhere" (4:161). Rome laid bare for him the fragility of life's crust, but rather than follow Miriam into unknown territory, a cultural world predicated on the reality of that pit, Hawthorne retreats to the old "obsessions" as if they were a saving plank on which, if he trod carefully enough, he might span it.

Dark as its ending was, *The Scarlet Letter* had looked ahead to a better time. In returning its characters to a simpler, more innocent America, *The Marble Faun* seeks to escape time altogether. If Rome constituted the fullness of human experience, America was blessed by having *less* of it, a molehill of crime being preferable to a mountain. It would be centuries before America became the object-lesson Rome was. In any case, Hawthorne felt in 1859–60, America would last *his* time, as indeed it did for another year.

Epilogue: Last Words

Hawthorne was a man so peculiarly constituted—his mind and body were so finely interwoven, as it were—as almost to make it seem that he might live if he would firmly resolve to do so.

—Julian Hawthorne, *Nathaniel Hawthorne and His Wife*

What does it mean then, what can it all mean?

—Lily Briscoe in Virginia Woolf, *To the Lighthouse*

"We know something of that time now" (13:17), Hawthorne wrote in "Septimius Felton," the first of the three unfinished "Elixir of Life" manuscripts, begun in Concord in 1861 early in one war and set initially in 1775, also in Concord, at the outbreak of another. On May 16, 1861, Hawthorne spoke of the war "interrupt[ing] my literary industry" and quenching the popular taste for romances, "even if I could write one" (18:379). Ten days later he praised its juvenating effect; the war lifted his "flagging" spirits, engaged him "in the heroic sentiment of the time," and made him "feel that [he] had a country" again (18:380). With little confidence in the genuine and stable unity of the Union (18:381, 591; *NHW* 2:269)—"If I have any wishes on the subject," he told Henry Bright, "it is that New England might be a nation by itself" (18:543)—and only mixed enthusiasm for the abolitionist cause (18:381, 591; *NHW* 2:271), Hawthorne followed the war with a rush of adrenalin but no steadfast commitment of mind and heart. By the spring of 1863, fourth months before Gettysburg and the fall of Vicksburg, events had filled him with "a sense of infinite weariness. I want the end to come, and the curtain to drop, and then to go to sleep" (18:543).

He might almost have been referring to the end of his life. His "physical energy" had been "on the wane" ever since his return to America (*NHW* 2:269), and by "the spring and summer of 1863," though "he seemed to have no definite disease,...he grew thinner, paler, and more languid day by day," and "no longer...seemed to find any sufficient interest in life" (*NHW* 2:329). He appears to have known he was slowly dying and to have met the fact with unprotesting submission, even (according to Julian) with "gentle sport" (*NHW* 2:334). Death failed to terrify him less because he had a strong faith in immortality than because he had lost much of his appetite for living.

It is not surprising that a man in this condition should write of death and empathize with the wish to evade it, provided youth and energy could be indefinitely preserved. The subject came home to him in the most literal way, Thoreau having told him of a previous occupant of his house "who was resolved never to die" (18:499). To meditate on death was inevitably to meditate on the meaning of life—on the shape and achievements of one's own life, but also on life itself. There is very little concern with an afterlife in the "Elixir of Life" manuscripts ("Septimius Felton," "Septimius Norton," and "The Dolliver Romance")[1] or in the several "Studies" for them in which Hawthorne made notes about his material. His impelling theme, before he lost his way in complications of plot, was how to live. "So much trouble of preparation to live," Septimius Felton complains, "and then no life at all; a ponderous beginning, and nothing more" (13:7). Life on these terms hardly seems worthwhile to Septimius, but it has been granted and he must decide what to do with it.

In developing Thoreau's anecdote into a book, Hawthorne's challenge, as he recognized in one of the Studies for "Dolliver," was to find "some particular reason for which [his protagonist] wishes to live" (13:531). One of Septimius's first thoughts is that living is an apprenticeship to the art of life from which "we are snatched away…before we have learned the alphabet" (13:12). "The way truly to live and answer the purposes of life," Septimius thinks, "was not to gather up thoughts into books, where they grow so dry, but to live, and still be going about full of green wisdom, ripening ever, not in maxims cut and dry, but in wisdom ready for daily occasions like a living fountain; and that to be thus, it was necessary to live long on earth, drink in all its lessons, and not to die on the attainment of some smattering of truth" (13:14).

"Ripening ever" suggests living for its own sake with a consciousness of endless becoming, a happy formulation of the naturalism to which Hawthorne had always been attracted but which, in the end, he had always resisted. He would resist it again. Although Hawthorne is unsure what Septimius wants, a note in Study 7 indicates what he *doesn't* want: the repetition of the "small and mean necessities of life—feeding, getting up, going to bed, dressing ourselves in an interminable series;—seeing the wretched old sun rise forever" (13:513).

It may seem paradoxical that a man contemptuous of life should try to extend it, but immortality for Septimius is not the experience of daily living prolonged indefinitely so much as an *idea*, like Ethan Brand's Unpardonable Sin, that separates him from the multitude and marks him out by an unparalleled fate; it is a way of transcending the mundane, not of perpetuating it. Hawthorne knows such a motive is shadowy, but his efforts to give it more familiar substance— Septimius is "a man of high purposes, which he hates to leave unaccomplished"

(13:532); Septimius is "dissatisfied much with death, on noble grounds, because it so breaks off and brings to naught all human effort, so as to make man a laughing stock to whoever created him" (13:507); Dr. Dolliver wants to live "over again in order to correct some great error…in his past life, which he fears will be of very bad influence on mankind, & therefore he lives again to grub up this evil by the root" (13:533); and so on—all have the air of expedients and are abandoned. The theme that truly concerns him is the renunciation of common life in the name of a proud ideal. The irony is that in seeking to live forever Septimius involves himself in austere denials that empty his life *of* life. Death, one Study has him realize, is what "gave warmth of life" and "kept the sap running, which would otherwise petrify" (13:503).

In setting ordinary happiness against devotion to an extraordinary purpose, "Septimius Felton/Norton," Hawthorne's penultimate romance, returns to the theme of *Fanshawe*, his first. The trio of Fanshawe, Ellen Langton, and Edward Wolcott is replicated by that of Septimius, the schoolmistress Rose Garfield, and the yeoman farmer (soon to be soldier) Robert Hagburn. Unlike Septimius, who feels life "a failure, because we do not live long enough" (13:12), Hagburn is content to fill his allotted span with "what this life has, toil, enjoyment, suffering, struggle, fight, rest," then submit to annihilation (13:8). For Hagburn, the richness of daily life is itself life's purpose and reward. Initially engaged to Septimius, Rose comes to realize, or is led by Septimius's indifference to realize, that Hagburn is the proper choice; Hawthorne so fully agreed that in developing the story he deleted the engagement and recast Rose from fiancée to half sister. In a rare moment of happiness with Rose, Septimius feels that "she reconciled him, in some secret way, to life as it was, to imperfection, to decay" (13:56), but imperfection is not what he or other Hawthornean males desire. Like Fanshawe or Owen Warland, Septimius believes he has "some high lonely path, in which, to make any progress, to come to any end, he must walk unburthened by the affections" (13:41).

Septimius's quest will fail, of course, but is the attempt noble—a protest against the meanness of everyday life—or is his "history [that] of a mind," as Hawthorne says, "bewildered in certain errors" (13:16)? Would a life like Robert Hagburn's have been better? In one of the earliest views of him, Septimius is shown "with his head bent down, brooding, brooding, with his eyes fixed on some chip, some stone, some common plant, any commonest thing, as if it were the clue and index to some mystery," about which his speculations find "no end" (13:6). Adapting the lines for his poem "Hawthorne," Robert Lowell adds a conclusion that epitomizes Hawthorne's lifelong exasperation with the real: "The disturbed eyes rise / furtive, foiled, dissatisfied / from meditation on the true / and insignificant."[2] Though endlessly absorbing, life is resistant to the meanings one would distill from it. It simply is—and then it isn't any longer.

Julian Hawthorne felt that the Septimius manuscripts fail because Hawthorne "could not bring himself into sympathy with Septimius's infatuation" (*NHW* 2:301). It may be that he had too much sympathy. Outwardly he was a Robert Hagburn who married, fathered children, found happiness in the common way, and consented to live with "imperfection" and "decay"; yet inwardly he was a Septimius whose most intense life was solitary and who may have wondered whether a rosy-minded "New England girl" and the family she bore him were "enough...to engross a man's life and higher purposes" (13:43). Like his village uncle of thirty years before, Hawthorne seems to have found the solid realities of domestic life melting away at the last even as he gauged the terrible price of loneliness and egotism he might have paid without them. Julian's chapters on this period show Hawthorne a devoted and appreciative father, but with an element of detachment, of irony, and of the village uncle's feeling that his chosen life and impending death are somehow things apart from the essential *him*.

"Our story is an internal one" (13:15), Hawthorne announces in "Septimius Felton"; it turns out to be anything but that. Hawthorne's gift was never for sustained narrative, yet as with "The American Claimant," his initial command of situation and theme gives way to an increasingly intricate and bizarre plot. On his way to the Battle of Concord, Septimius meets and reluctantly kills a young British officer, who, dying, gives him a manuscript with cryptic instructions for an elixir of life. The complications arising from this episode are romantic confection—the officer's fiancée comes incognito to Concord; she befriends Septimius with the aim of killing him, falls in love with him, drinks the elixir he eventually brews (which proves poisonous through a mistake in his recipe), and dies—but they are comparatively tidy alongside the materials Hawthorne imports from the Claimant manuscripts, including the inevitable bloody footstep. Simpler and less melodramatic, "The Dolliver Romance" is also less interesting. Hawthorne knew he lacked energy and life enough to complete it, and to his credit (and financial loss) he resisted James T. Fields's encouragement to persevere, telling Fields that in doing so he "should smother myself in mud of my own making" (18:641).

That some recent Hawthorneans should speak well of the "Elixir of Life" manuscripts reflects a generous impulse to reclaim Hawthorne's final years from imputations of depression and failed powers.[3] They are right to feel that Hawthorne's talent survived almost to the last, but they are looking in the wrong place for evidence of it. Even as he labored on the late romances, digging himself deeper into pits of obfuscation, Hawthorne was elsewhere writing some of his most limpid prose. *Our Old Home* is a quiet masterpiece. Although its source is the English notebooks, the changes Hawthorne made in the published text are, as Julian says, "just the right changes" (*NHW* 2:304), and the chapters are enriched by a substantial amount of new writing and fashioned with a mastery that transforms journal observation into high art.

The Marble Faun notwithstanding, the implication of Hawthorne's later years is that the more fruitful line of development after his English residence, whether in fiction or nonfiction prose, was toward a discerning realism mellowed and refined by the gentle humor and irony that was always, from the time of "The Old Manse," his most engaging style. His mistake on returning to America was to think that he could and should continue to write romance; his vexation was to find that he could not. When he sets romance aside, in the *Atlantic Monthly* essays that would develop into *Our Old Home*, he shows a greater command of structure, language, and tone than ever before except in *The Scarlet Letter* and portions of *The Blithedale Romance*, and yet he openly deprecated the sketches as if they were a literary by-blow. Flattery aside, James T. Fields was right in commending them; "I don't think even your pen did a better thing in its way," he wrote of the comparatively modest "Leamington Spa" (Mellow 560). It is unfortunate that Fields did not go further and tell Hawthorne, "Forget romance. You did that wonderfully in the past. But *this* is where your present and future lie." Echoing Julian's suggestion that the weakened Hawthorne might have lived for a time had he chosen to, John Updike finds his death "as much a spiritual as a physical event."[4] Though not yet 60, Hawthorne seems to have acquiesced in, even welcomed death as if from a consciousness that he had outlived his cultural and literary time, indeed that he had outlived what he took to be his writerly self.

NOTES

Preface

1. Millicent Bell, "The Obliquity of Signs: The Scarlet Letter," Massachusetts Review, 23 (Spring 1982): 13.

Chapter 1

1. Julian Hawthorne, "The Salem of Hawthorne," *Century Magazine* 28 (May 1885): 4.
2. W. C. Brownell, *American Prose Masters* (1909; Cambridge, MA: Harvard University Press, 1967), 54. See Millicent Bell, "The Obliquity of Signs: *The Scarlet Letter*," *Massachusetts Review* 23 (Spring 1982): 13.
3. E. P. Whipple, unsigned review of *The House of the Seven Gables, Graham's Magazine* 38 (June 1851): 467.
4. Bliss Perry, "Hawthorne at North Adams," in *The Amateur Spirit* (Boston: Houghton Mifflin, 1904), 123.
5. This side of Hawthorne revived temporarily in England in his solitary or male-only ramblings through Liverpool and London and through the English countryside.
6. *Hawthorne's Lost Notebook, 1835–1841,* transcript and preface by Barbara S. Mouffe, introduction by Hyatt H. Waggoner (University Park: Pennsylvania State University Press, 1978), ms. leaf 8.
7. Dan McCall, *Citizens of Somewhere Else: Nathaniel Hawthorne and Henry James* (Ithaca, NY: Cornell University Press, 1999), 22.
8. Brownell, *American Prose Masters,* 54.
9. Brownell, *American Prose Masters,* 54.
10. Charles Feidelson, *Symbolism and American Literature* (Chicago: University of Chicago Press, 1953), 8; Paul de Man, *Blindness and Insight* (Minneapolis: University of Minnesota Press, 1983), 216.
11. Nina Baym, *The Shape of Hawthorne's Career* (Ithaca, NY: Cornell University Press, 1976), 117.
12. de Man, *Blindness and Insight,* 222.
13. I. A. Richards, *Practical Criticism* (New York: Harcourt, Brace, 1929), 260.
14. Ann Douglas, *The Feminization of American Culture* (New York: Knopf, 1977), 245.
15. Yvor Winters, "Maule's Curse, or Hawthorne and the Problem of Allegory," in *In Defense of Reason* (Denver: Alan Swallow, 1937), 158.
16. William Dean Howells, *Literary Friends and Acquaintance* (New York: Harper & Brothers, 1900), 118.
17. Henry James, *The Europeans,* in *Henry James: Novels, 1871–1880* (New York: Library of America, 1983), 971.
18. Sarah Orne Jewett, *The Country of the Pointed Firs* (1896; New York: Norton, 1982), 76.

19. Jewett, *The Country of the Pointed Firs*, 77.

20. Philip Rahv, "The Dark Lady of Salem," in *Image and Idea* (New York: New Directions, 1949), 26. In a similar vein, Irving Howe remarks, "His acute moral sense had been long detached from the traditional context of orthodox faith, but it found little else in which to thrive, certainly no buoying social vision—which may explain why he turned so often to allegory, the literary mode in which it might be possible to represent the moral sense as an independent force." Howe, *Politics and the Novel* (New York: Horizon Press, 1957), 164.

21. George Parsons Lathrop, "The Novel and Its Future" (1874), in *Documents of American Realism and Naturalism*, ed. Donald Pizer (Carbondale: Southern Illinois University Press, 1998), 28.

22. Richard H. Brodhead calls *The House of the Seven Gables* Hawthorne's "effort to write a new sort of realistic fiction" located within "a new kind of reality." *Hawthorne, Melville, and the Novel* (Chicago: University of Chicago Press, 1976), 70. Millicent Bell argues (rightly, I believe) that "Hawthorne has misled critics" who take his preface at face value. "Hawthorne and the Real," in *Hawthorne and the Real: Bicentennial Essays*, ed. Bell (Columbus: Ohio State University Press, 2005), 6.

23. See, for example, Henry T. Tuckerman, "Nathaniel Hawthorne," *Southern Literary Messenger* 17 (June 1851): 348. Hereafter cited in the text as Tuckerman.

24. Brodhead, *Hawthorne, Melville, and the Novel*, 81.

25. Harriet Beecher Stowe, *The Minister's Wooing* (1859; New York: Penguin, 1999), 120. Hereafter cited in the text as *MW*.

26. William James, *The Varieties of Religious Experience* (Cambridge, MA: Harvard University Press, 1985), 367.

27. Emily Dickinson's poem "Of course—I prayed" (#581) is an eleven-line deconstruction of nearly two and a half centuries of New England piety.

28. Rita K. Gollin discusses Hawthorne and the problem of belief in "'The Fairest Hope of Heaven': Hawthorne on Immortality," *Nathaniel Hawthorne Review* 31 (2005): 75.

29. John Updike, *Self-Consciousness* (New York: Fawcett, 1989), 239.

30. F. O. Matthiessen, *American Renaissance* (New York: Oxford University Press, 1941), 326.

31. Stowe, *Sunny Memories of Foreign Lands*, in *The House of the Seven Gables*, ed. Robert S. Levine (New York: Norton, 2006), 331.

32. Johann Wolfgang von Goethe, quoted in Walter Benjamin, *The Origins of German Tragic Drama*, trans. John Osborne (London: Verso, 1998), 161.

33. Edwin H. Cady, *The Light of Common Day* (Bloomington: Indiana University Press, 1971), 8.

34. James, *The Varieties of Religious Experience*, 119, 120.

35. Octavius B. Frothingham, *Recollections and Impressions, 1822–1890* (New York: Putnam's, 1891), 42.

36. McCall, *Citizens of Somewhere Else*, 29.

37. Northrop Frye, *Fables of Identity: Studies in Poetic Mythology* (New York: Harcourt, Brace, 1963), 152.

38. Mary's mother, Katy, also has faculty but, though conventionally religious, is a practical woman lacking spirituality apart from reverence for the memory of her saintly husband.

39. Matthiessen, *American Renaissance*, 322.

40. Richard Poirier, *A World Elsewhere: The Place of Style in American Literature* (New York: Oxford University Press, 1966), xxi.

41. Frye, *Fables of Identity*, 152.

42. Gollin, "The Fairest Hope of Heaven," 75.

43. Joseph Conrad, *Heart of Darkness*, in *"Youth" and Other Stories*, vol. 16 of *Complete Works* (Garden City, NY: Doubleday, Page, 1926), 149. Hereafter cited in the text as *HD*.

44. Brodhead, *Hawthorne, Melville, and the Novel*, 200.

45. Henry D. Thoreau, *A Week on the Concord and Merrimack Rivers*, ed. Carl F. Hovde et al. (Princeton: Princeton University Press, 1980), 382.

46. Newton Arvin, *Walt Whitman* (New York: Macmillan, 1938), 197–98.

47. Friedrich Nietzsche, *Beyond Good and Evil*, trans. Marianne Cowan (Chicago: Henry Regnery, 1955), 42. Hereafter cited in the text as *BGE*.

48. As John Updike observes, "late works are [haunted by] the author's previous works: he is burdensomely aware that he has been cast, unlike his ingénue self, as an author who writes in a certain way, with the inexorable consistency of his own handwriting." Updike, "Late Works," in *Due Considerations* (New York: Knopf, 2007), 60.

49. For an account of Delia Bacon, see James Shapiro, *Contested Will: Who Wrote Shakespeare* (New York: Simon and Schuster, 2010), 83–110. Nina Baym discusses Hawthorne and Bacon in "Delia Bacon: Hawthorne's Last Heroine," *Nathaniel Hawthorne Journal* 20, 2 (1994): 1–9.

Chapter 2

1. *The Writings of Henry D. Thoreau, Journal*, vol. 1, *1837–1844*, ed. Elizabeth Hall Witherell et al. (Princeton: Princeton University Press, 1981), 34.

2. See Gloria C. Erlich, *Family Themes and Hawthorne's Fiction: The Tenacious Web* (New Brunswick, NJ: Rutgers University Press, 1984), xvii, 8–9. Hereafter cited in the text as Erlich.

3. For a valuable discussion of the Salem Hawthorne knew, see Margaret B. Moore, *The Salem World of Nathaniel Hawthorne* (Columbia: University of Missouri Press, 1998).

4. Elizabeth Palmer Peabody, [Epistolary Thoughts on Hawthorne, 1838–1886], in *Hawthorne in His Own Time*, ed. Ronald A. Bosco and Jillmarie Murphy (Iowa City: University of Iowa Press, 2007), 26.

5. Edwin Haviland Miller, *Salem is My Dwelling Place: A Life of Nathaniel Hawthorne* (Iowa City: University of Iowa Press, 1991), xiii.

6. Quoted in Arlin Turner, *Nathaniel Hawthorne, A Biography* (New York: Oxford University Press, 1980), 40.

7. Julian Hawthorne, "The Salem of Hawthorne," *Century Magazine* 28 (May 1885): 6.

8. William Dean Howells, *Literary Friends and Acquaintance* (New York: Harper, 1900), 38.

9. Howells, *Literary Friends and Acquaintance*, 51, 54, 55.

10. Andrew Preston Peabody, untitled review, in *Hawthorne: The Critical Heritage*, ed. J. Donald Crowley (New York: Barnes and Noble, 1970), 64. See also Crowley, "Historical Commentary," *Twice-Told Tales* (9:511).

11. Edgar A. Dryden, *The Poetics of Enchantment* (Ithaca, NY: Cornell University Press, 1977), 9.

12. Miller, *Salem is My Dwelling Place*, xiv.

13. Brenda Wineapple, *Hawthorne: A Life* (New York: Knopf, 2003), 12.

14. Charles Fenno Hoffman, unsigned review, *American Monthly Magazine* (1838), in Crowley, *Hawthorne*, 62.

15. Julian Hawthorne, *Hawthorne and His Circle* (New York: Harper & Brothers, 1903), 33.

16. Annie Fields, quoted in Rita K. Gollin, "Annie Fields's Nathaniel Hawthorne," *Hawthorne's Women: Engendering and Expanding the Hawthorne Tradition*, ed. John L. Idol, Jr. and Melinda M. Ponder (Amherst: University of Massachusetts Press, 1999), 141.

17. Frederick C. Crews, *The Sins of the Fathers* (New York: Oxford University Press, 1966), 12. Hereafter cited in the text as Crews.

18. Oliver Wendell Holmes, "At the Saturday Club," in *The Complete Poetical Works* (Boston: Houghton Mifflin, 1895), ll. 113–14.

19. Quoted in Wineapple, *Hawthorne*, 58.

20. Hyatt H. Waggoner, *Hawthorne: A Critical Study*, rev. ed. (Cambridge, MA: Harvard University Press, 1963), 10. See also Nina Baym, *The Shape of Hawthorne's Career* (Ithaca, NY: Cornell University Press, 1976), 65–66; hereafter cited in the text as Baym.

21. See Philip Young, *Hawthorne's Secret: An Un-Told Tale* (Boston: Godine, 1984).

22. Jeremy Taylor, quoted in Neal Frank Doubleday, *Hawthorne's Early Tales: A Critical Study* (Durham, NC: Duke University Press, 1972), 155.

23. Taylor, quoted in Doubleday, *Hawthorne's Early Tales,* 158.

24. *Hawthorne's Lost Notebook, 1835-1841,* transcript and preface by Barbara S. Mouffe, introduction by Hyatt H. Waggoner (University Park: Pennsylvania State University Press), 1978, [notebook p. 25]; Waggoner, introduction, 25.

25. Stephen Nissenbaum, *Sex, Diet, and Debility in Jacksonian America: Sylvester Graham and Health Reform* (Westport, CT: Greenwood, 1980), 26, 12. T. Walter Herbert, Jr. observes that during his Salem years Hawthorne was "long...devoted to a pattern of life—cultivating his own fancies in a compulsive bookish solitude—well recognized as conducive to prurient lassitude, and in particular to masturbation." Herbert, *Dearest Beloved: The Hawthornes and the Making of Middle-Class Family* (Berkeley: University of California Press, 1993), 144.

26. S. A. Tissot, *A Treatise on the Diseases Produced by Onanism,* in *The Secret Vice Exposed!* ed. Charles Rosenberg and Carroll Smith-Rosenberg (New York: Arno Press, 1974), 74, 46. See James N. Mancall, *"Thoughts Painfully Intense": Hawthorne and the Invalid Author* (New York: Routledge, 2002).

27. John Todd, *The Student's Manual* (1835; London: William Tegg, 1853), 71, 70, 71.

28. See Sylvester Graham, *A Lecture to Young Men on Chastity* (1834; Boston: Charles H. Pierce, 1848); and Nissenbaum, *Sex, Diet, and Debility in Jacksonian America,* 30.

29. Sigmund Freud, "Creative Writers and Day-Dreaming," in *The Standard Edition of the Complete Psychological Works of Sigmund Freud,* ed. James Strachey et al., trans. James Strachey (London: Hogarth Press and the Institute of Psycho-Analysis, 1953-74), 9:147.

30. John W. Shroeder, "Alice Doane's Story: An Essay on Hawthorne and Spenser," *Nathaniel Hawthorne Journal* 4 (1974): 133.

31. Lawrence Buell, *New England Literary Culture* (Cambridge: Cambridge University Press, 1986), 69. Buell is referring to the "conservative" Romantic role generally, not to Hawthorne in "Alice Doane's Appeal." See also Stanley Brodwin, "Nathaniel Hawthorne and the Function of History: A Reading of 'Alice Doane's Appeal,'" *Nathaniel Hawthorne Journal* 4 (1974): 118.

32. Hyatt H. Waggoner argues similarly when he observes that Hawthorne "found in the past of New England a way of projecting and objectifying the concerns, the tensions, and the deep feelings that haunted him from the personal past of his childhood." *Hawthorne,* 66-67.

33. Waggoner, *Hawthorne,* 55.

34. Lea Newman, *A Reader's Guide to the Short Stories of Nathaniel Hawthorne* (Boston: G. K. Hall, 1979), 5; see also Shroeder, "Alice Doane's Story," 134.

35. Northrop Frye, *Fables of Identity: Studies in Poetic Mythology* (New York: Harcourt, Brace, 1963), 36.

36. Peter Brooks, *Reading for the Plot: Design and Intention in Narrative* (New York: Knopf, 1984), 6. See M. H. Abrams, *Natural Supernaturalism: Tradition and Revolution in Romantic Literature* (New York: Norton, 1971).

37. For a discussion of this subject, see Rita K. Gollin, *Nathaniel Hawthorne and the Truth of Dreams* (Baton Rouge: Louisiana State University Press, 1979).

38. Q. D. Leavis, "Hawthorne as Poet," in *Hawthorne: A Collection of Critical Essays,* ed. A. N. Kaul (Englewood Cliffs, NJ: Prentice-Hall, 1966), 36.

39. Jane Tompkins, *Sensational Designs: The Cultural Work of American Fiction, 1790-1860* (New York: Oxford University Press, 1985), 10, 11.

40. E. A. Duyckinck (unsigned review), "Nathaniel Hawthorne," *United States Magazine and Democratic Review* 16 (April 1845): 381.

41. Years later Hawthorne would have the same reaction to monkeys when he took Julian to the London zoo (21:315).

42. Philip Young has argued that the devil's words from "Young Goodman Brown" are "a magical account of the origin of [Hawthorne's] insight into human culpability, and of his vision of the world." *Hawthorne's Secret,* 69.

43. Edmund Wilson, *The Wound and the Bow: Seven Studies in Literature* (New York: Oxford University Press, 1965), 240.

44. Thomas Mann, "Tonio Kröger," *Death in Venice and Seven Other Stories*, trans. H. T. Lowe-Porter (New York: Vintage, 1954), 99.

45. See Chandler Robbins, *Remarks on the Disorders of Literary Men* (Boston, 1825).

46. Erik H. Erikson, *Identity: Youth and Crisis* (New York: Norton, 1968), 172–73.

47. Michael Davitt Bell, *The Development of American Romance: The Sacrifice of Relation* (Chicago: University of Chicago Press, 1980), 130.

48. Mann, "Tonio Kröger," 133.

49. Erikson, *Identity*, 169.

50. In 1836–37, especially, Bridge feared that Hawthorne, despondent over his dealings with would-be publishers, might commit suicide. His generous subvention of *Twice-Told Tales* was prompted partly by a sense of urgency.

51. Erikson, *Identity*, 170

52. Alison Easton, *The Making of the Hawthorne Subject* (Columbia: University of Missouri Press, 1996), 86–87.

53. Mann, "Tonio Kröger," 134.

54. For a still valuable discussion of "The Story Teller," see Nelson F. Adkins, "The Early Projected Works of Nathaniel Hawthorne," *Papers of the Bibliographical Society of America* 39 (1945): 119–55.

55. Biographer Megan Marshall views this relationship as a de facto engagement. *The Peabody Sisters: Three Women Who Ignited American Romanticism* (Boston: Houghton Mifflin, 2005), 358. Vocationally, Hawthorne owed much to Elizabeth Peabody's energy and devotion, but given Hawthorne's tastes and distastes with women, the notion of an engagement seems dubious.

Chapter 3

1. Arlin Turner, *Nathaniel Hawthorne: A Biography* (New York: Oxford University Press, 1980), 21.

2. Gloria C. Erlich, *Family Themes and Hawthorne's Fiction: The Tenacious Web* (New Brunswick, NJ: Rutgers University Press, 1984), 69.

3. Henry Adams, *The Education of Henry Adams*, in *Novels, Mont St Michel, The Education*, ed. Ernest Samuels and Jayne B. Samuels (New York: Library of America, 1983), 727. Hereafter cited in the text as Adams.

4. Anne Bradstreet, "Contemplations," *The Complete Works of Anne Bradstreet*, ed. Joseph R. McElrath, Jr. and Allan P. Robb (Boston: Twayne, 1981), 168, l. 14.

5. Surveying this period, Larry J. Reynolds finds a "remarkable" similarity between Hawthorne's "sociopolitical outlook" and those of Emerson, Thoreau, Margaret Fuller, and Bronson Alcott (Reynolds, *Devils and Rebels: The Making of Hawthorne's Damned Politics* [Ann Arbor: University of Michigan Press, 2008], 112). I doubt this as a matter of practical content and, still more, of spirit. Emerson, Thoreau, and Fuller, even Alcott in his fashion, were preachers of awakening; Hawthorne felt the "great want" of the period was "sleep!" (10:29). What separated Hawthorne's "morning" from the others', aside from his native skepticism, was the Edenic self-sufficiency of his life at the Manse, which left him indifferent to a millennial future. Having turned away from the historical settings and psychological themes of the Salem period, Hawthorne found a usable source of material in "reform," especially for sketches aimed for the *Democratic Review*. His concern with reform, however, was neither deeply thoughtful nor abiding.

6. Margaret Fuller, *Margaret Fuller's 1842 Journal: At Concord with the Emersons*, ed. Joel Myerson, *Harvard Library Bulletin* 21 (1973): 325. See also "The Hall of Fantasy" (10:182–83).

7. Henry D. Thoreau, *Walden*, ed. J. Lyndon Shanley (Princeton: Princeton University Press, 1971), 186. Hereafter cited in the text as *W*.

8. See Leo Marx, *The Machine in the Garden* (New York: Oxford University Press, 1964), 11–33.

9. Thoreau, *A Week on the Concord and Merrimack Rivers*, ed. Carl F. Hovde et al. (Princeton: Princeton University Press), 382.

10. David M. Robinson, *Natural Life: Thoreau's Worldly Transcendentalism* (Ithaca, NY: Cornell University Press, 2004), 76.

11. Thoreau, *Journal*, ed. John C. Broderick et al. (Princeton: Princeton University Press, 1981–), 3:370. Hereafter cited in the text as *TJ* with volume and page.

12. See Robert Milder, *Reimagining Thoreau* (Cambridge: Cambridge University Press, 1995), 130–38.

13. T. Walter Herbert, *Dearest Beloved: The Hawthornes and the Making of the Middle-Class Family* (Berkeley: University of California Press, 1993), 144.

14. Sophia Hawthorne, "Sophia Peabody Hawthorne's *American Notebooks*," ed. Patricia Dunlavy Valenti, in *Studies in the American Renaissance*, ed. Joel Myerson (Charlottesville: University Press of Virginia, 1996), 132. Hereafter cited in the text as *SPHAN*.

15. Valenti, introduction to "Sophia Peabody Hawthorne's *American Notebooks*," 116.

16. Herbert, *Dearest Beloved*, 145.

17. Harriet Beecher Stowe, *The Minister's Wooing* (1859; New York: Penguin, 1999), 78. Hereafter cited in the text as *MW*.

18. Phyllis Cole, *Mary Moody Emerson and the Origins of Transcendentalism* (New York: Oxford University Press, 1998), 8.

19. Megan Marshall, *The Peabody Sisters: Three Women Who Ignited American Romanticism* (Boston: Houghton Mifflin, 2005), 259.

20. Marshall, *The Peabody Sisters*, 260. Unlike Marshall, biographer Patricia Dunlavy Valenti denies that Sophia was "invested" in her invalidism, yet even Valenti notes that after a happy sojourn in Cuba in the early 1830s (she had accompanied her sister Mary, who served as tutor in a wealthy island family) Sophia "returned to Salem and her parents' home to repress and repudiate the person she had become": "no wonder her headaches recurred with greater ferocity than ever before." Valenti, *Sophia Peabody Hawthorne: A Life*, vol. 1, *1809–1847* (Columbia: University of Missouri Press, 2004), 107, 86.

21. Sophia Hawthorne, in "A Sophia Hawthorne Journal, 1843–1844," ed. John J. McDonald, *Nathaniel Hawthorne Journal* 4 (1974): 23.

22. Elizabeth Palmer Peabody, [Epistolary Thoughts on Hawthorne, 1838–1886], *Hawthorne in His Own Time*, ed. Ronald A. Bosco and Jillmarie Murphy (Iowa City: University of Iowa Press, 2007), 28.

23. Valenti, *Sophia Peabody Hawthorne*, 196.

24. Quoted in Valenti, *Sophia Peabody Hawthorne*, 170.

25. Thomas Woodson, introduction, *The Letters, 1813–1843* (15:29).

26. McDonald, "A Sophia Hawthorne Journal," 8, 12, 18.

27. Sophia Peabody to sister Elizabeth Peabody, in Brenda Wineapple, *Hawthorne: A Life* (New York: Knopf, 2003), 117.

28. Luanne Jenkins Hurst, "The Chief Employ of Her Life: Sophia Peabody Hawthorne's Contribution to Her Husband's Career," in *Hawthorne and Women: Engendering and Expanding the Hawthorne Tradition*, ed. John L. Idol, Jr. and Melinda M. Ponder (Amherst: University of Massachusetts Press, 1999), 45–54.

29. Leland S. Person, Jr., "Hawthorne's Love Letters: Writing and Relationship," *American Literature* 59 (May 1987): 213.

30. Woodson, introduction (15:30).

31. Quoted in Valenti, *Sophia Peabody Hawthorne*, 142.

32. Larry J. Reynolds, "Hawthorne's Labors in Concord," in *The Cambridge Companion to Nathaniel Hawthorne*, ed. Richard H. Millington (Cambridge: Cambridge University Press, 2004), 19.

33. Lea Newman, *A Reader's Guide to the Short Stories of Nathaniel Hawthorne* (Boston: G. K. Hall, 1979), 83; Philip Young, *Hawthorne's Secret: An Un-Told Tale* (Boston: Godine, 1984), 65.
34. Valenti, *Sophia Peabody Hawthorne*, 240.
35. In McDonald, "A Sophia Hawthorne Journal," 13.
36. The inconsistencies in capitalization are Hawthorne's.
37. Person, "Hawthorne's Love Letters," 221.
38. Valenti, *Sophia Peabody Hawthorne*, 227.
39. Joel Pfister situates "The Birth-mark" within a larger cultural discourse that represents "the female body as pathological." *The Production of Personal Life: Class, Gender, and the Psychological in Hawthorne's Fiction* (Stanford, CA: Stanford University Press, 1991), 38. Thomas R. Mitchell sees the story as Hawthorne's wishful but guilt-ridden abortion fantasy. "'The Birth-mark': Hawthorne's Abortion Fantasy," paper delivered at Nathaniel Hawthorne Society Conference, Concord, MA, June 2010. See Young, *Hawthorne's Secret*, 61.
40. Nina Baym, "Thwarted Nature," in *American Novelists Revisited: Essays in Feminist Criticism* (Boston: G. K. Hall, 1982), 61, 65.
41. In McDonald, "A Sophia Hawthorne Journal," 8.
42. Reynolds, "Hawthorne's Labors in Concord," 21.
43. Valenti, *Sophia Peabody Hawthorne*, 227.
44. Baym, "Hawthorne's Women: The Tyranny of Social Myths," *Centennial Review* 15 (1977): 252. Zenobia and Miriam hardly qualify as "artless."
45. If Sophia "ignited her husband's creativity by her very presence as the female, transcendental other," as Patricia Valenti claims, the writings at the Manse would be consistently better than they are and not, like woodcarver Drowne's everyday figureheads, workmanlike but without brilliance. *Sophia Peabody Hawthorne*, 183.
46. Philip Rahv, "The Dark Lady of Salem," in *Image and Idea* (New York: New Directions, 1949), 25. By "of Salem" Rahv means created by the Salemite Hawthorne. In another respect, his title is inapt, for the figure had its origins in the Concord period and is absent from *The House of the Seven Gables*, Hawthorne's Salem romance.
47. See Baym, "Thwarted Nature," 58-77.
48. In Frederick C. Crews's words, "Hawthorne's plot…encourages suspicions which his explicit moralizing condemns as narrowly materialistic." *The Sins of the Fathers: Hawthorne's Psychological Themes* (New York: Oxford University Press, 1966), 117.

Chapter 4

1. Nina Baym, "Nathaniel Hawthorne and His Mother: A Biographical Speculation," *American Literature* 54 (March 1982): 2.
2. Roberta Weldon, *Hawthorne, Gender, and Death: Christianity and Its Discontents* (New York: Palgrave Macmillan, 2008), 1.
3. Weldon, *Hawthorne, Gender, and Death*, 1.
4. Brenda Wineapple, *Hawthorne: A Life* (New York: Knopf, 2003), 212.
5. Philip Rahv, "The Dark Lady of Salem," *Image and Idea* (New York: New Directions, 1949), 23.
6. Nina Baym, *The Shape of Hawthorne's Career* (Ithaca, NY: Cornell University Press, 1976), 124. See also Richard H. Brodhead, *Hawthorne, Melville, and the Novel* (Chicago: University of Chicago Press, 1976), 50.
7. T. E. Hulme, *Speculations* (New York: Harcourt, Brace, 1924), 117.
8. Darrel Abel, *The Moral Picturesque: Studies in Hawthorne's Fiction* (West Lafayette, IN: Purdue University Press, 1988), 189.
9. D. H. Lawrence, "Nathaniel Hawthorne and *The Scarlet Letter*," in *Studies in Classic American Literature* (1923; New York: Viking Press, 1961), 91.

10. E. P. Whipple, review of *The Scarlet Letter, Graham's Magazine* 36, 4 (May 1850); rpt. in *Nathaniel Hawthorne: The Contemporary Reviews*, ed. John L. Idol and Buford Jones (Cambridge: Cambridge University Press, 1994), 125.

11. Hamilton Wright Mabie, "A Typical Novel," *Andover Review* 4 (1885); rpt. in *Documents of Modern Literary Realism*, ed. George J. Becker (Princeton: Princeton University Press, 1963), 306.

12. Mabie, "A Typical Novel," 306.

13. Millicent Bell, "The Obliquity of Signs," *Massachusetts Review* 23 (Spring 1982): 12.

14. Edward S. Reed, *From Soul to Mind: The Emergence of Psychology from Erasmus Darwin to William James* (New Haven: Yale University Press, 1997), 2, 14, 15–16.

15. W. C. Brownell, *American Prose Masters* (1909; Cambridge, MA: Harvard University Press, 1967), 67.

16. Brodhead takes this view in *Hawthorne, Melville, and the Novel*.

17. Bell, "The Obliquity of Signs," 12.

18. Sacvan Bercovitch sees it as defusing dissent by diverting it "into the gradualism of process." *The Office of the Scarlet Letter* (Baltimore: Johns Hopkins University Press, 1991), 29.

19. George Bailey Loring, "Hawthorne's *Scarlet Letter*," *Massachusetts Quarterly Review* 3, 12 (September 1850); rpt. in Idol and Jones, *Nathaniel Hawthorne*, 137. Hereafter cited in the text as Loring.

20. Harry Levin, *The Power of Blackness* (New York: Knopf, 1958), 40.

21. Friedrich Nietzsche, "The Genealogy of Morals," in *The Birth of Tragedy and The Genealogy of Morals*, trans. Francis Golffing (Garden City, NY: Doubleday, 1956), 155.

22. Whipple, "Nathaniel Hawthorne," *Atlantic Monthly* 5 (May 1860): 615.

23. A. N. Kaul, *The American Vision* (New Haven: Yale University Press, 1972), 185–86.

24. Amy Schrager Lang, *Prophetic Woman: Anne Hutchinson and the Problem of Dissent in the Literature of New England* (Berkeley: University of California Press, 1987), 93.

25. See Thomas R. Mitchell, *Hawthorne's Fuller Mystery* (Amherst: University of Massachusetts Press, 1998).

26. Sigmund Freud, *Civilization and Its Discontents*, trans. James Strachey (1929; New York: Norton, 1962), 50, 44, 50.

27. Freud, *Civilization and Its Discontents*, 51.

28. Perry Miller, *The Transcendentalists: An Anthology* (Cambridge, MA: Harvard University Press, 1967), 475.

29. Bercovitch, *The Office of the Scarlet Letter*, 118.

30. Frederic I. Carpenter, "Scarlet A Minus," *College English* 5 (January 1944): 174. See Emerson, "Self-Reliance," *CWE* 2:42.

31. See Terence Martin, *The Instructed Vision: Scottish Common Sense Philosophy and the Origins of American Fiction* (Bloomington: Indiana University Press, 1961), 145. In 1833 Hawthorne did charge out James Marsh's edition of Coleridge's *Aids to Reflection* (*HR* #109), a seminal text for Transcendentalists, but the only tale of his to show a marked impress of Romantic thought is "The Artist of Beautiful," and even its claims are aesthetic (on behalf of the imagination) rather than moral or intellectual. As V. L. Parrington long ago observed, "The buried voice of God that the Transcendentalists professed to have discovered in instinct, [Hawthorne] greatly distrusted." Parrington, *Main Currents in American Thought*, vol. 2, *1800–1860: The Romantic Revolution in America* (1927; New York: Harcourt Brace, n.d.), 435.

32. Ralph Waldo Emerson, *Memoirs of Margaret Fuller Ossoli*, by R. W. Emerson, W. H. Channing, and J. F. Clarke, 2 vols. (Boston: Roberts, 1874), 1:227, 228.

33. William Faulkner, "1699–1945: The Compsons," in *The Portable Faulkner*, ed. Malcolm Cowley (New York: Viking Press, 1946), 743.

34. Rahv, "The Dark Lady of Salem," 27.

35. See Jane Swisshelm, review of *The Scarlet Letter, Saturday Visiter* [*sic*], September 28, 1850; rpt. in *The Scarlet Letter and Other Writings*, ed. Leland S. Person (New York: Norton,

2005), 274; and Orestes Brownson, "Literary Notices and Criticism," *Brownson's Quarterly Review* 4 (October 1850); rpt. in Person, *The Scarlet Letter and Other Writings*, 251.

36. See Bercovitch, *The Office of the Scarlet Letter*.
37. Quoted in Mitchell, *Hawthorne's Fuller Mystery*, 126.
38. I am indebted to Barbara Barrow for this idea.
39. Miller, "The Romance and the Novel," in *Nature's Nation* (Cambridge, MA: Harvard University Press, 1967), 248.
40. Wineapple, *Hawthorne*, 228.

Chapter 5

1. Quoted in Brenda Wineapple, *Hawthorne: A Life* (New York: Knopf, 2003), 220.
2. Margaret B. Moore, *The Salem World of Nathaniel Hawthorne* (Columbia: University of Missouri Press, 1998), 2.
3. T. S. Eliot, "Tradition and the Individual Talent," in *The Sacred Wood* (London: Methuen, 1960), 49.
4. Michael J. Colacurcio, *The Province of Piety: Moral History in Hawthorne's Early Tales* (Cambridge, MA: Harvard University Press, 1986), 19.
5. Leonard N. Neufeldt, *The Economist: Henry David Thoreau and Enterprise* (New York: Oxford University Press, 1989), 24.
6. William Dean Howells, *Literary Friends and Acquaintance* (New York: Harper, 1900), 53.
7. Howells, *Literary Friends and Acquaintance*, 54.
8. Lawrence Buell remarks that "for the average New Englander of our period who thought at all about the matter, the sense of Puritan origins was probably more a mood inspired by special occasions than a constant, indwelling magnetic force." *New England Literary Culture* (Cambridge: Cambridge University Press, 1986), 195.
9. Buell, *New England Literary Culture*, 211.
10. Herbert Marcuse, *Eros and Civilization* (Boston: Beacon Press, 1955), 32.
11. Historically, this would have been "Major Hathorne"—Hawthorne himself added the *w* to the family name. His misspelling in "Main-street" seems a pointed effort at public identification with his ancestor.
12. Friedrich Nietzsche, *The Genealogy of Morals*, in *The Birth of Tragedy and The Genealogy of Morals*, trans. Francis Golffing (Garden City, NY: Doubleday, 1956), 225. Hereafter cited in the text as Nietzsche.
13. Q. D. Leavis, "Hawthorne as Poet," in *Hawthorne: A Collection of Critical Essays*, ed. A. N. Kaul (Englewood Cliffs, NJ: Prentice-Hall, 1966), 35.
14. Giles Gunn, *Thinking Across the American Grain* (Chicago: University of Chicago Press, 1992), 23.
15. Gunn, *Thinking Across the American Grain*, 1.
16. Rufus Choate, "The Importance of Illustrating New-England History By a Series of Romances like the Waverley Novels," in *Works of Rufus Choate*, 2 vols., ed. Samuel Gilman Brown (Boston: Little, Brown, 1862), 1:338, 340.
17. See Buell, *New England Literary Culture*, 193–213.
18. Joseph A. Conforti, *Imagining New England: Explorations of Regional Identity from the Pilgrims to the Mid-Twentieth Century* (Chapel Hill: University of North Carolina Press, 2001), 182.
19. Conforti, *Imagining New England*, 189.
20. Michael Davitt Bell, *Hawthorne and the Historical Romance of New England* (Princeton: Princeton University Press, 1971), 57.
21. Bell, *Hawthorne and the Historical Romance of New England*, 58.
22. See Bell, *Hawthorne and the Historical Romance of New England*, 59.
23. Frederick C. Crews, *The Sins of the Fathers* (New York: Oxford University Press, 1966), 33.

24. Colacurcio, *The Province of Piety*, 24.
25. Henry James, *The Europeans*, in *Novels: 1871–80* (New York: Library of America, 1983), 902–3.
26. Harriet Beecher Stowe, *The Minister's Wooing* (1859; New York: Penguin, 1999), 16, 61, 62, 64. Hereafter cited in the text as *MW*.
27. Crews, afterword, *The Sins of the Fathers: Hawthorne's Psychological Themes* (1966; rpt. Berkeley: University of California Press, 1989), 276.
28. Gloria C. Erlich, *Family Themes and Hawthorne's Fiction: The Tenacious Web* (New Brunswick, NJ: Rutgers University Press, 1984), 8–9.
29. Choate, "The Importance of Illustrating New-England History By a Series of Romances like the Waverley Novels," 1:324.
30. See Perry Miller, "Declension in a Bible Commonwealth," in *Nature's Nation* (Cambridge, MA: Harvard University Press, 1967), 14–49.
31. Wineapple, *Hawthorne*, 237.
32. Clark C. Griffith, "Substance and Shadow: Language and Meaning in *The House of the Seven Gables*," *Modern Philology* 51 (February 1954): 187.
33. Kenneth Burke, *The Philosophy of Literary Form*, rev. ed., abridged by the author (New York: Random House, 1957), 40.
34. With Clifford, as Mellow puts it, "Hawthorne was exorcising the spirit of an overly refined and ineffectual man…that in certain negative respects bore a resemblance" to himself (Mellow 353).
35. James, *Roderick Hudson*, in *Novels: 1871–80*, 167, 176.
36. F. O. Matthiessen and T. Walter Herbert, Jr. also see Holgrave as one of Emerson's disaffected youths. Matthiessen, *American Renaissance* (New York: Oxford University Press, 1941), 331; and Herbert, *Dearest Beloved: The Hawthornes and the Making of the Middle-Class Family* (Berkeley: University of California Press, 1993), 100.
37. Millicent Bell, "Hawthorne and the Real," in *Hawthorne and the Real: Bicentennial Essays*, ed. Bell (Columbus: Ohio State University Press, 2005), 18.
38. Richard H. Brodhead, *The School of Hawthorne* (New York: Oxford University Press, 1986), 57.
39. Thomas R. Mitchell, "In the Whale's Wake," in *Hawthorne and Melville: Writing a Relationship*, ed. Jana L. Argersinger and Leland S. Person (Athens: University of Georgia Press, 2008), 259. Wineapple calls *Seven Gables* "a book of middle age" (*Hawthorne*, 235).
40. Mitchell, "In the Whale's Wake," 259.
41. Quoted in Herbert, *Dearest Beloved*, 278.
42. Herbert, *Dearest Beloved*, xvi.

Chapter 6

1. Henry D. Thoreau, *Walden*, ed. J. Lyndon Shanley (Princeton: Princeton University Press, 1971), 91. Hereafter cited in the text as *W*.
2. N. Kaul, *The American Vision* (New Haven: Yale University Press, 1972), 204.
3. Thomas R. Mitchell, "In the Whale's Wake," in *Hawthorne and Melville: Writing a Relationship*, ed. Jana L. Argersinger and Leland S. Person (Athens: University of Georgia Press, 2008), 175. In its themes and tensions—and, I would add, its spirit—*The Blithedale Romance*, as Larry J. Reynolds notes, is a "response to his life in Concord during 1842–45" as much as to Brook Farm. Reynolds, "Hawthorne's Labors in Concord," in *The Cambridge Companion to Nathaniel Hawthorne*, ed. Richard H. Millington (Cambridge: Cambridge University Press, 2004), 10.
4. Richard H. Brodhead, *Hawthorne, Melville, and the Novel* (Chicago: University of Chicago Press, 1976), 92. Hereafter cited in the text as Brodhead.

5. Sigmund Freud, *Civilization and Its Discontents*, trans. James Strachey (1929; New York: Norton, 1962), 60.

6. "To read this novel, as to exist within its world as a character," Richard H. Millington remarks of this passage, "is to find everywhere manifest the fragility of the self and of the communities we build around it." Millington, *Practicing Romance: Narrative Form and Cultural Engagement in Hawthorne's Fiction* (Princeton: Princeton University Press, 1992), 166.

7. Virginia Woolf, *To the Lighthouse* (1927; New York: Harcourt, Brace, 1981), 97.

8. Woolf, *To the Lighthouse*, 112.

9. Nina Baym, *The Shape of Hawthorne's Career* (Ithaca, NY: Cornell University Press, 1976), 197.

10. Marilyn French, *Shakespeare's Division of Experience* (New York: Summit, 1981), 22. Hereafter cited in the text as French.

11. Elizabeth Cady Stanton, *The Woman's Bible* (1895; rpt. New York: Arno Press, 1972), Part I, 25.

12. Irving Howe, *Politics and the Novel* (New York: Horizon, 1957), 171.

13. Paul John Eakin, *The New England Girl: Cultural Ideals in Hawthorne, Stowe, Howells, and James* (Athens: University of Georgia Press, 1976), 69.

14. "'The Impulses of Human Nature': Margaret Fuller's Journal From June through October 1844," ed. Martha L. Berg and Alice De V. Perry, *Proceedings of the Massachusetts Historical Society* 102 (1990): 81. Hereafter cited in the text as *MFJ*.

15. Hawthorne, "Mrs. Hutchinson," in *Hawthorne: Tales and Sketches* (New York: Library of America, 1982), 19.

16. Quoted in Patricia Dunlavy Valenti, *Sophia Peabody Hawthorne: A Life*, vol. 1, *1809–1847* (Columbia: University of Missouri Press, 2004), 82.

17. Quoted in Charles Capper, *Margaret Fuller: An American Romantic Life. The Public Years* (New York: Oxford University Press, 2007), 186.

18. Margaret Fuller, "Mariana," in *Margaret Fuller, American Romantic*, ed. Perry Miller (New York: Doubleday, 1963), 17.

19. Fuller, "Mariana," 17.

20. Ralph Waldo Emerson, *Memoirs of Margaret Fuller Ossoli*, by R. W. Emerson, W. H. Channing, and J. F. Clarke, 2 vols. (Boston: Roberts, 1874), 1:203, 228. Hereafter cited in the text as *MMFO*.

21. See also Capper, *Margaret Fuller*, 136–37, 158.

22. Although "patched together" by Coverdale in afterthought, the conversation between Zenobia and Westervelt is presented in the mode of objective dialogue (3:104).

23. See Samuel Chase Coale, "Mysteries of Mesmerism: Hawthorne's Haunted House," in *A Historical Guide to Nathaniel Hawthorne*, ed. Larry J. Reynolds (New York: Oxford University Press, 2001), 51–52.

24. Richard H. Brodhead, *The School of Hawthorne* (New York: Oxford University Press. 1986), 150.

25. Henry James, *The Bostonians* (New York: Oxford University Press, 1994), 131.

26. See Brodhead, *Hawthorne, Melville, and the Novel*, 111.

27. Millington, *Practicing Romance*, 154, 155.

28. E. P. Whipple, unsigned review of *The Blithedale Romance*, *Graham's Magazine* 41 (September 1852): 334.

29. Richard Poirier, preface, *The Comic Sense of Henry James* (Oxford University Press, 1967), 9.

30. Philip Rahv, "The Dark Lady of Salem," in *Image and Idea* (New York: New Directions, 1949), 37.

31. James McIntosh, "The Instability of Belief in *The Blithedale Romance*," *Prospects* 9 (1984): 77.

32. See Paul John Eakin's incisive discussion of Fuller in *The New England Girl*, 51–60.

33. Rahv, "The Dark Lady of Salem," 30.

34. Richard H. Brodhead, *Cultures of Letters: Scenes of Reading and Writing in Nineteenth-Century America* (Chicago: University of Chicago Press, 1993), 49, 50. See also Baym, *The Shape of Hawthorne's Career*, 196–97.

Chapter 7

1. Henry Arthur Bright, [On First Meeting Hawthorne in America, 1852], *Hawthorne in His Own Time*, ed. Ronald A. Bosco and Jillmarie Murphy (Iowa City: University of Iowa Press, 2007), 61.
2. See Raymona E. Hull, *Nathaniel Hawthorne: The English Experience, 1853–1864* (Pittsburgh: University of Pittsburgh Press, 1980), 190. Hull's fine, intelligent book is a foundational work for anyone studying this period.
3 Matthew Arnold, *Culture and Anarchy*, ed. J. Dover Wilson (1932; Cambridge: Cambridge University Press, 1963), ch. 3.
4. Henry James to Thomas Sergeant Perry, quoted in Leon Edel, *Henry James: The Untried Years: 1843–1879* (New York: Lippincott, 1953; rpt. New York: Avon, 1978), 264.
5. Ralph Waldo Emerson, *English Traits*, in vol. 5 of *The Complete Works of Ralph Waldo Emerson (Centenary Edition)* (Boston: Houghton Mifflin, 1903), 98, 233.
6. Hawthorne was hardly alone in this view of the English. Paul Langford notes that "the cult of John Bull, assiduously promoted from at least the 1790s, and with roots that went back much further, had no parallel elsewhere.... John Bull seemed a flesh and blood character who might walk off the pages of a novel or out of a vulgar cartoon into everyday life. Foreigners thought they beheld him wherever ordinary Englishmen were to be found" (*Englishness Identified: Manners and Character, 1650–1850* [Oxford: Oxford University Press, 2000], 11). Washington Irving had included a portrait of John Bull in *The Sketch Book* (1819–20). Nina Baym also makes this point: Hawthorne "chiefly perceived England as the most massively actual and materialistic culture he could ever have imagined. Repeatedly, he characterizes the English as a 'beef and ale' people, by which he means to suggest their physical substantiality and their lack of imagination" (*The Shape of Hawthorne's Career* [Ithaca, NY: Cornell University Press, 1976], 219).
7. Matthew Arnold, *Discourses in America*, vol. 4 of *Works* (London: Macmillan, 1903), 366.
8. Washington Irving, *The Sketch Book of Geoffrey Crayon, Gent.*, ed. Haskell Springer (Boston: Twayne, 1978), 9.
9. Peter Mandler, *The English National Character* (New Haven: Yale University Press, 2006), 58.
10. Langford, *Englishness Identified*, 43–50.
11. Emerson, *English Traits*, 88.
12. Raymond Williams, *Culture and Society, 1780–1950* (1958; London: Chatto and Windus, 1961), 16.
13. Emerson, *English Traits*, 221.
14. Emerson, *English Traits*, 65–66.
15. See Raymond Williams's discussion of the term "culture" in his introduction to *Culture and Society*, 13–19.
16. J. Dover Wilson, editor's introduction to Arnold, *Culture and Anarchy*, xxiv.
17. G. M. Young, *Victorian England: Portrait of an Age*, 2nd ed. (New York: Oxford University Press, 1964), 77.
18. Young, *Victorian England*, 153.
19. I borrow the term and idea from F. Scott Fitzgerald's story "May Day," in *The Stories of F. Scott Fitzgerald* (New York: Scribner's, 1951), 87.
20. *Plato's Symposium*, trans. Benjamin Jowett (Indianapolis: Bobbs-Merrill, 1956), 32.

Chapter 8

1. Bryan Homer, *An American Liaison: Leamington Spa and the Hawthornes, 1855–1864* (Madison, NJ: Fairleigh Dickinson University Press, 1998), 20.

2. John Updike, *Memories of the Ford Administration* (New York: Fawcett Crest, 1992), 241. Updike's fictional conversation between Hawthorne and United States minister James Buchanan is a masterpiece of insight and delight.

3. Terence Martin, "Hawthorne's Public Decade and the Values of Home," *American Literature* 46 (May 1974): 143.

4. James Boswell, *The Life of Samuel Johnson* (London, 1791), 1:228–29.

5. Nina Baym, *The Shape of Hawthorne's Career* (Ithaca, NY: Cornell University Press, 1976), 217.

6. Rita K. Gollin and John L, Idol, Jr., *Prophetic Pictures: Nathaniel Hawthorne's Knowledge and Use of the Visual Arts* (Wesport, CT: Greenwood, 1991), 31.

7. John Ruskin, *The Genius of John Ruskin: Selections from His Writings*, ed. John D. Rosenberg (Boston: Houghton Mifflin, 1963), 35.

8. *The Genius of John Ruskin*, 33.

9. *The Genius of John Ruskin*, 33.

10. Barbara Novak, *American Painting of the Nineteenth Century: Realism, Idealism, and the American Experience*, 2nd ed. (New York: Harper and Row, 1979), 98.

11. T. Walter Herbert, *Dearest Beloved: The Hawthornes and the Making of the Middle-Class Family* (Berkeley: University of California Press, 1993), 144.

12. Herbert, *Dearest Beloved*, 231, 232.

13. Henry James, preface to *The American*, vol. 2 of the *Novels and Tales of Henry James* (New York: Scribner's, 1907), vii. Hereafter cited in the text as *The American*.

14. Larry J. Reynolds, *Devils and Rebels: The Making of Hawthorne's Damned Politics* (Ann Arbor: University of Michigan Press, 2008), 218.

15. Quoted in Raymona E. Hull, *Nathaniel Hawthorne: The English Experience, 1853–1864* (Pittsburgh: University of Pittsburgh Press, 1980), 204.

Chapter 9

1. *The Complete Notebooks of Henry James*, ed. Leon Edel and Lyall H. Powers (New York: Oxford University Press, 1987), 141.

2. Henry James, *The Ambassadors* (New York: Scribner's, 1907), 1:217.

3. James, *William Wetmore Story and His Friends* (Boston: Houghton Mifflin, 1903), 7.

4. Richard H. Brodhead, introduction, *The Marble Faun* (New York: Penguin, 1990), xi.

5. Paul S. Baker, *The Fortunate Pilgrims: Americans in Italy, 1800–1860* (Cambridge, MA: Harvard University Press, 1964), 81.

6. Sophia Hawthorne, *Notes in England and Italy* (New York: G. P. Putnam, 1869), 543.

7. Baker, *The Fortunate Pilgrims*, 203.

8. Nathalia Wright, *American Novelists in Italy: The Discoverers: Allston to James* (Philadelphia: University of Pennsylvania Press, 1965), 206.

9. Wright, *American Novelists in Italy*, 206.

10. A. W. Schlegel, *Lectures on Dramatic Art and Literature*, trans. John Black (London: Bohn, 1846), 24, 25.

11. Schlegel, *Lectures on Dramatic Art and Literature*, 24.

12. Wright, *American Novelists in Italy*, 206.

13. Nina Baym, *The Shape of Hawthorne's Career* (Ithaca, NY: Cornell University Press, 1976), 22.

14. James, *Roderick Hudson* (1878 edition) (New York: Penguin, 1986), 159. Hereafter cited in the text as *RH*.

15. Baker, *The Fortunate Pilgrims*, 141.

16. Jenny Franchot, *Roads to Rome: The Antebellum Protestant Encounter with Catholicism* (Berkeley: University of California Press, 1994), 235, 236.

17. George S. Hillard, *Six Months in Italy*, 2 vols. (Boston: Ticknor, Reed, and Fields, 1853), 1:160.

18. Sophia Hawthorne, *Notes in England and Italy*, 503.

19. Hillard, *Six Months in Italy*, 1:122.

20. Harriet Beecher Stowe, *The Minister's Wooing* (1859; New York: Penguin, 1999), 15, 56, 62. Hereafter cited in the text as *MW*.

21. William James, *The Varieties of Religious Experience* (Cambridge, MA: Harvard University Press, 1985), 15. Hereafter cited in the text as *VRE*.

22. James, *The Ambassadors*, 1:46.

23. See Baker, *The Fortunate Pilgrims*, 159.

24. Orestes Brownson, "Literary Notices and Criticisms," *Brownson's Quarterly Review* (1850), rpt. in *The Scarlet Letter and Other Writings*, ed. Leland S. Person (New York: Norton, 2005), 253.

25. See George S. Hillard's description of the environs of the Pantheon. *Six Months in Italy*, 1:314–15.

26. Philip Larkin, *Collected Poems* (New York: Farrar, Straus and Giroux, 1998), lines 48, 55–57, 62.

27. Terence Martin, "Hawthorne's Public Decade and the Values of Home," *American Literature* 46 (May 1974): 144.

28. David B. Kesterson, "*The Marble Faun* as Transformation," in *Nathaniel Hawthorne Journal* (1978), ed. C. E. Frazer Clark, Jr. (Detroit: Gale, 1978), 75.

Chapter 10

1. Philip Rahv, "The Dark Lady of Salem," in *Image and Idea* (New York: New Directions, 1949), 26.

2. Millicent Bell, "*The Marble Faun* and the Waste of History," *Southern Review* 35 (1999): 359; see *The Marble Faun* (4:110).

3. See Evan Carton, "*The Marble Faun*": *Hawthorne's Transformations* (New York: Twayne, 1992), 15.

4. Hyatt H. Waggoner, *Hawthorne: A Critical Study*, rev. ed. (Cambridge, MA: Harvard University Press, 1963), 209; Frederick C. Crews, *The Sins of the Fathers* (New York: Oxford University Press, 1966), 225.

5. Friedrich Schiller, "*Naïve and Sentimental Poetry*" *and* "*On the Sublime*," trans. Julius A. Elias (New York: Ungar, 1966), 111. Hereafter cited in the text as Schiller.

6. Lea Newman, "Sophia's Enduring Influence: Hawthorne's Creative Resurgence and the Genesis of *The Marble Faun*," *Nathaniel Hawthorne Review* 26 (2000): 1–12.

7. Richard H. Millington, *Practicing Romance: Narrative Form and Cultural Engagement in Hawthorne's Fiction* (Princeton: Princeton University Press, 1992), 203.

8. T. Walter Herbert calls the model "the leading embodiment of corrupt patriarchy." *Dearest Beloved: The Hawthornes and the Making of the Middle-Class Family* (Berkeley: University of California Press, 1993), 259. See also Millington, *Practicing Romance*, 179.

9. M. H. Abrams, *Natural Supernaturalism* (New York: Norton, 1971), 334.

10. F. O. Matthiessen, *American Renaissance* (New York: Oxford University Press, 1941), 441.

11. Harriet Beecher Stowe, *The Minister's Wooing* (1859; New York: Penguin, 1999), 199.

12. Herbert, *Dearest Beloved*, 219.

13. Bell, "*The Marble Faun* and the Waste of History," 366.

14. Albert Camus, *The Myth of Sisyphus and Other Essays*, trans. Justin O'Brien (1955; New York: Random House, 1959), 21.

15. Milton R. Stern, *Contexts for Hawthorne: "The Marble Faun" and the Politics of Openness and Closure in American Literature* (Urbana: University of Illinois Press, 1991), 130.

16. Rahv, "The Dark Lady of Salem," 36.

17. Rahv, "The Dark Lady of Salem," 38.

18. Judith W. Mann, "Artemisia and Orazio Gentileschi," in *Orazio and Artemisia Gentileschi*, ed. Keith Christiansen and Judith W. Mann (New York and New Haven: Metropolitan Museum of Art and Yale University Press, 2001), 249.

19. Elizabeth Cropper, "Life on the Edge: Artemisia Gentileschi, Famous Woman Painter," in Christiansen and Mann, *Orazio and Artemisia Gentileschi*, 275.

20. R. Ward Bissell, *Artemisia Gentileschi and the Authority of Art* (University Park: Pennsylvania State University Press, 1999), 126.

21. Patrizia Cavazzini, "In Her Father's House," in Christiansen and Mann, *Orazio and Artemisia Gentileschi*, 311.

22. Bissell, *Artemisia Gentileschi and the Authority of Art*, 21.

23. In the Florentine Academy of Fine Arts, Hawthorne "was much struck with a picture (by Fabricio Gentile, or Gentileschi, or some such name) of the Adoration of the Magi" (14:323). Hawthorne was mistaken in the attribution—the painting was by Gentile da Fabriano (14:817). David R. Mayer takes the entry as a Freudian "slip of the pen" that signifies a surfacing of the repressed. See Mayer, "Artemisia Gentileschi as Artist Model for Miriam in Hawthorne's *The Marble Faun*," *Nathaniel Hawthorne Review* 31 (Fall 2005): 19–22, 27, 28. Hawthorne's mention of Gentileschi could as easily have referred to Orazio as to Artemisia. Mayer's 2005 article confirmed my own shock of recognition when I saw Gentileschi's paintings in an exhibition at the St. Louis Art Museum a few years earlier.

24. Mary D. Garrard, *Artemisia Gentileschi: The Image of the Female Hero in Italian Baroque Art* (Princeton: Princeton University Press, 1989), 312.

25. Joseph Campbell, "Transformations of the Hero," in *The Making of Myth*, ed. Richard Ohmann (New York: Putnam, 1962), 122.

26. E. P. Whipple, "Nathaniel Hawthorne," *Atlantic Monthly* 5 (May 1860): 621–22. Nina Baym also makes this point. *The Shape of Hawthorne's Career* (Ithaca, NY: Cornell University Press, 1976), 234.

27. Friedrich Nietzsche, "Twilight of the Idols," in *The Portable Nietzsche*, ed. and trans. Walter Kaufmann (New York: Viking, 1954), 491.

28. Nietzsche, *The Genealogy of Morals*, in *The Birth of Tragedy and The Genealogy of Morals*, trans. Francis Golffing (Garden City, NY: Doubleday, 1956), 170.

29. Nietzsche, *The Genealogy of Morals*, 151.

30. On the tradition of the "femme forte," see Garrard, *Artemisia Gentileschi*, 165–69.

31. See Thomas R. Mitchell, *Hawthorne's Fuller Mystery* (Amherst: University of Massachusetts Press, 1998), 233.

32. Nietzsche, "The Antichrist," in *The Portable Nietzsche*, 638.

33. Mitchell, *Hawthorne's Fuller Mystery*, 222–28, 238–40.

34. James R. Mellow, for one, finds her "an almost monstrous character" (Mellow 524).

35. John Milton, "Areopagitica," in *John Milton: Complete Poems and Major Prose*, ed. Merritt Y. Hughes (New York: Odyssey, 1957), 728.

36. Millington, *Practicing Romance*, 186.

37. Richard H. Brodhead, introduction, *The Marble Faun* (New York: Penguin, 1990), xvi.

Epilogue

1. Unless otherwise indicated, all references to the "Elixir of Life" manuscripts will be to "Septimius Felton."

2. Robert Lowell, "Hawthorne," *For the Union Dead*, in *"Life Studies"; and "For the Union Dead"* (1964; rpt. New York: Noonday, 1967), 38.

3. See Brenda Wineapple, *Hawthorne: A Life* (New York: Knopf, 2003), 363; and Magnus Ullén and David Greven, "Late Hawthorne: A Polemical Introduction," *Nathaniel Hawthorne Review*, 35 (Fall 2009): 3.

4. John Updike, "Late Works," in *Due Considerations* (New York: Knopf, 2007), 58.

LIST OF ILLUSTRATIONS

Four quadrants with pictures (clockwise from top left) of Salem, Concord, Liverpool, and Rome

A top left quadrant: Nathaniel Hawthorne, Birthplace, Salem, MA. Library of Congress Prints and Photographs Division Washington, D.C.

B top right quadrant: Concord River at Old Bridge, Concord, MA, ca. 1900. Courtesy Concord Free Public Library.

C bottom right quadrant: George's Dock Basin, Liverpool, ca. 1850. Courtesy National Museums, Liverpool.

D bottom left quadrant: Interior of the Pantheon, Rome, Giovanni Paolo Panini (1691–1765).

Section I: America

Bowdoin College, ca. 1823. Provided by Bowdoin College Museum of Art, Brunswick, Maine, Gift of Harold L. Berry, Class of 1901.

Sophia Amelia Peabody at the age of 36. Etching by S. A. Schoff, opposite page 242, volume 1 of Julian Hawthorne's *Nathaniel Hawthorne and His Wife*, 1884. Courtesy of Peabody Essex Museum, Salem, MA.

Portrait of Nathaniel Hawthorne by Charles Osgood, 1840. Courtesy Peabody Essex Museum, Salem, MA, Gift of Professor Richard C. Manning.

The Emerson House, Concord. Library of Congress Prints and Photographs Division Washington, D.C.

Margaret Fuller, head-and-shoulders portrait, facing left. Library of Congress Prints and Photographs Division, Washington, D.C.

Hawthorne's Old Manse—home in Salem, Mass. Library of Congress Prints and Photographs Division Washington, D.C.

Salem Custom House, ca. 1850. Courtesy National Park Service, Salem Maritime National Historic Site.

Una and Julian Hawthorne, ca. 1850, daguerreotype by unknown photographer.

Portrait of Nathaniel Hawthorne by George P.A. Healy, 1852/3. Courtesy the New Hampshire Historical Society.

10. The Wayside, Concord (house Hawthorne bought in 1852). Courtesy Concord Free Public Library.

II. England and Italy (after Chapter 6)

Sketch of St. Giles, London, ca. 1850.

Francis Bennoch, 1857. Sketch from the front matter of *The Modern Scottish Minstrel, Volume V.*

"John Bull's Alien Act." Political cartoon, ca. 1850.

Delia Bacon, daguerreotype, unknown photographer, 1853.

The Roman Forum, ca. 1850.

The Piazza San Pietro in Rome at the time of a Papal Blessing, 1850 (oil on canvas), Chernetsov, Grigori Grigor'evich (1801–65) / State Russian Museum, St. Petersburg, Russia / The Bridgeman Art Library.

Faun of Praxiteles , Capitoline Museum, Rome.

18. *Judith Slaying Holofernes*, Gentileschi, Artemisia (1597–c.1651) / Museo e Gallerie Nazionali di Capodimonte, Naples, Italy / The Bridgeman Art Library.

19. *The Transfiguration*, 1516–1520 (oil on canvas), Raphael (1483–1520) / Pinacoteca, Vatican City.

20. Photographic portrait of Nathaniel Hawthorne, ca. 1860–1865, by Matthew Brady. Library of Congress Prints and Photographs Division, Washington, D.C.

INDEX

Abel, Darrell, 95, 106
Abrams, M. H., 250
Adams, Henry, 58
Allori, Cristofano, 256
Arnold, Matthew, 171, 172, 196
Arvin, Newton, 25
Auden, W. H., 231–32

Bacon, Delia, 26–27
Baker, Paul S., 220
Baym, Nina, 10, 24, 40, 43, 83, 84, 87, 88, 91, 93, 141, 201, 225, 284n.6
Bell, Michael Davitt, 50, 121–22
Bell, Millicent, x, 97, 99, 133, 244, 253
Bennoch, Francis, 110, 169, 170, 182–83, 200
Bercovitch, Sacvan, 108, 280n.18
Bissell, R. Ward, 256
Bradstreet, Anne, 59
Bridge, Horatio, 4, 30, 50, 54–55, 124–25, 277n.50
Bright, Henry A., 167, 182
Brodhead, Richard H., 15, 25, 135, 139, 144, 151, 164, 165, 222, 267, 274n.22
Brooks, Peter, 44
Brownell, W. C., 4, 8, 9, 98
Brownson, Orestes, 111, 238–39
Buell, Lawrence, 118, 121, 276n.31, 281n.8
Burke, Kenneth, 126, 127–28
Burns, Robert, 174

Campbell, Joseph, 258
Camus, Albert, 254
Cady, Edwin H., 20
Carpenter, Frederic I., 108
Cenci, Beatrice, 232–33, 258–59, 260
Choate, Rufus, 121, 125
Cilley, Jonathan, 4, 33

Clarke, James Freeman, 147, 148, 150, 161–62
Colacurcio, Michael J., 24, 116, 123
Conforti, Joseph A, ix, 121
Conrad, Joseph, 24
Cooper, James Fenimore, 210
Crews, Frederick C., 24, 34, 36, 42, 123–24, 279n.48
Cropper, Elizabeth, 256

De Man, Paul, 9, 11
Dickinson, Emily, 25, 28, 29, 101, 231, 274 n. 27
Douglas, Ann, 12
Dryden, Edgar A., 33
Duyckinck, Evert A., 46

Eakin, Paul John, 145
Easton, Alison, 51
Edwards, Jonathan, 96
Eliot, T. S., 116
Emerson, Mary Moody, 67
Emerson, Ralph Waldo, 25, 35, 59, 61, 71, 72, 74, 75, 102–03, 108, 109, 111, 124, 130, 132, 133, 137, 150, 151, 171, 172, 180
Erikson, Erik H., 49–50
Endicott, John, 118–19, 120–22
Erlich, Gloria C., 28, 37

Faulkner, William, 110, 154
Fields, Annie, 34
Fields, James T., 134–35
Fitzgerald, F. Scott, 137, 284n.19
Florence, 221, 247–48
Forster, E. M., 188
Franchot, Jenny, 229
French, Marilyn, 142, 149

Freud, Sigmund, 40, 41, 44, 102, 105–06, 137, 139, 142
Frothingham, Octavius Brooks, 20–21
Frye, Northrop, 21, 23, 41, 44, 154
Fuller, Margaret, 69, 104–05, 109, 112, 144–50, 161–62, 259, 261

Gentileschi, Artemisia, 255–57
Gibson, John, 233
Goethe, Wolfgang Johann von, 19–20, 161–62
Gollin, Rita K, 24
Griffith, Clark C., 127
Graham, Sylvester, 39
Guercino, 160
Gunn, Giles, 120

Hawthorne, Elizabeth Manning (mother), 90–92
Hawthorne, Elizabeth Manning (Ebe, sister), 29, 30, 37, 48, 50, 51, 135, 186
Hawthorne, Julian, 3–4, 29, 33, 34, 37, 68–69, 81, 87, 116, 134, 135, 146, 149, 166, 168, 171, 173, 190, 201, 204–205, 215, 227, 239, 268, 271
Hawthorne, Nathaniel
  on aristocracy, 171, 178–79, 195, 209–10
  and Catholicism, 234–39
  cavern image in, 32–33, 35–36, 44–47, 56, 245–50
  theme of concealment and exposure in, 31–35
  and Concord, 57–64, 138, 215, 239, 241–42, 282n.3
  on connoisseurship, 128–29, 171, 185–87, 203, 222–23, 227–28
  as consul in Liverpool, 167–69, 199–200
  and death, 17–18, 90–93, 160–63, 268–69, 272
  on English character, 171–73, 177–85
  on English poverty, 188–95
  and feminism, 103–06, 112–13, 144–150
  and history, 93–95, 116–29, 225–26
  courtship of and marriage to Sophia Peabody Hawthorne, 55, 65–71, 76, 78–85, 85, 133–36
  dark heroines in, 26, 85–89, 105–06, 113–14, 140–44, 162–63, 254–62
  theme of guilt in, 31–44, 46–47, 91, 216
  incest theme in, 36–37, 41–43
  influence of Sophia Peabody (Hawthorne) on, 65–71
  and literary realism, 7–8, 12–20, 54–55, 96–101, 156–57, 203–09, 219
  on marriage, 48–53, 55–56, 132–34, 165, 271
  and mesmerism, 150–54, 160

  and naturalism, x–xi, 20–21, 24–27, 60–64, 97–101, 140, 156–66, 218–19, 231–33, 250–54, 269
  on painting and sculpture, 186–87, 203–07, 225, 227–34
  on the permanence of sin, 106–11, 159–60, 261–62
  and reform, 60, 72–76, 93–94, 111–13, 130–31, 158–60, 188–89,
  and religion, 18, 20–21, 229–32
  and romance, 3, 8–13, 21–26, 154–60, 174–77, 202, 212–19, 269–72
  and Rome, 224–27, 240–41, 243–45, 253–54, 267
  and Salem, 28–30, 44–47, 80, 115–17, 124–29, 134, 215
  on sectionalism and the Civil War, 215, 268
  and sexuality, 36–39, 82–89, 109–11, 181–83, 232–33
  and Transcendentalism, 60, 108–09, 130–31
  and women, 21–22, 47–48, 66–67, 73–74, 83–84, 110, 131, 140–44, 163–65, 183–85, 190–91, 210–12, 234, 259–65
  writings:
  "Alice Doane's Appeal," 41–44, 117, 244
  "American Claimant Manuscripts," 207, 219
  The American Notebooks, 4–8 and passim
  "The Ancestral Footstep," 186, 207–14
  "The Artist of the Beautiful," 49, 84–85, 124, 125, 127
  "The Birth-mark," 7, 83–84, 88
  The Blithedale Romance, 3, 81–82, 84, 137–66
  "Buds and Bird-Voices," 58–59, 75
  "The Canterbury Pilgrims, 51
  "The Christmas Banquet," 76, 77–78, 80–81
  "The Custom-House," 14, 22, 116, 199–200
  "The Devil in Manuscript," 40, 50
  "The Dolliver Romance," 269, 270, 271
  "Drowne's Wooden Image," 86
  "Earth's Holocaust," 72–73, 103
  "Egotism; or, The Bosom Serpent," 7, 62, 76, 78–80
  "Endicott and the Red Cross," 91, 121–22
  The English Notebooks, 201–03 and passim
  "Ethan Brand," 8–11, 269
  "Etherege," 167, 197, 207, 215–17
  "Elixir of Life" manuscripts, 268–69
  "Fancy's Show Box," 37–41, 78, 257
  Fanshawe, 20, 48–50, 270
  "Fragments from the Journal of a Solitary Man," 48, 50–51, 56, 128
  The French and Italian Notebooks, 221–22, 244, and passim
  "The Gentle Boy," 98, 123
  "Grimshawe," 20, 207, 217–19
  "The Hall of Fantasy," 60, 72
  "The Haunted Mind," 35–36, 40, 47–48, 56

The House of the Seven Gables, 14–23, 43, 52, 75, 113–14, 116, 117, 126–34, 142, 178, 186, 208, 213–14
"The Intelligence Office," 77, 78, 80
"Little Annie's Ramble," 46–47
"Little Daffydowndilly," 59
"Main-street," 14, 123, 125–26, 132
The Marble Faun, 26, 211, 212, 225–27, 237–38, 239, 240, 242, 243–67, 272
"The Maypole of Merry Mount," 118–20, 248–49
"The Minister's Black Veil," 32, 47, 79, 91
"Monsieur du Miroir," 7
Mosses from an Old Manse, 72, 80; see individual stories
"Mrs. Hutchinson," 94, 145
"My Kinsman, Major Molineux," 44, 45, 46, 98, 240
"The New Adam and Eve," 7, 73–74, 85
"The Old Apple-Dealer," 7
"The Old Manse," 12, 30, 32–33, 74–75
Our Old Home, 39, 170–71, 175–97, 199, 201, 209, 271–72
"Passages from a Relinquished Work," 54, 124
"The Procession of Life," 77
"Rappaccini's Daughter," 81–82, 86–89
"Roger Malvin's Burial," 91, 98
The Scarlet Letter, 31–32, 90–114, 141–42, 195
"A Select Party," 71
"Septimius Felton," 13–14, 49, 95, 268–71
"Sights from a Steeple," 200
"Sir William Phips," 93
"Sketches from Memory," 6
"The Story Teller," 53–55
"The Village Uncle," 51–53, 133, 271
"Wakefield," 201
"The Wedding Knell," 51
Twice-Told Tales, 54–55; see individual stories
"Young Goodman Brown," 44, 45–47, 98
Hawthorne, Sophia Peabody, 34, 37, 47, 55–56, 65–71, 76, 80–83, 85, 86, 116, 127, 132, 136, 145–46, 149, 224, 230–31, 248, 252, 263–64
Hawthorne, Una, 82–83, 85, 113, 240–41, 252–53
Heller, Erich, 47
Herbert, T. Walter, 63, 66, 136, 211, 253, 276n.25, 286n.8
Hillard, George S., 35, 229, 233
Hoffman, Charles Fenno, 34
Holmes, Oliver Wendell, 33, 35
Homer, Bryan, 199
Hosmer, Harriet, 259
Howe, Irving, 273–74n.20
Howells, William Dean, 12, 13, 117, 220
Hudson Rivers artists, 206
Hulme, T. E., 94

Hunt, Leigh, 128, 185–86
Hurst, Luanne Jenkins, 69
Hutchinson, Anne, 94, 102–03, 108

Irving, Washington, 170, 173–74, 177, 210

James, Henry, ix, xi, 5, 9, 14, 46–47, 97, 117, 156, 165, 170, 171–72, 181, 182, 185, 207, 210, 221, 224–25, 244; *writings: The American*, 212–13; *The Ambassadors*, 220–21, 238; "A Passionate Pilgrim," 208–09; *The Bostonians*, 152; *The Europeans*, 11, 12, 123; "The Jolly Corner, 217: *Roderick Hudson*, 129, 226, 240; *William Wetmore Story and His Friends*, 220
James, William, 17, 20, 21, 234, 236–38
Jewett, Sarah Orne, 13
Johnson, Samuel, 174–77, 201

Kaul, A. N., 103, 138
Kazin, Alfred, 8
Keats, John, 163
Kesterson, David B., 242

Lander, Louisa, 211–12, 222
Lang, Amy Schrager, 103–04
Langford, Paul, 177, 178, 284n.6
Lansdowne, Henry Petty-Fitzmaurice, Marquess of, 179, 182
Laocoön, 229–30, 252
Larkin, Philip, 239
Lathrop, George Parsons, 14, 15
Lawrence, D. H., 95
Leamington Spa, 187
Leavis, Q. D, 46, 120
Levin, Harry, 100
Liverpool, 169, 173, 188
London, 167, 170, 172–73, 200–01, 223
Longfellow, Henry Wadsworth, 29
Loring, George Bailey, 3, 99, 106–10
Lowell, Robert, 270

Mabie, Hamilton Wright, 96, 99
Manchester Arts Exhibition, 180, 186–87, 203–05
Mann, Judith W., 255
Mann, Mary Peabody, 35
Mann, Thomas, 47–50, 53
Marcuse, Herbert, 111, 119, 140
Marshall, Megan, 67–68, 277n.55
Martin, Terence, 200, 240

Marx, Leo, 62
Matthiessen, F. O., 19, 251
Mayer, David R., 257, 287n.23
McCall, Dan, 7, 22
McIntosh, James, 159
Mellow, James R., 31, 48, 58, 70, 91, 135, 217–219, 243, 282n.34, 287n.34.
Melville, Herman, 7, 19, 25, 32, 33, 34 46, 71, 85, 98, 101, 135, 181, 188, 189, 192–93, 195–96, 232, 243, 250, 251, 254
Millington, Richard H., 153, 248, 266, 283n.6
Miller, Edwin H., 30, 33
Miller, Perry, 113, 125
Milnes, Richard Monckton, 170
Milton, John, 120, 262, 264
Mitchell, Thomas R., 135, 138, 261, 279n.39
Mitford, Mary Russell, 201
Moore, Margaret B., 116

Nelson, Admiral Horatio, 181
Nero, 186
Neufeldt, Leonard N., 116–17
Newman, Lea, 43, 247
Nietzsche, Friedrich, 24, 25–26, 90, 100–01, 117–18, 119, 120, 132–33, 246, 258–59, 260
Nissenbaum, Stephen, 38

Ossoli, Angelo, 149, 261

Pantheon, 226, 239, 261
Paris, 223
Parrington, V. L., 280n.31
Pater, Walter, 254
Peabody, Andrew Preston, 33
Peabody, Elizabeth, 26, 30, 54, 55, 68, 69, 79, 113, 128, 263
Perry, Bliss, 4
Person, Leland S, Jr., 69
Perugino, 229
Pfister, Joel, 279n.39
Pierce, Franklin, 241
Plato, 195, 197
Poirer, Richard, 23, 157
Porte, Joel, 31
Pousin, Nicholas, 160
Powers, Hiram, 167, 222
Pre-Raphaelites, 204

Rahv, Philip, 13, 86, 93, 110, 113, 159, 162, 243, 255, 279n.46
Raphael, 228–29, 232–33
Reed, Edward S., 8

Reynolds, Larry J., 24, 76–77, 83, 277n.3, 282n.3
Richards, I. A., 11
Ripley, George, 137
Robbins, Chandler, 38
Robinson, David, 62
Robinson, Edwin Arlington, 115
Ruskin, John, 203, 205–06

Schroeder, John W., 41
Scott, Sir Walter, 105, 173–74
Schlegel, A.W., 225
Schiller, Friedrich, 245, 246–47
Shakespeare, William, 26–27, 174
Snow, Caleb, 121
Sodoma, 230–31, 232, 251
Sophocles, 48
Stanley, Edward Henry Smith, Lord, 179
Stanton, Elizabeth Cady, 141, 143
Stern, Milton R., 255
Stoddard, R .H., 5
Story, William Wetmore, 128, 221–22, 224, 254
Stowe, Harriet Beecher, 16–18, 19, 21–22, 66–67, 115, 123, 236, 252
Swisshelm, Jane, 106, 111

Taylor, Jeremy, 37–38, 78
Tennyson, Alfred, Lord, 170, 181
Thoreau, Henry David, 25, 28, 57, 60–64, 138, 198, 269
Tissot, S.A., 38
Titian, 87, 233
Todd, John, 38
Tompkins, Jane, 45–46
Trollope, Anthony, 202, 204, 205
Tuckerman, Henry T., 20
Turner, Arlin, 58
Turner, J. M. W., 205–06

Updike, John, ix, xi, 14, 18, 90, 198, 199, 207, 272, 275n.48, 285n.2
Upham, Charles W., 127

Valenti, Patricia Dunlavy, 65, 82, 84, 278n.20, 279n.45
Venus de Medici, 234

Waggoner, Hyatt H., 3, 43, 276n.32
Weldon, Roberta, 92
Whipple, E. P., 4, 94–95, 96, 150, 154, 259
Whitman Walt, 25
Williams, Raymond, 122, 179–80

Wilson, Edmund, 48
Wilson, J. Dover, 189
Wineapple Brenda, 33, 92, 114, 127, 135
Winters, Yvor, 12
Woodson, Thomas, 34, 70, 145, 170
Woolf, Virginia, 140, 250, 268

Wright, Nathalia, 224–25

Young, G. M., 189, 191
Young, Philip, 36, 276n.42